standard catalog of
JAPANESE MOTORCYCLES
1959-2007

Doug Mitchel

©2007 Doug Mitchel
Published by

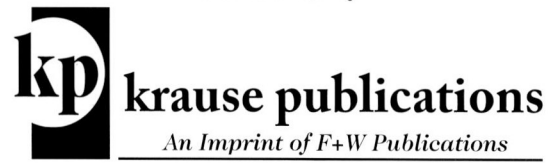

kp krause publications
An Imprint of F+W Publications

700 East State Street • Iola, WI 54990-0001
715-445-2214 • 888-457-2873
www.krausebooks.com

Our toll-free number to place an order or obtain
a free catalog is (800) 258-0929.

All rights reserved. No portion of this publication may be reproduced
or transmitted in any form or by any means, electronic or mechanical,
including photocopy, recording, or any information storage and
retrieval system, without permission in writing from the publisher,
except by a reviewer who may quote brief passages in a critical
article or review to be printed in a magazine or newspaper, or
electronically transmitted on radio, television, or the Internet.

Library of Congress Control Number: 2007924541

ISBN-13: 978-0-89689-564-5
ISBN-10: 0-89689-564-5

Designed by Paul Birling
Edited by Tom Collins

Printed in China

Dedication

To: Joe Bortz, an old friend and new collector

Contents

Introduction 7
Price Guide 387

HONDA 1959 - 2007

Introduction 8	1971 35	1984 65	1997 93
1959 9	1972 37	1985 67	1998 95
1960 11	1973 39	1986 70	1999 97
1961 13	1974 41	1987 74	2000 99
1962 14	1975 43	1988 75	2001 101
1963 15	1976 45	1989 76	2002 103
1964 17	1977 47	1990 78	2003 105
1965 18	1978 50	1991 80	2004 107
1966 20	1979 52	1992 82	2005 109
1967 23	1980 55	1993 84	2006 111
1968 27	1981 57	1994 86	2007 113
1969 30	1982 59	1995 89	
1970 32	1983 62	1996 91	

KAWASAKI 1963 - 2007

Introduction 114	1974 131	1986 154	1998 172
1963 114	1975 133	1987 155	1999 174
1964 115	1976 135	1988 158	2000 177
1965 115	1977 137	1989 159	2001 179
1966 116	1978 138	1990 160	2002 181
1967 118	1979 140	1991 162	2003 182
1968 119	1980 142	1992 163	2004 185
1969 121	1981 144	1993 164	2005 187
1970 123	1982 146	1994 165	2006 189
1971 125	1983 148	1995 166	2007 192
1972 127	1984 150	1996 168	
1973 129	1985 152	1997 169	

SUZUKI

1963 - 2007

Introduction....194	1974...........213	1986...........235	1998...........263
1963...........195	1975...........215	1987...........239	1999...........267
1964...........196	1976...........217	1988...........241	2000...........270
1965...........197	1977...........218	1989...........243	2001...........273
1966...........198	1978...........220	1990...........244	2002...........275
1967...........199	1979...........222	1991...........245	2003...........277
1968...........202	1980...........224	1992...........250	2004...........281
1969...........204	1981...........227	1993...........252	2005...........283
1970...........205	1982...........228	1994...........253	2006...........286
1971...........206	1983...........230	1995...........254	2007...........288
1972...........209	1984...........233	1996...........258	
1973...........211	1985...........233	1997...........260	

YAHAMA

1961 - 2007

Introduction....290	1972...........316	1984...........343	1996...........363
1961...........291	1973...........319	1985...........345	1997...........365
1962...........292	1974...........323	1986...........347	1998...........367
1963...........293	1975...........325	1987...........349	1999...........369
1964...........294	1976...........327	1988...........351	2000...........371
1965...........296	1977...........329	1989...........353	2001...........374
1966...........298	1978...........330	1990...........355	2002...........377
1967...........302	1979...........332	1991...........356	2003...........378
1968...........305	1980...........334	1992...........356	2004...........379
1969...........307	1981...........337	1993...........358	2005...........381
1970...........310	1982...........339	1994...........359	2006...........383
1971...........313	1983...........341	1995...........361	2007...........386

ACKNOWLEDGMENTS

I must once again extend my gratitude to all the owners and collectors who generously donated their time and energy and allowed me to photograph their motorcycles. In addition, many others offered their reference materials and model details that were used to create this work. Without these helpful friends, my life would be complete chaos.

Keith Campbell and Joe Brown at Hourglass Racing

Jim Kersting, his family, and their collection

John Parham and Jeff Carstensen at J&P Cycles

Brad Powell at www.bradbikes.net

Larry Klein at GT Motors

Mark Pawelski and Michelle Wagner at Fox Valley Cycles

Buzz and Pixie Walneck

The editor also thanks Fox Valley Motorsports (Yamaha) of Appleton, Wisconsin, Green Bay Cycles (Kawasaki) of Green Bay, Wisconsin and Team Motorsports of Green Bay (Honda and Suzuki), De Pere, Wisconsin, for their assistance.

NOTE:

When I suggested this title to the publisher, I was confident that adequate materials were available to compile every year-by-year model listing in detail. The further I got into the project, the more gaps I found in these materials. I hope the reader can understand that finding accurate information on more than 150 years of motorcycle history is a daunting task.

What you are reading now is the result of nearly a year of searching, scrounging and begging for facts and figures that were reliable. While the Internet has become a terrific tool for certain things, not all of the information found there can be verified. I attempted to use factory brochures and materials as often as they could be found. Period magazines were another boon for data, but my collection that spans the entire period was also found to have some gaps.

My only hope is that any incorrect or missing data in this book will be seen as an innocent mistake, not a deliberate attempt to misguide the world of collectors and fans of the Japanese motorcycle.

If you find any missing or incorrect information, please contact the publisher so they can pass the word along to me for future corrections.

Introduction

Until the latter part of the 1950s, the motorcycle market in the United States was comprised of two stateside manufacturers and a handful of British and German brands. The U.S. builders' roots could be traced back to the turn of that century while the European brands came along a bit later. The classic Indian brand succumbed to market pressures in 1953, leaving only Harley-Davidson as the sole American maker of two-wheeled transportation.

In June of 1959, a fresh face entered the fray on these shores. The Honda brand started out slowly, but grew rapidly as buyers embraced the simple and efficient machines from this Japanese manufacturer. Within five years, Honda was joined by three more Japanese builders, as Kawasaki, Suzuki and Yamaha offered their own brand of diminutive, yet highly capable motorcycles.

Initially, many scoffed at these spindly craft from across the pond, but it didn't take long for their positive aspects to become apparent, and sales began to thrive. People responded with a keen interest to the well-designed motorcycles that offered much in the way of fun with a minimal fuss. All four makers began their U.S. sales with small, single-cylinder machines that were easy to ride and maintain. Each year saw bigger and more powerful variations roll onto the showroom floors. Honda set a new level of performance with their 1969 CB750 model that was powered by an inline, four-cylinder motor.

The introduction of this now classic Honda opened the floodgates, and each of the other Japanese builders followed suit with bigger models of their own. What was first viewed as a momentary blip on the sales charts became a serious threat to the fabled Milwaukee-made cycles.

Once the dominant player in the motorcycle market, Harley-Davidson was being swallowed whole by the Japanese models. A recovery of the marque in the mid 1980s returned Harley-Davidson to its former glory, but dark days were encountered on their journey.

The history of all four Japanese companies began well before their foray into the motorcycle field, but served them well as industrial leaders. What was learned in other, related arenas was easily translated into the assembly of two-wheeled machines that the American market was yearning to ride.

In contrast to the wobbly offerings first shipped here by the four Japanese manufacturers, today's sales catalogs are full of exciting and capable machines. The variety and scope of their lineups is only rivaled by their performance and quality. Every year sees the release of newer, more powerful craft, carrying better chassis designs and creature comforts into the marketplace.

Only a few visionaries would have guessed that the unknown names from overseas would grow to be worldwide and world-class builders today.

HONDA

Introduction

Born near the city of Hamamatsu City, Japan, Soichiro Honda discovered his interest in mechanical devices at an early age. His high level of mechanical aptitude allowed him to create a car of his own design, and he soon began to put his plans into action. Once grade school was complete, he moved to Tokyo to begin work in a small automobile repair facility.

In 1946 he began what would become the foundation of the Honda Motor Company. Using the money he had saved over the years, he set up a business to create and develop his own line of motorcycles. The Honda Technical Research Institute he created would prove to be fertile ground for his technical abilities, and allowed him to expand his reach in the market.

When World War II had come to an end, he was able to acquire a quantity of 500 small motors that he fitted to bicycle frames, thus creating his first two-wheeled machines. This took place only one year after he founded the Honda Technical Research Institute.

His first motorized cycles paved the way for the formation of the Honda Motor Company, Ltd. Honda was 41 years of age when he formed the company, but he retained the dreams of a younger man in his heart. With starting capital of one million yen in 1948, he set out to produce his first real motorcycle. By joining forces with a financial guru named Takeo Fujisawa, his two-wheeled company was brought to life.

The 1949 D-Type Dream was the fruit of their labors. The E-Type Cub would soon follow. It was powered by a four-stroke engine, and was the first of its type from Honda. In 1952, after only five years as a corporate entity, Honda Motor Company began exporting his machines to other markets. The new F-Type Cub was a great success and allowed many overseas countries to experience the pleasure of riding Mr. Honda's two-wheeled creation.

By 1959, the name Honda was common in overseas markets, as well as the winner's circle at races around the world. The dominance of his machines was growing and the United States became his biggest export destination. It was on June 4, 1959, when the doors opened at 4077 Pico Boulevard in Los Angeles, California.

This unassuming building would be the home for American Honda Motor Company, Inc., where 12 employees began their trek deep into the U. S. marketplace. With a newly minted ad campaign that claimed, "You meet the nicest people on a Honda," the world of motorcycling in America would be changed forever.

The management team at Honda believed that the U. S. manufacturers were not in touch with what American riders wanted in a motorcycle. In the space of less than a year, Honda was outselling all other brands except two. One year later they were the number one seller in the country, and had no intention of vacating that coveted position.

STANDARD CATALOG OF ® JAPANESE Motorcycles

HONDA

1959

Unlike many of the motorcycle builders at the turn of the 20th century in the U. S., Honda entered the American market with a variety of machines. Soichiro Honda began his dream with a single model in 1946, but by the time his company reached the American shores, he was armed with a catalog of two-wheeled fun. Two different models were released on June 4, 1959, and would soon be followed by six more before the first year of U. S. operations ended.

The CA92/C92 Benly Touring model featured 124cc of displacement and the overhead cam design was a radical departure from most builders, proving Honda's ability to design machines that met with the public's demands. The power plant, which was brought to life at the touch of a button, thanks to the electric start, was only a part of the complete electrical system found on the fledgling model. Of course a kick-start lever was in place to allow the rider to be on his way when the battery wouldn't cooperate.

A four-speed transmission gave the rider plenty of choices for journeys on diverse American roadways. Drum brakes mounted on both wheels provided adequate stopping power. The pressed steel backbone of the frame allowed plenty of rigidity while still being light. The 1959 model year would be the only season for the CA92 Benly, but improved versions would soon follow. As with many of the early Honda models, a "C" prefix was used on a Japanese specification machine that was sold in the USA and other markets. The "CA" designation pertained to USA/North American specification cycles that were also sold in markets outside of America.

The second model to be released in 1959 was the CA71/C71 Dream Touring 250. This model was powered by a 247cc, parallel twin, overhead cam (OHC) motor. The CA71 featured tubular chrome handlebars while the C71 had bars formed from pressed steel. The C71 had a slightly larger fuel tank, but both models had chrome insets on each side of the tank.

First released in August 1959, the C100 Super Cub pounced onto the sales floor. These step-through bikes were designed to entice new riders to the world of motorcycling, and were the models featured in Honda's ultra successful "You meet the nicest people on a Honda" ad campaign.

Powered by 49cc, single-cylinder motors, their power was not excessive, but was enough to get you and a friend around town. Although most of the C100s featured a two-person saddle,

One of the first Hondas to be sold in the USA was the Benly. Its success would quickly lead to the introduction of many more.

American Honda

HONDA

some early examples were built with solo pillions. Three speeds were available through an automatic clutch, and a kick-starter was the only way to bring the machine to life. A complete set of lights permitted riding during the day and after the sun had set.

Trimmed in choices of Scarlet Red and White, Blue and White, Black and White or an all-Black option, the Super Cub offered plenty of style. With claims of 200 miles per gallon, the C100 was an efficient way to have fun.

Bowing on September 1, 1959 was the CA95 Benly Touring 150. With a 154cc parallel twin motor, and four speeds on tap, this Benly version looked and rode more like a real motorcycle than its smaller siblings. The center of the fuel tank was matched in the color chosen by the buyer, and the sides were trimmed with large chrome panels and small rubber kneepads. A square headlight was wrapped in an enclosure that included the integrated speedometer. The final drive chain was fully enclosed, and the muffler was delivered with flat sides, finished in chrome. Black wall tires and the short rear fender brace help to set the 1959 Benly models apart.

Three additional Dream models also entered the fray on September 1, 1959. The CE71 Dream Sport 250 featured a 247cc, OHC, parallel twin engine, four-speed transmission and a single carburetor. The fuel tank on the CE71 Dream Sport was always finished in silver, and was fitted with rubber kneepads but lacked chrome panels. The rest of the sheet metal was painted black or maroon depending on which color was ordered.

Early examples of this model rolled on 18-inch wheels, while later entries had 16-inch hoops at each end.

Two more entrants for 1959 also arrived on September 1. The CA76/C76 Dream Touring 300 models were the biggest kids in the Honda sandbox. Motivation came from a 305cc, OHC, dry sump, parallel twin motor that rowed through a four-speed transmission. A single carburetor fed the twin cylinders in efficient fashion.

Available in White, Black, Blue or Scarlet Red, the fuel tanks were all mated with chrome panels inset on each side of the receptacle.

The CA76 featured high-rise tubular handlebars while the C76 had a set of low-rise, pressed steel bars. Both models featured the square headlights found on other Hondas.

The smooth nacelle that was fitted to the lights also held the speedometer.

The CB92 Benly Super Sport arrived on November 1, 1959. This model met with the needs of pseudo-racers everywhere. The 124cc, OHC, parallel twin motor stirred a four-speed transmission and sipped fuel through a single carburetor.

A small clear windscreen was fitted just above the square headlight, adding to the racer image of the Super Sport. The fuel tank, front fender and side covers were all finished in silver, with a choice of red or blue hardware. The red version was paired with a black saddle while the blue option came with a red pillion. Alloy was used to form the fuel tank, fenders and side covers of the early iterations.

1959 HONDA

Model	Product Code	Engine Type/Displacement	Transmission	Year(s) Available
C100 Super Cub	001	OHV Single/49cc	3-Speed	1959-62
CA92/C92 Benly Touring 125	203	OHC Parallel Twin/124cc	4-Speed	1959
CB92 Benly Super Sport 125	205	OHC Parallel Twin/124cc	4-Speed	1959-62
CA95 Benly Touring 150	206	OHC Parallel Twin/154cc	4-Speed	1959-63
CA71/C71 Dream Touring 250	255	OHC Parallel Twin/247cc	4-Speed	1959-60
CE71 Dream Sport 250	257	OHC Parallel Twin/247cc	4-Speed	1959-1960
CA76/C76 Dream Touring 300	260	OHC Parallel Twin/305cc	4-Speed	1959-60

HONDA
1960

It was only Honda's second year of sales in the United States, but model changes were found throughout the line. With the exception of the CA92/C92 Benly Touring 125 model, the remaining 1959 team was carried over into the new model year. And 1960 would be the first year for numerous additions and the last year for many others.

First in the new model lineup was the CSA76/CS76 Dream Sport 300. Only available for one year, it included an amalgam of features not seen before on a Honda motorcycle.

Driven by a 305cc, OHC, parallel twin motor, both versions featured a pair of upswept exhaust pipes, one on each side of the chassis. The CSA76 steered with a set of high-rise tubular handlebars dipped in chrome. The CS76 had a set of painted, pressed steel, low-rise bars.

Both bikes had four-speed transmissions, and were offered in the usual hues of White, Black, Blue and Scarlet Red. Chrome side panels adorned the fuel tanks as well as a set of rubber kneepads.

Another new face for 1960, released on July

Model year 1960 saw Honda release several additional models to the US market, one of which was the Sport Cub.

American Honda

HONDA

1, was the C102 Super Cub. It was identical to the C100 Super Cub, except for the addition of an electric starter. The kick-start C100 was still available.

For 1960, the CA71 Dream Touring 250 was joined by the CA72. The CA72 was built with high-rise tubular handlebars, and although the fuel tank was the same shape, it was fitted with chrome panels and rubber kneepads.

A new addition to the family was the CA77 Dream Touring 305, which was released to the dealers in August of 1960.

The latest model featured a 305cc, OHC parallel twin motor, and a fuel tank that was larger than the early CA72. A pair of low mounted exhaust pipes set the CA77 apart from the CSA77/CS77 models.

The CSA76/CS76 was only a single year model and the CSA77/CS77 would arrive in September, and would run until 1963. The 77 versions were identical to the 76 series scheduled to be replaced but were often fitted with white-wall tires.

A late entry in the 1960 models was the C110 Super Sports Cub. First available late in 1960, the C110 was fitted with the same 49cc motor as the C100 and C102, but featured a more traditional motorcycle chassis. Not a step-through model the Super Sports Cub carried a standard solo saddle that was devoid of a rear hand strap.

The three-speed transmission was also manually shifted, unlike the automatic boxes found on the C100 and C102. Color options were all based on a white tank and side covers. Contrasting frame and fender colors were Scarlet Red, Blue and Black.

The 1960 model year would be the last for the CA71 Dream Touring 250, CE71 Dream Sport 250, and the CA76/C76 Dream Touring 300 models. All four had been introduced in 1959.

1960 HONDA

Model	Engine	Displacement	Transmission
C100 Super Cub	OHV Single	49cc	Three-Speed, Auto
C102 Super Cub	OHV Single	49cc	Three-Speed, Auto
C110 Super Sports Cub	OHV Single	49cc	Three-Speed, Manual
CB92 Benly Super Sport 125	OHC Parallel Twin	124cc	Four-Speed
CA95 Benly Touring 150	OHC Parallel Twin	154cc	Four-Speed
CA71/C71 Dream Touring 250	OHC Parallel Twin	247cc	Four-Speed
CE71 Dream Sport 250	OHC Parallel Twin	247cc	Four-Speed
CA72 Dream Touring 250	OHC Parallel Twin	247cc	Four-Speed
CA76/C76 Dream Touring 300	OHC Parallel Twin	305cc	Four-Speed
CSA76/CS76 Dream Sport 300	OHC Parallel Twin	305cc	Four-Speed
CA77 Dream Touring 305	OHC Parallel Twin	305cc	Four-Speed
CSA77/CS77 Dream Sport 305	OHC Parallel Twin	305cc	Four-Speed

HONDA 1961

The new model year consisted of many carryovers from 1959, but also added six new entrants to the Honda team. Missing from the 1961 offerings were the CA71/C71 Dream Touring 250, CE71 Dream Sport 250, CA76/C76 Dream Touring 300 and CSA76/CS76 Dream Sport 300.

February saw the CB72 Hawk 250 makes its debut. This sportier model featured the same 247cc OHC motor used on other Hondas, but took in fuel through a pair of carburetors. The chassis of the CB72 was formed of tubular steel versus the pressed-steel varieties used on other Hondas. Improved telescopic front forks were on hand to assist in the ride and handling. Early models were fitted with flat handlebars while later entries had low-rise style bars.

March saw four new models being pushed onto the sales floors. Smallest of the new models were the CA100T Trail 50/C100T Trail Cub. Designed more for off-road uses, these 49cc machines came devoid of front fenders and could be had with optional skid plates and rear mounted luggage racks. A small black plastic engine guard was standard.

The step-through layout was accented by a solo saddle and was sold in Scarlet Red or an all-chrome version. The chrome model came with accents of red and had a black seat.

The second March release was the CB92R Benly Super Sports Racer 125. Based on the CB92 Benly, the "R" version was equipped as a mini-racing machine.

The racing saddle, chrome megaphone exhaust pipes and added horsepower provided the feel of a real racing machine. Behind a clear windscreen, the speedometer of the CB92 was replaced with a tachometer in the headlight nacelle.

The final March entry was the C77 Dream Touring 305. A virtual twin to the CA77 introduced in 1960, the C77 wore low-rise handlebars that were formed of pressed steel and painted, versus the tubular high-rise bars on the CA77. A small tire pump, located beneath the seat was also added to the C77.

April of 1961 saw the last new model being introduced for the year. The CB77 Super Hawk 305 wore a pair of telescopic front forks in place of the pressed-steel affairs used on most other Hondas at the time.

Early Super Hawks wore flat bars with lower fork legs to match the unit color chosen. Later versions used low-rise bars and all silver fork lowers.

The 305cc parallel twin motor was also fitted with a pair of carburetors to enhance performance. A four-speed transmission was still the standard application.

1961 HONDA

Model	Engine	Displacement	Transmission
C100 Super Cub	OHV Single	49cc	Three-Speed, Auto
CA100TTrail 50 and C100T Trail Cub	OHV Single	49cc	Three-Speed, Auto
C102 Super Cub	OHV Single	49cc	Three-Speed, Auto
C110 Super Sports Cub	OHV Single	49cc	Three-Speed, Manual
CB92 Benly Super Sport 125	OHC Parallel Twin	124cc	Four-Speed
CB92R Benly S.S. Racer 125	OHC Parallel Twin	124cc	Four-Speed
CA95 Benly Touring 150	OHC Parallel Twin	154cc	Four-Speed
C72 Dream Touring 250	OHC Parallel Twin	247cc	Four Speed
CA72 Dream Touring 250	OHC Parallel Twin	247cc	Four-Speed
CB72 Hawk 250	OHC Parallel Twin	247cc	Four-Speed
C77 Dream Touring 305	OHC Parallel Twin	305cc	Four-Speed
CA77 Dream Touring 305	OHC Parallel Twin	305cc	Four-Speed
CSA77/CS77 Dream Sport 305	OHC Parallel Twin	305cc	Four-Speed
CB77 Super Hawk 305	OHC Parallel Twin	305cc	Four-Speed

HONDA
1962

The step-through design and high mounted front fender made the Trail model useful both on and off paved surfaces.

Stuart Covington

Model year 1962 would be the final year for the C100 Super Cub, CA100T Trail50/C100T Trail Cub, C102 Super Cub, C110 Super Sports Cub and both the CB92 Benly Super Sport 125 and CB92R Benly Super Sports Racer 125.

To fill the void left by the departing C100 and C102 Super Cub models, the CA100 and CA102 Honda 50s were added to the lineup. A "Honda 50" logo was placed on the front cowl and a seat base emblem also helped to identify the latest versions. The taillight was also enlarged, and was mounted with a bracket.

For the rider who still desired a machine for rugged adventures, the C105T Trail 55 took the spot left by the CA100T and C100T. The C105T Trail 55 now came with the chrome luggage rack as standard equipment and had a larger saddle. An engine with six additional cubic centimeters of displacement was also installed on the 1962 model.

The departing C110 Super Sports Cub would barely be missed with the rollout of the CA110 Sport 50 model. Chrome panels on the sides of the fuel tank dressed up the latest version and an aluminum cylinder head helped with cooling on the 49cc motor. The CA110 Sport 50 was fitted with a 3-speed manual transmission up to serial no. C110-218191, but would add another gear starting with the subsequent serial number. The new tank badge read "Honda 50" to assist in differentiating one model from another.

A brand new model was offered up in 1962 in the form of the CL72 Scrambler 250. An upswept, baffled straight pipe exhaust suggested off-road use. The 247cc motor was fed with a pair of carburetors, and 4-speeds were on duty.

1962 HONDA

Model	Transmission	Displacement	Engine
C100 Super Cub	Three-Speed,	Auto49cc	OHV Single
CA100Honda 50	Three-Speed,	Auto49cc	OHV Single
CA100TTrail 50 andC100T Trail Cub	Three-Speed,	Auto49cc	OHV Single
C102 Super Cub	Three-Speed,	Auto49cc	OHV Single
CA102Honda 50	Three-Speed,	Auto49cc	OHV Single
C105TTrail 55	Three-Speed,	Auto54cc	OHV Single
C110 Super Sports Cub	Three-Speed,	Manual49cc	OHV Single
CA110Sport 50	Three-Speed or Four-Speed,	Manual49cc	OHV Single
CB92 Benly Super Sport 125	Four-Speed	124cc	OHC Parallel Twin
CB92RBenly S.S. Racer 125	Four-Speed	124cc	OHC Parallel Twin
A95Benly Touring 150	Four-Speed	154cc	OHC Parallel Twin
CA72 Dream Touring 250	Four-Speed	247cc	OHC Parallel Twin
CB72Hawk 250	Four-Speed	247cc	OHC Parallel Twin
CL72 Scrambler 250	Four-Speed	247cc	OHC Parallel Twin
C77 Dream Touring 305	Four-Speed	305cc	OHC Parallel Twin
CA77 Dream Touring 305	Four-Speed	305cc	OHC Parallel Twin
CSA77/CS77 Dream Sport 305	Four-Speed	305cc	OHC Parallel Twin
CB77 Super Hawk 305	Four-Speed	305cc	OHC Parallel Twin

HONDA
1963

In 1962, the "thrifty nifty" Honda 50 (that's what the ad copy said!) took riders to the beach—and elsewhere.

April of 1963 saw the following models come in as replacements for the departing versions. With the CA105T Trail 55 appearing, few noticed the loss of the C105T Trail 55.

The new CA105T featured an upswept exhaust, and later models would include a chrome front fender. The CA95 Benly Touring 150, first seen in 1959, was being supplanted by a newer version of the same machine. The new version featured larger rubber kneepads on the tank, and smaller chrome panels. A more pronounced taillight, white wall tires and a tubular exhaust set the newer version apart from the old.

The April 1963 release of the latest CA72 Dream Touring 250 would see the shape of the fuel tank altered from the model sold until then.

Another changing of the guard was applied to the CA77 Dream Touring 305. Released in April of 1963, the latest iteration featured a differently shaped fuel tank than the previous model.

A completely new machine was released to dealers in September of 1963. The CA200 Honda 90/C200 Touring 90 was powered by an 87cc engine shifting through the four speeds with a manual clutch. Starting the single cylinder was accomplished via the use of a kick-start pedal only. Sold in White, Black or Scarlet Red, the fuel tank was trimmed with chrome panels and rubber kneepads. A "Honda 90" badge was also applied to the tank.

1963 HONDA

Model	Engine	Displacement	Transmission
CA100 Honda 50	OHV Single	49cc	Three-Speed, Auto
CA102 Honda 50	OHV Single	49cc	Three-Speed, Auto
C105T Trail 55	OHV Single	54cc	Three-Speed, Auto
CA105T Trail 55	OHV Single	54cc	Three-Speed, Auto
CA110 Sport 50	OHV Single	49cc	Three-Speed or Four-Speed, Manual
CA200 Honda 90 and C200 Touring 90	OHV Single	87cc	Four-Speed
CA95 Benly Touring 150	OHC Parallel Twin	154cc	Four-Speed
CA95 Benly Touring 150	OHC Parallel Twin	154cc	Four-Speed
CA72 Dream Touring 250	OHC Parallel Twin	247cc	Four-Speed
CA72 Dream Touring 250	OHC Parallel Twin	247cc	Four-Speed
CB72 Hawk 250	OHC Parallel Twin	247cc	Four-Speed
CL72 Scrambler 250	OHC Parallel Twin	247cc	Four-Speed
C77 Dream Touring 305	OHC Parallel Twin	305cc	Four-Speed
CA77 Dream Touring 305	OHC Parallel Twin	305cc	Four-Speed
CA77 Dream Touring 305	OHC Parallel Twin	305cc	Four-Speed
CB77 Super Hawk 305	OHC Parallel Twin	305cc	Four-Speed

HONDA　　　　　　　　　　　　　　　　　　　　　　　　　STANDARD CATALOG OF ® JAPANESE MOTORCYCLES

America's largest selling 2nd car
(on two wheels)

If you see more and more sporty red Hondas these days, don't be surprised. Not that Honda owners don't have a car. It's just that they've been spoiled. Running errands on a Honda is more fun. And you save a lot of money.

Take the price, for instance: $245 (plus a modest set-up charge). Could anything be lower? Look what you've got going for you in a Honda. A 4-stroke 50cc OHV engine that conjures up 225 miles to a gallon of gas. At 45 mph you hardly know the motor's there. Even a double load can't ruffle it.

Other things count, too: 3-speed transmission, automatic clutch, dual cam-type brakes on both wheels, even an optional push-button starter for the ultimate in ease. But the biggest thing is the sheer fun of owning a Honda. And meeting the nicest people. How about making your 2nd car a Honda? You'll have lots of company. For address of your nearest dealer or other information, write: American Honda Motor Co., Inc., Dept. P, 100 West Alondra, Gardena, California.

HONDA world's biggest seller!

© 1963 AMERICAN HONDA MOTOR CO., INC

In 1963, Honda's motorcycle was positioned as an alternative to the second family car for Americans.

HONDA 1964

Although similar to the CA105T Trail 55, the new CT200 Trail 90 was enhanced in several ways. A larger engine displacement delivered more horsepower, and an extra gear was installed for versatility. The front suspension on the new 90 was of the bottom link design, and a pair of dual overlay rear sprockets was installed on the rear wheel.

The S90 Super 90, released in October of 1964 wore the stylings of a bigger motorcycle along with many common features of its larger siblings. The 89cc single-cylinder motor shifted through four speeds manually. Examples of the S90 built between October 1964 and March 1968 wore painted silver fenders and were only sold in solid White, Black or Scarlet Red colors.

Those built after March of 1968 featured chrome fenders and were available in Candy Blue or Candy Red paint, as well as White and Black solids.

Designated the CA95 or Benly Touring 150, this Honda was modified only slightly from the previous year's edition.

Stuart Covington

The Honda 50 took over where the Super Cub left off but was virtually the same machine with a new name.

Stuart Covington

1964 HONDA

Model	Engine	Displacement	Transmission
CA100 Honda 50	OHV Single	49cc	Three-Speed, Auto
CA102 Honda 50	OHV Single	49cc	Three-Speed, Auto
CA105T Trail 55	OHV Single	54cc	Three-Speed, Auto
CA110 Sport 50	OHV Single	49cc	Three-Speed or Four-Speed, Manual
CA200 90 and C200 Touring 90	OHV Single	87cc	Four-Speed
CT200 Trail 90	OHV Single	87cc	Four-Speed, Auto
S90 Super 90 (New for 1964!)	OHV Single	89cc	Four-Speed, Manual
CA95 Benly Touring 150	OHC Parallel Twin	154cc	Four-Speed
CA72 Dream Touring 250	OHC Parallel Twin	247cc	Four-Speed
CB72 Hawk 250	OHC Parallel Twin	247cc	Four Speed
CL72 Scrambler 250	OHC Parallel Twin	247cc	Four-Speed
C77 Dream Touring 305	OHC Parallel Twin	305cc	Four-Speed
CA77 Dream Touring 305	OHC Parallel Twin	305cc	Four-Speed
CB77 Super Hawk 305	OHC Parallel Twin	305cc	Four-Speed

HONDA
1965

Honda's CA100 opened the doors for many new riders who longed for adventure on the open road, or at least while tooling around town.

Stuart Covington

Making its debut for 1965 was the S65 Sport 65, which was released on the first of April. Powered by a single cylinder 63cc overhead-cam engine, it had four manual gears on hand for the rider's selection. A high-mounted exhaust pipe was covered by a slotted heat shield. Sold in White, Black or Scarlet Red, the S65 wore a saddle of black and white vinyl. A red tank badge was accented with a silver wing.

Also new for 1965 was the CB160 Sport 160. It carried an extra seven ccs over the CA95 Benly Touring 150, and was packaged in a sportier format. Taking the place of the valanced fenders of the Benly, the CB160 wore wheel-hugging sheet metal between the telescopic front forks. A torpedo-shaped exhaust was used to allow for free breathing. The 161cc parallel twin motor inhaled through a pair of Keihin carburetors and shifted through a four-speed transmission.

Whether the color choice was Black, Scarlet Red, Blue or White, the fenders and side covers were finished in silver. When buying the Blue and Silver model, the saddle was covered in matching blue vinyl, while the rest of the hues came with a standard black mount.

An enhanced CL77 Scrambler 305 was rolled out for 1965 as well. Assembled with a fuel tank, side covers and fenders painted in silver, the bike could be ordered in three hues. The frame, upper forks and headlight bucket were sold in Blue, Black or Red. An upswept exhaust featured two separate tubes with a common muffler. A slotted, wrap-around heat shield was applied midway along the length. The 305cc OHC parallel twin sported dual carbs and sent the power through a four-speed transmission.

Pushing the performance envelope was the new CB450 Super Sport. It was a new model and so Honda applied a fresh series of identification

1965 HONDA

Model	Engine	Displacement	Transmission
CA100 Honda 50	OHV Single	49cc	Three-Speed, Auto
CA102 Honda 50	OHV Single	49cc	Three-Speed, Auto
CA105T Trail 55	OHV Single	54cc	Three-Speed, Auto
CA110 Sport 50	OHV Single	49cc	Three-Speed or Four-Speed, Manual
S65 Sport 65 and CS65	OHC Single	63cc	Four-Speed
CA200 Honda 90 and C200 Touring 90	OHV Single	87cc	Four-Speed
CT200 Trail 90	OHV Single	87cc	Four-Speed, Auto
S90 Super 90	OHV Single	89cc	Four-Speed, Manual
CA95 Benly Touring 150	OHC Parallel Twin	154cc	Four-Speed
CB160 Sport 160	OHC Parallel Twin	161cc	Four-Speed
CA72 Dream Touring 250	OHC Parallel Twin	247cc	Four-Speed
CB72 Hawk 250	OHC Parallel Twin	247cc	Four-Speed
CL72 Scrambler 250	OHC Parallel Twin	247cc	Four-Speed
CA77 Dream Touring 305	OHC Parallel Twin	305cc	Four-Speed
CB77 Super Hawk 305	OHC Parallel Twin	305cc	Four-Speed
CL77 Scrambler 305 (New for 1965!)	OHC Parallel Twin	305cc	Four-Speed
CB450 Super Sport and CB450K0 (New for 1965!)	DOHC Parallel Twin	444cc	Four-Speed

numbers. The KO letters used in the identification marked that this would be the first year for the model.

The CB450KO featured a 444cc, parallel twin motor with dual overhead cams. Dual constant velocity (CV) carburetors were employed for delivery of the fuel and air mix. A four-speed transmission with manual clutch was on hand for gear selection.

The only colors sold on the 1965 models were black with silver accents.

The fuel tank, upper fork tubes and headlight nacelle were all black, while the side covers and both fenders were finished in silver. The tubular frame was also done in black. The K0 and K1 models wore chrome panels and rubber kneepads on the fuel tank.

For some, the inexpensive Honda 50 was an introduction to motorcycles in 1965.

The price is only half the story. Let's face it. Honda is way out front in popularity. Nobody's even close. And for good reason. A Honda 50 is powered by a relentless 4-stroke, OHV engine that coaxes 200 miles from a gallon of gas. A paragon of economy. And it cruises at a comfortable 40 mph.

If that isn't enough, a Honda 50 has 3-speed transmission, dual cam-type brakes on both wheels for extra safety, even an optional push-button starter. About service? Honda has the largest parts and service organization in the country. Though you'll rarely need it. Hondas hold up. That goes for all 14 models. Choose a Honda. Most everybody does.

Honda—the world's biggest seller. For information, write: American Honda Motor Co., Inc., Dept. FZ, 100 W. Alondra, Gardena, Calif.

HONDA
ABOUT $215*

*PLUS DEALER'S SET-UP AND TRANSPORTATION CHARGES © 1965 AMERICAN HONDA MOTOR CO., INC.

MAY 1965

HONDA

STANDARD CATALOG OF ® JAPANESE MOTORCYCLES

CA-77 DREAM

Did you ever see a Dream running?

Here's one. The Honda Dream Touring model. So named because it performs like one. In either the 250 cc or 305 cc version. The Honda Dream purrs — doesn't roar — yet comes on with all the aplomb of a charging tiger when your throttle hand gives the command.

Perfect for open-road touring or city riding, the Honda Dream is comfortable, quiet and remarkably vibration-free. Just the ticket for the rider who wants power and ready response in a touring bike. And the Dream's heavy-duty shock absorbers make mirages out of bumps in the road.

Honda's rugged OHV four-stroke engine, twin cylinders, four-speed constant-mesh transmission, electric starter, smooth clutch and unerring brakes: that's the stuff Dreams are made of.

Be a smooth operator. Get a Honda Model CA-77. It's a Dream.

HONDA
world's biggest seller!

TECHNICAL SPECIFICATIONS — HONDA DREAM TOURING	
Engine .... 4-stroke OHC twin-cylinder	Maximum Speed .... 90 MPH (Approx.)
Brake Horsepower .... 23.0 HP @ 7,500 RPM	Fuel Consumption .... 102 Miles Per Gallon
Bore & Stroke .... 60 x 54mm	Transmission .... 4-Speed, Constant Mesh
Compression Ratio 8.2:1	Clutch .... Wet Multiplate-Type
Weight .... 372 lbs.	Shock Absorbers .... Heavy Duty Hydraulic-Type

The Honda Dream Touring, one of 14 Honda models to choose from, starts at about $560, plus dealer's set-up and transportation charges. For the address of your nearest dealer or other information, write: Dept. FX, American Honda Motor Co., Inc., 100 West Alondra Blvd., Gardena, California 90247.   © 1965 AMERICAN HONDA MOTOR CO., INC.

Stylish and with plenty of chrome, this Honda was a staple in the company's lineup, the 1965 CA-77 Dream.

STANDARD CATALOG OF ® JAPANESE Motorcycles

HONDA
1966

Among the models that would be departing by the end of the year were the CA200 Honda 90/C200 Touring 90 and the CT200 Trail 90. Farther up the food chain, the CA95 Benly Touring 150, CA72 Dream Touring 250 and the CB72 Hawk 250 would be de-listed from the catalogs.

The CM91 Honda 90 was a larger version of their CA102 Super Cub that was first seen in 1960. A bump in the displacement brought the number to 89cc, and the CM91 was still brought to life with a button or kick-start pedal. The three-speed gearbox remained an automatic.

The new CT90 Trail 90/CT90K0 replaced the CA105T Trail 55. Growing from 54 to 89ccs and carrying the newest K0 designation would help to track future changes to the model. The upswept, chrome exhaust system would remain in place on the K0 and K1 models. Early examples wore a pair of dual overlay sprockets on the rear wheel that were mated to the four-speed automatic transmission. Later models would feature an eight-speed dual-range transmission.

The 1966 CA160 Touring 160 was sold alongside the CA95 Benly Touring 150, which was on its way out in 1966. The new machine displaced a few more ccs and wore tires with thin white walls in place of the wider black-walls used on the Benly. The rear fender strut was also different on the new CA160.

The CL160 Scrambler was based on the CB160 Sport of the previous year. Built more for all around use, the CL160 had a set of dual exhaust pipes that were wrapped in a heat shield, a unit that became a large muffler. Carrying a weight of 282 lbs., the CL160 was shown with a top speed of 76 mph. The 161-cc engine was the same as found in the CB160, but was geared differently for off-road use. Both an electric and kick-starter were included to get things moving. The fenders and side covers were painted silver, while the options for the remaining sheet metal was Silver, Candy Orange and Candy Blue.

These models could be found at the 1,700 United States Honda dealers.

Back for another round of fun was the CB160 Sport. The 161cc engine and features of larger machines made the CB160 a great choice for all levels of riders.

Greg Mazza

HONDA

STANDARD CATALOG OF® JAPANESE Motorcycles

In 1966, the Honda 65 became an important part of the wedding party.

A memorable Honda ad line appeared in 1966—"You Meet the Nicest People on a Honda."

1966 HONDA

Model	Engine	Displacement	Transmission
CA100 Honda 50	OHV Single	49cc	Three-Speed, Auto
CA102 Honda 50	OHV Single	49cc	Three-Speed, Auto
CA110 Sport 50	OHV Single	49cc	Three-Speed orFour-Speed, Manual
S65 Sport 65 and CS65	OHC Single	63cc	Four-Speed
CA200 Honda 90 and C200 Touring 90	OHV Single	87cc	Four-Speed
CT200 Trail 90	OHV Single	87cc	Four-Speed, Auto
S90 Super 90	OHV Single	89cc	Four-Speed, Manual
CM91 Honda 90	OHC Single	89cc	Three-Speed, Auto
CT90 Trail 90 (CT90KO)	OHC Single	89cc	Four-Speed (early) Eight-Speed (late)
CA95 Benly Touring 150	OHC Parallel Twin	154cc	Four-Speed
CA160 Touring 160 (New for 1966)	OHC Parallel Twin	161cc	Four-Speed
CB160 Sport 160	OHC Parallel Twin	161cc	Four-Speed
CL160 Scrambler 160 (New for 1966)	OHC Parallel Twin	161cc	Four-Speed
CA72 Dream Touring 250	OHC Parallel Twin	247cc	Four-Speed
CB72 Hawk 250	OHC Parallel Twin	247cc	Four-Speed
CA77 Dream Touring 305	OHC Parallel Twin	305cc	Four-Speed
CB77 Super Hawk 305	OHC Parallel Twin	305cc	Four-Speed
CL77 Scrambler 305	OHC Parallel Twin	305cc	Four-Speed
CB450 Super Sport and CB450KO	DOHC Parallel Twin	444cc	Four-Speed

HONDA

1967

The first new model released to dealers for 1967 was the CL90 Scrambler. March 1st saw this 89cc model hit the sales floors. Both fenders and exhaust were chrome, and the heat-shielded exhaust pipe rode mid-level on the right side of the chassis. You could choose Candy Red, Candy Blue or Black, with a fuel tank finished in Silver. A manual clutch allowed changes between the four-speeds.

Although the CL160 Scrambler was departing, the CL160D and Scrambler 160D were right behind to fill its shoes. The major difference between the models was the addition of electric start to the "D." Where the previous variant wore an all silver motif, the new version could be purchased in Silver, Candy Orange or Candy Blue.

July saw the debut of the CL125A Scrambler. High-mounted exhaust allowed for some mild off-road riding with less chance of causing fires, and the slotted heat shield kept the rider's legs from doing the same thing. This Honda came with a pair of chrome fenders and a Candy Blue or Bright Yellow frame and upper fork legs. The headlight bucket and gas tank were always finished in Metallic Silver. The overhead-cam twin engine pulled air through a single CV carb and shifted with a four-speed transmission.

The CL77 carried the exhaust high to avoid setting brush fires while being ridden off-road and the heat shield protected the rider's legs.

Terry Mitchell

The Dream Touring 305 continued to be one of Honda's more successful offerings.

HONDA
STANDARD CATALOG OF JAPANESE Motorcycles

The CB450 was considered a large motorcycle from Honda, although it was dwarfed by machines from other manufacturers.
Chris and Jennifer Christensen

Several 1967 Honda models were featured in this ad including the 90, Sport 50, Trail 90 and Roadster.

One month later, the SS125A Super Sport joined the fray. Powered by the same 124cc twin-cylinder motor as the CL 125, the Super Sport had a low mounted exhaust. The fuel tank was formed with more angular contours. The fenders were always finished in Silver. The frame, upper forks, headlight bucket, swing arm and shock covers were available in Candy Red, Candy Blue or Black. A side cover emblem of "SS125" was done in Red and White.

The final entrant for 1967 would be a one-year-only model. The CB450D Super Sport 450 had an evil twin in name only óthe CL450 Scrambler 450.

In June 1967, this model arrived with a 444cc dual-overhead-cam parallel twin motor fitted with a pair of upswept exhaust pipes, one on each side of the machine. The requisite heat shield was also used on each length of pipe.

Two chrome fenders were blended with upper forks and a headlight nacelle of black. Metallic Silver, Candy Red or Candy Blue would cover the fuel tank and side covers. The side covers were tattooed with a short section of angled checkerboard stripe with "450" accenting the black and white graphic.

Slotted beneath the Black Bomber was the 305cc Super Hawk, but the "big bike" design was still present.

Vintage Memories, Inc.

1967 HONDA

Model	Engine	Displacement	Transmission
CA100 Honda 50	OHV Single	49cc	Three-Speed, Auto
CA102 Honda 50	OHV Single	49cc	Three-Speed, Auto
CA110 Sport 50	OHV Single	49cc	Three-Speed or Four-Speed, Manual
S65 Sport 65 and CS65	OHC Single	63cc	Three-Speed
S90 Super 90	OHV Single	89cc	Four-Speed, Manual
CL90 Scrambler 90	OHC Single	89cc	Four-Speed, Manual
CM91 Honda 90	OHC Single	89cc	Three-Speed, Auto
CT90 and Trail 90	OHC Single	89cc	Four-Speed (early) Eight-Speed (late)
CL125A Scrambler	OHC Parallel Twin	124cc	Four-Speed
SS125A Super Sport	OHC Parallel Twin	124cc	Four-Speed
CA160 Touring	OHC Parallel Twin	161cc	Four-Speed
CB160 Sport	OHC Parallel Twin	161cc	Four-Speed
CL160 Scrambler	OHC Parallel Twin	161cc	Four-Speed
CL160D Scrambler	OHC Parallel Twin	161cc	Four-Speed
CA77 Dream Touring 305	OHC Parallel Twin	305cc	Four-Speed
CB77 Super Hawk 305	OHC Parallel Twin	305cc	Four-Speed
CL77 Scrambler 305	OHC Parallel Twin	305cc	Four-Speed
CB450 Super Sport	DOHC Parallel Twin	444cc	Four-Speed
CB450D Super Sport	DOHC Parallel Twin	444cc	Four-Speed
CL450 Scrambler	DOHC Parallel Twin	444cc	Four-Speed

HONDA

STANDARD CATALOG OF® JAPANESE Motorcycles

Take your pick of a Honda. The Trail 90 left. Or the Rally, one of the Honda Custom Group. These models feature a special type of tank, pipe, handlebars, seat. Ride off on your personalized Honda. Wild.

Honda shapes the world of wheels
You've got to hand it to Honda. New designs. New colors. Altogether 20 models to put a glint in your eye. That famous four-stroke engine takes everything in stride. Won five out of five '66 Grand Prix Championships, 50cc to 500cc. A world's record. With Honda, performance counts as well as style. And that tells it like it is. Any questions? See your local Honda dealer for a safety demonstration ride. **HONDA**

For a free color brochure and safety pamphlet write: American Honda Motor Co., Inc., Dept. QF, Box 50, Gardena, California 90247. ©1967, AHM.

Honda was mod, colorful and trendy in 1967 with its "fab gear" Honda 90 cycles.

STANDARD CATALOG OF® JAPANESE Motorcycles   HONDA

1968

The expanding interest in the multiple use scramblers saw Honda roll out their 450 version for 1968.
Rick Darke Photo

To comply with the state of Nevada's five-horsepower restriction, a CL90L Scrambler was introduced in 1968. The "L" model was almost identical to the standard CL90, but had Red and White "5HP" appliqués of the air filter housing.

Released to dealers in January of 1968, the CL175 Scrambler was built around a tubular steel chassis backbone. It featured both chrome fenders and chrome exhaust. The latest version would replace the CL160 Scrambler, in its final year of sales. The CL175 also used a five-speed transmission, one of many 1968 models to do so.

Another fresh face for 1968 was the CA175 (CD175) Touring. A 174cc engine hung from the pressed-steel frame, and a four-speed gearbox was included. Both the tank and side cover emblems read "Honda 175." Two new 350cc models included the CB350 Super Sport made its debut with great fanfare from both Honda and the motorcycle press. *Cycle Illustrated* was impressed by the CB350's 10,500 redline and its five-speed transmission. The engine produced an impressive 36 hp. The semi-double loop frame was crafted from pressed steel, and provided ample rigidity for the nimble machine. A pair of gleaming chrome megaphone exhausts added a sporty flair. The headlight bucket and side covers were White, while the fuel tank was sold in Candy Blue, Candy Red or Green with a White lower half. Another "350" first seen in 1968 was the CL350 Scrambler. It was a close match to the CB350, but was fitted with high-mounted, exhaust pipes that were covered with slotted heat shields and a black muffler guard.

HONDA

The 1968 CL350 Scrambler provided the more experienced rider with added power in a dual-purpose format. Rick Darke Photo

Buyers were also calling for increasing power in street machines and the CL450 answered the call in 1968. Rick Darke Photo

Two-tone paint was again found on the dual-purpose 350. The color choices were Daytona Orange, Candy Blue or Candy Red teamed with a lower section of White. Side covers and headlight shell were also White. Early CL350's featured upper fork legs of Black, while later versions wore colors that matched the primary paint. The same 325cc motor of the CB was used on the CL and it shifted through five speeds.

Honda's CB450 Super Sport was headed for retirement by the end of 1968. The CB450K1 Super Sport debuted in April 1968. Chrome fenders replaced the painted ones used on the exiting model, and several additional cosmetic changes were also seen.

The new K1 had a free-standing speedometer and tachometer, just above the headlight. The on- and off-road CL450K1 Scrambler was also introduced in February of 1968, and was equipped as most other Honda Scramblers. A pair of high exhaust pipes was finished in all-chrome including the two-piece heat shield. The headlight bucket and upper fork legs were delivered in Black. Chrome fenders were used over both tires. The same 444cc, DOHC parallel twin motor rested in the frame as in the CB450K1. A "Honda 450" emblem, complete with the corporate wing was applied to the fuel tank that was sold in Candy Red, Candy Blue or Metallic Silver.

1968 HONDA

Model	Engine	Displacement	Transmission
CA100 Honda 50	OHV Single	49cc	Three-Speed, Auto
CA102 Honda 50	OHV Single	49cc	Three-Speed, Auto
CA110 Sport 50	OHV Single	49cc	Three-Speed or Four-Speed, Manual
P50 Little Honda	OHC Single	49cc	Automatic
S65 Sport 65 and CS65	OHC Single	63cc	Four-Speed
S90 Super 90	OHV Single	89cc	Four-Speed, Manual
CL90 Scrambler	OHC Single	89cc	Four-Speed, Manual
CL90L (5hp) Scrambler	OHC Single	89cc	Four-Speed, Manual
CM91 Honda 90	OHC Single	89cc	Three-Speed, Auto
CT90 Trail	OHC Single	89cc	Four-Speed (early) and Eight-Speed (late)
CL125A Scrambler	OHC Parallel Twin	124cc	Four-Speed
SS125A Super Sport	OHC Parallel Twin	124cc	Four-Speed
CA160 Touring	OHC Parallel Twin	161cc	Four-Speed
CB160 Sport	OHC Parallel Twin	161cc	Four-Speed
CL160D Scrambler	OHC Parallel Twin	161cc	Four-Speed
CA175 Touring (CD175)	OHC Parallel Twin	174cc	Four-Speed
CL175 Scrambler (CL175K0) (New for 1968)	OHC Parallel Twin	174cc	Five-Speed
CA77 Dream Touring 305	OHC Parallel Twin	305cc	Four-Speed
CB77 Super Hawk 305 (Final year of sale)	OHC Parallel Twin	305cc	Four-Speed
CL77 Scrambler 305 (Final year of sale)	OHC Parallel Twin	305cc	Four-Speed
CB350 Super Sport (CB350K0) (New for 1968)	OHC Parallel Twin	325cc	Five-Speed
CL350 Scrambler (CL350K0) (New for 1968)	OHC Parallel Twin	325cc	Five-Speed
CB450 Super Sport (CB450K0) (Final year of sale)	DOHC Parallel Twin	444cc	Four-Speed
CB450K1 Super Sport (New for 1968)	DOHC Parallel Twin	444cc	Five-Speed
CL450K1 Scrambler (New for 1968)	DOHC Parallel Twin	444cc	Five-Speed

HONDA

1969

STANDARD CATALOG OF® JAPANESE Motorcycles

The appearance of Honda's big CB750-4 in 1968 set the motorcycle world at a new tilt and would forever change the way we rode.

Ray Landy

The year 1969 would see the world of two-wheeled transportation change forever. Honda's introduction of their CB750 set the standards for performance and smoothness. Four-cylinder engines had been used in other motorcycles as early as 1911 but they lacked the Honda's technical prowess. The smallest of the 1969 models was the CL70 Scrambler. A 72cc, overhead-cam engine delivered power to a four-speed transmission.

The CT90 Trail was supplanted by the CT90K1. Changes included the telescopic front forks in place of the pressed steel variety. The eight-speed, dual range transmission with an automatic clutch was standard through 1979. Honda replaced the CA175 Touring with the CA175K3 version. The K3 would be built around a tubular steel chassis instead of the pressed-steel type. The cylinders were more vertical than the CA175.

The CB175K3 Super Sport was first seen in June 1969 and would change within the model year. A two-tone fuel tank was used on the entire 1969 run of CB175K3s. Early models wore either Candy Blue or Candy Red on the top half of the tank, while White graced the lower section. Later models saw the color segment extended lower with the "Honda" name in that field. Later offerings wore pleated vinyl on the saddle while early examples were non-pleated. Later models also had covered coil springs on the rear shocks. A 174-cc, overhead-cam, parallel twin engine shifted through a five-speed transmission, and used a 12-volt electrical system. Drum brakes were used at both ends.

The CL175 Scrambler was upgraded to the CL175K3. The new K3 included fenders, fuel tank, side covers and headlight shell that were all painted the same hue, depending on what color was selected. Candy Blue and Candy Orange were the paint options. The front fender was mounted high above the front tire versus the rubber-hugging version. The frame was now an all-tubular layout and the cylinders were more upright in the engine. The CB350K0 Super Sport was replaced by the CB350K1. The seat was now covered with pleated vinyl, and a single reflector was added to the front fender. A rectangular tail light lens was also used in place of the oval style.

The newly minted CB450K2 Super Sport took the place of the K1. A differently shaped fuel tank was now seen wearing a gold accent stripe. Just below this stripe were new metal tank badges, replacing the earlier painted trim. The rectangular tail light lens was also applied to the 1969 CB450.

The CL450 was altered from the previous K1 to the latest K2 model. "450 DOHC" side-cover emblems were done in gold for 1969. The pleated seating surface and rectangular tail light were new.

The CB750 Four (CB750K0) model was released on the June 6, 1969 and embodied the best of everything Honda had to offer while it surpassed anything else on the market. Displacing 736cc, and breathing through a set of four carburetors, the spent gases departed through a four-into-four exhaust. Honda claimed the bike produced 68 hp and could run up to 125 mph.

The new CB750 had only one overhead cam. Both electric start and a kick-start pedal were available. A four-into-four throttle cable system was used to control the bank of carbs. With the power on tap, Honda offered a single hydraulic disc up front was joined with an internally-expanding rear drum brake on the rear wheel. A double loop, steel tube frame held everything in place and both ends were fully suspended.

Displacing 735cc into an inline-four configuration, the CB750's engine was a model of modern efficiency and smoothness. Ray Landy

1969 HONDA

Model	Engine	Displacement	Transmission
CA100 Honda 50	OHV Single	49cc	Three-Speed, Auto
CA102 Honda 50	OHV Single	49cc	Three-Speed, Auto
CA110 Sport 50	OHV Single	49cc	Three-Speed orFour-Speed, Manual
S65 Sport 65 or CS65	OHC Single	63cc	Four-Speed
CL70 Scrambler (CL70K0)	OHC Single	72cc	Four-Speed, Manual
S90 Super 90 or CS90	OHV Single	89cc	Four-Speed, Manual
CL90 Scrambler	OHC Single	89cc	Four-Speed, Manual
CL90L (5hp) Scrambler	OHC Single	89cc	Four-Speed, Manual
CM91 Honda 90	OHC Single	89cc	Three-Speed, Auto
CT90K1 Trail	OHC Single	89cc	Eight-Speed, Auto
SS125A Super Sport	OHC Parallel Twin	124cc	Four-Speed
CA160 Touring	OHC Parallel Twin	161cc	Four-Speed
CB160 Sport	OHC Parallel Twin	161cc	Four-Speed
CA175 Touring	OHC Parallel Twin	174cc	Four-Speed
CA175K3 Touring or CD175K3	OHC Parallel Twin	174cc	Four-Speed
CB175K3 Super Sport	OHC Parallel Twin	174cc	Four-Speed
CL175 Scrambler	OHC Parallel Twin	174cc	Five-Speed
CL175K3 Scrambler	OHC Parallel Twin	174cc	Five-Speed
CA77 Dream Touring 305	OHC Parallel Twin	305cc	Four-Speed
CB350 Super Sport (CB350K0)	OHC Parallel Twin	325cc	Five-Speed
CB350K1 Super Sport	OHC Parallel Twin	325cc	Five-Speed
CL350 Scrambler (CB350K0)	OHC Parallel Twin	325cc	Five-Speed
CL350K1 Scrambler	OHC Parallel Twin	325cc	Five-Speed
CB450K1 Super Sport	DOHC Parallel Twin	444cc	Five-Speed
CB450K2 Super Sport	DOHC Parallel Twin	444cc	Five-Speed
CL450K1 Scrambler	DOHC Parallel Twin	444cc	Five-Speed
CL450K2 Scrambler	DOHC Parallel Twin	444cc	Five-Speed
CB750 Four (CB750K0) (New model)	SOHC Inline Four	736cc	Five-Speed

HONDA

STANDARD CATALOG OF JAPANESE MOTORCYCLES

1970

One of the hues seen on the 1970 CB750 was Candy Ruby Red, proving to be a popular choice for the big Honda.

Vintage Memories, Inc.

The CA100, first sold in 1962 would disappear after 1970. The slightly more powerful C70M would supplant the tiny machine. The latest CL70K1 Scrambler now carried fuel in a revised tank that was finished in Silver Metallic with the winged Honda logo. The speedometer was housed as an individual gauge. Rear shock springs were now enclosed in tubular housings.

The CT90K2 wore a pair of gray side covers to better accent its gray shroud. New for 1970 was the CB100 Super Sport. Powered by a 99cc OHC engine, it was designed to mimic the bigger street-going models. The CL100 Scrambler was close to being a clone of the CB100, but featured a few altered details. The upswept exhaust of the CL100 was covered with a two-piece heat shield, and the fuel tank carried different contours. For 1970, the CB175 K4 was seen with a two-tone fuel tank decorated with white Honda "wing" on both sides and the word "Honda" in black.

STANDARD CATALOG OF® JAPANESE MOTORCYCLES　　　　　　　　　　　　　　　　　　　　　　　HONDA

The CB750 would continue to dominate the market for big motorcycles for several years until other manufacturers caught up.

Vintage Memories, Inc.

The CL175K3 Scrambler would last until March of 1970 when the K4 Scrambler took over. Changes on the K4 included chrome fenders that hugged the tires, a black heat shield on the muffler and a white tank stripe that had a new shape. The pillion and fuel tank were also re-designed for the 1970. The CB350K2 Super Sport was enhanced with a few minor upgrades. The front fender braces now connected to the lower end of the front fork tubes from their previous location further up the legs. The latest color scheme included the two-tone tank seen on other 1970 models with matching side covers, upper fork legs and headlight shells. Candy Blue Green, Candy Gold and Candy Ruby Red were the 1970 options.

The CL350K2 Scrambler also experienced some cosmetic changes. A different profile of the fuel tank was augmented by a white accent stripe, and the selected unit color, applied to the tank, side covers, upper forks and headlight bucket. The black heat shield on the muffler was exchanged for a perforated chrome version.

The CB450K3 Super Sport had become a motorcycle that many magazine editors of the day considered to be a perfect. With a weight just over 420 lbs., and 45 hp on tap, the latest CB450 was both nimble and stable.

An hydraulic front disc brake was installed on the 1970 model that enhanced performance over the drum brake used before. A major improvement on the 1970 CB450 was the front fork "borrowed" from its big brother the CB750. The geometry led to nearly perfect road handling and comfort. The rear shocks were nitrogen-pressurized De Carbon units.

Candy Gold paint was accented by black trim, whereas other hues wore gold trim against their selected colors.

Brad Powell Collection

33

HONDA

STANDARD CATALOG OF® JAPANESE Motorcycles

Late in 1970, the K0 became the K1, and incremental changes were seen including revised side covers and badges.

Brad Powell Collection

The 450 Scrambler did not receive the same revisions as the Super Sport, but did get a few minor revisions. Fuel tank graphics included a white, tapered stripe but the side covers were unchanged.

The CB750K0 remained on the books until the CB750K1 was released.. A new version of the side cover badge was also seen on the K1.

1970 HONDA

Model	Engine	Displacement	Transmission
CA100 Honda 50	OHV Single	49cc	Three-Speed, Auto
C70M Honda 70 (C70MK0)	OHC Single	72cc	Three-Speed, Auto
CL70K1 Scrambler	OHC Single	72cc	Four-Speed, Manual
CL90L (5hp) Scrambler	OHC Single	89cc	Four-Speed, Manual
CT90K2 Trail	OHC Single	89cc	Eight-Speed
CB100 Super Sport (CB100K0)	OHC Single	99cc	Five-Speed
CL100 Scrambler (CL100K0)	OHC Single	99cc	Five-Speed
CA175K3 Touring (CD175K3)	OHC Parallel Twin	174cc	Four-Speed
CB175K4 Super Sport	OHC Parallel Twin	174cc	Five-Speed
CL175K3 Scrambler	OHC Parallel Twin	174cc	Five-Speed
CL175K4 Scrambler	OHC Parallel Twin	174cc	Five-Speed
CB350K2 Super Sport	OHC Parallel Twin	325cc	Five-Speed
CL350K2 Scrambler	OHC Parallel Twin	325cc	Five-Speed
CB450K3 Super Sport	DOHC Parallel Twin	444cc	Five-Speed
CL450K3 Scrambler	DOHC Parallel Twin	444cc	Five-Speed
CB750 Four (CB750K0) (Through Sept. 21)	SOHC Inline Four	736cc	Five-Speed
CB750K1750 Four	SOHC Inline Four	736cc	Five-Speed

HONDA
1971

The CL70K2 retained the Silver Metallic fuel tank that was trimmed with tapered stripes to match the unit color chosen. Candy Red joined the Candy Sapphire Blue and Candy Topaz Orange that were first offered in 1970.

The CT90K3 received a few minor cosmetic changes for 1971. Bright Yellow was replaced by Summer Yellow on the order sheet. The exhaust system now featured black piping covered by chrome heat shields.

The CB100K1 had an altered saddle contour and a strip of chrome was added to the lower edge. Side cover "CB100" badges were molded plastic versus the previous adhesive art. The lower third of the fuel tank was finished in white with "Honda" falling within that zone. Changes included a new one-pieced heat shield, perforated with cylindrical openings. The front fender was now suspended with a pair of curved supports. A molded plastic CL100 badge was also used on the side covers.

The CB175K5 Super Sport was almost identical to the K2 model it replaced. The side cover emblems had the same shape and size, but now featured a chrome background with the white "175" on a field of black. All CL175K5 models featured a few more changes. The 1971 exhaust heat shield was now all chrome. The cooling slots were

Strato Blue Metallic was a new color choice for the 1971 CL350. The tank stripe's color scheme had been revised as well.

Steve Henkel

Taking one step closer to their biggest CB750 was the CB450 model.

American Honda

HONDA

STANDARD CATALOG OF JAPANESE MOTORCYCLES

Carrying a smaller version of the 750's inline-four motor in its frame, the CB500 arrived for 1971 and was a great choice for someone wanting a big bike in a slightly smaller package.

American Honda

horizontal in front section, and cylindrical at the muffler. New colors were Strato Blue Metallic and Poppy Yellow Metallic.

The CB350K3 was the recipient of a new fuel tank and graphics package. The updated fuel receptacle now featured a reverse backswept black accent stripe. The CL350 was virtually unchanged for 1971 save the color choices and tank graphics. Both the CB and CL 450 models were upgraded cosmetically, but no alterations were made on the mechanical side. The CL variant did have a new one-piece muffler and a newly vented heat shield, also done in one section, replacing the previous two-piece unit. Strato Blue Metallic and Poppy Yellow Metallic joined the old standby Candy Topaz Orange. The side covers also wore the "Double Overhead Cam 450" designation.

Almost identical in design to its bigger brother the CB750, the CB500 was downsized in every dimension. With the tank half full, the CB500 tipped the scales at only 427 lbs., about 80 lbs. lighter than the 750. The smaller and lighter CB500 was equipped just as well as the CB750.

Front disc brakes, a wide and comfortable saddle and a list of comfort and convenience features made this a great Honda. The four-into-four exhaust was different from the 750 version in both size and megaphone design.

With a top speed just shy of 100 mph, the CB500 would provide adequate power for almost any rider, especially those who didn't need the levels delivered by the 750.. List price in 1971 was $1,345.

1971 HONDA

Model	Engine	Displacement	Transmission
C70M Honda 70 (C70MKO)	OHC Single	72cc	Three-speed, auto
CL70K2 Scrambler	OHC Single	72cc	Four-speed, manual
CT90K3 Trail	OHC Single	89cc	Eight-Speed
CB100K1 Super Sport	OHC Single	99cc	Five-Speed
CL100K1 Scrambler	OHC Single	99cc	Five-Speed
CL100S Scrambler	OHC Single	99cc	Five-Speed
CB175K5 Super Sport	OHC Parallel Twin	174cc	Five-Speed
CL175K5 Scrambler	OHC Parallel Twin	174cc	Five-Speed
CB350K3 Super Sport	OHC Parallel Twin	325cc	Five-Speed
CL350K3 Scrambler	OHC Parallel Twin	325cc	Five-Speed
CB450K4 Super Sport	DOHC Parallel Twin	444cc	Five-Speed
CL450K4 Scrambler	DOHC Parallel Twin	444cc	Five-Speed
CB500K0 500 Four (New For 1971)	SOHC Inline Four	498cc	Five-Speed
CB750K1 750 Four	SOHC Inline Four	736cc	Five-Speed

HONDA
1972

Very few changes were made to the 1972 CB750, except for the reflectors on the front forks and the Flake Sunrise Orange paint.
David Bloom

Honda introduced the C70K1 for the latest sales year. It featured the traditional molded front shroud that added a touch of style to the compact model. The solo seat was joined by a luggage rack that added carrying capacity to the fuel-efficient model. The CL70K3 Scrambler saddle was covered in a different vinyl pattern. The heat shield and exhaust were mounted at a slightly higher location and the shield's venting was revised. Fuel tanks on the 1972 models were finished in Special Silver Metallic with a set of red and black stripes. An auxiliary fuel tank was found to the left of the rear-mounted luggage rack. The black band was removed from the Honda logo on the shroud, and only Mars Orange was sold for 1972.

The CB100K2 Super Sport received only cosmetic changes. The CB175K6 was back with a 2.4-gallon fuel tank decorated with a shapely black stripe that held the "Honda" name. The 282-lb. dry weight allowed the CB175K6 to be propelled to a top speed of 76 mph.

The Scrambler crowd had the CL175K6 with many cosmetic changes but nothing in the mechanical department. The CB350F was a downsized version of its sibling, the CB500.

A set of Keihin carbs was used but this time 20mm versions handled the incoming blend. A single overhead cam motor was used to power the CB350F, and a front disc brake was used to slow it down. The tachometer wore a redline of 10,000 rpm. The speedometer and tachometer were joined by a small panel of warning lamps. Even with their new inline-four cylinder brother join-

HONDA

STANDARD CATALOG OF® JAPANESE MOTORCYCLES

The Honda lineup in 1972 included the XL-250 (left) and the SL-175 (right), the motorcycles that freed riders, according to the ad.

No city limits.

Cities can be inhuman. They squeeze you. They choke you. And they limit you.

Motorcycles free you. Especially the new single-cylinder Honda XL-250 and SL-125 K1.

They're rugged dirt machines that are also suitable for road riding. So they get you out to the country without a hitch.

They each have a USDA-approved spark arrestor/muffler to protect the countryside and people's ears. They're powered by famous, dependable Honda four-stroke engines to protect your peace of mind. And they're backed by strong Honda warranties to protect you.

The Honda dealer in your city will have the new XL-250 and Motosport™125 soon. Drop by. There's no limit to the ways he can get you out of town.

Honda.

ing the family, the CB350K4 would return for another year of fun. The painted headlight shell was replaced by a black version for 1972 and the "350" side cover badges were enlarged. CL350K4 models would receive a few minor tweaks for 1972. A reshaped fuel tank was mounted to the chassis and a pair of angular slots was cut into the side covers. The 350 Scrambler would also see a few new styling touches to set it apart from the 1971 models. The fuel tank now carried a more oval profile. The CB450K5 was back for 1972. Its upper fork legs were chrome and the headlight bucket was black. The CL450K5 also received a few alterations including a more oval contour applied to the fuel tank as was white and orange striping. For 1972 the CB750 wore a black instead of color-matched headlight housing. The upper fork legs were also changed from the color keyed choice to chrome for 1972. A different taillight was incorporated as new, enlarged side reflectors on the front forks.

1972 HONDA

Model	Engine	Displacement	Transmission
C70K1 Honda 70 (C70MK1)	OHC Single	72cc	Three-Speed, Auto
CL70K3 Scrambler	OHC Single	72cc	Four-Speed, Manual
CT90K4 Trail	OHC Single	89cc	Eight-Speed
CB100K2 Super Sport	OHC Single	99cc	Five-Speed
CL100K2 Scrambler	OHC Single	99cc	Five-Speed
CL100S2 Scrambler	OHC Single	99cc	Five-Speed
CB175K6 Super Sport	OHC Parallel Twin	174cc	Five-Speed
CL175K6 Scrambler	OHC Parallel Twin	174cc	Five-Speed
CB350F Four	SOHC Inline Four	347cc	Five-Speed
CB350K4 Super Sport	OHC Parallel Twin	325cc	Five-Speed
CL350K4 Scrambler	OHC Parallel Twin	325cc	Five-Speed
CB450K5 Super Sport	DOHC Parallel Twin	444cc	Five-Speed
CL450K5 Scrambler	DOHC Parallel Twin	444cc	Five-Speed
CB500K2 500 Four	SOHC Inline Four	498cc	Five-Speed
CB750K2 750 Four	SOHC Inline Four	736cc	Five-Speed

HONDA
1973

Powered by a 325cc parallel-twin engine, the 350G made a great choice for the mid-level rider.

Rick Youngblood

The CT70 was gone, and only the 90cc version would remain in 1974.

The CL100S3 Scrambler wore a white stripe on the fuel tank and a badge on the side cover reading ì100S.î Its blacked-out exhaust was fitted with a chrome heat shield. In 1973, a slightly larger CL125S Scrambler joined the CL100S3 in the Honda lineup. A 122cc engine and different trim set the two apart. In September 1972, the new CB125S make its debut and it was powered by a single-cylinder, 122cc OHC mill. Both Candy Topaz Orange and Candy Peacock Green were decorated with a White and Black tank graphics. A pair of chrome fenders were used on this Honda series.

The only changes seen on the 1973 CB175K7 Super Sport and CL175K7 Scrambler were a chrome grab rail behind their saddles, and the instrument panels were angled back towards the rider for better visibility.

The CB350G Super Sport was another offering for 1973. Unlike the CB350F, a 325cc parallel twin motor drove the G, and a pair of CV carburetors and a five-speed transmission was a part of the deal. A set of black and white tank graphics topped off paint choices of Candy Orange, Tyrolean Green Metallic or Iris Purple Metallic. A hydraulic front disc brake was a nice addition.

The latest CB450K6 wore new tank stripes and was sold in Brier Brown Metallic or Tyrolean Green Metallic. A chrome rail be-

HONDA

The Honda Scrambler 175 K6 and Super Sport 175 K6 were part of the ways people could "Experience Honda" in 1973.

Four Honda cycles were in this 1973 ad including the SL-350 (top left), the CL-350 K4 (top right), the CB-350 G (bottom left) and the CB-350 K4 (bottom right).

hind the seat and angled instruments were among the changes. An additional warning light pod was also installed between the tach and speedometer.

The CB500K2 was in its last year of sale in 1973, but wore a black side panel on the fuel tank and also had its enlarged instruments angled to better meet the rider's vision.

Honda's big CB750 Four was back. Striping on the fuel tanks was now black with white with gold accents. Paint options were Flake Sunrise Orange, Candy Bacchus Olive and Maxim Brown Metallic. No other changes were made to the popular CB, but something would need to be done soon as the Kawasaki began to encroach on Honda's earlier domination. The release of the more powerful Kawasaki Z-1 would stir up competition and soon Honda and other companies had more models that made the scene.

1973 HONDA

Model	Engine	Displacement	Transmission
C70K1 Honda 70 (C70MK1)	OHC Single	72cc	Three-Speed, Auto
CL70K3 Scrambler	OHC Single	72cc	Four-Speed, Manual
CT90K4 Trail	OHC Single	89cc	Eight-Speed
CL100S3 Scrambler	OHC Single	99cc	Five-Speed
CB125S	OHC Single	122cc	Five-Speed
CL125S Scrambler	OHC Single	122cc	Five-Speed
CB175K7 Super Sport	OHC Parallel Twin	174cc	Five-Speed
CL175K7 Scrambler	OHC Parallel Twin	174cc	Five-Speed
CB350F Four (CB350F0)	SOHC Inline Four	347cc	Five-Speed
CB350G Super Sport	OHC Parallel Twin	325cc	Five-Speed
CB350K4 Super Sport	OHC Parallel Twin	325cc	Five-Speed
CL350K4 Scrambler	OHC Parallel Twin	325cc	Five-Speed
CL350K5 Scrambler	OHC Parallel Twin	325cc	Five-Speed
CB450K6 Super Sport	DOHC Parallel Twin	444cc	Five-Speed
CL450K5 Scrambler	DOHC Parallel Twin	444cc	Five-Speed
CB500K2 500 Four	SOHC Inline-Four	498cc	Five-Speed
CB750K3 750 Four	SOHC Inline-Four	736cc	Five-Speed

STANDARD CATALOG OF® JAPANESE Motorcycles

HONDA

1974

Freedom Green Metallic was chosen for this 1974 CB750 and still looks classic today.

Norm Dank

Several new street models were added to the 1974 catalog, and some returning machines received minor alterations. The CT90K5 Trail 90 was one such machine. For the 1974 models, turn signal housings were chrome.

The CB125S1 returned, and was treated to a few new goodies for 1974. The drum brake on the front wheel was upgraded to a mechanical disc, and the 1974 would have a speedometer and tachometer as well. Honda engineers were assigned the task of creating a small machine that was capable of doing almost everything and it would also have to retail for less than $700. Based on the chassis used on the CB125, the new CB200 was fitted with a 198cc twin-cylinder motor. Weighing in at just over 300 lbs., the CB200 was small and solid.

The dual purpose variation was the CL200 Scrambler. Powered by the same 198cc, vertical twin mill, there were a few changes on the CL. A drum brake was found on both wheels instead of the front disc, rear drum combination on the CB. The CL200 was also fitted with a high-mounted exhaust system. Both the exhaust pipes and heat shield were plated in chrome

The CB360K0 and CB360G were powered by the same 356cc parallel twin engine and they shared both the chassis and the bodywork. The CB360G had a front wheel disc brake to set it apart from the CB360KO.

A dual purpose version of the 360 was also sold. The CL 360 Scrambler featured high-mounted

HONDA

STANDARD CATALOG OF® JAPANESE Motorcycles

Honda CB-750 K4 motorcycles were shown in action in this 1974 magazine ad.

exhaust, front drum brake and Muscat Green Metallic paint. The "CL360" emblems on each side panel were finished in yellow and white.

Moving up the food chain, a pair of 450 models remained in the catalog for 1974. The CB450K7 received different tank stripes that were a combination of black and gold. Colors offered in 1974 were Candy Orange and Maxim Brown Metallic. The CL450K6 Scrambler was seen wearing a fuel tank from earlier (K1-K4) models and different graphics of white and black. Candy Sapphire Blue Flake was the single color choice.

The two-piece muffler was now black with a pair of chrome heat shields. The exhaust was chrome with chrome shields. A chrome rail was located behind the saddle and the instrument cluster was leaned back at a steeper angle.

Weighing 454 lbs. when it was fully fueled, the CB550 produced 37.8 hp at 8,000 rpm. The single overhead cam motor displaced 544ccs, and was oiled with a wet sump lubrication system. A five-speed gearbox provided plenty of ratios to match the rider's needs, and it was capable of reaching 100 mph in top gear.

The big CB750 was back in the latest K4 trim. Modifications were trifling, and included wider white stripes on the fuel tank. Numeration on the speedometer was printed in increments of 20. Flake Sunrise Orange was again available, along with Freedom Green Metallic and Boss Maroon Metallic.

1974 HONDA

Model	Engine	Displacement	Transmission
CT90K5 Trail 90	OHC Single	89cc	Eight-Speed
CB125S1	OHC Single	122cc	Five-Speed
CB200 (CB200K0)	OHC Parallel Twin	198cc	Five-Speed
CL200 Scrambler	OHC Parallel Twin	198cc	Five-Speed
CB360 (CB360K0) Replaced CB350	OHC Parallel Twin	356cc	Six-Speed
CB360G Replaced CB350G	OHC Parallel Twin	356cc	Six-Speed
CL360 Scrambler (CL360K0) Dual Purpose	OHC Parallel Twin	356cc	Five-Speed
CB450K7 Super Sport	DOHC Parallel Twin	444cc	Five-Speed
CL450K6 Scrambler	DOHC Parallel Twin	444cc	Five-Speed
CB550 (CB550K0) 550 Four (New Model for 1974)	SOHC Inline-Four	544cc	Five-Speed
CB750K4 750 Four	SOHC Inline-Four	736cc	Five-Speed

STANDARD CATALOG OF® JAPANESE Motorcycles

HONDA
1975

Honda released the GL1000 for 1975. The touring machine was smoother and faster than anything else on the market, carving its own niche within moments of its debut.

Jerry Boody

The Trail 90, now in its K6 form would receive a few slight of changes. Tahitian Red would now be found on the frame shroud and side cover to match the body. Returning for 1975 was the CB125, now bearing the S2 designation. A different side cover badge was finished in white and yellow. The chrome cover seen on the rear shocks of the 1974s was also removed.

The CB200T, previously listed as a "K0" was now shown as "T0." New side cover "CB200T" art wore white and yellow paint. Only minor changes were applied to the 360cc models. The CB360K0 was now the CB360T0, and sported white and yellow "CB360T" badges on the side covers. The first of the new 1975 models was the CB400F Super Sport. Part of its allure was due to the serpentine four-into-one exhaust. The in-line-four cylinder motor was built with a single overhead cam and displaced 408cc. The CB400 Super Sport models would be seen with low, drag style handlebars. This design provided a more sporting riding crouch without being uncomfortable. A six-speed gearbox allowed the rider to keep the CB400 in the proper ratio. Rear drum and front disc brakes handled the deceleration.

HONDA

The 360cc models took over where the 350cc versions left off and the CB360T featured a parallel twin engine.

Doug King

Carrying a retail price tag of $1,395, the smallest Super Sport was purchased by those who sought performance on a lighter scale.

The CB500T offered a new engine to those wanting something different. The 498cc power plant was designed in parallel twin configuration, and was controlled by double overhead cams. The gearbox provided a choice of five ratios. The 1975 CB500T also carried gauges with white numerals on a black background.

Joining the CB550 Four was the CB550F Super Sport model, and it shared many design traits seen on the CB400 Super Sport. The 544cc engine controlled the valves with a single overhead cam, and fed each cylinder with its own Keihin 22mm carburetor. Only five speeds were found within the gearbox. The surface of both instruments was dark green with white numerals.

The CB750F Super Sport was powered by the same SOHC engine as the CB750K, the Super Sport exhaled through a serpentine four-into-one exhaust much like the two smaller Super Sports. The fuel tank, seat and integrated rear cowling were all unique to the 750 Super Sport.

The CB750K5 received a few minor changes, and continued to be a favorite among buyers seeking a larger machine. The GL1000 Gold Wing abandoned the previous path of building bigger and bigger inline-four motors. The new GL was driven by a horizontally opposed four-cylinder engine. Displacing 999ccs, the monster mill offered the GL Gold Wing a top speed of more than 130 mph.

The styling of the Gold Wing was conservative at best, and held a few surprises. The "fuel tank" was actually a storage compartment that opened for access to the electronics and accessories. Fuel was actually held in a five-gallon receptacle mounted beneath the saddle. The liquid cooled engine drew air through the front mounted radiator that was placed just in front of the frames' down tubes. A retail sticker in the neighborhood of $3,000 assured that only the serious rider would apply, but those that did were rewarded with a smooth motorcycle that handled terrifically.

1975 HONDA

Model	Engine	Displacement	Transmission
CT90K6 Trail 90	OHC Single	89cc	Eight-Speed
CB125S2	OHC Single	122cc	Five-Speed
CB200T (CB200T0)	OHC Parallel Twin	198cc	Five-Speed
CB360T (CB360T0)	OHC Parallel Twin	356cc	Six-Speed
CL360 Scrambler (CL360K1)	OHC Parallel Twin	356cc	Six-Speed
CB400F Super Sport (CB400F0)	SOHC Inline-Four	408cc	Six-Speed
CB500T (CB500T0)	DOHC Parallel Twin	498cc	Five-Speed
CB550F Super Sport (CB550F0)	SOHC Inline-Four	544cc	Five-Speed
CB550 (CB550K1) 550 Four	SOHC Inline-Four	544cc	Five-Speed
CB750F Super Sport (CB750F0)	SOHC Inline-Four	736cc	Five-Speed
CB750K5 750 Four	SOHC Inline-Four	736cc	Five-Speed
GL1000 Gold Wing (GL1000K0) (Flat-four, shaft)	SOHC Opposed-Four	999cc	Five-Speed

HONDA
1976

A Limited Edition version of the GL1000 was offered in 1976, and it was lavishly trimmed in gold along with a variety of unique features.

Pete Boody

The CT90 was back for 1976, and only minor changes were made. Shiny Orange paint was the only color and the ìHondaî decal on the shroud was yellow. The rear shocks also featured exposed coil springs and were chrome.

Also returning was the CB125S. Aquarius Blue was the color selected and the "Honda" appliqué on the tank was red with white outlines. The ì125Sî markings on the side covers were finished in red and white. A dark brown seat was installed and instrumentation was reduced to a speedometer only. The 122cc single-cylinder motor was now constructed using a two-piece head and still had a five-speed gearbox.

The CB200T wore new colors, Parakeet Yellow and Shiny Orange, with side covers of black.

The CB360T featured a silver points cover, and new fuel tank graphics. Candy Sapphire Blue or Candy Ruby Red both had tank stripes of black and white.

One new model for 1976 was the CJ360T. Wearing bodywork reminiscent of the 750 Super Sport, the CJ was a better-dressed version of the CB360T it was based on. A two-into-one exhaust helped to distinguish the two machines. The sleek fuel tank, altered saddle and rear cowling pre-

HONDA

Black side panels replaced the color matched versions used on the '75 CB400F, but the mid-size model remained very popular.

American Honda

sented the family resemblance to the bigger 750. Candy Antares Red was applied to the tank, rear cowl and front fender.

The CB400F Super Sport touted a few cosmetic modifications to set it apart from the 1975s. Parakeet Yellow replaced Varnish Blue in the catalog, but Light Ruby Red was still listed. Previous side covers matched the fuel tank, but 1976 models wore black.

CB500Ts remained for a final year. Changes were green instrument faces, and the addition of Candy Antares Red to the Glory Brown Metallic paint checklist.

Incremental changes continued on the CB550F Super Sports for 1976. Instrument faces were now finished with Light Green, and the seat was wrapped in brown. The 1976 colors were Flake Sapphire Blue and Shiny Orange. The CB550K was seen with the light green instrument faces, and only Candy Garnet Brown was sold.

New for 1976 was the CB750A Hondamatic. Taking styling cues from other 750 models and mixing in a two-speed, automatic gearbox, form and function were united. The 736cc inline-four engine was retained but it breathed through a four-into-one exhaust that was found on the Super Sport. Wire wheels and aluminum rims held the rubber in place. Muscat Green Metallic or Candy Antares Red were the choices in 1976.

The CB750F Super Sport was seen in Sulfur Yellow or Candy Antares Red and had the light green instrument faces. The CB750K models were only sold in Candy Antares Red and also featured the latest in light green instrumentation.

The GL1000, introduced in 1975 was only the recipient of a new color option, Sulfur Yellow, and had its gauge faces modified to the newest Light Green design.

To spice up the Gold Wing offerings, a Limited Edition model was also sold alongside the standard model. A wide array of decorative alterations set the Limited apart from the debut model. Gold striping and badges highlighted Candy Brown paint. Rims and the spoke wheels were also anodized in gold. The radiator shroud was chrome plated and the saddle took on a two-tier design. Located inside the faux fuel tank was a limited edition tool kit that came with a leather storage bag. The key fob was also finished in the same golden leather as the tool storage bag.

1976 HONDA

Model	Engine	Displacement	Transmission
CT90 Trail 90	OHC Single	89cc	Eight-Speed
CB125S	OHC Single	122cc	Five-Speed
CB200T	OHC Parallel Twin	198cc	Five-Speed
CB360T	OHC Parallel Twin	356cc	Six-Speed
CJ360T	OHC Parallel Twin	356cc	Five-Speed
CB400F Super Sport	SOHC Inline-Four	408cc	Six-Speed
CB500T 500 Twin	DOHC Parallel Twin	498cc	Five-Speed
CB550F Super Sport	SOHC Inline-Four	544cc	Five-Speed
CB550K 550 Four	SOHC Inline-Four	544cc	Five-Speed
CB750A 750 Hondamatic	SOHC Inline-Four	736cc	Two-Speed Automatic Gearbox
CB750F Super Sport	SOHC Inline Four	736cc	5-Speed
CB750K 750 Four	SOHC Inline-Four	736cc	5-Speed
GL1000 Gold Wing	SOHC Opposed-Four	999cc	5-Speed
GL1000 Ltd. Gold Wing	SOHC Opposed-Four	999cc	5-Speed Limited Edition

HONDA
1977

With the exhaust muffler mounted to the right side of the CB550F, the left side was exposed.

Sheri Fowler

The GL1000 received a few changes along with some new colors for 1977. Handlebars were slightly taller and reshaped to improve ergonomics. Instrument faces were black with green numerals. The contoured saddle used on the Limited Edition model was melded to the standard issue Gold Wing. Candy Antares Red returned, Candy Sirius Blue or Black were the latest color choices.

The Hondamatic now exhaled through a four-into-two exhaust, replacing the four-into one system of the debut model. Gold pinstripes were applied to the side covers and fuel tank, accenting the Candy Sword Blue or Candy Presto Red.

The CB750F Super Sport was the first model seen wearing Honda's Comstar wheels. These five-spoke rims were formed from aluminum components, saving weight and bringing a more modern look to the big 750.

A second disc brake was added to the front wheel, bringing a new level of stopping power to the sporting 750. The lower sections of the fork legs and the motor were blacked out on the 1977 versions. Candy Presto Red and Black were offered with a tank stripe of red with contrasting gold pinstripes. New color options were offered

HONDA

STANDARD CATALOG OF JAPANESE MOTORCYCLES

The world's best touring bike for the money.

"World's best" is not a phrase to be taken lightly. Yet the Honda GL-1000 motorcycle is a superlative expression of the grand touring machine which easily outclasses other similar bikes.

The heart of the bike is a powerful 999cc liquid-cooled, horizontally-opposed, overhead-cam, four-cylinder engine that delivers smooth-yet-awesome power through a sophisticated shaft drive system.

You'll notice an obvious absence of lateral torque reaction as you accelerate, thanks to an advanced counter-rotating alternator rotor that offsets the natural torque reaction of the crankshaft. The result is predictable straight-line power every time you throttle up.

Attention to precise engineering detail is obvious everywhere you look. Braking, for example, is handled by huge double hydraulic discs up front, a single disc at the rear. Fuel economy and exact throttle response come from the four constant-velocity carburetors.

The unique center storage compartment houses electrical components, coolant reservoir, plus space for small personal gear. Instrumentation includes warning lights for vital functions, plus an electric fuel gauge.

Even though the GL-1000 is one of the largest motorcycles you can buy, you'll be amazed at its comfort, agility and ease of handling due to its low center of gravity.

The minute you get on the bike, you know this is a machine designed for many thousands of miles of traveling, in no way merely a means of transportation. That's why GL-1000 buyers become believers overnight. It's that kind of a masterpiece.

You're probably thinking that the best of its kind is also the most expensive. The Honda GL-1000 lists at $2,938.* That's over $1,000 less than the most popular European sports tourer.**

That's why we call it the world's best touring bike for the money. A lot of people call it the world's best touring bike. Period.

HONDA GOING STRONG!

The Honda GL-1000 was posed by a tropical-looking ocean front setting in this 1977 ad.

on the CB750K. Candy Alpha Red or Excel Black found a gold tank stripe outlined with Red and White pinstripes. Side cover badges were finished in gold.

The 1977 model year would be the last one for the CB550F Super Sport. Instrument faces were Dark Blue, the seat was again covered in black with the rubber fork boots deleted. Candy Sword Blue and Candy Presto Red were both trimmed with a gold tank stripe.

The CB550K was in its penultimate year with Excel Black the only color, with a tank highlight-

A taller set of handlebars and recessed fuel cap were hallmarks of the last CB400 Super Sport.

Vintage Memories, Inc.

48

ed by a red stripe with gold pin striping. The side cover badges still read ì550Four Kî but were now finished in gold.

The CB400 Super Sport would also see its final year of sale, and only minor changes were employed.

The fuel tank cap was now recessed and the previous flat handlebars were raised to add comfort. Candy Antares Red models were trimmed with gold and orange tank stripes while the Parakeet Yellow version wore black and red accents.

Neither the CB200 nor CB360T were available in 1977.

Strangely enough, the CB125S was not seen in the official *Honda Motorcycle Identification Guide* for 1977, but would return in 1978.

The CT90 Trail 90 was back for another year. Shiny Orange was the same as in 1976, but the "Honda" logo on the frame was black.

In its penultimate year of production, the 1977 CB750F returned with only minor changes.

Doug Mitchel

1977 HONDA

Model	Engine	Displacement	Transmission
CT90 Trail 90	OHC Single	89cc	Eight-Speed
CB125S	OHC Single	122cc	Five-Speed
CJ360T	OHC Parallel Twin	356cc	Five-Speed
CB400F Super Sport	SOHC Inline Four	408cc	Six-Speed
CB550F Super Sport	SOHC Inline Four	544cc	Five-Speed
CB550K 550 Four	SOHC Inline Four	544cc	Five-Speed
CB750A 750 Hondamatic	SOHC Inline Four	736cc	Two-Speed Automatic
CB750F Super Sport	SOHC Inline Four	736cc	Five-Speed
CB750K 750 Four	SOHC Inline Four	736cc	Five-Speed
GL1000 Gold Wing	SOHC Opposed Four	999cc	Five-Speed

HONDA
1978

STANDARD CATALOG OF ® JAPANESE Motorcycles

Expanding their range of automatic gearbox models, Honda introduced the Hawk for 1978.

Ed Fleck

The CT90 Trail 90 was still around for 1978, and in keeping with the annual flip-flop, the "Honda" logo on the frame tube was again white. Bright Yellow replaced Shiny Orange as the only color. The handlebars, rear shock coil springs and both wheel hubs were now black.

Changes to the CB125S were minimal, including new side cover emblems that read "CB125S" and were yellow and white.

New was the CM185T Twinstar. This new model offered a bit more engine than the CB125S, but was still a simple motorcycle. Power came by a 181cc overhead cam parallel twin motor, and shifted through a four-speed gearbox. Two-into-two exhaust gave the spent gases an easy exit. A set of "buckhorn" bars reached back to the rider's hands for a comfortable grip, and the two-level saddle offered accommodations for rider and passenger. The CB400A Hawk Hondamatic shifted through a two-speed, semi- automatic transmission. The rider made selection of the two gears, but no manual clutch was required. The tachometer was supplanted by a series of gear indicator lights in the housing. The 395cc parallel twin engine featured three-valve heads and a set of 28mm Keihin constant velocity carburetors.

For those buyers who sought a middleweight machine that could be shifted manually, the CB400TI Hawk I was right up their alley. The same power plant was used on the Hondamatic, but the engine was fed by a pair of 32mm Keihin CV carbs. It shifted with a five-speed gearbox. The Hawk I had spoke wheels instead of the

Comstars, and was kick-start only. A drum brake on both wheels was another cost saving measure. Gauges were limited to a single speedometer and warning lights.

The CB400TII Hawk II looked like its siblings. It wore the same Comstar wheels as the Hondamatic, and the same fuel tank. The big differences were its kick start and an electric start as well as a hydraulic front disc brake. Another new model for 1978 was the CX500. Driven by a longitudinally mounted, 80-degree, V-twin engine, it was a new direction for Honda.

A mechanical drum brake on the rear wheel was joined by an 11-inch disc up front, grabbed by a hydraulic caliper. Comstar wheels were also used on the new CX500. The gauges were mounted in a housing that morphed into the headlight bezel. A speedometer, tachometer, temperature gauge and indicator lights were included.

A fuel tank holding 4.9 gallons was trimmed with a red stripe outlined with white. Both side covers bore "CX500" badges. The mildly stepped saddle was finished off with a passenger grab rail and a small cowling that ensconced the tail light. The CB550K was the only model in that displacement range. The other semi-automatic model, the CB750A was back for its final year of sale.

The CB750F Super Sport retained the black mill for 1978 as well as the matching fork lowers. The "750 Four" badges used on the side covers were of a more artistic style and stood alone. The GL1000 Gold Wing would receive several upgrades in 1978, but they were only cosmetic. A newly designed exhaust system was finished in all chrome and provided better breathing for the 999cc motor. Wheels were changed from spokes to Comstars and an instrument pod was added to the top of the "fuel" tank. Faces of the gauges were now black with red markings.

When equipped with accessories like the back rest and passenger pads, the 395cc Hawk was ready for the open road.

Ed Fleck

1978 HONDA

Model	Engine	Displacement	Transmission
CT90 Trail 90	OHC Single	89cc	Eight-Speed
CB125S	OHC Single	122cc	Five-Speed
CM185T Twinstar	OHC Parallel Twin	181cc	Four-Speed
CB400A Hawk Hondamatic	OHC Parallel Twin	395cc	Two-Speed Automatic
CB400TI Hawk I	OHC Parallel Twin	395cc	Five-Speed
CB400TII Hawk II	OHC Parallel Twin	395cc	Five-Speed
CX500	OHV V-Twin	496cc	Five-Speed
CB550K 550 Four	SOHC Inline Four	544cc	Five-Speed
CB750A 750 Hondamatic	SOHC Inline Four	736cc	Two-Speed Automatic
CB750F Super Sport	SOHC Inline Four	736cc	Five-Speed
CB750K 750 Four	SOHC Inline Four	736cc	Five-Speed
GL1000 Gold Wing	SOHC Opposed Four	999cc	Five-Speed

HONDA

1979

STANDARD CATALOG OF JAPANESE Motorcycles

Of Honda's new models for 1979, the CBX stole the show with its amazing six-cylinder engine and sporting nature.

Steve Passwater

The year 1979 would be the final one for the CT90 Trail model. Changes to the CB125S were minor, the biggest was the replacement of the front disc brake with a leading shoe drum. Twinstar CM185T was in the last year of sale for 1979, receiving only cosmetic modifications. With the CB400A removed from the catalog, both the Hawk I and II were unaltered from the previous year. The 400cc family grew by two with the CM400A Hondamatic and CM400T. The CM400A featured Honda's two-speed, semi-automatic transmission while the CM400T rowed through your choice of five gears. Both 400s breathed through new "shorty" exhausts and featured blacked-out Comstar wheels with silver alloy rims. The CX500 line expanded to three models in 1979, proving the popularity of the 80-degree V-twin that bowed a year earlier.

Suspended from the frame and taking the place of traditional frame tubes, the CBX motor was both powerful and rigid.
Steve Passwater

The two new CX500 models were added for 1979, with both powered by the same 496cc, V-twin mill found in the standard CX500. The CX500C Custom featured a teardrop fuel tank, deeply sculpted saddle and pullback handlebars.

The third CX500 model for 1979 was the Deluxe. The Deluxe stood apart with full-length exhaust canisters and a pair of chrome fenders. Taller handlebars and a cushier, chrome trimmed saddle provided a compliant and comfortable riding posture. The CB650 was introduced to satisfy the needs of many riders. A 627cc, SOHC inline-four engine shifted through a five-speed gearbox and delivered the power to the rear wheel via chain drive. With a dry weight of 437 lbs., the CB650 delivered ample power in a fairly lightweight package.

The CB750A Hondamatic was removed from the lineup after 1978 as the majority of riders preferred to shift their own gears.

All three 750 models, CB750K, CB750K Limited Edition and CB750F were now powered by a 749cc, DOHC, 16-valve engine that delivered improved performance. A set of four 30mm Keihin carburetors fed its expanded dimensions. The new design was 1.5 inches narrower and one half inch shorter than the previous SOHC engine.

The new CB750K and Limited Edition models were fairly similar, but had some major differences. The base model K rolled on chrome spoke wheels. The Limited Edition CB750K was painted in two-tone Candy Muse Red and Red with gold stripes. Perhaps the most exciting entry in the 750 class was the CB750F. Still powered by the same engine as the other two entries, it used cosmetic alterations seen on previous Super Sports from Honda. Carburetor jetting was adjusted to better suit the CB750F's demands as was the altered breathing characteristics of the four-into-two exhaust.

The F model also wore different bodywork and graphics than the other two 750s. A sweeping fuel tank blended directly into the side covers that swept back to meet with the duck tail housing that wrapped around the brake light. When ordered in Black, the machine was trimmed with a set of swooping red and orange stripes. When opting for the Pleiades Silver Metallic, black and red stripes were applied.

HONDA

The CBX Super Sport instantly won the accolades of every enthusiast on the block with its massive inline six-cylinder engine. The CBX was their first civilian Honda offered with an inline six. Dual overhead cams and four valves per cylinder metered the 1047cc beast. Honda claimed an output of 103 hp. An enormous 5.3 gallon fuel tank was hoisted on top of the frame's backbone, and was required to slake the CBX's thirst. Slowing the 606-lb. marvel was handled by three rotors squeezed by hydraulic calipers. The GL1000 continued to offer the touring rider a primary choice for long distance rides. Turn signals on the 1979s were now rectangular, as was the tail light, borrowed from the CBX parts bin.

Despite its size, the CBX cut a graceful profile and stood out as a one-of-a-kind machine in 1979.

Steve Passwater

1979 HONDA

Model	Engine	Displacement	Transmission
CT90 Trail 90	OHC Single	89cc	Eight-Speed
CB125S	OHC Single	122cc	Five-Speed
CM185T Twinstar	OHC Parallel Twin	181cc	Four-Speed
CB400TI Hawk I	OHC Parallel Twin	395cc	Five-Speed
CB400TII Hawk II	OHC Parallel Twin	395cc	Five-Speed
CM400A Hondamatic	OHC Parallel Twin	395cc	Two-Speed Semi-Automatic
CM400T	OHC Parallel Twin	395cc	Five-Speed
CX500	OHV V-Twin	496cc	Five-Speed
CX500C Custom	OHV V-Twin	496cc	Five-Speed
CX500D Deluxe	OVH V-Twin	496cc	Five-Speed
CB650 New Model	SOHC Inline Four	627cc	Five-Speed
CB750F Super Sport	DOHC Inline Four	749cc	Five-Speed
CB750K 750 Four	DOHC Inline Four	749cc	Five-Speed
CB750K Limited Edition	DOHC Inline Four	749cc	5-Speed
GL1000 Gold Wing	SOHC Opposed Four	999cc	5-Speed
CBX Super Sport Inline-Six	DOHC Inline Six	1047cc	5-Speed

HONDA

1980

The CT90 Trail had taken a new form and became the CT110 for 1980, but few changes were implemented. Only four speeds were available in contrast to the previous eight-speed arrangement. Ignition was now fired with points. The 1980 models saw a set of color-matched fenders in place of chrome. CM200T Twinstar took over where the CM185 had been and was powered by a 194cc parallel twin engine, for the most part an enlarged CM185T. Truncated mufflers were the only physical alteration between the two. The 400cc class lost the Hawk I and Hawk II, but was filled by the CB400T, a smaller version of the CB750F. Solid black Comstar wheels were fitted to both ends and a chrome fender was applied at the front end. A single piston brake caliper grabbed the disc that was attached to the front wheel. A rear drum remained on duty out back.

The 395cc parallel twin featured three-valve heads and a six-speed gearbox. The CM400A returned with only some altered cosmetics. Entering the 400cc fray as an entry-level model, the CM400E. Wire wheels replaced the Comstars, a front wheel drum brake was used instead of the disc and instrumentation was limited to a speedometer only.

The base CB650 was simplified and sported wire wheels and a front disc brake. A set of chrome panels was added to the airbox along with an altered saddle and side covers. A four-into two exhaust was included in the blend of the base CB650.

Slotting in above that version was the new CB650C Custom. A pair of black Comstar wheels and a four-into-four exhaust set the Custom apart from the lower level 650. The CB750K Limited Edition was only intended as

Black Comstar wheels and a silver motor are hallmarks of the 1980 CB750F model.

M&R Cycle Specialists

HONDA

The sleek bodywork of the 750 Super Sport included the upturned "duck tail" rear fender, an instant classic.

M&R Cycle Specialists

a single-year model. Expanding the family of "custom" offerings was the CB750C. Its teardrop tank, stepped saddle and pullback bars were all part of the appearance package. A single disc brake was found on the front Comstar and a drum was used on the aft wheel. The CB750F Super Sport now had blacked-out Comstar wheels and an 85 mph speedometer. The CB750K lost the taillight cowling and the stop light was now supported on a bracket jutting from the rear fender. The 85 mph speedometer was commonly applied to all motorcycles of the period due to government restrictions. The 1980 CB900C Custom was powered by a larger displacement DOHC, four-valve engine. A new variation was the dual-range, five-speed gearbox. It gave the rider 10 speeds to choose from.

The new CB900C was shaft driven adding smoothness and reducing maintenance needs. A four-into-four exhaust was all chrome.

All 1980 CBXs were limited to 98 hp. Air adjustable front forks were added to the 1980 CBX and the Comstar wheels were black. Even the mighty CBX was forced to wear an 85-mph speedometer.

A horizontally opposed-four cylinder engine would still power the GL, but displacement was increased to 1085cc. The all-silver Comstar wheels were replaced with highlighted black versions. A pair of single piston hydraulic brakes and solid disc brakes adorned the front wheel. The GL family grew by one with the debut of the Interstate.

By adding a full coverage fairing, hard saddlebags and rear storage box to the naked Gold Wing, a new touring king was crowned. The equipment choices added 100 lbs. to the already ponderous 636-lb. base reading. An AM/FM radio, complete with helmet intercoms, could be added to the GLI. The Clarion audio system was designed to fit the Gold Wing. The entire assembly was easily removed with a key for safety and security.

1980 HONDA

Model	Engine	Displacement	Transmission
CT110 Trail 90	OHC Single	105cc	Four-Speed
CB125S	OHC Single	122cc	Five-Speed
CM200T Twinstar	OHC Parallel Twin	194cc	Four-Speed
CB400T Hawk	OHC Parallel Twin	395cc	Six-Speed
CM400A Hondamatic	OHC Parallel Twin	395cc	Two-Speed Semi-Automatic
CM400E	OHC Parallel Twin	395cc	Five-Speed
CM400T	OHC Parallel Twin	395cc	Five-Speed
CX500C Custom	OHV V-Twin	496cc	Five-Speed
CX500D Deluxe	OVH V-Twin	496cc	Five-Speed
CB650	SOHC Inline Four	627cc	Five-Speed
CB650C Custom	SOHC Inline Four	627cc	Five-Speed
CB750C Custom	DOHC Inline Four	749cc	Five-Speed
CB750F Super Sport	DOHC Inline Four	749cc	Five-Speed
CB750K 750 Four	DOHC Inline Four	749cc	Five-Speed
CB900C Custom	DOHC Inline Four	902cc	Five-Speed Dual-Range Gearbox
GL1100 Gold Wing	SOHC Opposed Four	1085cc	Five-Speed
GL1100I Gold Wing Interstate	SOHC Opposed Four	1085cc	Five-Speed
CBX Super Sport Reduced Hp	DOHC Inline Six	1047cc	Five-Speed

HONDA
1981

The CB125S trundled on, and wore Black paint with gold and red stripes. The CM200T Twinstar was back for 1981. The previous 6-volt system was upped to 12 and a capacitor discharge ignition was new. A chrome grab rail was added behind the seat.

CB400T Hawk models got a few cosmetic upgrades, and still looked a lot like their larger siblings. A new design was applied to the front fender and it was now painted to match the chosen body color. The rear taillight cowl had a bolder spoiler molded into it to complete the big brother effect. Black Comstar wheels were now highlighted on the edges and a dual-disc front brake seized the rotor. Joining the CM400 family was the CM400C Custom. Shifting through a five-speed gearbox versus the semi-automatic two-speed was about the only mechanical difference.

Other minor contrasts were in the dual-piston front brake and Black Comstar wheels with highlights. The entry level CM400E claimed a few small victories in the modification department. The speedometer now resided atop a chrome base, and the turn signal housings were chrome versus black.

The CX500 side of the Honda clan was joined by two new members and minor changes were applied to the Custom and Deluxe versions. The CX500C Custom steered through a pair of leading axle front forks in 1981 and 1982. The CX500 Deluxe delivered more ride control with the addition of air adjustable front forks in 1981.

The new GL500 Silver Wing was introduced as a new 1981 model. Based on the chassis and power train of the CX500 models, the Silver Wing wore all new modular saddle and storage design that allowed the rider to reconfigure the machine. By replacing the rear section of the saddle with a small trunk, a moderate amount of travel gear could be stowed. Another choice involved installing a large trunk with a back rest for the rider.

The pair of rear coil over shocks used on the CX models was upgraded to Honda's Pro-Link rear suspension that resided between the frame tubes, and delivered a more compliant and adjustable ride. Taking mid-level touring to the next level, the GL500 Silver Wing Interstate version also was introduced during the 1981 model year.

Rolling on the same chassis and suspension as the base Silver Wing, the Interstate provided the rider with protection from the elements by

The finest ride in Honda's catalog was that of the GL1100 Interstate, bringing comfort and technology to the forefront.
American Honda

The CB400T bore a striking resemblance to the larger 750 and 900 models in the 1981 Honda catalog.
American Honda

HONDA

employing a full coverage fairing. The Interstate also expanded the stowage capacity by allowing for a set of hard saddlebags to join the modular seat and rear storage compartments. The GL500 Interstate was slowed with a pair of slotted disc brakes on the front wheel. The CB650 was among the models now fitted with adjustable air suspension. Along with the air suspension, "CB650" logos on the side covers were redesigned, and the Black paint was replaced by the color Cosmo Black Metallic. Adjustable air also was found on the leading axle forks of the CB650C Custom.

Joining the other Super Sports for 1981 was the new CB900F, making an immediate dent in the sport bike market. American Honda

The CB750F Super Sports now featured a front fender, complete with its own small ducktail spoiler, and painted in a unit color. A pair of front disc brakes were slotted and squeezed by twin-piston calipers. The CB750K models were fitted with air adjustable front forks and newly shaped mufflers.

All-new for 1981 was the CB900F Super Sport. Built in the same tradition as the CB750F model, the 900F touted higher performance and sexier bodywork to the sport-minded rider. A four-into-two exhaust was mated to the 902cc, 16-valve engine to save weight and enhance breathing. A trio of disc brakes was on board to slow the Super Sport. Having lost some of its power for 1980, the CBX was pointed in a more "sport-touring" direction for 1981. The big six-cylinder monster was fitted with a sleek frame-mounted fairing and hard-sided saddlebags that were easily detached.

The tail section was also smoother and devoid of the ducktail used on the previous units. Every inch of the new bodywork was covered in Magnum Silver Metallic and highlighted with black stripes that were outlined in red. The added weight of the new trim gave Honda reason to upgrade the front disc brakes to internally vented rotors for added cooling. Rear coil over shocks were replaced with the adjustable Pro-Link suspension.

1981 HONDA

Model	Engine	Displacement	Transmission
CB125S	OHC Single	122cc	Five-Speed
CM200T Twinstar	OHC Parallel Twin	194cc	Four-Speed
CB400T Hawk	OHC Parallel Twin	395cc	Six-Speed
CM400A Hondamatic	OHC Parallel Twin	395cc	Two-Speed Semi-Automatic
CM400C Custom	OHC Parallel Twin	395cc	Five-Speed
CM400E	OHC Parallel Twin	395cc	Five-Speed
CM400T	OHC Parallel Twin	395cc	Five-Speed
CX500C Custom	OHV V-Twin	496cc	Five-Speed
CX500D Deluxe	OHV V-Twin	496cc	Five-Speed
GL500 Silver Wing	OHV V-Twin	496cc	Five-Speed
GL500 Silver Wing Interstate (Full coverage fairing)	OHV V-Twin	496cc	Five-Speed
CB650	SOHC Inline Four	627cc	Five-Speed
CB650C Custom	SOHC Inline Four	627cc	Five-Speed
CB750C Custom	DOHC Inline Four	749cc	Five-Speed
CB750F Super Sport	DOHC Inline Four	749cc	Five-Speed
CB750K	DOHC Inline Four	749cc	Five-Speed
CB900C Custom	DOHC Inline Four	902cc	Five-Speed Dual-Range Gearbox
CB900F Super Sport (New for 1981!)	DOHC Inline Four	902cc	Five-Speed
GL1100 Gold Wing	SOHC Opposed Four	1085cc	Five-Speed
GL1100I Gold Wing Interstate	SOHC Opposed Four	1085cc	Five-Speed
CBX Super Sport (Full fairing and bags)	DOHC Inline Six	1047cc	Five-Speed

STANDARD CATALOG OF® JAPANESE MOTORCYCLES

HONDA

1982

Blowing onto the scene for 1982 was the turbocharged CX500T. Based on the existing CX500 model, it brought new levels of technology to the fold.

Tom O'Roark

Driven by a 49cc two-stroke engine, the MB5 was designed for a multitude of uses. From a sporty pit bike to a street legal form of miserly transport, the MB5 did it all.

The CM200T Twinstar saw mainly cosmetic changes as it was being phased out.

Honda's CM250C Custom was added for 1982. Powered by a 234cc, parallel twin engine, its appearance was similar to the CM200T. Unlike the CM200T the CM250C rowed through five speeds. The first of the new 450cc models was the CB450SC Nighthawk. It would be the smallest of the new Nighthawk family and wore distinctive sheet metal and graphics. The Hawk was now powered by a 447cc engine. The CM450A Hondamatic had also grown to the 447cc dimension for 1982 and a few other alterations were found. With the exception of the newly installed 447cc engine, the CM450E was unchanged.. All of the latest 450 models now carried the Hondamatic's oil cooler. The CX500D departed. Built using the Pro-Link-equipped

HONDA

Uniquely designed Comstar wheels graced the CX500 Turbo, and the gold anodizing helped to sell the machine as the specialty item it was.

Tom O'Roark

GL500 chassis, the CX500TC brought a new level of sophistication to Honda. Faced with the challenges of finding a turbocharger small enough for the motorcycle, a unit from IHI was selected for duty. Oil capacity was increased through the use of finned sump to keep things slippery. A digital computerized fuel injection design meted out fuel to meet with the power demands of the blown mill. The engine displaced one more cc than the CX500C but still delivered the power to the rear wheel via the drive shaft.

The CX500TC was wrapped in sleek bodywork with unique Comstar wheels anodized in gold. When compared to the complexity of the Turbo, the FT500 Ascot seemed almost primitive. Named for the famous dirt track in Southern California, it provided simplicity and performance.

Powered by a single-cylinder, 498cc OHC engine, the FT500 was brought to life with the touch of a button and it exhaled through a two-into-one exhaust. The 1982 GL500 Silver Wing models received a vacuum-operated fuel valve, complete with a reserve now installed on the smaller touring machines.

The 1982 CB650 was joined by a new Nighthawk. Changes to the CB650 included a second piston up front. Joining the Honda fray was the CB650SC Nighthawk. The SOHC in-line-four engine and its styling set this cycle apart from other non-Nighthawks in the catalog. The 750cc division saw three new faces, with changes made to the returning members as well. The CB750C stopped with a second set of pistons being added to each of its two front calipers. The CB750F Super Sport saw even fewer alterations. The first new 750 entrant was another version of the Nighthawk. It shared many cosmetic cues with the smaller 650 and 450 models.

Two brand new 750s were sold for the first time in 1982, and except for sharing a power plant, they were nothing alike. The VF750C Magna and VF750S Sabre were both powered by four-cylinder V-four engines. A 90-degree divide between the banks was used and four-valves were found atop each cylinder. Liquid cooling, a shaft drive and a six-speed gearbox were all used.

The VF750C was designed in the "cruiser" or "custom" theme. A deeply sculpted, two-person saddle was matched to a set of pull-back handlebars. A low-rise backrest complete with an aluminum "sissy bar" also graced the V45 Magna layout. A shortened rear fender and minimalist front fender were both finished in chrome. Cast wheels were used to keep both tires in place and a duo of grooved disc brakes were used up front. The VF750S Sabre looked much different than its sibling. A more sedately sculpted saddle featured a rear grab-rail that was finished off with a contoured tail section. Different cast wheels were used and a chrome fender was found on the front. The Sabre rode with Honda's Pro-Link suspension at the rear and required an inch longer wheelbase. Riders found a clock that doubled as a stopwatch, trip meter, fuel and temperature gauges.

The 1982 CB900C models were fitted with slotted front brake discs and dual piston calipers. The naked GL1100 rolled on larger rubber both fore and aft, and dual piston calipers compressed slotted discs up front. Self-canceling turn-signals found their way into the GL1100's network as well.

The Aspencade took the Interstate's level of comfort up a notch and bristled with more toys and storage capability. An enlarged passenger backrest

Ready to ride off into the sunset in comfort, the CBX was discontinued after the 1982 model year.

Steve Searles

included storage pouches on both sides for easy access to small items. The Type II audio system put the controls at the rider's fingertips by placing them on the handlebars.

The Interstate had the newest slotted front disc brakes and dual-piston calipers, and was sold in the same colors as the base GL1100.

Once the CBX had been detuned, then shifted into "sport touring" mode, buyer interest began to wane. The once mighty six-cylinder machine would see its final year of sale in 1982. A rear passenger grab rail was also installed, but all else remained the same as the CBX rode into its final sunset.

The addition of the Pro-Link rear suspension softened the ride but not the blow to the performance edge the 1979 delivered.

Steve Searles

1982 HONDA

Model	Engine	Displacement	Transmission
MB5 (MB50)	Two-Stroke Single	49cc	Five-Speed
CB125S	OHC Single	122cc	Five-Speed
CM200T Twinstar	OHC Parallel Twin	194cc	Four-Speed
CM250C Custom	OHC Parallel Twin	234cc	Five-Speed
CB450SC Nighthawk (New For 1982)	SOHC Parallel Twin	447cc	Six-Speed
CB450T Hawk	SOHC Parallel Twin	447cc	Six-Speed
CM450A Hondamatic	SOHC Parallel Twin	447cc	Two-Speed Semi-Automatic
CM450C Custom	SOHC Parallel Twin	447cc	Six-Speed
CM450E	SOHC Parallel Twin	447cc	Six-Speed
CX500C Custom	OHV V-Twin	496cc	Five-Speed
CX500TC Turbo	Turbocharged Twin	OHV V-Twin	497cc Five-Speed
FT500 Ascot (New For 1982)	OHC Single	498cc	Five-Speed
GL500 Silver Wing	OHV V-Twin	496cc	Five-Speed
GL500 Silver Wing Interstate	OHV V-Twin	496cc	Five-Speed
CB650	SOHC Inline Four	627cc	Five-Speed
CB650SC Nighthawk (New For 1982)	SOHC Inline Four	627cc	Five-Speed
CB750C Custom	DOHC Inline Four	749cc	Five-Speed
CB750F Super Sport	DOHC Inline Four	749cc	Five-Speed
CB750K 750 Four	DOHC Inline Four	749cc	Five-Speed
CB750SC Nighthawk (New For 1982)	DOHC Inline Four	749cc	Five-Speed
VF750C V45 Magna (New For 1982)	DOHC V-Four	748cc	Six-Speed
VF750S V45 Sabre (New For 1982)	DOHC V-Four	748cc	Six-Speed
CB900C Custom	DOHC Inline Four	902cc	Five-Speed Dual-Range Gearbox
CB900F Super Sport	DOHC Inline Four	902cc	Five-Speed
GL1100 Gold Wing	SOHC Opposed Four	1085cc	Five-Speed
GL1100A Aspencade (New version In 1982)	SOHC Opposed Four	1085cc	Five-Speed
GL1100I Gold Wing Interstate	SOHC Opposed Four	1085cc	Five-Speed
CBX Super Sport (Final year of sale)	DOHC Inline Six	1047cc	Five-Speed

HONDA

1983

STANDARD CATALOG OF® JAPANESE Motorcycles

From the bikini fairing to the racy red, white and blue palette, the CB1100F was easy to spot, even at rest.

Brad Powell Collection

The 1983 CM250C used a belt drive in place of the chain. The CM250C engine was painted black with highlighted cooling fins, silver heads and external cases. The 450 clan found the CB450T and CM450C missing. The CB450SC Nighthawk was given a few alterations. Cast alloy wheels replaced the Comstars and the speedometer was now showing a top speed of 105. The CM450A also featured cast alloy wheels and the triple-digit speedometer. A blacked out motor with silver accents was installed in the CM450E and the 105mph speedometer was also installed.

The Ascot family grew by one and only minor changes were made to the FT500. A 120-mph speedometer was visible.

The new entry was the VT500FT Ascot. Powered by a 491cc, V-twin engine, the latest iteration delivered a different power band to the rider. Liquid cooled, the engine sent power through a six-speed gearbox and exhaled through a two-into-one exhaust that was finished in black chrome. Cast alloy wheels and a front disc brake completed the hardware parade.

One of the two new Shadows was the

VT500C, powered by a 491cc, V-twin OHC liquid-cooled engine. Shaft drive and a six-speed transmission were all a part of the latest machine. Cast alloy ComCast wheels were replacing the previous Comstars across the model line and the VT500C Shadow was one of the machines wearing the cast hoops.

The Nighthawk grew by one model in 1983 with the debut of the CB550SC. Both the 550 and 750 versions of this bike benefited from a new engine architecture that included hydraulic valve lash adjusters. A rated 572ccs were on tap in the inline-four, 16-valve engine. The CB650SC Nighthawk stayed on to carry the torch for 650 buyers. The inline-four engine was bumped to 655cc, and hydraulic valve adjusters were now a part of the design. Honda's new "TRAC" anti-dive forks were installed on the 650 Nighthawk for more control under hard braking. Shaft drive, cast alloy wheels and triple disc brakes rounded out the 1983 model.

The CX and GL models had their displacement bumped to 674cc for 1983. The CX650C rolled off of showroom floors wearing a new fuel tank, saddle and wheels. The turbo-fed CX650TC changed little outside of the enlarged mill. Both versions of the GL were upgraded to 674cc engines for 1983. A set of cast alloy wheels was found on the latest versions. Gone were the CB750C and the revered CB750F Super Sport. In their stead, the CB750SC Nighthawk would remain the only inline-four powered model. The big Nighthawk now showed a top speed of 150 mph on its speedometer and rode on cast alloy, ComCast wheels that were black with highlighted "spokes."

The 1983 VF750C V45 Magnas and the VF750S V45 Sabres also saw the addition of a 150 mph speedometer. Front brake discs were still grooved, but they changed from straight to curved slots.

One of the new models from Honda was the sporty VF750F Interceptor. By canting the 748cc, V-four motor at a different angle in the frame and wrapping the bike in sleek bodywork, this Honda had a distinct racing image. Final chain drive and a 16-inch front hoop also played into the sporting nature of the Interceptor.

Although similar in appearance to its smaller offspring, the VT500C, the VT750C Shadow packed a lot more punch. Two spark plugs were used in each of the V-twin's heads to ensure complete burn. The 45-degree engine layout included three-valve heads and, although liquid cooled, this motorcycle sported cylinder fins like an air-cooled model. Honda claimed an output of 67 hp.

The big Super Sport was always done in white, with panels of red or blue.

Brad Powell Collection

Another one year only model was the CB1000 Custom, stepping in to fill the void left by the deleted CB900C.

Jeff Kalin

HONDA

The turbocharged CX was back for 1983, but was now built around the bigger 650cc motor. Colors were also changed in the turbo's final year of sale.

Matt Jonas

Riding in to replace the CB900C was the new CB1000C Custom. A 973cc, inline-four engine featured dual overhead cams and four valves per cylinder. The five-speed gearbox featured a sub-transmission that provided another five gear ratios.

For the sport rider who wanted all the cubic inches Honda could muster, the CB1100F Super Sport was introduced in 1983. Its combination of an inline four-cylinder engine that displaced 1,062ccs made the loss of the 750, 900 and CBX Super Sports easier to accept. A Black Charcoal four-into-two exhaust saved some weight over a four-into-four system and provided greater cornering clearance.

Triple disc brakes were on hand to slow the speed-hungry machine. A five-speed gearbox and chain drive completed the performance aspects of the big Super Sport. The CB1100F was also a one-year-only model.

The Gold Wing GL1100 now rolled on 11-spoke cast wheels and control was enhanced with the assistance of Honda's "TRAC" anti-dive forks. A 150 mph top speed was indicated. The Aspencade also got the 11-spoke wheels and TRAC anti-dive forks.

The VF1100C V65 Magna had a 1098cc, V-four, DOHC engine rated at 105 hp and it had no equals.

1983 HONDA

Model	Engine	Displacement	Transmission
CM250C Custom	OHC Parallel Twin	234cc	Five-Speed
CB450SC Nighthawk	SOHC Parallel Twin	447cc	Six-Speed
CM450A Hondamatic	SOHC Parallel Twin	447cc	Two-Speed Semi-Automatic
CM450E	SOHC Parallel Twin	447cc	Six-Speed
FT500 Ascot	OHC Single	498cc	Five-Speed
VT500C Shadow	OHC V-Twin	491cc	Six-Speed
VT500FT Ascot	OHC V-Twin	491cc	Six-Speed
CB550SC Nighthawk	DOHC Inline-Four	572cc	Six-Speed
CB650SC Nighthawk	SOHC Inline-Four	655cc	Six-Speed
CX650C Custom	OHV V-Twin	674cc	Six-Speed
CX650TC Turbo (Final year)	OHV V-Twin	674cc	Five-Speed
GL650 Silver Wing	OHV V-Twin	674cc	Five-Speed
GL650I Silver Wing Interstate	OHV V-Twin	674cc	Five-Speed
CB750SC Nighthawk	DOHC Inline-Four	749cc	Five-Speed
VF750C V45 Magna	DOHC V-Four	748cc	Six-Speed
VF750F Interceptor (New for 1983)	DOHC V-Four	748cc	Five-Speed
VF750S V45 Sabre	DOHC V-Four	748cc	Six-Speed
VT750C Shadow (New for 1983)	SOHC V-Twin	749cc	Six-Speed
CB1000C Custom (New for 1983)	DOHC Inline-Four	973cc	Five-Speed Dual-Range
CB1100F Super Sport (One-year-only model)	DOHC Inline-Four	1062cc	Five-Speed
GL1100 Gold Wing	SOHC Opposed-Four	1085cc	Five-Speed
GL1100A Aspencade	SOHC Opposed-Four	1085cc	Five-Speed
GL1100I Gold Wing Interstate	SOHC Opposed-Four	1085cc	Five-Speed
VF1100C V65 Magna (New for 1983)	DOHC V-Four	1098cc	Six-Speed

HONDA
1984

Changes were minimal to the CB125S, in its second last year. A circular headlight and a 12-volt electrical system rounded out the modifications seen on the '84 models.

A smaller VF500C V30 Magna appeared. A 498cc V-four motor produced 64 hp and delivered more ponies per liter than its bigger sibling. A primary difference on the V30 was the final chain drive in place of the shaft used on the other Magnas. Weighing only 401 lbs. dry, the V30 Magna fit the needs of less experienced riders. Another new entry shared the 498cc V-four engine found in the V30 Magna, but was packaged as a sport bike. The VF500F Interceptor was a reduced version of the VF750F and the new VF1000F. The mini-Interceptor tipped the scales at 408 lbs. and carried a horsepower rating of 68. The VF500F shared some key components with the 750 version in the air-adjustable front shocks with TRAC anti-dive and the Pro-Link rear suspension. Virtually untouched for 1984, the VT500C Shadow returned. The VT500FT remained for its final year of sale and a three-tone tank decal was applied in place of the two-tone version seen on 1983 models. Only cosmetic changes were applied to the CB650SC Nighthawk.

In an effort to level the playing field, a steep tariff was placed on imported motorcycles displacing more than 750ccs. To comply with this new ruling, Honda began selling 700cc machines in 1984. One all-new model to meet with the ruling was the CB700SC Nighthawk S. The 696cc was divided into four cylinders, arranged inline.

With a dry weight of only 470 lbs., the new Nighthawk S delivered terrific performance from the revised class of bikes. The bikini fairing, fuel tank, side covers and tail section were all treated to a two-tone paint scheme of either black and red or black and blue.

A reduced capacity 699cc engine was installed in the latest VF700C Magna, and except for a change in the wheel design, the mid-range Magna remained unchanged.

Introduced in 1983 and instantly garnering a multitude of awards, the VF750F returned along with its detuned twin, the VF700F Interceptor.

An all-new model in the Interceptor family was the 498cc VF500F and the smaller sibling carried the bloodlines proudly.

Steve Passwater

HONDA

Honda used "Follow the Leader" as a tag for its 1984 ad featuring the Nighthawk S.

The VF700F Interceptor used the bigger 750 version, but sold for $800 less. The VF700S Sabre had also been reduced to 699cc to meet the new guidelines. The next victim of the 700cc ruling was the VT700C Shadow. The smaller 694cc power plant was the only change listed for the 1984 model.

To help to ease the pain caused by the loss of several models, the VF1000F Interceptor was introduced. By applying the successful formula used to build the VF750F and increasing some key dimensions, the bigger Interceptor was everything its younger brother was and more. Displacing 998cc, and fitted with larger valves, the VF1000F produced 113 hp, 27 more than the VF750F.

An aluminum radiator replaced the brass model that was also found on the 750. A 17-inch rear wheel was employed and front fork tubes were 41mm units, complete with improved TRAC anti-dive control. By adding another 100cc, Honda offered two machines to the buyer. The VF1100C V65 Magna was little changed save for colors. New for 1984 was the VF1100S V65 Sabre. By installing the 1098cc engine used in the Magna into a larger and longer frame, the V65 Sabre was born. Additional tweaks gave the Sabre even more power than the V65 Magna.

All three models in the Gold Wing family received complete makeovers and emerged better than ever. The increase ito 1182cc and every facet of the design was rejuvenated to meet with increasing competition from Yamaha and Kawasaki. Chassis geometry and altered wheel sizes brought the latest "Wing" closer to the ground and improved the cornering clearance.

The Aspencade also housed an on-board air compressor that was used to supply the GL's air-ride suspension, as well as fill a beach ball if required. The Aspencade also had the luxury of a fine audio system that could be augmented with a CB radio. All controls for the sound system were mounted with the fairing towers near the grips for easy access at speed. When fully equipped, the Aspencade tipped the scales over at 755 lbs.

The Interstate was still well-equipped but paled in comparison to the Aspencade.

1984 HONDA

Model	Engine	Displacement	Transmission
CB125S	OHC Single	124cc	Five-Speed
VF500C V30 Magna	DOHC V-Four	498cc	Six-Speed
VF500F Interceptor	DOHC V-Four	498cc	Six-Speed
VT500C Shadow	OHC V-Twin	491cc	Six-Speed
VT500FT Ascot	OHC V-Twin	491cc	Six-Speed
CB650SC Nighthawk	SOHC Inline-Four	655cc	Six-Speed
CB700SC Nighthawk S (New for 1984)	DOHC Inline-Four	696cc	Six-Speed
VF700C V45 Magna (Reduced displacement)	DOHC V-Four	699cc	Six-Speed
VF700F Interceptor (Reduced displacement)	DOHC V-Four	699cc	Five-Speed
VF700S V45 Sabre (Reduced displacement)	DOHC V-Four	699cc	Six-Speed
VT700C Shadow (Reduced displacement)	SOHC V-Twin	694cc	Six-Speed
VF750F Interceptor	DOHC V-Four	748cc	Six-Speed
VF1000F Interceptor (New for1984)	DOHC V-Four	998cc	Five-Speed
VF1100C V65 Magna	DOHC V-Four	1098cc	Six-Speed
VF1100S V65 Sabre (New for1984)	DOHC V-Four	1098cc	Six-Speed
GL1200 Gold Wing (Redesigned)	SOHC Opposed-Four	1182cc	Five-Speed
GL1200A Aspencade (Redesigned)	SOHC Opposed-Four	1182cc	Five-Speed
GL1200I Gold Wing Interstate (Redesigned)	SOHC Opposed-Four	1182cc	Five-Speed

STANDARD CATALOG OF® JAPANESE Motorcycles

HONDA
1985

The CB125S1 was in its final year in 1985. A rectangular headlight replaced the round 1984 unit, and changes to the striping were the only revisions. The CMX250C Rebel cruised onto the scene for 1985 and was an instant success in the expanding "cruiser" market. Riding on a chassis that provided a 26-inch saddle height, the new Rebel was especially appealing to smaller riders. A 234cc, parallel-twin engine was joined by a five-speed gearbox. A set of classic spoke wheels measured 15 inches at the rear and 18 inches at the front, adding to the traditional styling. After being pulled from the 1984 catalog, the CB450SC Nighthawk was back for 1985.

Fresh graphics and a revised instrument cluster graced the VF500C V30 Magna, and Candy Andromeda Red was replaced by Candy Wineberry Red. The VF500F Interceptor also received new gauges, and altered graphics for 1985. The VT500C Shadows now wore polished engine covers and enlarged cooling fins on the cylinders.

A more aggressive two-place saddle was extended to include a backrest for improved passenger comfort. Chrome was applied to the round headlight housing. With only one face to be seen in the 650 class, the Nighthawk did not receive much attention for 1985. Improvements to the

Stepping in to replace the missing Interceptors was the race inspired VF1000R of 1985.

American Honda

67

HONDA

STANDARD CATALOG OF JAPANESE Motorcycles

Back for a second year was the CB700SC Nighthawk and was almost identical to the premier edition 1984 models.

American Honda

TRAC anti-dive system and revised brake rotors were the most useful changes.

Nighthawk S models were mostly unchanged with the exception of a white outline around the red or blue color panels used. Speedometer faces were now printed with their speeds listed in increments of 10, beginning at the 5 mph mark.

Adding some comfort and appearance features to the VF700C Magna improved the breed. Cast wheels were now comprised of five individual spokes. A rear sissy bar complete with padded backrest was now a standard feature on the 700 Magna. The 1985 edition would be the final year for the VF700F Interceptor production A more easily adjusted TRAC system on the front forks and revisions to the brake rotors and calipers joined revised handlebars and mirrors.

The 1985 VF700S Sabre models featured Pro-Link rear suspension complete with roller bearings in the linkage. All 1985 700 Sabres were finished in Black with Monte Rosa Silver metallic insets. VT700C Shadow models also now featured polished engine covers. Quelling the tears of those missing their beloved Interceptors was the new VF1000R, a true race-inspired machine powered by a 998cc, 90-degree V-four motor that pumped out 117 hp. Part of the horsepower equation was the 36mm CV carburetors and 11.1 compression. A box-section frame of steel and a swingarm of box-section aluminum provided stiffness and light weight resulting in dry weight of only 525 lbs. A 6.2-gallon fuel tank was cloaked in a wind-tunnel tested fairing that looked racy. Black, star-shaped Comstar wheels were teamed with a pair of floating rotor front disc brakes and stout 41mm fork legs. The lower fork legs were finished in red to match the seat and front fender.

The VF1100C Magnas now included more easily adjustable

One of the V65 models for 1985 was the Magna. The 1098cc, V-four motor was mounted in a cruiser style machine.

American Honda

68

brake and clutch levers, improved self-canceling turn-signals that employed push-to-cancel switches. The 1100 Sabre also received the screw-adjustment levers and self-canceling turn-signals. The same colors used on the VF700S Sabre applied to the bigger 1100 model.

The addition of the VT1100C grew that family tree to three different models bearing the Shadow name. The 500cc and 700cc varieties were still sold alongside the 1100. Displacing 1099cc, the new Shadow was fired with two spark plugs per cylinder and carried the rider on a 29.1 inch saddle height. A chubby 15-inch rear tire was slowed by a drum while the taller 18-inch front rubber was anchored by a brace of discs. Without fluids the VT1100C weighed a moderate 531 pounds.

Touring riders wanted more than a plush chassis and powerful motor, and the better dressed models outsold the stripped-down Gold Wing by a wide margin, forcing its retirement. Improvements to the Aspencades and Interstates included lower gear ratios for smoother take-offs, better ventilation and altered self-canceling turn signals.

For those for whom even the lavish accoutrements of the Aspencade weren't enough, the Limited Edition would fill their every need. A bevy of electronic enhancements dazzled the senses. An on-board travel computer, electronic cruise-control, and computerized fuel injection were the biggest hitters on the field. Cornering lights and rear mounted stereo speakers added another layer of frosting to the cake. An interior light on the rear trunk and special tool kit rounded out the long list of desirable features. Sold in very limited numbers, the 1985 GL1200L was truly a limited edition.

The tiny CB125 would see its final year of sale for 1985 as buyers were drawn to bigger machines from Honda.

American Honda

1985 HONDA

Model	Engine	Displacement	Transmission
CB125S1 (Final year)	OHC Single	124cc	Five-Speed
CMX 250C Rebel (26" seat height)	OHC Parallel Twin	234cc	Five-Speed
CB450SC Nighthawk	SOHC Parallel Twin	447cc	Six-Speed
VF500C V30 Magna	DOHC V-Four	498cc	Six-Speed
VF500F Interceptor	DOHC V-Four	498cc	Six-Speed
VT500C Shadow	OHC V-Twin	491cc	Six-Speed
CB650SC Nighthawk	SOHC Inline-Four	655cc	Six-Speed
CB700SC Nighthawk S	DOHC Inline-Four	696cc	Five-Speed
VF700C V45 Magna	DOHC V-Four	699cc	Six-Speed
VF700F Interceptor	DOHC V-Four	699cc	Five-Speed
VF700S V45 Sabre	DOHC V-Four	699cc	Six-Speed
VT700C Shadow	SOHC V-Twin	694cc	Five-Speed
VF1000R (New for 1985)	DOHC V-Four	998cc	Five-Speed
VF1100C V65 Magna	DOHC V-Four	1098cc	Six-Speed
VF1100S V65 Sabre	DOHC V-Four	1098cc	Six-Speed
VT1100C Shadow	SOHC V-Twin	1099cc	Five-Speed
GL1200A Aspencade	SOHC Opposed-Four	1182cc	Five-Speed
GL1200I Gold Wing Interstate	SOHC Opposed-Four	1182cc	Five-Speed
GL1200L Gold Wing Limited Edition	SOHC Opposed-Four	1182cc	Five-Speed

HONDA
1986

Sold to the consumer and raced on tracks across the USA, the 750 Interceptor was a winner in both realms.

American Honda

The 250 Rebel was now the smallest street bike that Honda sold. Marching beside its brother, the CMX250 Limited wore Gold as badge of distinction. The Limited was festooned with swirling gold artwork on the tank and rear fender. Cylinder head covers plus fuel cap and carburetor covers were also finished in gold.

The 1986 production year would be the final one for the CB450SC Nighthawk. A CMX450C Rebel was introduced for 1986 to expand the offerings in the now popular segment. By enlarging the cooling fins of the existing Hawk 450 engine, the Rebel appealed to a new audience of riders. A six-speed gearbox was fed by the 447cc, SOHC parallel twin mill. A Honda wing on the tank and "Rebel Four-Fifty" decal on the battery cover added to the decor.

The VF500F Interceptor would see its final year of sale. Cosmetic alterations included all-black wheels, and a seat, front fender and lower fork legs wearing red. The VT500C Shadow would be gone at the end of the 1986 model year. Honda's first tariff beater, the CB700SC Nighthawk S, bowed out after 1986 with only cosmetic changes for its final run. A chrome side stand was the only change found on the 1986 VF700C Magna.

The VFR700F and VFR750F Interceptors were new and set the performance bar at a new level. The 700 variant was sold to comply with the remaining tariffs, and the 750 was designed to crush the racing world into submission. Both V-four motors featured gear-driven cams and claimed more than 100 hp for the 750. Honda listed a dry weight for either machine at less than

440 lbs., partly due to their all-aluminum chassis and rear swing arm assemblies. The four-valve, liquid-cooled engines displaced 698cc or 748cc, and a six-speed transmissions with chain drive was part of both equations. The VFR700F2 was also sold in 1986. F2 instrumentation was also housed in angular pods versus the round gauges seen on the other two models.

Honda wasted no time in modifying the VT700C Shadow for 1986. The new Shadow was longer, lower and more radical. A revised wheelbase of 63 inches and a saddle height of only 27.4 inches added to the mystique. The rather small fuel tank was joined to another holding cell under the saddle. A pair of cast, five-spoke rims and exaggerated pull-back handlebars completed the stage.

With only this year remaining on its agenda, the VF1000R was little changed. A fork bridge, finished in anodized gold, was found on the front forks. Model year 1986 found the VF1100C V65 Magna in its twilight year. An unaltered chassis and drive train left the appearance to do all the dirty work.

All brake discs now included inner-opening cut-outs and a fiber-optic anti-theft system was included in the package. The VT1100C Shadow was mostly unchanged but an all-black model was offered alongside the black and silver and the side covers were finished in the same silver and black paint. A gold "Shadow" side-cover decal replaced the silver used in 1985.

A year of evolutionary changes was on hand for the Gold Wings. Dolby noise reduction was added to the sound system on the Aspencade, and a splash guard was added to the rear fender.

The GL1200SE-I Aspencade was introduced for 1986. This best-dressed model imbibed all the

Adding some flash to the 450 Rebel's equation was the Limited Edition version of the same.

American Honda

The SE-I version of the Gold Wing Aspencade took luxury and convenience to unseen levels.

American Honda

HONDA

Another model to sing its swan song was the CB700S Nighthawk that appeared when the tariffs were initiated.

American Honda

qualities of a "standard" Wing and added some extras to set it apart. The Pearl Splendor Ivory and Camel Beige Metallic paint was one-of-a-kind. Power from a fuel-injected engine added to the recipe and allowed easier starting and smoother acceleration. A comprehensive bank of electronics was at the driver's fingertips and there was a tank-mounted display and control panel.

Dolby noise reduction and a pair of angular speakers were also added to the sound system on the SE-I. A pair of angular speakers were added to the tops of the rear box for added passenger enjoyment. Both ends of the suspension could be easily adjusted with the onboard air compressor system. An extensive tool kit also awaited the buyer of the SE-I Aspencade, along with miles of open-road adventure.

1986 HONDA

Model	Engine	Displacement	Transmission
CMX 250C Rebel	OHC Parallel Twin	234cc	Five-Speed
CMX250CD Rebel Limited	OHC Parallel Twin	234cc	Five-Speed
CB450SC Nighthawk	SOHC Parallel Twin	447cc	Six-Speed
CMX450C Rebel (New for 1986)	SOHC Parallel Twin	447cc	Six-Speed
VF500F Interceptor (Final year)	DOHC V-Four	498cc	Six-Speed
VT500C Shadow	DOHC V-Twin	491cc	Six-Speed
CB700SC Nighthawk S (Final year)	DOHC Inline-Four	696cc	Five-Speed
VF700C V45 Magna	DOHC V-Four	699cc	Six-Speed
VFR700F Interceptor	DOHC V-Four	698cc	Six-Speed
VFR700F2 Interceptor (Special paint)	DOHC V-Four	698cc	Six-Speed
VT700C Shadow	SOHC V-Twin	694cc	Six-Speed
VFR750F Interceptor	DOHC V-Four	748cc	Six-Speed
VF1000R (Final year)	DOHC V-Four	998cc	Five-Speed
VF1100C V65 Magna	DOHC V-Four	1098cc	Six-Speed
VT1100C Shadow	SOHC V-Twin	1099cc	Five-Speed
GL1200A Aspencade	SOHC Opposed-Four	1182cc	Five-Speed
GL1200I Gold Wing Interstate	SOHC Opposed-Four	1182cc	Five-Speed
GL1200SE-I Aspencade SE-I	SOHC Opposed-Four	1182cc	Five-Speed

25 YEARS OF RACING HISTORY JUST HIT THE STREETS.

Honda won its first World Championship way back in 1961. And from the high banks of Daytona to Gran Prix courses the world over, no other manufacturer has dominated racing the way we have.

And we've stayed the Superbike leader by following one simple rule: If you want to be out front on the race track or on the street, you've got to be out front in technology.

That's the reason why we totally redesigned the Interceptor™ for 1986.

THE MOST POWERFUL 750 YOU CAN BUY.

The VFR750 Interceptor™ has even more power than ever before. The new V-4, with four valves per cylinder and 10.5:1 compression ratio, now puts out an incredible 104 horsepower! And it has more power throughout the mid-range than any conventional engine in its class.

Throughout the new V-4 we saved weight everywhere we could. Sometimes even down to fractions of a gram. The result is an engine that's even lighter and more compact than our original V-4.

THE INTERCEPTOR. STRICTLY FOR THOSE WHO DEMAND THE BEST.

Next we went after every engine's two worst enemies: Excess heat and friction.

The new V-4 is not only water-cooled but oil-cooled as well. Our unique lubrication system draws oil directly from the oil cooler as well as from the sump so that the V-4 runs up to 54° cooler than conventional engines.

What's more, the V-4's camshafts are gear-driven for 30% less friction than chain-driven cams.

Last, we coupled that power to a close-ratio six-speed transmission to give you a gear for any situation.

Add more power, lose weight, heat and friction, and you've got the ultimate experience for experienced riders.

THE INTERCEPTOR FRAME. A LESSON IN ADVANCED GEOMETRY.

With an engine this strong, the new Interceptor needed a frame to match.

We had just the one. The same frame design we use on our World Championship Gran Prix machines. It's a composite frame that's rigid, yet lightweight. The massive twin spars are made of 28 x 69mm extruded aluminum alloy box tubing, keeping the Interceptor's total dry weight to just 437 pounds.

What's more, since the Interceptor's V-4 engine is much narrower than in-line fours, so is its frame and fairing. And that gives the Interceptor the most aerodynamically efficient design of any motorcycle on the market.

In 1983, the original Interceptor set new standards for all Superbikes. The 1986 Interceptor just raised them.

This year, if you're not on one, you'll be behind one.

RIDE LIKE A PRO.

That means using your head. And riding safely. Always wear a helmet and eye protection. Read your owner's manual carefully. Maintain your machine in safe running condition. Follow the rules of the road and always use common sense. Never drink and ride. Always ride at a safe speed. If you're riding a new or unfamiliar machine, take it extra easy.

Doing the right things makes riding a lot safer. And more fun.

HONDA MOTORCYCLES
FOLLOW THE LEADER

The VFR750 Interceptor has a 12-month unlimited mileage warranty. See your local Honda dealer for complete details. California version differs slightly due to emissions equipment. †SAE net taken at the crankshaft. Specifications and availability subject to change without notice. For a free brochure, see your Honda dealer. Or write: American Honda, Dept. 199, P.O. Box 7055, No. Hollywood, CA 91609-7055. ©1986 American Honda Motor Co., Inc. (5/86)

In 1986, Honda introduced the powerful Interceptor to the world.

HONDA
1987

The 250 Rebel remained a popular choice for those just getting their feet wet in motorcycling, or whose feet needed to be closer to the ground. The 1987 production year would be the last year for the small Rebel until its return almost a decade later. Artwork on the red models was a combination of gray, silver and white.

The CMX450C Rebel returned for another round. Splashier tank graphics and polished control levers were about the only modifications made. An enlarged fuel tank decal now read "Rebel Honda." With a 598cc, inline-four engine producing 83 hp and a slippery set of bodywork, the CBR600F Hurricane broke all records in the 600 class. The new engine was employed as a stressed-member of the "diamond-type" frame and helped to keep dry weight just below 400 lbs. The inline engine was liquid cooled, featured 16 valves and shifted through a six-speed gearbox. A four-into-one exhaust handled spent fumes. Three disc brakes were mounted to the 17-inch front and rear wheels. The Hurricane itself was sold in Pearl Crystal White with Fighting Red or Black with Monza Red. The 600 Hurricane was one of many Hondas to use this technology and name.

The VF700C Magna also returned, with numerous changes. New styling exaggerated the Magna's cruiser status and vented side covers. A small chin spoiler was also added to the front down tubes of the frame. An upswept four-into-four exhaust was fitted with four individual mufflers.

The 1987 VFR700F2 featured a digital ignition system as the only hardware upgrade. Having been redesigned for the 1986 model year, the VT700C Shadow returned in 1987 wearing only different graphics. Honda also whipped up a little something named the CBR1000 Hurricane. Similar in design to the smaller 600cc model, the 998cc-version produced 130 hp and claimed a top speed nearing 160 mph. The Hurricane was as sleek as it was fast. The 16-valve, inline-four motor was liquid cooled and sent its power through a choice of six speeds with chain final drive. A trio of drilled disc brakes slowed the 490-lb. machine to a halt. Three different two-tone options were sold in 1987. The cruiser class was still dominated by Honda's VT1100C Shadow. A pair of elongated exhaust pipes swept backwards towards the new shaft drive and accented the long look of the machine. One gear was removed from the gearbox for a new total of four.

Only two versions of the GL1200 Gold Wing were sold in 1987, and changes were minimal. A redesign of the plush king and queen saddles now included three-stage foam for increased comfort.

The Aspencade had three new two-tone color combos on the menu. Candy Wineberry Red with Dusky Red Metallic, Black with Tempest Gray or Pleiades Silver Metallic with Spiral Blue Metallic. The Interstate was still available in solid colors, Pearly Beige Metallic or Amethyst Gray Metallic.

1987 HONDA

Model	Engine	Displacement	Transmission
CMX 250C Rebel	OHC Parallel Twin	234cc	Five-Speed
CMX450C Rebel	SOHC Parallel Twin	447cc	Six-Speed
CBR600F Hurricane (New for 1987)	DOHC Inline-Four	598cc	Six-Speed
VF700C V45 Magna	DOHC V-Four	699cc	Six-Speed
VFR700F2 Interceptor	DOHC V-Four	698cc	Six-Speed
VT700C Shadow	SOHC V-Twin	694cc	Six-Speed
CBR1000F Hurricane	DOHC Inline-Four	998cc	Six-Speed
VT1100C Shadow	SOHC V-Twin	1099cc	Four-Speed
GL1200A Aspencade	SOHC Opposed-Four	1182cc	Five-Speed
GL1200I Gold Wing Interstate	SOHC Opposed-Four	1182cc	Five-Speed

STANDARD CATALOG OF® JAPANESE Motorcycles   HONDA

1988

Both 250 and 450 versions of the Rebel were gone for 1988, but Honda released their new Interceptor VTR to get the beginning rider on the street. Sporty panels were wrapped around a liquid-cooled, V-twin motor that displaced 250cc and a Pro-Link rear suspension. A seat height of only 29.9 inches made it easy for smaller riders to get in on the fun, too. The six-speed gearbox led to a final chain drive and the entire package only weighed 330.8 lbs.

The CBR600F Hurricane was seen with Fighting Red paired with Pearl Crystal White or Medium Gray Metallic with Granite Blue Metallic.

A fresh member of the cruiser genre was the VT600C Shadow VLX. Powered by a liquid-cooled V-twin engine that displaced 583cc, the VLX had a four-speed gearbox and chain drive. The VLX had only one rear shock which rode beneath the lower frame rails. This arrangement gave the illusion of a hard tail chassis with the comfort of suspension. A triangular air cleaner sat nestled in the V of the motor, all of which was silver.

The new NT650 Hawk GT was built around a 647cc V-twin engine. The Hawk GT featured an aluminum spar frame that was both lighter and stiffer than previous designs. The rigidity of this new design was proven by the application of a single-sided swingarm on the rear end. This combination provided a terrific all-around machine that was both sporty and comfortable. Big enough for highway use, yet nimble enough for local errands, the Hawk GT filled a new niche for Honda. A pair of disc brakes was mounted to the six-spoke alloy rims and a two-into-one exhaust routed the gases cleanly on their way. The V45 Magna returned to its former glory as the VF750C guise. Except for the increased displacement, the V45 Magna was mostly the same as the 1987 version.

Called a "modern classic" in the sales brochure, the VT600C was brand new for 1988 and continued to build on the success of the cruiser models.

American Honda

The chin spoiler returned but was now color-matched to the fuel tank chosen. With the displacement limits removed, the VT700C Shadow appeared in 1988 as the VT800C. Outside the enlarged V-twin engine, changes were few. Wire wheels replaced the cast units seen before and two tone fuel tank paint was mated to chrome on the side covers. Modifications to the CBR1000F Hurricane were also limited to new color options.

The returning VT1100C Shadow only had a few details altered. The silver stripe found on the fuel tank was now removed and black spark plug wires were installed. Frames on the 1988 models matched the selected color of the sheet metal.

The flat-four engine in the Gold Wing had increased to 1200cc, and accessories had grown to meet with riders' growing demands. Not only

HONDA

For the entry-level rider who wanted something sporty, the Interceptor VTR was right up their alley and new for 1988.

American Honda

When loaded with all required fluids, the 1988 Gold Wing tipped the scales at a high 882 lbs. To ease the burden of moving the new GL into spaces or a garage, a reverse gear was installed. It was a system that supplied a running GL with enough power in neutral to feed a mechanism that propelled the machine backwards. If the machine fell over while being reversed a shut-off switch killed the motor to prevent further damage. A full compliment of electronic wares was installed on the latest Gold Wing and everything was easier to use. Three 296mm brake discs, one on the rear wheel and two up front, slowed the bikes. Twin-piston calipers were on hand to anchor the discs. The front rotors were dressed with plastic covers that also helped direct air onto the calipers for cooling assistance. A cast-aluminum 18-inch wheel was held in the front forks while a 16-inch rim rolled out back.

did Honda jump displacement to 1520cc for 1988, but they did so by adding another pair of cylinders. The opposed-six was even smoother and more powerful than any previous iteration, leaving the competition scratching their heads in wonder. Everything that shone on the Wings was polished to a new luster.

1988 HONDA

Model	Engine	Displacement	Transmission
VTR250 Interceptor (New for 1988)	DOHC V-Twin	249cc	Six-Speed
CBR600F Hurricane	DOHC Inline-Four	598cc	Six-Speed
VT600C Shadow VLX (New for 1988)	SOHC V-Twin	583cc	Four-Speed
NT650 Hawk GT (New for 1988)	SOHC V-Twin	647cc	Five-Speed
VF750C V45 Magna	DOHC V-Four	748cc	Six-Speed
VT800C Shadow	SOHC V-Twin	800cc	Four-Speed
CBR1000F Hurricane	DOHC Inline-Four	998cc	Six-Speed
VT1100C Shadow	SOHC V-Twin	1099cc	Four-Speed
GL1500 Gold Wing (New engine)	SOHC Opposed-Six	1520cc	Five-Speed

1989

Returning for round two was the Interceptor VTR. Mechanical changes were non-existent but coloration now saw white wheels replacing the blue of 1988.

The needs of the small sport bike market were improved with the CB400F CB-1. With an inline-four motor slung beneath the chassis, the CB-1 had a resemblance to the Hawk GT, but lacked the spar frame and single-sided swingarm. Within the walls of the 399cc, dual-overhead cam engine were gear-driven camshafts and liquid cooling. A four-into-one exhaust was finished in black chrome and made a nice contrast to the Pearl Presto Blue paint. A six-speed gearbox provided plenty of ratios for spirited riding.

The GB500 looked like an antique, but the Tourist Trophy was a modern machine. A single-cylinder, 499cc overhead cam engine was similar to a multitude of British machines that had been powered by "thumper" engines in their heyday and the GB embodied that emotion. A two-into-one exhaust handled the departing gases and the muffler was finished in chrome. Starting the GB was accomplished via electric start or kick-start pedal.

It had been many moons since Honda included kick starting on a street-going machine. The solo saddle was truncated by a small rear cowling that, along with the classic fuel tank, were draped in Black Green Metallic paint and offset with gold pinstripes. Everything about the Tourist Trophy said "classic," right down to the spoke wheels at either end. Low-mounted handlebars and a 5-speed gearbox completed the list of features.

CBR600F models were no longer called "Hurricane," but "CBR" instead. Graphics were the only revision to the 1989 models with Pearl Crystal White being paired with Winter Lake Blue Metallic or Terra Blue and Fighting Red. "CBR" decals replaced the previous "Hurricane" on the fuel tank.

The only change to the 1989 VT600C Shadow VLX was a script-style logo on the tank.

First seen in 1989, the XL600V Transalp was kind of a gentleman's dual-purpose bike. Plenty of ground clearance and protective shrouds gave the impression of an off-road machine, but the full-frontal fairing and comfortable saddle looked like open road features. Powered by a 583cc, liquid-cooled V-twin engine, the Transalp shifted through a five-speed gearbox and had an exhaust that exited high under the tail section. Pearl Crystal White was trimmed with red and blue stripes.

The NT650 Hawk GT returned unchanged but was now finished in Italian Red paint.

With Honda's domination of the large touring bike market with its GL1500, there was no reason to add a new model to that facet of the field. For those wanting a touring machine, but not quite as opulent or pricey, the PC800 Pacific Coast was introduced for 1989. The 800cc, SOHC V-twin mill and its shaft drive were all housed within a set of full-coverage bodywork. Beneath the saddle, a spacious storage compartment carried the things a medium distance rider needed. Pearl Pacific White paint melded with sections of Ocean Gray Metallic.

The shrinking cruiser segment still included the VT1100C Shadow as one of its own, and the only change was the application of a script logo on the fuel tank. Black was replaced by Indian Lake Blue Metallic in 1989.

With the GL1500 an all-new model in 1988, only a few alterations were applied to the 1989 model. Perhaps the biggest change was that the Gold Wing was to be assembled in the USA beginning this year. The "1500/6" emblem went missing from the saddlebags as of 1989, and color-keyed front brake housings were used when buying the Commodore Blue-Green Metallic and Triton Blue Metallic or Martini Beige with Haze Brown Metallic paint. A silver cover was still found when purchasing the Candy Wineberry Red and Burgundy Red Metallic option.

1989 HONDA

Model	Engine	Displacement	Transmission
VTR250 Interceptor	DOHC V-Twin	249cc	Six-Speed
CB400F CB-1 (New for 1989)	DOHC Inline-Four	399cc	Six-Speed
GB500 Tourist Trophy (New for 1989)	OHC Single	499cc	Five-Speed
CBR600F	DOHC Inline-Four	598cc	Six-Speed
VT600C Shadow VLX	SOHC V-Twin	583cc	Four-Speed
XL600V Transalp (New for 1989)	OHC V-Twin	583cc	Five-Speed
NT650 Hawk GT	SOHC V-Twin	647cc	Five-Speed
PC800 Pacific Coast (New for 1989)	SOHC V-Twin	800cc	Five-Speed
VT1100C Shadow	SOHC V-Twin	1099cc	Four-Speed
GL1500 Gold Wing (Assembled in USA)	SOHC Opposed-Six	1520cc	Five-Speed

HONDA
1990

The RC30 was as close to race bike as many buyers would ever see in their garage. The combination of technology and trim made the RC30 truly unique.

Matt Jonas

The Interceptor VTR would make its final appearance for 1990 and a 17-inch front rim would now be fitted with an external disc brake.

The CB-1 would be sold for $400 less in 1990. The GB500 Tourist Trophy was another return model with no changes, but a $500 reduction was made to its sticker price.

An additional 10 hp was added to the output of the 1990 CBR600F but it was otherwise unchanged. Only the VT1100C was left in the cruiser lineup, but changes in that market segment would soon alter the balance of sport and custom offerings.

Another returning model was the NT650 Hawk GT. No changes were seen in either features or color for the 1990 version.

Last applied to a Honda in 1986, the VFR750F moniker was back, and affixed to a better version of the V-4-powered sport bike.

Influenced by the RC30, the VFR chassis now featured a twin spar design and single-sided swing arm. The latest iteration of the V-4 engine was more compact yet produced over 100 hp.

Rigid 41mm front forks were joined by a single, gas-charged shock absorber on the cast aluminum swing arm. A set of 17-inch rims were mounted to both axles with radial tires keeping them off the pavement. A saddle height of 30.8 inches and wet weight of 540 lbs. was deftly managed by the bike's expertly designed chassis and geometry. As good as the latest VFR was, Honda also sold the VFR750R RC30. For a mere $14,998, and for the first time in the U.S., buyers could ride home on this exotic bike.

The RC30 was full of race-level technology and weight saving materials. The 748cc engine was similar in appearance to that used in the VFR, but within the alloy cases you found little in common. A close-ratio gearbox, titanium connecting rods and an entirely different top-end set the RC30 apart. The light alloy chassis steered with a set of 43mm front forks and a single-sided swing arm. Weight-saving materials meant the RC30 with a full-tank weight of only 475.5 lbs. was 65 lbs. lighter than the VFR.

The cockpit of the RC30 was all business and tucked behind the race-inspired fairing and windscreen. The tachometer showed a redline of 12,500 rpm and the speedometer ran all the way up to 185 mph. Clip-on handlebars continued the race bike in street clothing motif as did the thinly padded pillion with no passenger allowance. Model year 1990 was the only year of sale in the states for the RC30.

The PC800 Pacific Coast had been upgraded with 62 minor changes according to Honda. The most obvious of which were a taller windscreen. Last sold in the U.S. in 1988, the CBR1000F returned in 1990, but was stripped of the "Hurricane" moniker. Only incremental alterations were made including revised fairing contours and radial tires.

First sold in 1990, the new ST1100 was actually classified as a 1991 model by Honda. Assembled around a steel chassis, the ST1100 ran with a 1084cc V-4 engine that was liquid cooled. A five-speed gearbox fed the power into a shaft drive to keep things neat and quiet. The camshafts were driven by rubber belts to quiet engine operations.

Aerodynamic bodywork included a pair of quick-release saddlebags, each capable of swallowing a full-face helmet. When the bags were removed from the bike, small panels flipped into place, concealing the mounting hardware from view. An enormous 7.7-gallon fuel tank provided the rider and passenger with long runs between fill-ups.

The VT1100C Shadow was the only remaining cruiser in the Honda catalog for 1990, and was delivered without changes.

A Special Edition GL1500 was sold with Pearl White paint subtly accented with Eagle Silver Metallic and Ocean Gray Metallic. An aerodynamic rear trunk spoiler was joined by brake and running lights that were now integrated into the contours. Passengers could adjust the position of their footrests. An advanced audio system was installed complete with illuminated switches on both the handlebars and radio. An automatic volume control and intercom were both a part of the latest package.

1990 HONDA

Model	Engine	Displacement	Transmission
VTR250 Interceptor (Final year of sale)	DOHC V-Twin	249cc	Six-Speed
CB400F CB-1	DOHC Inline-Four	399cc	Six-Speed
GB500 Tourist Trophy	OHC Single	499cc	Five-Speed
CBR600F	DOHC Inline-Four	598cc	Six-Speed
XL600V Transalp	OHC V-Twin	583cc	Five-Speed
NT650 Hawk GT	SOHC V-Twin	647cc	Five-Speed
VFR750F VFR	DOHC V-Four	748cc	Six-Speed
VFR750R RC30 (New for 1990)	DOHC V-Four	748cc	Six-Speed
PC800 Pacific Coast	SOHC V-Twin	800cc	Five-Speed
CBR1000F	DOHC Inline-Four	998cc	Six-Speed
ST1100 (New for 1990)	DOHC V-Four	1084cc	Five-Speed
VT1100CShadow	SOHC V-Twin	1099cc	Four-Speed
GL1500 Gold Wing	SOHC Opposed-Six	1520cc	Five-Speed
GL1500SE Gold Wing	SOHC Opposed-Six	1520cc	Five-Speed

HONDA

1991

STANDARD CATALOG OF ® JAPANESE Motorcycles

Added to the mix for 1991 was the 750cc Nighthawk. The naked bike delivered terrific performance in a simple package that appealed to a wide variety of buyers.

American Honda

A 234cc parallel twin engine resided beneath sleek bodywork that belied the simple nature of the new CB250. Simple spoke wheels and Passion Red paint were complimented by silver "Nighthawk" graphics. The comfortable two-person seat was paired with a set of handlebars that kept the rider in a mild crouch.

CBR600F fans would applaud the new version of Honda's compact sport bike. The 1991 CBR600F2 was loaded with new power and performance yet sold for the same price as last year's model. The 600 class was proving to be most popular and upgrades to the CBR pushed it to the head of the class.

The frame was new and held the motor further back and lower than before. The perimeter design was crafted in rectangular section steel and employed the motor as a stressed member for added rigidity with less weight. Overall, the new CBR600F2 weighed eight pounds less than the 1990 model. While retaining the same characteristics as the previous motor, the F2's mill was smaller, lighter and spun up to 13,000 rpm. The combined efforts of the designers resulted in a compact engine that delivered seven more horsepower, while saving space and weight. Achieving more than 100 ponies from a 599cc mill was quite a feat, even for Honda. The 34mm, flat-slide carbs replaced the 32mm units on the 1990 models, and drew breath through a larger 6.2-liter airbox. Spent gases flowed through a four-into-two-into-one exhaust. Lightweight, six-spoke alloy rims were used at both ends and 60 series radial tires added to the handling of the improved F2. All of this performance was available in one of two color combinations: Ross White with Fighting Red or Black with Real Blue, Light Blue and Pink graphics.

With the Interceptor VTR missing from the '91 catalog, it was up to the new 250 Nighthawk to serve the entry-level rider.

American Honda

Returning for another few rounds was the VT600C Shadow VLX. With the exception of the new Black paint, it was unchanged. The NT650 Hawk GT also returned in 1991, but was unchanged, including the Italian Red paint.

80

STANDARD CATALOG OF ® JAPANESE MOTORCYCLES   HONDA

Another new naked bike for 1991 was the CB750 Nighthawk. Motivated by a 747cc, in-line-four engine that was based on the European CBX750F, it provided a stable and powerful mount for those wanting something simpler. A five-speed transmission sent power to the rear wheel via chain drive, and five-spoke alloy rims kept the rubber in place. Candy Bourgogne Red paint was trimmed with silver "Honda" wing and "Nighthawk" graphics.

The hugely popular VFR750F was only given gold wheels for 1991, leaving the remaining details unchanged. The PC800 Pacific Coast went on hiatus until the 1994 model year. The big CBR1000F was also unchanged except for Passion Red with Checker Black Metallic paint.

The ST1100, although sold in the spring of 1990, was officially released for 1991. Only Black was sold in the spring while Sparkling Silver Metallic was added in the fall of 1990.

The VT600C had returned in 1991 but the VT1100C would be a no-show until 1992.

Gold Wing buyers were once again faced with a decision when deciding to ride home a GL1500. Three different variations were offered, each wearing a different blend of goodies. The Aspencade was a 10th Anniversary model and wore gold emblems and a commemorative number plate and logo. Black was the only color sold, and a chrome front brake cover was also a part of the appearance package. The Interstate was also a 10th Anniversary model. Stripped of the reverse-gear and cruise control, the GL1500I did include the Hondaline AM/FM radio unit as standard equipment. Rear passenger floorboards were replaced with foot pegs. Cinnamon Beige Metallic with Valiant Brown Metallic was the only color listed. Another SE model was also part of the Gold Wing lineup and it remained as the fully-equipped version sold in 1990. Sunflash Gold Metallic was complimented by Valiant Brown Metallic. Some 10th Anniversary badges and a number plate were a part of the plan.

Basically an all new version of the 1990 model, the CBR600 sold for the same MSRP, delivering terrific value to the 1991 edition.

American Honda

Honda's liter bike listings were few, but the CBR1000F made up for any shortcomings in the entry list.

American Honda

1991 HONDA

Model	Engine	Displacement	Transmission
CB250 Nighthawk (New for 1991)	OHC Parallel Twin	234cc	Five-Speed
CBR600F2 Super Sport	DOHC Inline-Four	599cc	Six-Speed
VT600C Shadow VLX	SOHC V-Twin	583cc	Four-Speed
CB750 Nighthawk (New for 1991)	DOHC Inline-Four	747cc	Five-Speed
NT650 Hawk GT (Final year of sale)	SOHC V-Twin	647cc	Five-Speed
VFR750F VFR	DOHC V-Four	748cc	Six-Speed
CBR1000F	DOHC Inline-Four	998cc	Six-Speed
ST1100	DOHC V-Four	1084cc	Five-Speed
GL1500A Gold Wing Aspencade	SOHC Opposed-Six	1520cc	Five-Speed
GL1500I Gold Wing Interstate	SOHC Opposed-Six	1520cc	Five-Speed
GL1500SE Gold Wing	SOHC Opposed-Six	1520cc	Five-Speed

HONDA
1992

STANDARD CATALOG OF® JAPANESE MOTORCYCLES

Actually an early release 1993 model, the CBR900RR took performance to new levels in a light and powerful package.

American Honda

The CB250 Nighthawk was now sold in choices of Passion Red or Myth Blue Metallic, but no other alterations were seen.

New colors and graphics were the only changes made to the CBR600F2. Black with Palette Purple or a solid Fighting Red finish were the 1992 options. The VT600C Shadow wore a new shade in its Candy Glory Red, and also sported new tank graphics.

The CB750 Nighthawk was available in your choice of Black or Candy Bourgogne Red. The 1992 VFR750F received a horsepower boost and mildly revised suspension. A silver "VFR" decal with purple outline adorned the fuel tank that, along with the rest of the bike, was delivered in Granite Blue Metallic. Metallic gray wheels replaced the gold rims seen in 1991.

Making its debut as an early release 1993 model, the CBR900RR took the performance race to new heights. Weighing only 408 lbs., but with the power of a much larger machine, the "RR" was a radical concept brought to life. Everything from the alloy chassis to the 11,000 rpm redline screamed "race bike" while the legal lighting proved it was street worthy. Wide tires and upgraded brakes ensured confidence when cornering or braking. The tires were also an advantage with acceleration.

After another brief hiatus, the Shadow 1100 was back for 1992 and custom paint was a new option for the buyer.

American Honda

For '92, the VFR750F received more horsepower and enhanced suspension along with altered graphics.

American Honda

The ST1100 was only sold in Candy Glory Red and the brake calipers and wheels were all finished in gray. A new version of the ST1100 would add the safety benefits of anti-lock brakes and traction control. The ST1100A was the official designation for this model, and gold wheels and brake calipers set it apart from the ST1100.

The VT1100C Shadow was "on" for another year, but only changes in the colors was made. In addition to four factory hues being shown, a new series of custom colors were offered. They allowed the rider to create a personal color combination to fit his or her desires. Twenty-four different combinations of colors and graphics were offered.

The four factory colors for 1992 were Cascade Silver Metallic, Candy Spectra Red, South Pacific Blue Metallic and Black.

The Aspencade and Interstate GL models were now offered in Candy Spectra Red or Cambridge Blue Metallic. The Interstate was also fitted with an improved AM/FM sound system complete with a 25-watt amplifier and an output jack. The SE was sold in a two-tone paint scheme of Barbados Blue Metallic and Laguna Blue Metallic.

Three variations of the Gold Wing were offered for 1992 with the SE at the top of the list.

American Honda

1992 HONDA

Model	Engine	Displacement	Transmission
CB250 Nighthawk	OHC Parallel Twin	234cc	Five-Speed
CBR600F2 Super Sport	DOHC Inline-Four	599cc	Six-Speed
VT600C Shadow VLX	SOHC V-Twin	583cc	Four-Speed
CB750 Nighthawk	DOHC Inline-Four	747cc	Five-Speed
VFR750F VFR	DOHC V-Four	748cc	Six-Speed
CBR900RR (Early release 1993)	DOHC Inline-Four	893cc	Six-Speed
ST1100	DOHC V-Four	1084cc	Five-Speed
ST1100A ABS-TCS (ABS/Traction Control)	DOHC V-Four	1084cc	Five-Speed
VT1100C Shadow	SOHC V-Twin	1099cc	Four-Speed
GL1500A Gold Wing Aspencade	SOHC Opposed-Six	1520cc	Five-Speed
GL1500I Gold Wing Interstate	SOHC Opposed-Six	1520cc	Five-Speed
GL1500SE Gold Wing	SOHC Opposed-Six	1520cc	Five-Speed

HONDA

STANDARD CATALOG OF® JAPANESE Motorcycles

1993

A brief time away from the sales floor, the CBR1000F was back in 1993 wearing new bodywork over the previous running gear.

American Honda

With the exception of three new colors being offered, the CB250 Nighthawk was unchanged. Black, Candy Bourgogne Red or Candy Tahitian Blue were available.

CBR600F2 models rolled on improved BT50 radial tires and featured revised graphics and colors. Two different three-color themes were sold, Black with Seed Silver Metallic and NR Red or Ross White, Real Blue and NR Red.

The standard VT600C Shadow VLX was finished in Black but wore carry-over graphics. Joining the VT600C was the VT600CD Shadow VLX Deluxe. While having the same mechanicals of the standard, the Deluxe was better dressed. A two-tone wardrobe featured Pearl Coral Reef Blue and Black paint. It was accented by chrome on the engine cases and valve covers. Handlebars were wider with a new shape, and the saddle was now a two-piece affair with upholstery buttons adding some texture to the theme.

Adding additional luster to the Shadow VLX was the Deluxe edition. It was suited with styling cues that helped to set it apart from other motorcycles in the genre.

American Honda

Only a third color was added to the game for the CB750 Nighthawk. Candy Tahitian Blue joined Black and Candy Bourgogne Red as buying options. The VFR750F also received nothing more than a few cosmetic tweaks. Pearl Crystal White paint and white wheels were the centerpieces of the latest arrangement. "Honda," "VFR750F," and the Honda "Wing" were all new graphics applied to the existing bodywork.

Two choices of three-color graphics were available for the 1993 CBR900RR; Ross White with Real Blue and NR Red graphics or Black with Seed Silver Metallic and NR Red.

After another model year on the bench, the CBR1000F returned wearing new clothes. A sleek set of bodywork was wrapped around the previous chassis and drive train. A linked braking system helped to keep things under control. Only one set of colors was sold for 1993. A lower cowl of gray was joined by Black, Red, Blitz Gray Metallic and Medium Gray Metallic surfaces on the rest of the panels.

Both versions of the ST1100 were in the 1993 lineup again, but neither the ST1100 nor ST1100A sported any alterations in appearance or running gear.

The VT1100C Shadow was entered into the Custom Color Program in 1992, and that was expanded in 1993 to include 26 combinations of colors and graphics. American Red, Pearl Coronado Blue and Pearl Glacier White joined the four colors listed in 1992.

After a year or so of receiving no improvements, the GL1500A Aspencade would receive a few new details. Air caps on the front shocks were now standard and needle bearing rocker arm pivots assisted in smooth and quiet operation of the opposed-six motor. The cruise control was also improved and held a selected speed with more accuracy. Black was also added to the color list, bringing the total array to three. The same Black option was added to the GL1500I Interstate list as well, but no other changes were seen.

Being at the top of its game, the SE Gold Wing needed little improvement, so Honda merely made the CB radio and rear speakers standard equipment. Three new hues were also added to the order sheets with Pearl Glacier White, Pearl Glacier White with Light Blue and Pearl Coronado Blue with Light Blue adding a new decision to the buyer's list.

Pearl Crystal White paint was applied to the body panels and wheels of the 1993 VFR750, but little else was changed.

American Honda

1993 HONDA

Model	Engine	Displacement	Transmission
CB250 Nighthawk	OHC Parallel Twin	234cc	Five-Speed
CBR600F2 Super Sport	DOHC Inline-Four	599cc	Six-Speed
VT600C Shadow VLX	SOHC V-Twin	583cc	Four-Speed
VT600CD Shadow VLX Deluxe (New version for 1993)	SOHC V-Twin	583cc	Four-Speed
CB750 Nighthawk	DOHC Inline-Four	747cc	Five-Speed
VFR750F VFR	DOHC V-Four	748cc	Six-Speed
CBR900RR	DOHC Inline-Four	893cc	Six-Speed
CBR1000F	DOHC Inline-Four	998cc	Six-Speed
ST1100	DOHC V-Four	1084cc	Five-Speed
ST1100A ABS-TCS	DOHC V-Four	1084cc	Five-Speed
VT1100C Shadow	SOHC V-Twin	1099cc	Four-Speed
GL1500A Gold Wing Aspencade	SOHC Opposed-Six	1520cc	Five-Speed
GL1500I Gold Wing Interstate	SOHC Opposed-Six	1520cc	Five-Speed
GL1500SE Gold Wing	SOHC Opposed-Six	1520cc	Five-Speed

HONDA

1994

For the buyer wanting a standard model with more muscle, the CB1000 was right up his alley and brand new for 1994.

American Honda

The CB250 Nighthawks soldiered on, and only two new colors were found in the revision listing. Candy Red Replaced Candy Bourgogne Red and Candy Tahitian Blue was overridden by Metallic Blue.

The CBR600F2 was also the recipient of new paint options for 1994 with no modifications made to the hardware. Three-color combinations were offered in Ross White with Black and Atomic Red, Black with Uranus Violet and Atomic Red or finally, Black, Uranus Violet with Chartreuse Yellow. Candy Glory Red was added to the list of available VT600C Shadow VLX hues, with no other alterations seen. Red with Pearl White or Teal with Pearl White were optional colors sold on the returning VT600CD Shadow VLX Deluxe.

Although only 300 copies of the RC30 were sold in 1990, Honda upped the ante with a new RVF750R RC45 in 1994. An all-new, 749cc, 90-degree V-4 engine featured titanium connecting rods, just as the RC30 had. Feeding this new mill was a computer-operated programmed fuel-injection system that was more accurate. A single-sided swing arm was

Continuing to make a terrific way to start riding, the 250 Nighthawk was still on the team for 1994.

American Honda

retained as was the racing style bodywork and fairing. Like the RC30, the RC45 was fitted with a solo saddle, keeping its racing intent clear. Ross White paint was mated with graphics of Sparkling Red and Purple.

Last seen as a 1988 model, the VF750C Magna was back in 1994. Although bearing the same name, it was an entirely new machine from the fuel tank down. The engine, wheels, exhaust and bodywork were all fresh on the machine, but the V-4 engine still throbbed beneath the saddle. Magna Red, Black and Pearl Shining Yellow were the available colors.

Another Honda bearing the same name as the previous model, yet riding with all new hardware, was the VFR750F VFR. Its intent was not changed, but the chassis, bodywork and running gear received modifications for 1994. The Pure Red paint was offset by black wheels and a N.A.R.T.-style intake vent on the side of the full-coverage fairing.

After slipping off the radar in 1991, the PC800 Pacific Coast was back in 1994. Save the Black-Z color, no other revisions were listed.

The featherweight CBR900RR rolled on an altered front tire and some new paint, but was otherwise unchanged. Ross White with Red and Black, or Black with Uranus Violet and Yellow were your latest choices.

Revised heavily for 1994, the VFR750 also sported new bodywork and black wheels.
American Honda

Bringing a new standard bike to the table, the CB1000 was a powerful example of what could be accomplished. A double-overhead cam, 998cc, liquid-cooled engine provided the motivation and a five-speed gearbox handled the distribution. Three-spoke alloy wheels finished in Gloss Black were fitted with triple disc brakes. A four-into-one exhaust was plated in chrome and matched to an aluminum muffler. Each rear shock carried a remote reservoir that provided a high degree of comfort and adjustability.

The CBR1000F was only trimmed with some

Another model to receive only incremental changes for '94 was the CBR1000F with new colors being one of the alterations.

American Honda

HONDA

STANDARD CATALOG OF *JAPANESE* Motorcycles

Still a popular purchase for the rider wanting a slightly smaller touring mount, the ST1100 was again sold in base and ABS equipped versions.

American Honda

new details for 1994. The upper section of the cowl now featured bumpers to protect the bodywork in case of a drop. The latest Matt Black, Ross White and Red color scheme was also altered in its pattern from the previous year.

Both ST1100 and ST1100A were now finished in Gloss Black but saw no other revisions. The VT1100C Shadow's Custom Color Program now claimed a few new shades, replacing earlier variants. Solid color models were only seen with the standard logo while two-tone versions could opt for the standard or secondary badges. The color choices of Cascade Silver Metallic and Pearl Glacier White were supplanted by Pearl Atlantis Blue and Pearl Bermuda Green in 1994.

The 1994 Aspencade and Interstate Gold Wings now featured a lower body cowling that was finished in the same color as the upper bodywork. Both versions were sold in Candy Spectra Red, Pearl Atlantis Blue or Black-Z. The SE retained the lower cowling in silver while the upper segments were seen in Pearl Bermuda Green, Pearl Atlantis Blue, Candy Spectra Red or Pearl Glacier White.

1994 HONDA

Model	Engine	Displacement	Transmission
CB250 Nighthawk	OHC Parallel Twin	234cc	Five-Speed
CBR600F2 Super Sport	DOHC Inline-Four	599cc	Six-Speed
VT600C Shadow VLX	SOHC V-Twin	583cc	Four-Speed
VT600CD Shadow VLX Deluxe	SOHC V-Twin	583cc	Four-Speed
RVF750R RC45 (New for 1994)	DOHC V-Four	749cc	Six-Speed
VF750C Magna (Returning model)	DOHC V-Four	748cc	Six-Speed
VFR750F VFR	DOHC V-Four	748cc	Six-Speed
PC800 Pacific Coast	SOHC V-Twin	800cc	Five-Speed
CBR900RR	DOHC Inline-Four	893cc	Six-Speed
CB1000 (New for 1994)	DOHC Inline-Four	998cc	Five-Speed
CBR1000F	DOHC Inline-Four	998cc	Six-Speed
ST1100	DOHC V-Four	1084cc	Five-Speed
ST1100A ABS-TCS	DOHC V-Four	1084cc	Five-Speed
VT1100C Shadow	SOHC V-Twin	1099cc	Four-Speed
GL1500A Gold Wing Aspencade	SOHC Opposed-Six	1520cc	Five-Speed
GL1500I Gold Wing Interstate	SOHC Opposed-Six	1520cc	Five-Speed
GL1500SE Gold Wing	SOHC Opposed-Six	1520cc	Five-Speed

STANDARD CATALOG OF ® JAPANESE MOTORCYCLES

HONDA

1995

Only two colors were offered for the CB250 Nighthawk, Black and Candy Red. No other changes were implemented.

The 1995 CBR600's now carried the F3 designation as minor modifications improved the breed. A dual-stage induction system aided in breathing and the headlight assembly was all-plastic to shave a few ounces from the overall weight. Two fresh color combinations were used as well as revised graphics. Black with Uranus Violet and Chartreuse Yellow was the first option with Ross White, Uranus Violet and Chartreuse Yellow following close behind.

Both versions of the VT600 Shadow received new fuel tanks and handlebars as well as revised art. The VT600C Shadow was sold in the same hues as last year while the Deluxe edition wore Candy Burgundy with Pearl White or Pearl Purple with Pearl White paint.

Having missed a year of sale, the CB750 Nighthawk returned for 1995 and featured some new bits. Whether you bought a Magna Red or Black model, the lower fork legs were now polished aluminum and the headlight bucket and support brackets were chrome.

The 1995 VF750 Magnas were sold in either Candy Glory Red or Pearl Shining Yellow. Joining the Magna crew was the VF750CD Deluxe. A small, bikini fairing was seen surrounding the headlight and two-tone paint was applied. Pearl Paragon Purple with Pearl Fadeless White or Black with Pearl Salem Mint were the choices. No other distinctions were made between the two models.

With the chassis and related changes being made in the previous year, the VFR750F was unchanged for 1995, including the Pure Red paint.

Another model returning with no changes was the PC800 Pacific Coast. Black-Z paint was the only one listed for 1995.

Returning for 1995 was the Pacific Coast, but no changes were made since its temporary disappearance.
American Honda

Changes to the ultra-light CBR900RR were minimal and included fresh graphics with altered paint and a revised fairing. Ross White was now joined with Uranus Violet and the Yellow and the Black combination seen in 1994 was carried over.

Besides being sold in Pure Red Pearl, the CB1000 would roll on without alteration.

The model year 1995 would prove to be the final one for the big naked bike as riders chose ei-

Improvements made to the F2 resulted in the release of the CBR600F3 as it continued to dominate that segment of the market.
American Honda

HONDA

A headlight mounted fairing and two-tone paint set the Deluxe Magna apart from the standard model but no mechanical alterations were employed.

American Honda

ther sport or cruising machines more often. The fully-faired CB1000F was only draped in new colors for 1995 with Gloss Black, Blitz Gray Metallic and Yellow laid onto the bodywork in the same pattern.

The ST1100s and ST1100As were both sold in Pure Red for 1995, and featured improved air intakes and windscreens that provided better protection than before.

VT1100 Shadows touted new artwork, and Pearl Royal Magenta replaced Pearl Bermuda Green in the paint department. Foregoing Japanese smoothness for more thump, the VT1100 motors were assembled with a single-pin crankshaft that added some of the familiar vibrations so well known in the U.S. built offerings. The VT1100C2 American Classic Edition, or A. C. E., would first be seen for 1995. The A. C. E. sported bodywork and exhaust that closely mimicked that of some Milwaukee-made machines. Wire wheels were installed in place of the cast spokes found on the Shadow and front and rear fenders now provided more coverage. Two-tone paint was again the catch of the day with four different hues on the hook. Black, American Red, Pearl Atlantis Blue and Pearl Royal Magenta were available.

All three variations on the Gold Wing theme wore 20th anniversary badges for 1995. Other revisions included suspension calibration and improved saddlebag and trunk liners. New colors were available for each model in the GL family with Candy Spectra Red, Pearl Royal Magenta and Pearl Sierra Green for the Aspencade. Candy Spectra Red and Pearl Sierra Green for the Interstate. The SE offered three different two-tone choices with Pearl Royal Magenta/Purple, Pearl Sierra Green/Toscana Green and Candy Spectra Red/Italian Red. For those seeking a monotone effect, Pearl Glacier White was offered as a solid hue.

1995 HONDA

Model	Engine	Displacement	Transmission
CB250 Nighthawk	OHC Parallel Twin	234cc	Five-Speed
CBR600F3 Super Sport (Updated for 1995)	DOHC Inline-Four	599cc	Six-Speed
VT600C Shadow VLX	SOHC V-Twin	583cc	Four-Speed
VT600CD Shadow VLX Deluxe	SOHC V-Twin	583cc	Four-Speed
CB750 Nighthawk (Returning model)	DOHC Inline-Four	747cc	Six-Speed
VF750C Magna	DOHC V-Four	748cc	Six-Speed
VF750CD Magna Deluxe (Bikini fairing)	DOHC V-Four	748cc	Six-Speed
VFR750F VFR	DOHC V-Four	748cc	Six-Speed
PC800 Pacific Coast (Returning model)	SOHC V-Twin	800cc	Five-Speed
CBR900RR	DOHC Inline-Four	893cc	Six-Speed
CB1000 (Final year of sale)	DOHC Inline-Four	998cc	Five-Speed
CBR1000F	DOHC Inline-Four	998cc	Six-Speed
ST1100	DOHC V-Four	1084cc	Five-Speed
ST1100A ABS-TCS	DOHC V-Four	1084cc	Five-Speed
VT1100C Shadow (Single pin crank)	SOHC V-Twin	1099cc	Four-Speed
VT1100C2 Shadow A. C. E. (Single pin crank)	SOHC V-Twin	1099cc	Four-Speed
GL1500A Gold Wing Aspencade	SOHC Opposed-Six	1520cc	Five-Speed
GL1500I Gold Wing Interstate	SOHC Opposed Six	1520cc	Five-Speed
GL1500SE Gold Wing	SOHC Opposed Six	1520cc	Five-Speed

HONDA
1996

The unchanged CB250 Nighthawk was again joined by the CMX250C Rebel. Last seen in 1987, the Rebel brought a higher level of "cruiser" to the small bike market. With only Magna Red listed for color, the Rebel was identical to the previous edition.

The CBR600F3 Super Sport wore new graphics and colors but offered no other changes. Ross White with Magna Red and Black accents or Uranus Violet with Pearl Shining Yellow and Ross White trim were offered. To mark the success of their racing efforts, a limited edition Smokin' Joe Replica—based on the controversial cigarette ad—was also marketed for 1996. The Pearl Paragon Blue or Pearl Shining Yellow versions bore the "Smokin' Joe" name and camel cartoon logo.

The VT600C Shadow VLX was only sold in Black while the Deluxe version listed three different two-tone choices. Red with Black, Black with Pearl Mint or Pearl Purple with Pearl White was listed.

The CB750 Nighthawk now had its motor finished in black with accents of polished heads and cooling fins. Black or Shining Yellow paint could be had on the bodywork. The VF750 models claimed new tank logos on the Magna that was now sold in Pure Red or Pearl Shining Yellow. The Deluxe now bore a scalloped paint arrangement on the fuel tank and retained the bikini fairing. The two-tone scallops were seen in Pearl Paragon Purple with Pearl Fadeless White or in Black and Pure Red.

The VFR750F was again a carryover model including the paint. For 1996 the Pacific Coast was finished in Magna Red.

The CBR900RRs were treated to a long list of upgrades to the motor and bodywork. Higher performance from the compact mill and enhanced aerodynamics earmarked the latest revisions. Only one color

Still at the top of the model listings was the Special Edition Gold Wing of 1996.
American Honda

Returning to the fray for 1996 was the 250cc Rebel, bringing up the lower end of the cruiser market for Honda.
American Honda

HONDA

By adding linked braking to the ST1100A it became one of the most safety conscious models on the market.

American Honda

powerful air-cooled alternator, the ST1100A was found with a linked-brake system to enhance the ABS and traction control already in place.

VT1100C Shadows replaced Pearl Royal Magenta with two new hues of Pearl Majestic Purple and Pearl Hot Rod Yellow. Pearl Majestic Purple, Pearl Hot Rod Yellow and Pearl Glacier White were added.

Minor changes of a full-logic audio system and the availability of Pearl Sparkling Blue were added to the GL1500A Aspencade's listing. No changes were seen for the 1996 GL1500I Interstate and would be the final year of sale for the mid-level trim package. Four new two-tone color selections were offered for the GL1500SE—Candy Spectra Red with Italian Red, Pearl Royal Magenta with Purple, Pearl Sierra Green with Toscana Green and Pearl Glacier White with Summer Blond Metallic.

combination was sold in the Glass Black with Pure Red and Atomic Red details.

The 1996 model year was the final year of sale for the CBR1000F and no changes whatsoever were shown.

Both the ST1100 and ST1100A were now fitted with 40 amp alternators. Along with the more

1996 HONDA

Model	Engine	Displacement	Transmission
CB250 Nighthawk	OHC Parallel Twin	234cc	Five-Speed
CMX250C Rebel (Returning model)	OHC Parallel Twin	234cc	Five-Speed
CBR600F3 Super Sport	DOHC Inline-Four	599cc	Six-Speed
CBR600SJR Smokin' Joe's Replica	DOHC Inline-Four	599cc	Six-Speed
VT600C Shadow VLX	SOHC V-Twin	583cc	Four-Speed
VT600CD Shadow VLX Deluxe	SOHC V-Twin	583cc	Four-Speed
CB750 Nighthawk	DOHC Inline-Four	747cc	Five-Speed
VF750C Magna	DOHC V-Four	748cc	Six-Speed
VF750CD Magna Deluxe (Scalloped paint)	DOHC V-Four	748cc	Six-Speed
VFR750F VFR	DOHC V-Four	748cc	Six-Speed
PC800 Pacific Coast	SOHC V-Twin	800cc	Five-Speed
CBR900RR	DOHC Inline-Four	893cc	Six-Speed
CBR1000F (Final year of sale)	DOHC Inline-Four	998cc	Six-Speed
ST1100	DOHC V-Four	1084cc	Five-Speed
ST1100A ABS-TCS (Linked braking)	DOHC V-Four	1084cc	Five-Speed
VT1100C Shadow	SOHC V-Twin	1099cc	Four-Speed
VT1100C2 Shadow A.C.E.	SOHC V-Twin	1099cc	Four-Speed
GL1500A Gold Wing Aspencade	SOHC Opposed-Six	1520cc	Five-Speed
GL1500I Gold Wing Interstate (Final year of sale)	SOHC Opposed-Six	1520cc	Five-Speed
GL1500SE Gold Wing	SOHC Opposed-Six	1520cc	Five-Speed

HONDA
1997

A new variation of the Gold Wing theme was the Valkyrie for 1997. It used the same flat-six engine as the Wing, but it was fed with a set of six individual carburetors.

American Honda

Both the CB250 Nighthawk and CMX250C Rebel were back for 1997 but no changes were made to the CB.

Engine enhancements on the CBR600F3 boosted horsepower ratings to 105 and a lightweight drive chain helped deliver the new found power to the rear sprocket. The VT600C Shadow VLX was only sold in Black and it seemed to be a fitting color for its final appearance. The Deluxe model would remain until the 1998 model year.

The VF750C Magna was now all-black while the VF750C2 (previously the CD) wore two-tone scalloped paint on the tank. The VFR750F VFR was in its final year of sale, and no alterations were seen.

A two-tone finish of Magna Red and Ostrich Black was applied to the 1997 PC800 and the molded front disc brake cover was removed. The self-canceling turn signals were replaced by a push-to-cancel system.

After a year of big changes to the CBR900RR in 1996, only graphics and paint would be revised for 1997. The 1997 CBR1100XX combined a terrific list of features and wrapped them in sleek bodywork that cheated the wind. The Black Bird, as it was also known, was motivated by a lightweight engine that displaced 1137cc, in an inline-four configuration. The upper crankcase and cylinder block were a single casting, providing simplicity and stiffness while saving weight. A linked braking system, like that used on the ST1100, allowed the XX to be slowed as easily as it was brought to speed. The pointed beak of the fairing lent itself to the given moniker of Black Bird, as did the Mute Black Metallic paint.

The ST1100 was unscathed, and even retained the Pure Red paint used on the 1996 models.

HONDA

The ST1100A was now tagged with the ABS II moniker. An improved anti-lock (ABS) system was tied to the linked braking introduced on the 1996 version.

The VT1100 Shadow was now the Shadow Spirit and featured oil and coolant lines that had been repositioned to be harder to see. This styling effort was teamed with five new color variations. An all-Black model was joined by four two-tone combinations. The VT1100C2, American Classic Edition, was seen in a Black-only model, or a two-tone edition. All switches were now marked with international symbols for use on both sides of the pond.

The Gold Wing clan had lost its Interstate member and changes to the remaining models would include hardware found on the latest opposed-six powered machines. Both the Aspencade and SE now featured the same internationally approved handlebar switches, and some new gearbox and clutch internals found on the new Valkyrie. The latest entry onto Honda's playing field was the Valkyrie. Powered by the same 1520cc, opposed-six cylinder motor from the Gold Wing, it was fed through a set of six carburetors, replacing the fuel injection used on the Gold Wing.

The GL1500C was stripped of all touring accessories, and featured simple trim commonly used on other cruisers.

Of course other cruisers weren't powered by the massive six-cylinder motor or were of the same enormous dimensions as the Valkyrie. The Valkyrie mill was tuned for performance and the six-into-six exhaust made noises like no other cruiser on the planet. A pair of full-coverage fenders covered the large rubber found at both ends.

Ergonomics of the Valkyrie were similar to those found on the Gold Wings with the large saddle and handlebars that reached back to greet the rider's grip.

For those seeking a bit more convenience, the GL1500CT Valkyrie Tourer provided everything the base model offered along with a wide windshield and a set of hard-sided saddlebags.

1997 HONDA

Model	Engine	Displacement	Transmission
CB250 Nighthawk (Final year of sale)	OHC Parallel Twin	234cc	Five-Speed
CMX250C Rebel (Final year of sale)	OHC Parallel Twin	234cc	Five-Speed
CBR600F3	DOHC Inline-Four	599cc	Six-Speed
VT600C Shadow VLX	SOHC V-Twin	583cc	Four-Speed
VT600CD Shadow VLX Deluxe	SOHC V-Twin	583cc	Four-Speed
CB750 Nighthawk	DOHC Inline-Four	747cc	Five-Speed
VF750C Magna	DOHC V-Four	748cc	Six-Speed
VF750C2 Magna Deluxe	DOHC V-Four	748cc	Six-Speed
VFR750F VFR (Final year of sale)	DOHC V-Four	748cc	Six-Speed
PC800 Pacific Coast	SOHC V-Twin	800cc	Five-Speed
CBR900RR	DOHC Inline-Four	893cc	Six-Speed
CBR1100XX Black Bird (New for 1997)	DOHC Inline-Four	1137cc	Six-Speed
ST1100	DOHC V-Four	1084cc	Five-Speed
ST1100A ABS II-TCS	DOHC V-Four	1084cc	Five-Speed
VT1100C Shadow Spirit	SOHC V-Twin	1099cc	Four-Speed
VT1100C2 Shadow A. C. E.	SOHC V-Twin	1099cc	Four-Speed
VT1100C2 Shadow A. C. E. Two-Tone	SOHC V-Twin	1099cc	Four-Speed
GL1500A Gold Wing Aspencade	SOHC Opposed-Six	1520cc	Five-Speed
GL1500SE Gold Wing	SOHC Opposed-Six	1520cc	Five-Speed
GL1500C Valkyrie (New for 1997)	SOHC Opposed-Six	1520cc	Five-Speed
GL1500CT Valkyrie Tourer (New for 1997)	SOHC Opposed-Six	1520cc	Five-Speed

HONDA
1998

With the exception of new colors, the CBR600F3 remained unaltered. Sparkling Red, Sparkling Red with Black or Black with Dark Crimson Red were the 1998 choices. For fans of Miguel Duhamel, a Smokin' Joe's Replica was also offered and it bore a copy of his signature on the fuel tank.

The VT600C was dropped, leaving only the Deluxe version behind. All-aluminum foot pegs were bound with wide rubber panels and Black with Jade Green or Ocean Gray Metallic with Black paint were the available color choices.

The CB750 Nighthawk was the only one left in the family with the sacking of the CB250. Only Black was sold with no other alterations listed. The VF750C Magna was another Black-only model with no additional changes. Only color differences were applied to the VF750C2 Magna with Black being mated to your choice of Terra Silver Metallic or Pearl Sparkling Blue.

The VT750C Shadow was last seen in 1983 but returned as an American Classic Edition for 1998. A 745cc V-twin engine powered the latest iteration and it was also all new in the cosmetics department. The latest ACE rolled on wire wheels.

The Pacific Coast was unchanged from 1997. Replacing the VFR750F was the all-new VFR800FI Interceptor. Built using a pivot-less frame and powered by a 781cc V-4 engine, the latest VFR would quickly prove itself to be a great all-around machine. The electronic fuel injection delivered flawless delivery regardless of rpm or speed and the linked braking provided a safer level of stopping power. For riders wanting a more purpose-built sport bike, the CBR900RR was both lighter and more powerful in 1998.

Power was boosted to 123 hp as well, creating a nearly unbeatable machine.

A new entry into the Honda lineup was the VTR1000F Super Hawk. The alloy frame cradled a 996cc, 90-degree V-twin power plant positioned it as a sport model. A frame-mounted ¾-size fairing provided rider protection but still allowed a view of the engine.

Climbing to the next rung of the performance ladder, the CBR1100XX was back with no changes for 1998. Both versions of the ST1100 were now sold in Black-Z only with no additional alterations listed.

A brace of new two-tone options were listed for the VT1100C Shadow Spirit but nothing mechanical was touched. The VT1100C2 Shadow

Seen here wearing the Pearl Coronado Blue and Pearl Ivory Cream finish, the 1998 Valkyrie was otherwise unchanged for 1998.

Bonzai Motorsports

95

HONDA

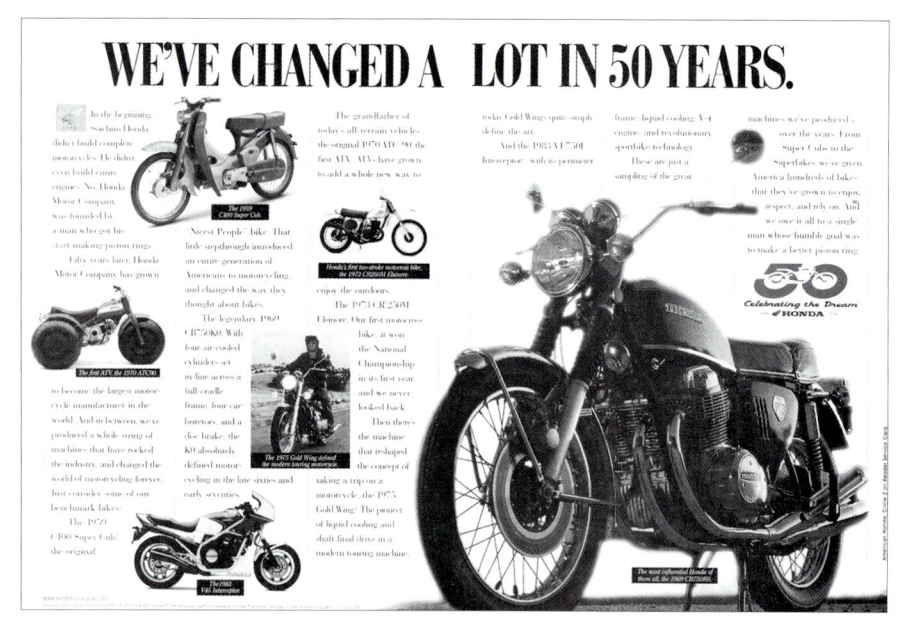

A 1998 ad celebrated 50 years of Honda motorcycles.

A. C. E. was unchanged in its all-black finish and black wall tires. Four new two-tone color combinations graced the VT1100C2 Shadow A. C. E.

Two new models joined the VT1100 family the first of which being the C3 Shadow Aero. With sheet metal that provided a more "classic" look the Aero was also the recipient of many chrome trim, a two-into-one exhaust and a rubber-mounted V-twin motor. The speedometer was housed in the oversized headlight housing and a two-piece saddle finished off the list of features. The final entry in the VT1100 clan was the ACE Tourer. By implementing cast-spoke rims, a windshield and a set of matching hard-sided saddlebags, the Tourer was ready for the open road. A different front fender was trimmed with a chrome splash guard and four different hues were offered.

Both the Aspencade and SE versions of the Gold Wing were fitted with revised cylinder head covers that featured fresh emblems. Tachometer and speedometer faces were now delivered with white faces.

Both versions of the Valkyrie were treated to new paint for 1998, but no other modifications were seen.

1998 HONDA

Model	Engine	Displacement	Transmission
CBR600F3	DOHC Inline-Four	599cc	Six-Speed
CBR600SE Smokin' Joe's Replica	DOHC Inline-Four	599cc	Six-Speed
VT600CD Shadow VLX Deluxe	SOHC V-Twin	583cc	Four-Speed
CB750 Nighthawk	DOHC Inline-Four	747cc	Five-Speed
VF750C Magna	DOHC V-Four	748cc	Six-Speed
VF750C2 Magna	DOHC V-Four	748cc	Six-Speed
VT750C Shadow A. C .E.	SOHC V-Twin	749cc	Six-Speed
VT750CD Shadow A. C. E. Deluxe	SOHC V-Twin	749cc	Six-Speed
PC800 Pacific Coast	SOHC V-Twin	800cc	Five-Speed
VFR800FI Interceptor	DOHC V-Four	781cc	Six-Speed
CBR900RR	DOHC Inline-Four	893cc	Six-Speed
VTR1000F Super Hawk (New for 1998)	DOHC V-Twin	996cc	Six-Speed
CBR1100XX Black Bird	DOHC Inline-Four	1137cc	Six-Speed
ST1100	DOHC V-Four	1084cc	Five-Speed
ST1100A ABS II	DOHC V-Four	1084cc	Five-Speed
VT1100C Shadow Spirit	SOHC V-Twin	1099cc	Four-Speed
VT1100C2 Shadow A. C. E.	SOHC V-Twin	1099cc	Four-Speed
VT1100C2 Shadow A. C. E. Two-Tone	SOHC V-Twin	1099cc	Four-Speed
VT1100C3 Shadow Aero	SOHC V-Twin	1099cc	Four-Speed
VT1100T Shadow A. C. E. Tourer	SOHC V-Twin	1099cc	Four-Speed
GL1500A Gold Wing Aspencade	SOHC Opposed-Six	1520cc	Five-Speed
GL1500SE Gold Wing	SOHC Opposed-Six	1520cc	Five-Speed
GL1500C Valkyrie	SOHC Opposed-Six	1520cc	Five-Speed
GL1500CT Valkyrie Tourer	SOHC Opposed-Six	1520cc	Five-Speed

STANDARD CATALOG OF ® JAPANESE MOTORCYCLES

HONDA
1999

The CB250 and CMX250C returned for 1999. No changes were made to the Nighthawk, and the Rebel was now only sold in Black. A third option in the 250cc segment was the CMX250C2 Rebel Two-Tone. Candy Glory Red with Black paint set the C2 apart from the C model.

The 1999 CBR600 models were revised to F4 status and the transformation was fairly dramatic. Nestled into a fresh chassis was a revamped 599cc motor that was smoother and more powerful than the last. Enhanced bodywork improved aerodynamics and a raft of other changes including three-spoke cast wheels saved weight. Black graphics accented your choice of Sunrise yellow or Italian Red.

The standard VT600C Shadow VLX were also back for 1999. A few revisions marked the latest version of the C, most obvious of which was the new saddle which now put the rider only 25.6 inches from the ground. The contours of the seat were now narrower in the front but wider and lower at the rear. The V-twin motor was fed through a single carburetor that was warmed by engine coolant. Both VT600C and VT600CD models were available in Black only. The VT600CD2 was offered in two-tone paint of Black with either Pearl Halcyon Silver or Pearl Sedona Red.

The VF750C Magna was also a repeat of 1998, with Italian Red added to the palette. A two-tone combination was sold for the VF750C2 in Black and Orange. The VT750C Shadow A. C. E. and VT750CD A. C. E. Deluxe were sold in the same configurations and colors as the year before. The VT750CD2 was sold in two-tone combinations of Black with Pearl Dark Red or Pearl Olive Green with Pearl Ivory.

The newest version of the Valkyrie was the Interstate which came complete with full coverage fairing, and a trio of hard storage compartments. American Honda

Still powered by a 996cc V-twin motor, the Super Hawk remained as Honda's sport-minded twin. American Honda

With a complete revamp under its belt in 1998, the VFR800FI returned in 1999 with no modifications. Having lost weight and gained power for 1998, the CBR900RR returned with no mechanical alterations. White was teamed with either Black or Pearl Shining Yellow.

VTR1000F Super Hawks were now finished in Mute Black Metallic or Pearl Shining Yellow in place of Italian Red.

A few minor tweaks were made to the CBR1100XX including an improved ram air system that boosted power, and a stacked, dual-taillight design. Mute Black Metallic was still the only hue offered for the Black Bird.

HONDA

ST1100 and ST1100 ABS II models returned with no changes.

There were now five different flavors on the VT1100 menu and gave the buyer very specific features depending on which model was chosen. The VT1100C Shadow Spirit saw no revisions except in the colors offered. An all-Black was sold alongside Black with either Twilight Silver or Blaze yellow. The C2 Shadow A. C. E. was seen wearing only Black while the C3 Shadow Aero had five options listed. Solid Black or Black mated to Pearl Vermont Green or Pearl Gray Blue were seen along with Somerset orange with Pearl White or finally, Pearl Sedona Red with Pearl Silver. The D2 designation pertained to the two-tone version of the Shadow and Black with Orange or Pearl Dark Red were the choices listed. The VT1100T Shadow A. C. E. Tourer was also back and sold in one of four different ensembles. Solid Black was shown on the brochure with Pearl Silver and Black, Pearl Vermont Green and Pearl White or Pearl Sedona Red and Black.

Gold Wing models for 1999 commemorated Honda's 50th anniversary by bearing special badges and ignition keys. The Aspencade was sold in the same hues as in 1998. The SE was available in Black-Z, Candy Spectra Red with Candy Dark Red, Pearl Merced Green with Dark Gray Green, Twilight Silver with Dark Silver or Glacier White with Metallic Gray.

A third trim level was made available in the Valkyrie lineup but only color changes effected the original variations. The latest edition was the GL1500CF Valkyrie Interstate. By adding a fork-mounted fairing, rear trunk and hard-sided saddlebags, the big opposed-six monster was ready for the highways and byways. It shared the same specially tuned motor found in the other Valkyrie models as well as the six individual carbs. Black, Black and Red or Pearl Sonoma Green with Metallic Gray were listed as options.

1999 HONDA

Model	Engine	Displacement	Transmission
CB250 Nighthawk	OHC Parallel Twin	234cc	Five-Speed
CMX250C Rebel	OHC Parallel Twin	234cc	Five-Speed
CMX250C2 Rebel 2-Tone	OHC Parallel Twin	234cc	Five-Speed
CBR600F4	DOHC Inline-Four	599cc	Six-Speed
VT600C Shadow VLX	SOHC V-Twin	583cc	Four-Speed
VT600CD Shadow VLX Deluxe	SOHC V-Twin	583cc	Four-Speed
CB750 Nighthawk	DOHC Inline-Four	747cc	Five-Speed
VF750C Magna	DOHC V-Four	748cc	Six-Speed
VF750C2 Magna	DOHC V-Four	748cc	Six-Speed
VT750C Shadow A. C. E.	SOHC V-Twin	749cc	Six-Speed
VT750CD Shadow A. C. E. Deluxe	SOHC V-Twin	749cc	Six-Speed
VT750CD2 Shadow A. C. E. Deluxe Two-Tone	SOHC V-Twin	749cc	Six-Speed
VFR800FI Interceptor	DOHC V-Four	781cc	Six-Speed
CBR900RR	DOHC Inline-Four	893cc	Six-Speed
VTR1000F Super Hawk	DOHC V-Twin	996cc	Six-Speed
CBR1100XX Black Bird	DOHC Inline-Four	1137cc	Six-Speed
ST1100	DOHC V-Four	1084cc	Five-Speed
ST1100A ABS II	DOHC V-Four	1084cc	Five-Speed
VT1100CShadow Spirit	SOHC V-Twin	1099cc	Four-Speed
VT1100C2 Shadow A. C. E.	SOHC V-Twin	1099cc	Four-Speed
VT1100C3 Shadow Aero	SOHC V-Twin	1099cc	Four-Speed
VT1100D2 Shadow A. C. E.	SOHC V-Twin	1099cc	Four-Speed
VT1100T Shadow A. C. E. Tourer	SOHC V-Twin	1099cc	Four-Speed
GL1500A Gold Wing Aspencade	SOHC Opposed-Six	1520cc	Five-Speed
GL1500SE Gold Wing	SOHC Opposed-Six	1520cc	Five-Speed
GL1500C Valkyrie	SOHC Opposed-Six	1520cc	Five-Speed
GL1500CF Valkyrie Interstate (New for 1999)	SOHC Opposed-Six	1520cc	Five-Speed
GL1500CT Valkyrie Tourer	SOHC Opposed-Six	1520cc	Five-Speed

HONDA 2000

Neither the CB250 or CMX250C saw any alterations, but the two-tone CMX250C2 was decked out in Pearl Halcyon Silver and Black paint for the 2000 model year.

The CBR600F4 was seen wearing fresh colors for 2000 but no modifications were made.

For the third consecutive year the CB750 Nighthawk was seen with no changes. The VF750C Magna only offered Black, and the C2 now wore Pearl Light Orange with Black. Two of the VT750 Shadows were also unaltered for 2000 while the two-tone CD2 offered Pearl Silver or Red with Black.

Efforts to curb emissions on the VFR800FI included adding an air injection system and three-way exhaust catalyzer. Mirrors were revised to fold for ease of use in confined spaces.

Honda took the RR formula to the next level for 2000 with the CBR929RR. A six-speed gearbox was mated to the 929cc engine and the entire machine weighed a scant 375 lbs., an amazing 21 lbs. less than the 900RR. A new fuel injection system was pressurized and electronically programmed. A titanium exhaust header led into a titanium muffler in an aluminum sleeve to further their weight loss plan.

A redesigned chassis and fresh bodywork kept the 929RR stiff and aerodynamically clean. Cast, three-spoke rims spared a few more ounces.

Fresh off the racetracks, the RVT1000R RC51 pulled into the Honda showroom for 2000. Positioned as a production super bike, the RC51 was packed with race-age technology. A 90-degree V-twin engine displaced 999cc, with each cylinder fed by a pair of fuel injectors. Four valves per cylinder provided adequate breathing for the jugs.

A close-ratio, six-speed gearbox kept the bike in the sweet spot and a twin-spar aluminum chassis held the whole package together. Only Pearl Shining Yellow was sold on the VTR1000F Super Hawk with no other revisions being made.

The CBR1100XX Black Bird was finished in Titanium Metallic but other changes were absent from the returning model. Candy Wineberry Red paint covered the bodywork of the ST1100 and ST1100A ABS II in 2000 and was the only modification listed.

The VT1100 family dwindled by one for 2000 and a new face was part of the remaining models. The VT1100C Shadow Spirit listed American Red with Black as a new combination but was otherwise unchanged. Joining the team for the new millennium was the VT1100C2 Shadow Sabre. Powered by the same 1099cc V-twin mill

The RC51 was Honda's latest attempt at putting a racing motorcycle in the showroom. Powered by a 999cc V-twin, the RC51 was an instant success both on and off track.

American Honda

HONDA

used in the other VT1100s, the Sabre claimed numerous styling tweaks that separated it from the others. Fully valanced fenders rode above wheels that were machined from aluminum in a three-spoke pattern. The bulk of the engine was now finished in black and was contrasted by a set of chrome, two-into-two pipes. Changes to the VT1100C3 Shadow Aero were limited to new hues and the VT1100T A. C. E. Tourer was now sold only in Black.

The year 2000 marked the 25th year of sale for the Gold Wing, and birthday badges and keys were introduced to celebrate the occasion. The Aspencade was sold in the same colors as the 1999 models while the SE was available with a pair of new two-tone options along with two carryovers. A lower saddle height of 28.9 inches graced the 2000 GL1500C Valkyrie and only three color

The Shadow Sabre was a new face in 2000. It was powered by a 1099cc V-twin engine teamed with hot-rod style that included plenty of chrome. American Honda

choices were shown. All Black, or Black with Red or Yellow were the latest wardrobe options for the otherwise naked Valkyrie. The hues for the Tourer were reduced to two for 2000 with Black or Black with Red being shown. The lower seat height also applied to the Tourer model.

2000 HONDA

Model	Engine	Displacement	Transmission
CB250 Nighthawk	OHC Parallel Twin	234cc	Five-Speed
CMX250C Rebel	OHC Parallel Twin	234cc	Five-Speed
CMX250C2 Rebel Two-Tone	OHC Parallel Twin	234cc	Five-Speed
CBR600F4	DOHC Inline-Four	599cc	Six-Speed
VT600C Shadow VLX	SOHC V-Twin	583cc	Four-Speed
VT600CD Shadow VLX Deluxe	SOHC V-Twin	583cc	Four-Speed
VT600CD2 Shadow VLX Deluxe Two-Tone	SOHC V-Twin	583cc	Four-Speed
CB750 Nighthawk	DOHC Inline-Four	747cc	Five-Speed
VF750C Magna	DOHC V-Four	748cc	Six-Speed
VF750C2 Magna	DOHC V-Four	748cc	Six-Speed
VT750C Shadow A. C. E.	SOHC V-Twin	749cc	Six-Speed
VT750CD Shadow A. C. E. Deluxe	SOHC V-Twin	749cc	Six-Speed
VT750CD2 Shadow A. C. E. Deluxe Two-Tone	SOHC V-Twin	749cc	Six-Speed
VFR800FI Interceptor	DOHC V-Four	781cc	Six-Speed
CBR929RR (New for 2000)	DOHC Inline-Four	929cc	Six-Speed
RVT1000R RC51 (New for 2000)	DOHC V-Twin	999cc	Six-Speed
VTR1000F Super Hawk	DOHC V-Twin	996cc	Six-Speed
CBR1100XX Black Bird	DOHC Inline-Four	1137cc	Six-Speed
ST1100	DOHC V-Four	1084cc	Five-Speed
ST1100A ABS II	DOHC V-Four	1084cc	Five-Speed
VT1100C Shadow Spirit	SOHC V-Twin	1099cc	Four-Speed
VT1100C2 Shadow Sabre (New for 2000)	SOHC V-Twin	1099cc	Four-Speed
VT1100C3 Shadow Aero	SOHC V-Twin	1099cc	Four-Speed
VT1100D2 Shadow A. C. E.	SOHC V-Twin	1099cc	Four-Speed
VT1100T Shadow A. C. E. Tourer	SOHC V-Twin	1099cc	Four-Speed
GL1500A Gold Wing Aspencade 25th Anniversary	SOHC Opposed-Six	1520cc	Five-Speed
GL1500SE Gold Wing 25th Anniversary	SOHC Opposed-Six	1520cc	Five-Speed
GL1500C Valkyrie	SOHC Opposed-Six	1520cc	Five-Speed
GL1500CF Valkyrie Interstate	SOHC Opposed-Six	1520cc	Five-Speed
GL1500CT Valkyrie Tourer	SOHC Opposed-Six	1520cc	Five-Speed

HONDA
2001

The 250cc Nighthawk and Rebel remained but the two-tone Rebel was eliminated.

Having added two notches in their victory belt with the CBR400F4 all they could do is improve the successful blend of power, comfort and handling. The 2001 version was fed with electronic fuel-injection and a 15 percent larger airbox assisted in the breathing and the exhaust was tuned for enhanced performance. A more rigid chassis delivered better handling to a machine that needed little help.

The 600cc Shadows lost a third of their lineup with the two-tone option removed from the catalog. The VT600C Shadow VLX and Deluxe remained with no changes from the 2000's.

Not even the price changed on the CB750 Nighthawk as it was sold again for 2001.

Only one variant of the VF750C Magna was listed for 2001, but it was given a few mechanical variations. Gear-driven cams were driven by chain, and an automatic cam-chain tension device kept things adjusted properly. A final chain drive saved some weight and complexity and therefore shaved a few dollars from the price tag. New for 2001 was the Shadow Spirit 750. Unlike the VT1100 version, the 745cc Spirit was styled more closely to the pending VTX1800 that was to be released in March 2001 as an early 2002 model. The VT750CD Shadow A. C. E. Deluxe was sold for another year but with only minor changes. The speedometer was now mounted atop the fuel tank.

VFR800FI Interceptors claimed no improvements for the 2001 model year, but according to most that rode one, none were required.

With the exception of a larger 17-inch front wheel and tire, the CBR929RR was the same

The Shadow A.C.E. was one of Honda's more popular models in the cruiser segment as it offered looks and power in a machine that could easily be modified to meet your own taste. American Honda

machine we saw last year. Bringing the street machines one step closer to the track, an Erion Racing edition was sold alongside the standard graphics model.

Having conquered the 2000 AMA Superbike series in 2000, the RC51 needed nothing and received exactly that in 2001.

Another Honda returning with no alterations was the VTR1000F Super Hawk. Only the return to red paint marked the 2001 models.

The CBR1100XX Black Bird was sold in Candy Red for 2001 and also had electronic fuel injection transplanted onto the motor.

Shadow Spirits now rowed through a five-speed gearbox and combined many features found on previous iterations to make the best example yet. Returning to its roots, the Shadow Aero was once again built using a staggered-crank motor in 2001, thus eliminating the vibrations installed in the 1995 edition single-pin motors. The final model in the 1100 Shadow family was the A. C. E. Tourer.

The Valkyrie crew was reduced to two models with the Tourer edition eliminated at the end of 2000. While a brand new Gold Wing was being introduced for 2001, the Valkyries were still pow-

HONDA

STANDARD CATALOG OF® JAPANESE Motorcycles

The Black Bird was now sold in Candy Red but was otherwise unaltered. American Honda

Powered by the larger 1099cc V-twin engine, the Aero still embodied the true spirit of the cruiser with more power on tap. American Honda

ered by the flat-six, 1520cc mill. Changes to the returning members were limited to colors.

Having ruled the roost in the big touring bike class for many years, the Gold Wing was starting to be upstaged by its rivals. Honda decided to push the bar higher with an all-new Gold Wing. While still embodying all the same traits as the previous versions, the latest "Wing" would be built using a stiffer chassis and be powered by a larger motor.

A bump to 1832cc, the opposed-six motor was still smoother than anything else on the market but now packed even more punch with eerie silence. The new engine was fed with a closed-loop fuel-injection system that delivered fuel precisely while providing more power and efficiency. Increased capacity of the fuel tank provided hours of painless riding on the open roads.

Push-button reverse made moving the 771-lb. beast easier when not at speed, but this weight was 24 lbs. fewer than in 2000. Radial rubber and ABS brakes also added to the comfort and safety of the latest GL.

Heated hand grips, a CD changer and improved sound system put the improved Gold Wing right back to the head of the class.

2001 HONDA

Model	Engine	Displacement	Transmission
CB250 Nighthawk	OHC Parallel Twin	234cc	Five-Speed
CMX250C Rebel	OHC Parallel Twin	234cc	Five-Speed
CBR600F4i (Fuel Injection)	DOHC Inline-Four	599cc	Six-Speed
VT600C Shadow VLX	SOHC V-Twin	583cc	Five-Speed
VT600CD Shadow VLX Deluxe	SOHC V-Twin	583cc	Five-Speed
CB750 Nighthawk	DOHC Inline-Four	747cc	Five-Speed
VF750C Magna	DOHC V-Four	748cc	Six-Speed
VT750CD Shadow A. C. E. Deluxe	SOHC V-Twin	749cc	Six-Speed
VT750 Shadow Spirit	SOHC V-Twin	745cc	Five-Speed
VFR800FI Interceptor	DOHC V-Four	781cc	Six-Speed
CBR929RR (17-inch front tire)	DOHC Inline-Four	929cc	Six-Speed
RVT1000R RC51	DOHC V-Twin	999cc	Six-Speed
VTR1000F Super Hawk	DOHC V-Twin	996cc	Six-Speed
CBR1100XX Black Bird	DOHC Inline-Four	1137cc	Six-Speed
ST1100	DOHC V-Four	1084cc	Five-Speed
ST1100A ABS II	DOHC V-Four	1084cc	Five-Speed
VT1100C Shadow Spirit	SOHC V-Twin	1099cc	Five-Speed
VT1100C2 Shadow Sabre	SOHC V-Twin	1099cc	Five-Speed
VT1100C3 Shadow Aero	SOHC V-Twin	1099cc	Five-Speed
VT1100T Shadow A. C. E. Tourer	SOHC V-Twin	1099cc	Five-Speed
GL1500C Valkyrie	SOHC Opposed-Six	1520cc	Five-Speed
GL1500CF Valkyrie Interstate (Final year of sale)	SOHC Opposed-Six	1520cc	Five-Speed
GL1800 Gold Wing (More displacement)	SOHC Opposed-Six	1832cc	Five-Speed

HONDA
2002

The CB250 Nighthawk was Black and the CMX250C Rebel was available in Black or Red with no additional changes to either model.

The Honda CBR600F4i received no fresh mechanicals but was dipped in your choice of Yellow or Red with Black, or Metallic Silver joined by Red. Both the standard and Deluxe versions of the VT600 Shadow were sold for another year without alterations.

The VFR800Fi Interceptor was greeted by a sister model complete with ABS braking. The additional hardware of the ABS version added 11 lbs. to the all-around machine, but was a welcome option for many riders. Fresh bodywork concealed a revised 781cc engine that claimed Honda's VTEC valve train. To fill the demand, color-matched, hard-sided bags were designed for the VFR and added a new level of usefulness to the capable Interceptor.

Introduced for the 2002 sales year was the 919 naked bike. Powered by a motor based on the CBR900RR, the 919 carried the inline-four in a chassis that utilized the engine as a stressed-member. Programmed-fuel-injection fed the four pots while a four-into-two exhaust traveled under the motor and exited high beneath the saddle. The 919 weighed only 427 lbs. dry, providing an ample horsepower-to-weight ratio. The six-speed transmission allowed plenty of gears for the rider's needs. A pair of fully-floating rotors with four-piston calipers slowed the 919 up front while another single-piston caliper was on duty out back.

The semi-matte Asphalt paint was a new trend, and would be pressed into action on other Honda models to come.

Taking the CBR929RR, bumping displacement and shaving weight resulted in the new CBR954RR. An extra 25cc in the engine, along with a long list of minor tweaks, provided a horsepower rating of 154, four more than the 929.

Five pounds of weight were also trimmed and a re-contoured fuel tank carried its load lower in the frame for improved distribution. The capacity of the tank was unchanged at 4.8 gallons. A titanium muffler was installed saving a few more precious ounces with the total weight now at 370 lbs. dry.

The RC51 had its debut in 2000, and instantly set the pace for open class machines.

The 2002 edition weighs eight pounds less and carries three extra ponies in the frame. A record-setting 120 hp. at the rear wheel is proof of Honda's ongoing efforts.

The CBR1100XX models now wore a cloak of Metallic Silver but were otherwise unchanged. ST1100s and ST1100As were also unaltered but now sported Candy Dark Red paint. VT1100 Shadows in the Spirit, Sabre and Aero trim levels all returned with new colors their only claim to fame. The Sabre was seen with new Pearl Flame paint in several colors that added another "hot rod" flair to the popular cruiser.

The big Valkyrie cruiser was the only model left in the lineup and was delivered sans any bags or windscreens.

The Gold Wing faction grew by one with the introduction of the ABS equipped version.

For cruiser buyers the VTX 1800 models rolled out in 2002. Driven by 1800cc V-twin mills, the VTX was the largest twin on the market. The C, R and S editions varied slightly from each other with two rolling on cast wheels and the third on spoke rims. Combining traditional cruiser styling with exaggerated dimensions and contemporary cues, the VTX family set yet another standard for the rest of the industry.

2002 HONDA

Model	Engine	Displacement	Transmission
CB250 Nighthawk	OHC Parallel Twin	234cc	Five-Speed
CMX250C Rebel	OHC Parallel Twin	234cc	Five-Speed
CBR600F4i	DOHC Inline-Four	599cc	Six-Speed
VT600C Shadow VLX	SOHC V-Twin	583cc	Five-Speed
VT600CD Shadow VLX Deluxe	SOHC V-Twin	583cc	Five-Speed
CB750 Nighthawk	DOHC Inline-Four	747cc	Five-Speed
VF750C Magna	DOHC V-Four	748cc	Six-Speed
VT750CD Shadow A. C. E. Deluxe	SOHC V-Twin	749cc	Six-Speed
VT750 Shadow Spirit	SOHC V-Twin	745cc	Five-Speed
VFR800Fi Interceptor	DOHC V-Four	781cc	Six-Speed
VFR800Fi ABS Interceptor (Anti-Lock Brakes)	DOHC V-Four	781cc	Six-Speed
CB900F 919 (New for 2002)	DOHC Inline-Four	919cc	Six-Speed
CBR954RR (New for 2002)	DOHC Inline-Four	954cc	Six-Speed
RVT1000R RC51	DOHC V-Twin	999cc	Six-Speed
VTR1000F Super Hawk	DOHC V-Twin	996cc	Six-Speed
CBR1100XX Black Bird	DOHC Inline-Four	1137cc	Six-Speed
ST1100	DOHC V-Four	1084cc	Five-Speed
ST1100A ABS II	DOHC V-Four	1084cc	Five-Speed
VT1100C Shadow Spirit	SOHC V-Twin	1099cc	Five-Speed
VT1100C2 Shadow Sabre	SOHC V-Twin	1099cc	Five-Speed
VT1100C3 Shadow Aero	SOHC V-Twin	1099cc	Five-Speed
GL1500CD Valkyrie	SOHC Opposed-Six	1520cc	Five-Spee
GL1800 Gold Wing	SOHC Opposed-Six	1832cc	Five-Speed
GL1800A ABS Gold Wing (Anti-Lock Brakes)	SOHC Opposed-Six	1832cc	Five-Speed
VTX1800C (New for 2002)	SOHC V-Twin	1795cc	Five-Speed
VTX1800R (New for 2002)	SOHC V-Twin	1795cc	Five-Speed
VTX1800S (New for 2002)	SOHC V-Twin	1795cc	Five-Speed

HONDA
2003

The 2003 CB250 Nighthawks were sold in Red while the CMX250C Rebel offered color choices of Black or Pearl Blue.

Metallic Silver with Black or Red appeared on the 2003 CBR6004i models but nothing else was modified from 2002.

An innovative twist in the expanding 600cc class was the CBR600RR. Much like the 954RR, the 600 combined the best features available and delivered them in a compact, lightweight machine. Borrowing heavily from Honda's own RC211V GP winning machine, it presented the street rider with a bevy of high-tech components. The inline-four motor displaced the same 599cc as the CBR6004i, but spun 800rpm faster due to lighter pistons. Dual-Stage Fuel Injection fed the beast and delivers a 15,000rpm redline. The aluminum chassis is more rigid than the 4i's but was similar in geometry. The 370-lb. dry weight was matched with a lower mounting point for the fuel tank that sharpened the already crisp handling. The 310mm front brake rotors were grabbed by four-piston calipers providing slowing power at a squeeze of the lever. Black, Black and Red or Pearl Yellow were the latest colors.

The VT600C Shadow VLX and VT600CD Shadow VLX Deluxe were back but sported no amendments. The 750 Nighthawks wore Red while the Magna saw Candy Blue. Both the VFR800Fi models offered Metallic Silver or Red for 2003.

The 919s added Smoke to the returning Asphalt as color choices. The 954RR gave riders their choice of Black with Metallic Titanium or Black with Red paint. The race-ready RC51 was as potent as ever and saw no modifications. The VTR1000F Super Hawk was again seen in the catalog but now wore a coat of Candy Blue. Even the mighty CBR1100XX received no changes save the Metallic Black paint.

The family of VT1100's shrank by one with the elimination of the Aero model. The remaining Spirit and Sabre were again unaltered.

Replacing the tried and true ST1100 was the completely new ST1300. Filling the same sport touring shoes as the 1100, the 1300 version left no stone unturned. Enhanced features included the chassis, swingarm and 1261cc V-4 engine.

The five-speed gearbox was filled with lower-ratio gearing and the previous carbs were supplanted by programmed-fuel injection.

HONDA

All the engine refinements led to 116 hp for the ST1300. The fairing and bodywork were also fresh for 2003 and provided the rider with a three-position saddle. For those who thought they'd miss the ABS system used on the ST1100A, the ST1300 was also sold with ABS as an option. Linked braking was found on both versions of the bigger ST. Metallic Dark Silver was the only hue listed for the revamped model.

For the cruiser buyer who found the VTX1800 a bit too daunting, the VTX1300 was rolled out for 2003. Using the same design formula, the VTX1300 featured the key styling features of the 1800, but reduced the entire package into a more compact format. The 1312cc V-twin engine drew breath through a single 38mm carburetor and exhaled through a two-into-two exhaust. The VTX1300S featured wire wheels while the VTX1300C rolled on a set of cast rims. The S model was actually sold in 2002 as an early-release 2003, but was still listed as a 2003 model.

The Valkyrie returned in 2003 but was a carry-over in features and color. Additional returning yet unchanged models were the GL1800 with or without ABS, and the three flavors of the VTX1800.

2003 HONDA

Model	Engine	Displacement	Transmission
CB250 Nighthawk	OHC Parallel Twin	234cc	Five-Speed
CMX250C Rebel	OHC Parallel Twin	234cc	Five-Speed
CBR600F4i	DOHC Inline-Four	599cc	Six-Speed
CBR600RR (New for 2003)	DOHC Inline-Four	599cc	Six-Speed
VT600C Shadow VLX	SOHC V-Twin	583cc	Five-Speed
VT600CD Shadow VLX Deluxe	SOHC V-Twin	583cc	Five-Speed
CB750 Nighthawk (Final year of sale)	DOHC Inline-Four	747cc	Five-Speed
VF750C Magna	DOHC V-Four	748cc	Six-Speed
VT750 Shadow Spirit	SOHC V-Twin	745cc	Five-Speed
VFR800Fi Interceptor	DOHC V-Four	781cc	Six-Speed
VFR800Fi ABS Interceptor	DOHC V-Four	781cc	Six-Speed
CB900F 919	DOHC Inline-Four	919cc	Six-Speed
CBR954RR	DOHC Inline-Four	954cc	Six-Speed
RVT1000R RC51	DOHC V-Twin	999cc	Six-Speed
VTR1000F Super Hawk	DOHC V-Twin	996cc	Six-Speed
CBR1100XX Black Bird (Final year of sale)	DOHC Inline-Four	1137cc	Six-Speed
VT1100C Shadow Spirit	SOHC V-Twin	1099cc	Five-Speed
VT1100C2 Shadow Sabre	SOHC V-Twin	1099cc	Five-Speed
ST1300 (New for 2003)	DOHC V-Four	1261cc	Five-Speed
ST1300 ABS (New for 2003)	DOHC V-Four	1261cc	Five-Speed
VTX1300C (New for 2003)	SOHC V-Twin	1312cc	Five-Speed
VTX1300S (New for 2003)	SOHC V-Twin	1312cc	Five-Speed
GL1500CD Valkyrie	SOHC Opposed-Six	1520cc	Five-Speed
GL1800 Gold Wing	SOHC Opposed Six	1832cc	Five-Speed
GL1800A ABS Gold Wing	SOHC Opposed-Six	1832cc	Five-Speed
VTX1800C	SOHC V-Twin	1795cc	Five-Speed
VTX1800R	SOHC V-Twin	1795cc	Five-Speed
VTX1800S	SOHC V-Twin	1795cc	Five-Speed

HONDA
2004

First shown as a concept bike, the amazing Rune appeared on showroom floors. The unique styling and exaggerated lines drew buyers who demanded something different.

American Honda

The 250 group retained both the Nighthawk and Rebel with no alterations outside of color. The CB250 Nighthawk was Red and the CMX250C Rebel had Black or Red shown on the option sheet.

Filling the vacant slot in the standard genre, the 599 was introduced for 2004. Powered by an inline-four motor based on the earlier CBR600F3, the 599 chassis provided an improved home for somewhat dated motor design. In a world dominated by fuel injection the 599 still sipped fuel through a set of four carbs. A dry curb weight of 420 lbs. allowed for nimble handling when combined with the rigid chassis and modern suspension. The 599 featured a comfortable pillion, mid-rise handlebars and exhaust that exited high on the frame. Asphalt Yellow paint was a terrific selling point for those that signed up.

Neither the CBR600F4i nor the CBR600RR received upgrades, but colors differed. A new twist on an old theme was the Shadow Aero, powered by a 745cc V-twin mill. Honda's cruiser lineup was heavy in the top-end models but the latest Aero helped those more timid riders to join in on the fun.

Metallic Silver was removed from the VFR800Fi and ABS order sheets, leaving only Red behind. The 919 lost its previous hues and gained Light Silver Metallic and Matte Uranium.

Beginning its journey as the flyweight CBR900RR, this pure sport machine grew into the 929, then 954 and would again grow and become the CBR1000RR. Borrowing heavily from the GP machine, the new RR bristled with lightweight and high-tech components. The 998cc engine was divided equally into four inline cylinders and 16 valves allowed for greater performance. Six speeds were encased within the transmission.

A dry weight of 396 lbs. did not dispel the intentions of the sporting machine. Returning with only Nicky Hayden paint in 2004, the RC51 was back with no other alterations. The 2003 revisions served the race-bred machine well and left little to the imagination.

The tried and true VTR1000F Super Hawk was back for another round and was now fitted with a pair of gold rims to accent the Black paint.

ST1300 and ST1300 ABS models featured a power-operated windshield that could be raised, lowered and adjusted for angle at a touch of a button. The saddle was still delivered with its own level of fine-tuning, making the ST1300s highly amenable to the sport-touring rider. Both versions of the VTX1300 returned for another year and wore either spoke or cast rims depending on your preference.

Honda showed a radically designed machine in 2003 and the Rune looked like nothing "production" but turned out to

Honda introduced the 599 for the buyer who desired a simple yet effective machine with no fairings or clutter.

American Honda

HONDA

STANDARD CATALOG OF® JAPANESE Motorcycles

With the original 900RR in its bloodline, the CBR1000RR was the latest entry into the liter bike category and was quickly accepted as the king of the hill.
American Honda

be just that. The enormous machine was powered by the Gold Wing's 1832cc flat-six mill, but was sheathed in exotic bodywork and alloy components. The six-into-two exhaust exited via canisters with triangular openings. A trailing-link front fork was slathered in chrome and the bulk of the exposed chassis was polished to a similar glow. A wheelbase of 68.9 inches was mated to a low saddle height of only 27.2 inches and helped to make the 794 lb. dry weight more manageable. Tail-dragger fenders were installed over both tires and accented the elongated fuel tank and space-age headlight. GL1800 Gold Wings saw no revisions and were sold in a wide array of colors for the 2004 model year.

Entering the VTX1800 clan was the 1800N. The N was clad in bodywork that borrowed from the Rune, but was not quite as radical. The C, R and S version remained on the roster each bringing a different twist to the same basic recipe.

The RC51 continued in its winning ways and still sold well, even with several inline-four sport bikes in the ranks.
American Honda

2004 HONDA

Model	Engine	Displacement	Transmission
CB250 Nighthawk	OHC Parallel Twin	234cc	Five-Speed
CMX250C Rebel	OHC Parallel Twin	234cc	Five-Speed
599 (New for 2004)	DOHC Inline-Four	599cc	Six-Speed
CBR600F4i	DOHC Inline-Four	599cc	Six-Speed
CBR600RR	DOHC Inline-Four	599cc	Six-Speed
VT600C Shadow VLX	SOHC V-Twin	583cc	Five-Speed
VT600CD Shadow VLX Deluxe	SOHC V-Twin	583cc	Five-Speed
VT750 Shadow Aero	SOHC V-Twin	745cc	Five-Speed
VFR800Fi Interceptor	DOHC V-Four	781cc	Six-Speed
VFR800Fi ABS Interceptor	DOHC V-Four	781cc	Six-Speed
CB900F 919	DOHC Inline-Four	919cc	Six-Speed
CBR1000RR (New for 2004)	DOHC Inline-Four	998cc	Six-Speed
RVT1000R RC51	DOHC V-Twin	999cc	Six-Speed
VTR1000F Super Hawk	DOHC V-Twin	996cc	Six-Speed
VT1100C Shadow Spirit	SOHC V-Twin	1099cc	Five-Speed
VT1100C2 Shadow Sabre	SOHC V-Twin	1099cc	Five-Speed
ST1300	DOHC V-Four	1261cc	Five-Speed
ST1300 ABS	DOHC V-Four	1261cc	Five-Speed
VTX1300C	SOHC V-Twin	1312cc	Five-Speed
VTX1300S	SOHC V-Twin	1312cc	Five-Speed
GL1800 Valkyrie Rune (New for 2004)	SOHC Opposed-Six	1832cc	Five-Speed
GL1800 Gold Wing	SOHC Opposed-Six	1832cc	Five-Speed
GL1800A ABS Gold Wing	SOHC Opposed-Six	1832cc	Five-Speed
VTX1800C	SOHC V-Twin	1795cc	Five-Speed
VTX1800N (New for 2004)	SOHC V-Twin	1795cc	Five-Speed
VTX1800R	SOHC V-Twin	1795cc	Five-Speed
VTX1800S	SOHC V-Twin	1795cc	Five-Speed

HONDA
2005

Extending their longevity, the 250 Nighthawk and Rebel both returned and were sold in Black, and the Rebel also listed Candy Orange as an option.

Both of Honda's successful 600cc sport bikes were again listed, but the RR version sported several enhancements with the F4i remaining unchanged. The CBR600RR lost 16 lbs. since 2004 and its lighter weight put it on par with the competition.

Other revisions include upside-down front forks, improved fuel injectors and ignition mapping. The frame was modified losing four pounds in the process. Although the exhaust was now fitted with a catalytic converter the overall system weight was down by a pound. Radial-mount front brake calipers and fresh bodywork were included on the list of refinements for the 2005 RR. A new black on black, tribal flame paint scheme was also an option.

The Shadow VLX was offered in base or Deluxe form, and the Deluxe carried chrome engine trim and two-tone paint while the standard was black and devoid of the engine glitter. The Shadow Spirit 750, fitted with bobbed fenders, shorty pipes and flame paint, fit into almost any cruiser buyer's budget. The Shadow Aero was another cost-conscious choice in the cruiser segment and delivered full fenders and a lower saddle height along with the 745cc V-twin engine.

The VFR800Fi Interceptors returned unchanged and could still be had with ABS braking as an option. Red and Light Metallic Silver were listed as 2005 hues. The 919 was back for another round and was sold in only Metallic Black.

The CBR1000RRs for 2005 benefited from several important changes. With a new chassis built using technology from the race-winning RC211V, the RR was stiffer, lighter and more nimble than before. A Honda Electronic Steering Damper kept handling secure and was joined by Honda's Unit Pro-Link rear suspension. Fuel injection was dual-stage and the exhaust now exited through a center-mounted high pipe that lived in the tail section.

To highlight their racing success, a Repsol replica paint ensemble was sold along with the three standard paint options.

RVT1000R RC51s were treated to Black and Metallic Gray paint, but no other changes were seen.

Another time-tested model, the VTR1000F Super Hawk was back and the Black body with gold wheels was replaced by Titanium sheet metal and matching rims.

The 2005 CBR1000RR was leaner than the '04 version and also claimed a variety of improvements.
American Honda

The 250cc Rebel pressed on as an entry level cruiser and appealed to both beginning and smaller riders.
American Honda

Available with a factory flame paint job, the Shadow Sabre took "cool" to a new level.
American Honda

HONDA

STANDARD CATALOG OF® JAPANESE Motorcycles

The 2005 Honda VTX1800F motorcycle was front and center in this 2005 Honda ad.

A new version of the recently introduced VTX1300 series rolled out was the VTX1300R. Joining the C and S styles, the R featured a longer set of handlebars, custom rims and a more shapely saddle.

Model year 2005 marked 30 years of production for the Gold Wing and the GL1800 was decorated with several birthday badges and light-up panel to celebrate the occasion.

The VTX1800 team was expanded with the F model's introduction in 2005. Designated as a sport cruiser, the F rolled on an 18-inch rear wheel and was steered with a set of low drag bars. The slimmed-down pillion was another styling cue on the latest of five VTX1800s being sold.

The VT1100 Shadow Spirit and Sabre wore fresh suits of color on unchanged mechanicals.

Candy Dark Red was the only color listed for the ST1300 whether fitted with ABS braking or not.

2005 HONDA

Model	Engine	Displacement	Transmission
CB250 Nighthawk	OHC Parallel Twin	234cc	Five-Speed
CMX250C Rebel	OHC Parallel Twin	234cc	Five-Speed
CBR600F4i	DOHC Inline-Four	599cc	Six-Speed
CBR600RR	DOHC Inline-Four	599cc	Six-Speed
VT600C Shadow VLX	SOHC V-Twin	583cc	Five-Speed
VT600CD Shadow VLX Deluxe	SOHC V-Twin	583cc	Five-Speed
VT750 Shadow Aero	SOHC V-Twin	745cc	Five-Speed
VFR800Fi Interceptor	DOHC V-Four	781cc	Six-Speed
VFR800Fi ABS Interceptor	DOHC V-Four	781cc	Six-Speed
CB900F 919	DOHC Inline-Four	919cc	Six-Speed
CBR1000RR	DOHC Inline-Four	998cc	Six-Speed
RVT1000R RC51	DOHC V-Twin	999cc	Six-Speed
VTR1000F Super Hawk (Final year of sale)	DOHC V-Twin	996cc	Six-Speed
VT1100C Shadow Spirit	SOHC V-Twin	1099cc	Five-Speed
VT1100C2 Shadow Sabre	SOHC V-Twin	1099cc	Five-Speed
ST1300	DOHC V-Four	1261cc	Five-Speed
ST1300 ABS	DOHC V-Four	1261cc	Five-Speed
VTX1300C	SOHC V-Twin	1312cc	Five-Speed
VTX1300R (New for 2005)	SOHC V-Twin	1312cc	Five-Speed
VTX1300S	SOHC V-Twin	1312cc	Five-Speed
GL1800 Gold Wing 30th Anniversary	SOHC Opposed-Six	1832cc	Five-Speed
GL1800A ABS Gold Wing 30th Anniversary	SOHC Opposed-Six	1832cc	Five-Speed
VTX1800C	SOHC V-Twin	1795cc	Five-Speed
VTX1800F (New for 2005)	SOHC V-Twin	1795cc	Five-Speed
VTX1800N	SOHC V-Twin	1795cc	Five-Speed
VTX1800R	SOHC V-Twin	1795cc	Five-Speed
VTX1800S	SOHC V-Twin	1795cc	Five-Speed

STANDARD CATALOG OF® JAPANESE Motorcycles

HONDA

2006

Honda had always placed the Gold Wing at the top of their list when it came to innovations, and for 2006 they brought new levels of sophistication to the big touring model. By adding five Option Packages available to the buyer, your Gold Wing could be perfectly suited to your own needs.

The most revolutionary step was the addition of an airbag. This would be the first ever application of the automotive safety feature used on a motorcycle. Creature comforts came in the form of satellite navigation and a premium audio system. A heated saddle and grips were other features to be found in one of the five individual packages.

For those seeking something a bit sportier, yet still able to swallow long distances whole, the ST1300 was the obvious choice. The ABS version was still an option.

The cruiser segment of Honda's catalog offered fewer choices than in years past. Five versions of the VTX1800 were still listed, each with its own profile that catered to unique slices of the audience. Three VTX1300 models were also in the composition and the slightly smaller machine delivered a unique experience.

The Shadow Sabre and Spirit carried 1099cc V-twin mills in their frames while the Spirit and 750 Aero utilized 745cc power plants. The VLX and VLX Deluxe retained the 600cc motors of the past and the Rebel continued to hold up the lower end of the cruiser genre for Honda.

Moving to the standard models, the 919 was still present and the 599 was back after being away for a year. The diminutive 250 Nighthawk was also still a choice for the smaller or beginning rider.

Sport bikes continued to be one of the market's fastest growing segments, and Honda still had a nice collection to suit nearly any rider. The CBR600F4i was joined by its sportier CBR600RR

After a year away, the 599 returned for 2006 in Metallic Black paint with no other alterations from the previous edition.

American Honda

The Honda 1000RR was lighter and faster for 2006 and was an attempt to continue the company's domination of the motorcycle marketplace.

American Honda

HONDA

The VTX1800 was still the largest V-twin cruiser sold by Honda and it was offered in five different variations.

American Honda

One of the two-tone choices for the 2006 Shadow Aero was Candy Orange with Dark Brown, and was only one of several offered.

American Honda

brother and both models still sat near the front of the middleweight class.

One step up was the Interceptor with standard or ABS braking aboard. The all-around machine remained a favorite of riders who rode in a variety of conditions whether across town or spanning the country.

For the buyer who needed a street legal race bike at home, the RC51 and CBR1000RR were there for the taking. The RC51 was unchanged from 2005 while the CBR1000RR bristled with improvements making it a dominant factor in the liter bike regime.

2006 HONDA

Model	Engine	Displacement	Transmission
CB250 Nighthawk	OHC Parallel Twin	234cc	Five-Speed
CMX250C Rebel	OHC Parallel Twin	234cc	Five-Speed
599	DOHC Inline-Four	599cc	Six-Speed
CBR600F4i	DOHC Inline-Four	599cc	Six-Speed
CBR600RR	DOHC Inline-Four	599cc	Six-Speed
VT600C Shadow VLX	SOHC V-Twin	583cc	Five-Speed
VT600CD Shadow VLX Deluxe	SOHC V-Twin	583cc	Five-Speed
VT750 Shadow Aero	SOHC V-Twin	745cc	Five-Speed
VFR800Fi Interceptor	DOHC V-Four	781cc	Six-Speed
VFR800Fi ABS Interceptor	DOHC V-Four	781cc	Six-Speed
CB900F 919	DOHC Inline-Four	919cc	Six-Speed
CBR1000RR	DOHC Inline-Four	998cc	Six-Speed
RVT1000R RC51	DOHC V-Twin	999cc	Six-Speed
VT1100C Shadow Spirit	SOHC V-Twin	1099cc	Five-Speed
VT1100C2 Shadow Sabre	SOHC V-Twin	1099cc	Five-Speed
ST1300	DOHC V-Four	1261cc	Five-Speed
ST1300 ABS	DOHC V-Four	1261cc	Five-Speed
VTX1300C	SOHC V-Twin	1312cc	Five-Speed
VTX1300R	SOHC V-Twin	1312cc	Five-Speed
VTX1300S	SOHC V-Twin	1312cc	Five-Speed
GL1800 Gold Wing	SOHC Opposed-Six	1832cc	Five-Speed
GL1800A ABS Gold Wing	SOHC Opposed-Six	1832cc	Five-Speed
VTX1800C	SOHC V-Twin	1795cc	Five-Speed
VTX1800F	SOHC V-Twin	1795cc	Five-Speed
VTX1800N	SOHC V-Twin	1795cc	Five-Speed
VTX1800R	SOHC V-Twin	1795cc	Five-Speed
VTX1800S	SOHC V-Twin	1795cc	Five-Speed

HONDA
2007

The interesting Honda VTX 1800N carried the model name Neo Retro— a bit of the classic cycle with a good deal of modern in its makeup.

The 25th anniversary edition of the Honda Interceptor came in a special paint scheme in 2007.

The 2007 Shadow Aero by Honda used a 745cc liquid-cooled V-twin engine.

The 2007 Honda CBR 1000RR used a 998cc engine and a cassette-type close ratio six-speed transmission.

In 2007, Honda CBR 1000RR buyers could get a Nicky Hayden Repsol replica edition cycle.

KAWASAKI

Introduction

With bloodlines that can be traced all the way back to 1878, the Kawasaki name had a strong grasp on the industrial market. Their early days as ship builders led them into locomotives and aircraft long before motorcycles became a part of their plan. After World War II came to an end, Kawasaki was one of many manufacturers who sought new ways to regain their footing in the industrial universe.

In 1950, they began producing a small 148cc engine that would find its way into motorcycle frames of other builders. By 1961, Kawasaki had built a motorcycle that was entirely their own, and the company joined forces with Meguro Manufacturing in 1962. Several models were created under this team umbrella, and it was only three years later when Kawasaki shipped their first motorcycles to the United States. With California being the most efficient point of importation, the first U.S. branch opened its doors there in 1964.

1963

The initial offerings from Kawasaki were few, but would open doors for additional models to follow.

The B8 and B8T were virtually the same machine, with one designed for off-road use and the other for street operation. A pressed steel backbone held the major components in place, and construction was simple yet durable. A two-stroke, 125cc motor was air-cooled and shifted through four-speeds.

A hydraulic front fork and rear shocks provided comfort to the rider. The B8 featured a solo saddle while the B8T had a two-person pillion. The B8T was fitted with a raised front fender, semi-knobby tires and a chrome luggage rack.

1963 KAWASAKI

Model	Engine	Displacement	Transmission	Features
B8	Single cylinder	125cc	Four-Speed	Off-road version
B8T	Single cylinder	125cc	Four-Speed	Touring version

KAWASAKI

1964

The second year of U.S. Kawasaki sales saw a third model enter the family. The SG was powered by a larger 250cc motor that was also of four-stroke design in contrast to the two-stroke B8/B8T.

The SG was considered quite basic and claimed a single saddle and a rear carrying rack. The bike was mostly black and due to its dowdy appearance, it was out of synch with other models of its day.

1964 KAWASAKI

Model	Engine	Displacement	Transmission	Features
B8	Single cylinder	125cc	Four-Speed	Off-road version
B8T	Single cylinder	125cc	Four-Speed	Touring version
SG	Single cylinder	250cc	Four-Speed	

1965

The 1965 B8 was offered in standard and touring form, and this B8T was one of the touring models.

Kersting Family Collection

In their third year of U.S. sales, Kawasaki added three new models to the family. Slotted in below the 125cc B8 models were the J1 and J1T. Both bikes were driven by an 85cc, single cylinder motor fitted with a rotary disc inlet valve. A four-speed gearbox was on hand to dole out the 7.5 horsepower. Like the B8 and B8T derivatives, the J1T was setup for touring with a two-person saddle, high-mounted exhaust and whitewall tires. The front fender was chrome and the chain drive was exposed.

The B8 clan grew by one with the addition of the B8S, which carried a slightly larger 150cc motor in its frame. The bigger mill produced 12 horsepower at 6500rpm, making it the sportiest of the B8 offerings.

1965 KAWASAKI

Model	Engine	Displacement	Transmission	Features
J1	Single cylinder	85cc	Four-Speed	Rotary Disc Inlet Valve
J1D	Single cylinder	85cc	Four-Speed	Electric Start
J1T	Single cylinder	85cc	Four-Speed	Touring Version
B8	Single cylinder	125cc	Four-Speed	Off-road version
B8T	Single cylinder	125cc	Four-Speed	Touring version
B8S	Single cylinder	150cc	Four-Speed	12hp @ 6500rpm
SG	Single cylinder	250cc	Four-Speed	

KAWASAKI

1966

STANDARD CATALOG OF® JAPANESE Motorcycles

Kawasaki's confidence in the American market grew for 1966, as did their model selection. Machines at both ends of the spectrum were now included in the catalog, and the 624cc W1 was the largest capacity machine being built by any Japanese manufacturer that year. "Fun people go Kawasaki" was the tagline used to entice new riders into the fold, and the expanding line of bikes seemed to be helping too.

Although no longer step-through models, the M10 and M11 still carried the 50cc engines in their frames. Only 2cc distinguished one engine from the other between the M10 and M11.

The M10 featured a two-person saddle while the M11 had room for only one, but provided a rack for small baggage.

Taking the J1T one notch higher was the D1. Powered by a 100cc engine, the D1 was otherwise identical to the J1T.

The C1 was next in line with a 115cc engine and a pressed-steel frame. The C1D went one step further and added an electric start to the equation.

The F1 and F1TR featured 175cc, single cylinder engines and the TR variation was meant for trail use. Both versions used a 25mm carburetor

Kawasaki's first big bike was the 1966 W1, displacing 624cc from a total of two cylinders.

Kersting Family Collection

1966 KAWASAKI

Model	Engine	Displacement	Transmission	Features
M10	Single cylinder	50cc	Three-Speed	Two-person saddle
M11	Single cylinder	50cc	Three-Speed	Solo Saddle
J1	Single cylinder	85cc	Four-Speed	Rotary Disc Inlet Valve
J1D	Single cylinder	85cc	Four-Speed	Electric Start
J1T	Single cylinder	85cc	Four-Speed	Touring Version
J1TR	Single cylinder	85cc	Four-Speed	Skid Plates and Trail Tires
D1	Single cylinder	100cc	Four-Speed	
C1	Single cylinder	115cc	Four-Speed	
C1D	Single cylinder	115cc	Four-Speed	Electric Start
B1	Single cylinder	125cc	Four-Speed	
B8	Single cylinder	125cc	Four-Speed	Off-road version
B8T	Single cylinder	125cc	Four-Speed	Touring version
B8S	Single cylinder	150cc	Four-Speed	12hp @ 6500rpm
F1	Single cylinder	175cc	Four-Speed	
F1TR	Single cylinder	175cc	Four-Speed	Trail Version
SG	Single cylinder	250cc	Four-Speed	
W1	Two cylinder	624cc	Four-Speed	Largest capacity engine

and shifted through a four-speed gearbox.

Carrying the banner as the biggest displacement Japanese motorcycle made, the W1 was also new for 1966. The 624cc, two-cylinder engine looked a lot like some British counterparts, but set the wheels in motion for the displacement war that would soon begin. A single Mikuni VM31 carburetor was used to meter the fuel and four speeds were available at the touch of the foot lever. An aluminum cylinder head and chain driven generator were only two of the features that made the W1 distinctive. The tubular steel chassis would become the norm for bikes of this nature, and held the machine together as best it could. Weighing a stout 471 lbs. held the W1's performance numbers down, and smaller machines soon were outperforming it on the road. Still in all, the W1 set a new standard for Japanese made cycles that would prove to be the start of a revolution.

Looking every bit the British motor that inspired it, the W1 powerplant was all Kawasaki, and set the stage for bigger models soon to follow.

Kersting Family Collection

FUN PEOPLE Go KAWASAKi

for the best of reasons!

SUPERIOR PERFORMANCE
- Plenty of low torque speed as well as high rpm power
- Oil dampened spring suspension eliminates bottoming of fork travel—the ultimate in rider comfort

BETTER STYLING
- Smart shiny appearance from every angle — yet never looks "chrome-y"
- Supersize tailight . . . largest in the industry
- Finished to the very highest standards

ADVANCED ENGINEERING DESIGN
- All engine parts are magnifluxed (x-rayed) to detect and prevent defects
- All engines have extreme heavy-duty 8 plate wet type clutches, full circle balanced crank assembly and needle bearings upper and lower ends
- New separate forced fuel feed system (for 2-stroke models)

COMPLETE SELECTION
- A full line. Two or four stroke models. Up to a dynamic 650 cc.

SEND FOR FREE NEW KAWASAKI BROCHURE
and the name of your nearest authorized Kawasaki dealer today

KAWASAKI
AIRCRAFT CO., LTD.
208 South LaSalle Street, Chicago, Illinois 60604
Main Office: Tokyo, Japan • West Coast Office: Los Angeles, Calif.

"Fun people go Kawasaki" was the claim in this 1966 ad, as the company did its best to counter the former "nicest people" campaign from Honda.

KAWASAKI 1967

Kawasaki's family portrait was extended for 1967 with the addition of several new models, each offered in various trim levels. The G1 was sold in both street and motocross versions, also known as the G1M. A 90cc engine drove the new machine while a four-speed gearbox provided the ratios.

The B8 and its variants were to leave the catalog for 1967 and not every change was an addition for that model year. Also gone for the 1967 model year was the F1 and F1TR.

Replacements for the soon-to-depart C1 was the C2—seen in both TR and SS trim. Both were sold as scrambler models, with the TR carrying more rugged tires and fender designs. New models were growing in displacement. The A1 and A1SS were fitted with 247cc, two-cylinder mills.

Five-speeds were included in the gearbox and the SS model was designated as the Street Scrambler, complete with high exhaust pipes. Built to compete in the Grand Prix Racing class, the A1R was equipped with a higher output motor, bigger brakes and lightweight alloy wheels.

Arriving to sell just beneath the remaining W1 price category was the A7 and A7SS. They carried 338ccs of two-cylinder power in their frames. The two-stroke motors were fed through Mikuni VM26 carburetors and used five-speed transmissions. The SS model rode with upswept exhaust pipes and more rugged gears and was intended for off-road riding. Some "scrambler" model designations were also referred to as "enduro" models. That name suggested the machines were able to be used on both paved and unpaved surfaces. The typically high-mounted or upswept exhaust stacks and the application of frame-mounted skid plates were often seen on the dual-purpose cycles.

The W1 stayed on but smaller Kawasaki machines overshadowed its lackluster output. Other Japanese makers also offered competition. While still the biggest Japanese engine sold, the W1 was not long for this motorcycle world. Late in the 1967 model year, a higher performance W2SS was released. Power on the SS version rose to 53 horses. It was joined with a 19-inch front wheel, trimmed fenders and a bit less weight.

1967 KAWASAKI

Model	Engine	Displacement	Transmission	Features
M10	Single cylinder	50cc	Three-Speed	Two-Person Saddle
M11	Single cylinder	52cc	Three-Speed	Solo Saddle
J1	Single cylinder	85cc	Four-Speed	Rotary Disc Inlet Valve
J1D	Single cylinder	85cc	Four-Speed	Electric Start
J1T	Single cylinder	85cc	Four-Speed	Touring Version
J1TR	Single cylinder	85cc	Four-Speed	Skid Plate & Trail Tires
G1	Single cylinder	90cc	Four-Speed	
G1M	Single cylinder	90cc	Four-Speed	Motocross Version
D1	Single cylinder	100cc	Four-Speed	
C1	Single cylinder	115cc	Four-Speed	
C1DL	Single cylinder	115cc	Four-Speed	Electric Start
C1D	Single cylinder	115cc	Four-speed	
C2SS	Single cylinder	115cc	Four-Speed	Two-Person Saddle
C2TR	Single cylinder	115cc	Four-Speed	Dual Drive Sprockets
B1/KC125	Single cylinder	125cc	Four-Speed	Base Model, No Superlube
F2	Single cylinder	175cc	Four-Speed	
F2TR	Single cylinder	175cc	Four-Speed	
A1	Two-cylinder	247cc	Five-Speed	Samurai
A1R	Two-cylinder	247cc	Five-Speed	Road Racing model
A1SS	Twin-cylinder	247cc	Five-Speed	Street Scrambler
SG	Single cylinder	250cc	Four-Speed	
A7	Two-cylinder	338cc	Five-Speed	Five-Speed
A7SS	Two-cylinder	338cc	Five-Speed	Street Scrambler
W1	Two-cylinder	624cc	Four-Speed	Largest Capacity Japanese Motor

KAWASAKI
1968

Sold in a variety of trim levels, the J1 series was based on an 85cc, single-cylinder engine. The TR was designed for both on- and off-road riding.

Brad Powell Collection

Model changes continued to flourish for the 1968 lineup, with a few new names as well as the departure of some others. A few of Kawasaki's earlier editions would also be phased out after the 1968 model year had closed.

First to be removed from the 1968 bench were the C1 models in all levels of trim. The C2 models would remain through the current year but be removed for 1969. People were slowly shifting towards larger motorcycles, and Kawasaki was not alone in its attempt to tailor the lineup to meet with U. S. demands. The slightly smaller D1 was to be removed after 1968, as was the J1 and its multitude of iterations.

The A1R road racer model was rolled into the pits permanently for 1968 as revised machines took to the racing circuit.

Having lagged in both sales and performance, the W1 would see its final sales year in 1968. The original model was improved, though, and would return as the W1SS and W2SS, also called the Commander, late in the model year. Both SS versions breathed through a pair of Mikuni VM28 carburetors and featured improved four-speed gearboxes. These versions carried less weight (458 lbs. versus 471) and addi-

KAWASAKI

The J1TR motor had a high-mounted exhaust that was joined by a front fender that provided additional clearance, both indications of the TR's off-road abilities.

Brad Powell Collection

tional horsepower, helping to boost sales in their remaining years. Smaller exhaust canisters and a more thinly padded saddle were also hallmarks of the W2SS. Of course, 1968 would also mark the year that Honda would debut its market-shaping CB750 to the world, making changes and improvements to the W1 mostly moot. The latest versions of the first W1 would last through the 1971 model year, the W2SS ending in 1970.

Returning models for 1968 were the F2 and F3. The F3 actually had a smaller, 169cc engine and replaced the F2TR while the F2 had a 238cc power plant slung in its frame. Both cycles were more like upgrades to the F1 that departed in 1967.

1968 KAWASAKI

Model	Engine	Displacement	Transmission	Features
M10	Single cylinder	50cc	Three-Speed	Two-Person Saddle
M11	Single cylinder	52cc	Three-Speed	Solo Saddle
J1	Single cylinder	85cc	Four-Speed	Rotary Disc Inlet Valve
J1D	Single cylinder	85cc	Four-Speed	Electric Start
J1T	Single cylinder	85cc	Four-Speed	Touring Version
J1TR	Single cylinder	85cc	Four-Speed	Skid Plate & Trail Tires
G1	Single cylinder	90cc	Four-Speed	
G1M	Single cylinder	90cc	Four-Speed	Motocross Version
D1	Single cylinder	100cc	Four-Speed	
C2SS	Single cylinder	115cc	Four-Speed	Two-Person Saddle
C2TR	Single cylinder	115cc	Four-Speed	Dual Drive Sprockets
B1/KC125	Single cylinder	125cc	Four-Speed	Base Model, No Superlube
F3	Single cylinder	169cc	Four-Speed	
F2	Single cylinder	238cc	Four-Speed	
F21M	Single cylinder	238cc	Four-Speed	
A1	Two-cylinder	247cc	Five-Speed	Samurai
A1R	Two-cylinder	247cc	Five-Speed	Road Racing Model
A1SS	Twin-cylinder	247cc	Five-Speed	Street Scrambler
SG	Single cylinder	250cc	Four-Speed	
A7	Two-cylinder	338cc	Five-Speed	Avenger
A7SS	Two-cylinder	338cc	Five-Speed	Street Scrambler, High Pipes
W1	Two-cylinder	624cc	Four-Speed	Largest Capacity Japanese Motor
W1СС	Two-cylinder	624cc	Four-Speed	Twin Mikuni VM28
W2SS	Two-cylinder	624cc	Four-Speed	Gauges In Headlight Nacelle

KAWASAKI
1969

Model year 1969 was the first appearance of the H1, and the triple carried itself well when compared to the 1969 Honda CB750.

Brad Powell Collection

The 1969 model year would see another wave of changes in the Kawasaki catalog, as well as the entry of one of the hottest machines of the day. It was true that the Honda CB750 was claiming the lion's share of the spotlight, but Kawasaki was not about to let that dampen their spirits.

New for 1969 were the GA1, GA2 and GA3, all of which followed in the footsteps of the G1 models. The single cylinder engines displaced 90cc and were accented with rotary valves to augment their two-stroke power. The GA3 sat at the top of the GA heap wearing De Carbon shocks and an upswept exhaust.

The F4 Sidewinder was another fresh entry, carrying 238cc under a shapely fuel tank. High mounted exhausts also suggested rugged off-road capabilities, but the low mounted front fender contradicted that thought.

As exciting as these new models may have been, they were all overshadowed by the mighty H1 that made its debut in 1969. Powered by a 499cc, three-cylinder engine, Kawasaki's new machine graced both the covers of *Cycle* and *Cycle World* magazines in April of 1969.

Called the "world's fastest touring 500" by

KAWASAKI

STANDARD CATALOG OF® JAPANESE Motorcycles

Also called the Sidewinder, the 1969 F4 featured a 238cc twin engine and shifted through a four-speed gearbox.

Brad Powell Collection

one and "Hottest production bike yet" by the other, it was obvious that Kawasaki had hit a home run, even with Honda's awesome CB750 making the rounds. Cranking out 60 horsepower from its bank of triple cylinders, the Mach III was unrivaled in the power to weight category. Each of the three cylinders was fed by its own Mikuni VM28SC carburetor. When all was perfectly synchronized, there was nothing on the street that could touch it. A five-speed gearbox offered plenty of gears to keep the H1 in the sweet spot, and in trained hands, the results were magical.

A 1969 H1 weighed 382 lbs., ran a 12.4-second quarter mile, and had a maximum velocity of 124 mph. All of these figures combined made the Mach II truly the king of the performance hill.

Sadly, the enormous output of the engine was somewhat hampered by a chassis that lacked the same precision and rigidity needed to keep things stable under intense cornering. This aspect of the design was fairly typical of the day since all manufacturers had the same grade of simple steel tubing to choose from. The elongated fuel tank on the H1 was graced with sculpted insets that helped to sell the aggressive nature of the bike. A true two-person saddle provided adequate comfort for long days on the open road, and an upright riding stance was typical for the period. The all-new Mach II retailed for $999 in 1969, compared to Harley's XLH at $1,795. The Mach II was the performance bargain of the century.

Still trying to save face in the big twin field, Kawasaki sold a high pipe version of the W2SS in the W2TT. Still fed by the dual Mikuni carbs, the TT's upswept exhaust was once again suggestive of more rugged riding. The single carb W1SS carried on.

1969 KAWASAKI

Model	Engine	Displacement	Transmission	Features
M10	Single cylinder	50cc	Three-Speed	Two-Person Saddle
M11	Single cylinder	52cc	Three-Speed	Solo Saddle
GA1	Single cylinder	90cc	Four-Speed	
GA2	Single cylinder	90cc	Five-Speed	
GA3	Single cylinder	90cc	Four-Speed	90SS
G1DL	Single cylinder	90cc	Four-Speed	Electric Start
G1M	Single cylinder	90cc	Four-Speed	Motocross Version
G1TRL	Single cylinder	90cc	Four-Speed	Trail Version
G3SS	Single cylinder	90cc	Five-Speed	
G3TR	Single cylinder	90cc	Five-Speed	Bushmaster
B1/KC125	Single cylinder	125cc	Four-Speed	Base Model, No Superlube
F3	Single cylinder	169cc	Four-Speed	Bushwhacker
F2	Single cylinder	238cc	Four-Speed	
F21M	Two-cylinder	238cc	Four-Speed	Green Streak racer
F4	Two-cylinder	238cc	Four-Speed	Sidewinder
A1	Two-cylinder	247cc	Five-Speed	Samurai
A1SS	Twin-cylinder	247cc	Five-Speed	Street Scrambler
SG	Single cylinder	250cc	Four-Speed	
A7	Two-cylinder	338cc	Five-Speed	Avenger
A7SS	Two-cylinder	338cc	Five-Speed	Street Scrambler, High Pipes
H1 Mach III	Three-cylinder	498cc	Five-Speed	
W1SS	Two-cylinder	624cc	Four-Speed	Single Mikuni VM28
W2SS	Two-cylinder	624cc	Four-Speed	Dual Mikuni VM28
W2TT	Two-cylinder	624cc	Four-Speed	Upswept Crossover Exhaust

KAWASAKI
1970

Back for another round of fun was the lightning fast 1970 Mach III.

Vintage Memories, Inc.

Model year 1970 would see many of Kawasaki's smaller motorcycles fade from view. With the success of several bigger machines being sold, it was obvious that the market would not be able to support the same array of sub-100cc machines.

First to go were the 50 and 52cc M10 and M11 models. The acceptance and uses of the diminutive bikes had been waning and it was time to send them out to pasture. In the 90cc class, Kawasaki still offered five different models, although several had been retired for the current sales year. The F4 Sidewinder was a 238cc, two-cylinder model aimed at the dual purpose market and was new for 1970. Another debut for 1970 was the Big Horn, powered by a 346cc single cylinder thumper that produced 35 hp and had easily detachable lighting when taking to the more rugged terrain.

Heading upstream, the W2TT was no longer offered, leaving the W1SS and W2SS in its wake. It would also be the final year for the twin-carb W2SS, leaving the W1SS to carry on for one year after.

KAWASAKI

High mounted pipes were a sign of the dual purpose machine, and the Samurai featured that design. Brad Powell Collection

Also designed as a dual-purpose machine, the Avenger carried a bigger 338cc engine in the frame. Brad Powell Collection

The G3TR was powered by one of Kawasaki's smaller 90cc engines. Brad Powell Collection

With nearly 100cc more displacement than the Samurai, the Avenger was better suited to two-person riding. Brad Powell Collection

The Mach III had rocked the motorcycle world in its debut year, and was little changed for 1970. To help prevent water from entering the distributor and fouling out the ignition, a revised cover was applied to the latest H1. The sleek fuel tank was carried over but would also be changed in the following year.

1970 KAWASAKI

Model	Engine	Displacement	Transmission	Features
GA1	Single cylinder	90cc	Four-Speed	
GA2	Single cylinder	90cc	Five-Speed	
GA3	Single cylinder	90cc	Four-Speed	90SS
G3SS	Single cylinder	90cc	Five-Speed	
G3TR	Single cylinder	90cc	Five-Speed	Bushmaster
G4TR	Single cylinder	100cc	Five-Speed	Trail Boss
G31M	Single cylinder	100cc	Five-Speed	Centurian
B1/KC125	Single cylinder	125cc	Four-Speed	Base Model, No Superlube
F21M	Two-cylinder	238cc	Four-Speed	Green Streak racer
F4	Two-cylinder	238cc	Four-Speed	Sidewinder
F21M	Single cylinder	238cc	Four-Speed	
F5	Single cylinder	346cc	Five-Speed	Big Horn
A1	Two-cylinder	247cc	Five-Speed	Samurai
A1SS	Twin-cylinder	247cc	Five-Speed	Street Scrambler
A7	Two-cylinder	338cc	Five-Speed	Avenger
A7SS	Two-cylinder	338cc	Five-Speed	Street Scrambler High Pipes
H1 Mach III	Three-cylinder	498cc	Five-Speed	
W1SS	Two-cylinder	624cc	Four-Speed	Single Mikuni VM28
W2SS	Two-cylinder	624cc	Four-Speed	Dual Mikuni VM28

KAWASAKI
1971

After culling the herd quite extensively in 1970, the 1971 lineup saw more upgrades to existing models than radical alterations.

The GA5A was a 100cc variant new to the G series of bikes, but was similar to the 90cc models that remained. Most of this Kawasaki segment was simply given an "A" suffix to delineate them from the previous editions.

Near the top of the Kawasaki food chain, the W2SS was deleted, leaving only the W1SS to trudge along for its final year.

The H1, first seen in 1969 was now dubbed the H1A, and was revised in several ways for the latest year. The sleek fuel tank was replaced with a more contoured style, changing the landscape immensely. Improvements to the CDI ignition delivered more consistent spark and engine breathing was also enhanced. Oddly enough, these "improvements" dropped the performance of the 1971 Mach III slightly. Alterations to the front fork and suspension did help in the handling department though, making the '71 easier to ride.

While reviewing period magazines for details, it appears that Suzuki advertising was run at a ratio of about 15:1 over Kawasaki, Yamaha and Honda. Whether Kawasaki was simply resting on their laurels of the H1's success, or simply taking a breather from massive ad campaigns is impossible to say, but seems a premature move with the sales of U. S.-bound machines still in their infancy.

The low-mounted exhaust forced the 1971 A1 to street duty only. This class was becoming crowded and the Samurai was forced out.

Brad Powell Collection

1971 KAWASAKI

Model	Engine	Displacement	Transmission	Features
GA1A	Single cylinder	90cc	Four-Speed	
GA2A	Single cylinder	90cc	Five-Speed	
G3SS	Single cylinder	90cc	Five-Speed	
G3TRA	Single cylinder	90cc	Five-Speed	Bushmaster
GA5A	Single cylinder	100cc	Five-Speed	
G4TRA	Single cylinder	100cc	Five-Speed	Trail Boss
G31M	Single cylinder	100cc	Five-Speed	Centurian
F6	Single cylinder	125cc	Five-Speed	
F7	Single cylinder	175cc	Five-Speed	
F8	Two-cylinder	247cc	Four-Speed	Sidewinder
F81M	Two-cylinder	247cc	Five-Speed	7.5:1 Compression ratio
F5A	Single cylinder	346cc	Five-Speed	Big Horn
A1B	Two-cylinder	247cc	Five-Speed	Samurai
A1SSB	Twin-cylinder	247cc	Five-Speed	Street Scrambler
A7B	Two-cylinder	338cc	Five-Speed	Avenger
A7SSB	Two-cylinder	338cc	Five-Speed	Street Scrambler, High Pipes
H1A Mach III	Three-cylinder	498cc	Five-Speed	
W1SS	Two-cylinder	624cc	Four-Speed	Single Mikuni VM28

KAWASAKI

STANDARD CATALOG OF® JAPANESE Motorcycles

KAWASAKI'S ADVANCED ENGINEERING... IS

"TUNABLE" HATTA FORKS—scaled down exclusively for the 175E. Spring tension can be 3-way adjusted with a simple twist of a screwdriver. Hard, intermediate, or soft.

Two full inches of height adjustment, provides increased rake to the front forks. Rugged, hydraulic action.

Three way adjustability at the axle to suit the riders needs. Greater rake increases high speed stability. Greater trail provides more maneuverability.

COMPLETELY ENCLOSED CARBURETOR—water can't touch it. Main jets can be changed from outside without removing cover.

COMPETITION MAGNETO CDI—(capacitor discharge ignition) Space age, solid state electronics—never needs to be adjusted or timed. With surface gap spark plug—expected life 5000 miles.

REAR SHOCKS—5 way adjustable to suit any riding condition—feature nitrogen pressurized oil dampening.

ROTARY DISC VALVE ENGINE—provides complete control of intake timing which means greater torque at lower rpms—more peak power, too.

THE ALL NEW 175E—This medium-sized competition machine is designed for the roughest off-the-road riding as well as freeway cruising. The 21.5 hp single, rotary disc valve engine features greater low-end torque, yet has a top speed of 80 mph. This lean and tough machine will take you where you want to go even through water up over the hubs. In every way the 175E has been built to take abuse!

K Kawasaki
1062 McGAW AVE. SANTA ANA, CALIF. 92705

THE MOTORCYCLE THAT ADVANCED ENGINEERING BUILT!

The 1971 Kawasaki 175E motorcycle was portrayed in a manner that depicted its engineering features.

STANDARD CATALOG OF® JAPANESE Motorcycles

KAWASAKI
1972

Kawasaki continued to trim the fat from the lineup in 1972, especially in the redundant smaller models segment. To replace some of the departing models, a few new machines at the other end of the rainbow stepped in.

In the 90cc range, the three G models from 1971 were carried over into 1972. In the 100cc category, the G3TRA was gone, leaving the GA5A, and renamed G4TRB in its stead. The G5, also known as the KE100, was new for 1972, but was a one year only model. The 125cc F6 became the F6A and was joined by the B1LA in the same class. The slightly larger, 175cc F7 returned as the F7A and was the only Kawasaki carrying that motor for 1972. The 247cc F8 Bison was also back, but was now the F8A. The 350cc Big Horn changed from the F5A to the F9, but was otherwise unaltered.

Based on the success of the 498cc Mach III, the S1 Mach I was fitted with a 250cc version of the three-cylinder mill and provided a nice stepping stone to the soon to follow larger machines. Seeing the fun in riding the triples, Kawasaki also saw fit to add the 346cc S2 Mach II to the 1972 catalog. The H1B and H1C were now listed, with the H1C using a front drum brake instead of the disc found on the H1B.

The W1 series was not gone for good, after a long, yet somewhat lackluster sales record.

Slotting in as the king of castle was the new H2 Mach IV for 1972. Taking the three-cylinder theory to

Taking the two-stroke triple to the next level, Kawasaki rolled out the 750cc Mach IV in 1972.
Vintage Memories, Inc.

127

KAWASAKI

Although never seen in printed Kawasaki literature, the H1C featured drum brakes on both wheels.

Sergei Traycoff

The 350cc S2 bore a strong resemblance to its larger sibling the H2 but was easier to maneuver due to the smaller dimensions.

Chris Bednas Collection

the next level, the H2 was motivated by a 748cc variant of the two-stroke power plant. Although similar in design to the smaller models, the engine of the Mach IV was unique and shared no components with the other variants. The chassis and running gear were about the same as used on the smaller triples, but gusseted and strengthened to contend with the awesome power the Mach IV produced.

Despite the niggling handling flaws that remained, the H2 was the fastest street-legal machine you could buy in 1972. The nearly flat saddle offered little in the way of grip when the throttle was twisted open wide. An improved front disc brake did its best to slow the mighty Mach IV down from speed, but braking had yet to develop as quickly as horsepower.

1972 KAWASAKI

Model	Engine	Displacement	Transmission
GA1A	Single cylinder	90cc	Four-Speed
GA2A	Single cylinder	90cc	Five-Speed
G3SS Bushmaster	Single cylinder	90cc	Five-Speed
GA5A	Single cylinder	100cc	Five-Speed
G4TRB Trail Boss	Single cylinder	100cc	Five-Speed
G5	Single cylinder	100cc	Five-Speed
B1LA	Single cylinder	125cc	Five-Speed
F6A	Single cylinder	125cc	Five-Speed
F7A	Single cylinder	175cc	Five-Speed
F8A Bison	Two-cylinder	247cc	Four-Speed
S1 Mach I	Three-cylinder	250cc	Five-Speed
F9 Big Horn	Single cylinder	346cc	Five-Speed
S2 Mach II	Three-cylinder	346cc	Five-Speed
H1B Mach III	Three-cylinder	498cc	Five-Speed
H2 Mach IV	Three-cylinder	748cc	Five-Speed

KAWASAKI 1973

Ushering in an era of better and faster motorcycles, the 1973 Kawasaki Z-1 not only raised the bar, it took it home for safekeeping.
Al Steier

The model year 1973 would see the Kawasaki lineup grow from 16 to 18 models, with many simply getting new designations. Another reduction in smaller machines was overshadowed by the entry of their biggest and best machine to date.

The G7S and G7T were new entries for 1973, both powered by 100cc, single cylinder motors.

The 250cc Bison (F8A) was gone for the new year while the 350cc Big Horn (F9A) remained. The F12MX featured a massive, 441cc, single cylinder lump in the frame and was another one year only model.

Continuing improvement on the triple cylinder models included adding a 277mm disc brake to the S2A's front wheel, which also had aluminum fork lowers. Minor changes were made to the Mach IV, but the release of their latest machine would make all others a moot point.

The sales of the Mach II and IV machines set the bar quite high in the performance world, and Kawasaki was proud to have done so. Even with those victories to their credit, they knew something even more potent was required to trump the Honda CB750. As early as 1967, Kawasaki engineers began toiling with the blend of traits that would result in the ultimate machine, capable of satisfying every level of riding needs. Using the codename T-103, the plans began for their next

KAWASAKI

STANDARD CATALOG OF JAPANESE Motorcycles

The G3SS had a 90cc single cylinder engine mounted in the frame and a low mounted exhaust, keeping it on the streets.

Brad Powell Collection

market dominating craft. As it was being developed, the "New York Steak" moniker was applied to the next ace up their sleeve.

The new machine had to be able to gobble up long stretches of highway in comfort, and also faster than a speeding Honda. Most motors being sold in the day ran with single overhead cam engines, but this design was a bit limiting in what it could do. Kawasaki chose to add a second cam and to boost displacement to 903cc for the new motor. A 750cc design was considered, but Kawasaki wanted more than what was already being offered. The new model was already being heavily developed in 1968, but Kawasaki wanted to be sure there was enough interest in a big four-cylinder bike, and let Honda do the market research.

By the end of 1971, the Z-1 was given the go ahead for production, and the first production models rolled off the line in February of 1972. The sleek fuel tank and rear "duck tail" fender have become classics in today's collector world, and looked great in 1973 too. The Maroon Metalflake with Orange trim panels appeared more like brown and orange to me, but very few other machines catch my eye today as quickly as correct '73 Z-1.

When fully loaded with fluids and fuel, the Z-1 weighed 539 lbs. Period ads claimed 82 hp at 8,500 rpm, easily overcoming any excess weight. When first introduced in 1972, the Z-1 carried a retail price tag of $1,895. If we knew then what we know now, we'd have all bought 10 of them and stored them away like a squirrel stores nuts.

1973 KAWASAKI

Model	Engine	Displacement	Transmission
GA1A	Single cylinder	90cc	Four-Speed
GA2A	Single cylinder	90cc	Five-Speed
G3SS Bushmaster	Single cylinder	90cc	Five-Speed
GA5A	Single cylinder	100cc	Five-Speed
G4TRC Trail Boss	Single cylinder	100cc	Five-Speed
G7S	Single cylinder	100cc	Five-Speed
G7T	Single cylinder	100cc	Five-Speed
B1LA	Single cylinder	125cc	Five-Speed
F6B	Single cylinder	125cc	Five-Speed
F7B	Single cylinder	175cc	Five-Speed
S1A Mach I	Three-cylinder	250cc	Five-Speed
F11M	Single cylinder	247cc	Five-Speed
F9A Big Horn	Single cylinder	346cc	Five-Speed
S2A Mach II	Three-cylinder	346cc	Five-Speed
F12MX	Single cylinder	441cc	Five-Speed
H1D Mach III	Three-cylinder	498cc	Five-Speed
H2A Mach IV	Three-cylinder	748cc	Five-Speed
Z1	Four-cylinder	903cc	Five-Speed

STANDARD CATALOG OF JAPANESE Motorcycles

KAWASAKI

1974

Model year 1974 would prove to be another period of revisions to the returning models, as well as the appearance of new listings. With the introduction of the Z1 in 1973 though, 1974 would be peaceful by comparison.

Variations in the 90cc segment were still being played with and for 1974 the G2S and G2T rolled into view. Based on the GA1A, the G2S had 10 fewer horsepower and shifted through a four-speed gearbox. The G2T was based on the GA2A and had an extra gear in the cases, bringing the total to five. The G5B was also added in 1974 and was for the most part a G4TR but lacked the dual range gearbox. Both the F6B and F7B were eliminated for 1974. Joining the ranks for 1974 was the 125cc KS125, also called the KE125.

Kawasaki's popular line of three-cylinder machines remained with some alterations being made to the format. The 250cc S1B came in at the lower end of the category, with the 346cc S2 replaced by the bigger 400cc S3 in 1974. The crankcases of the S3 were different than the S2 it replaced, and the square profile of the cooling fins helped to identify the two variations at a glance. By using Mikuni VM26SC carburetors and lowering compression to 6.5:1, the horsepower actually went up to 42 at 7,000 rpm. Rubber motor mounts made the more powerful S3 a smoother machine too. An extra bit of length was added to the wheelbase as well, bringing the new total to 53.7 inches.

The 498cc Mach II returned in H1E guise and was altered to include a CDI ignition and valves

Implementing two-stroke technology, the triple of the Mach III was almost unbeatable.

Mike Swistak

KAWASAKI

STANDARD CATALOG OF JAPANESE Motorcycles

The left side of the '74 Kawasaki H2 carried a single exhaust pipe and carved a classic profile.

Kersting Family Collection

and helped to calm the sometimes twitchy handling of the powerful H2.

A brand new street machine was also added in 1974 in the twin cylinder KZ400. The 399cc four-stroke engine brought a tamer model to the table. The triples were great, but some buyers steered clear of their quirky power band by starting out on the more traditional KZ400.

Having earned instant cult status in 1973, the Z-1 was little changed for the next year. The 1974 versions did wear different paint and the inline-four motor was now in its natural silver state versus the blacked-out version used on the debut model. Mild tweaks to the carburetion provided better performance when the motor was cold, but no other changes were seen. Combining the production of the 1973 and '74 models of the Z1, more than 80,000 units were built, one of Kawasaki's most popular editions ever.

that allowed oil to make its way to the main bearings. The bigger 748cc H2 gained a "B" designation along with revised bodywork that now utilized a new fuel tank and tail. A hydraulic steering damper was seen on the right side of the chassis

1974 KAWASAKI

Model	Engine	Displacement	Transmission
GA1A	Single cylinder	90cc	Four-Speed
GA2A	Single cylinder	90cc	Five-Speed
G2S	Single cylinder	90cc	Four-Speed
G2T	Single cylinder	90cc	Five-Speed
G3SS Bushmaster	Single cylinder	90cc	Five-Speed
GA5A	Single cylinder	100cc	Five-Speed
G5B	Single cylinder	100cc	Five-Speed
G4TRD Trail Boss	Single cylinder	100cc	Five-Speed
G7S	Single cylinder	100cc	Five-Speed
G7T	Single cylinder	100cc	Five-Speed
B1LA	Single cylinder	125cc	Five-Speed
KS125	Single cylinder	125cc	Five-Speed
KX250	Single cylinder	250cc	Five-Speed
S1B Mach I	Three-cylinder	250cc	Five-Speed
F11A	Single cylinder	247cc	Five-Speed
F9B Big Horn	Single cylinder	346cc	Five-speed
S3 Mach II	Three-cylinder	400cc	Five-Speed
KZ400D	Two-cylinder	398cc	Five-Speed
KX450	Single cylinder	441cc	Five-Speed
H1E Mach III	Three-cylinder	498cc	Five-Speed
H2B Mach IV	Three-cylinder	748cc	Five-Speed
Z1A	Four-cylinder	903cc	Five-Speed

KAWASAKI
1975

The lineup of 1975 models from Kawasaki would again be jostled in an ongoing effort to blend large and small machines.

The 90cc class lost the GA2A and G2S, leaving only two machines in the category. The G3T was a new 100cc model, and brought the number of those bikes to six for the model year. Moving up another rung on the displacement ladder, the KD125 and KX125A joined the game, adding to the two models that were carried over from 1974. Slotting in between the 125 and 250cc models, the KD175-A1 was another single cylinder machine in the Kawasaki lineup.

The triple-lung Mach I was back for another round and still carried 249cc in the frame. A new entry aimed at the beginning or budget minded buyer was the KZ400S. It was stripped of a few of the KZ400D's features to keep the price of admission lower.

The popularity of the smaller Kawasakis was waning, forcing certain models to be trimmed for the following model year.

Brad Powell Collection

KAWASAKI

The 903cc Z1 was back for another round in 1975 and was only slightly changed from the 1974 iteration.

Bill Turner

One model missing for 1975 was the 750cc Mach IV triple. This omission left a gap in the catalog between the 498cc Mach III and the dominating Z1-B. The Z1-B saw only minor alterations including the removal of the automatic chain oiler and revised front fork internals.

1975 KAWASAKI

Model	Engine	Displacement	Transmission
GA1A	Single cylinder	90cc	Five-Speed
G2T	Single cylinder	90cc	Five-Speed
G3SSE	Single cylinder	100cc	Five-Speed
G3T	Single cylinder	100cc	Five-Speed
G4TRE	Single cylinder	100cc	Five-Speed
G5C	Single cylinder	100cc	Five-Speed
G7SA	Single cylinder	100cc	Five-Speed
G7TA	Single cylinder	100cc	Five-Speed
B1LA	Single cylinder	125cc	Five-Speed
KD125	Single cylinder	125cc	Six-Speed
KS125A	Single cylinder	125cc	Five-Speed
KX125A	Single cylinder	125cc	Six-Speed
KD175A1	Single cylinder	175cc	Five-Speed
KH250B1 Mach I	Three-cylinder	250cc	Five-Speed
KT250	Single cylinder	250cc	Five-Speed
KX250A3	Single cylinder	250cc	Five-Speed
KH400A3	Three-cylinder	400cc	Five-Speed
KX400	Single cylinder	392cc	Five-Speed
KZ400D	Two-cylinder	398cc	Five-Speed
KZ400S	Twin-cylinder	398cc	Five-Speed
KH500A8 Mach II	Three-cylinder	489cc	Five-Speed
Z1B	Four-cylinder	903cc	Five-Speed

KAWASAKI
1976

The three-cylinder KH400 was carried near the lower end of the two-stroke models from Kawasaki.

The blend of available machines continued to change for 1976 as Kawasaki wrestled with their own line as well as those motorcycles sold by others. Finding the correct balance of big and small models was an ongoing battle, no matter who was making the cycles.

Smaller motorcycles continued to lose their grip on the sales floor, and for 1976, the GA1A, G3SA and G4TRE were all removed from the mix. The G2T was the only remaining 90cc model with your choice of four 100cc bikes still left to select. Additionally, four models continued to be sold at the 125cc level. A solitary 175cc cycle was offered, with the next model being a 250. The KX400A2 carried a 398cc single in the frame and was joined by a pair of 398cc twins.

The KZ400S2 was designated the "Special" and wore a retail price tag of only $995 in 1976.

Moving up the ladder, a new twin joined the team and displaced 745cc, and was sold as the KZ750.

Minor improvements continued to be made to the chart topping Z1 as well, and its name was changed to the KZ900. The 26mm carburetors replaced the previous 28mm models and the throttle linkage was upgraded. The air filter now caused less restriction to the air flow and a second disc brake helped to slow the big bike to a stop. In the handling department, the steering head received extra gusseting for added strength.

KAWASAKI

STANDARD CATALOG OF JAPANESE Motorcycles

A step up the ladder was Kawasaki's KH500 which had a motor displacing 499cc divided into a trio of cylinders.

Chris Bednas Collection

Adding to the recipe for 1976 was the KZ900 LTD. Based on the success of the standard KZ900, the LTD was more of a cruiser, although the classification was still in its infancy at the time. The LTD sported a third disc brake, a Jardine four-into-two exhaust system and special paint. The saddle was of a more deeply contoured shape as well, replacing the flatter unit used on the standard KZ900. The front brake calipers of the LTD were also mounted behind the lower fork legs instead of in front as they were on the other 900. Additional frame reinforcement aided in handling, and the new version of the classic Z1 was welcomed with open arms by the big bike buying crowd.

1976 KAWASAKI

Model	Engine	Displacement	Transmission
G2T	Single cylinder	90cc	Five-Speed
G3T	Single cylinder	100cc	Five-Speed
G7TA	Single cylinder	100cc	Five-Speed
KE100-A5	Single cylinder	100cc	Five-Speed
KH100-B7	Single cylinder	100cc	Five-Speed
B1LA	Single cylinder	125cc	Five-Speed
KD125	Single cylinder	125cc	Six-Speed
KE125A	Single cylinder	125cc	Five-Speed
KE125A3	Single cylinder	125cc	Six-Speed
KX125A3	Single cylinder	125cc	Six-Speed
KE175B1	Single cylinder	175cc	Five-Speed
KH250A5 Mach I	Three-cylinder	250cc	Five-speed
KT250	Single cylinder	250cc	Five-Speed
KX250A3	Single cylinder	250cc	Five-Speed
KH400A3	Three-cylinder	400cc	Five-Speed
KX400	Single cylinder	392cc	Five-Speed
KZ400D3	Two-cylinder	398 cc	Five-Speed
KZ400S2	Twin-cylinder	398 cc	Five-Speed
KH500A8 Mach III	Three-cylinder	498cc	Five-Speed
KZ750B1	Two-cylinder	745cc	Five-Speed
KZ900A4	Four-cylinder	903cc	Five-Speed
KZ900B1 Ltd	Four-cylinder	903cc	Five-Speed

KAWASAKI 1977

The 1977 Kawasakis were altered at both ends of the line but leaving most of the middle-range models the same. Gone for '77 were the G2T, G3T and G7TA, leaving only the KC90-C1 in the 90cc class. The advent of bigger cycles was quickly drawing down on the interest of the limited- use creations. The bulk of the 125cc and 175cc offerings were back for another year, with little more than changes to their designations.

New for 1977 was the KZ200. Powered by a single cylinder motor, the little KZ made a great entry-level motorcycle. I owned one that I bought new. It was not only my first motorcycle, but my initial exposure to riding anything with two wheels.

There were just two of the three-cylinder machines in the 1977 Kawasaki line with the KH250 Mach I and KH400 struggling to save face against the rising tide of rules against the smoky two-strokes.

Also joining the team for 1977 was the KZ650, sold in two varieties. A standard model was offered alongside a more rakish Limited Edition that featured the classic contoured seat and pullback bars. The big Z-1 had been sold in this level of trim in 1976, but was offered only in the standard style.

Bringing new levels of power and market domination to the fold were the new KZ1000 models from Kawasaki. With inline-four motors displacing 1015cc, the liter sized KZs were a force to be reckoned with. Sold in two versions, a buyer could grab a standard or Limited version in the first year of sale. The immediate acceptance of the big machines would quickly lead to other bikes being built on the same platform. Between the Z1 and the new KZ1000, Kawasaki was proving to the world it planned on staying on top of the performance charts in the USA.

1977 KAWASAKI

Model	Engine	Displacement	Transmission
KC90-C1	Single cylinder	90cc	Five-Speed
KE100-A6	Single cylinder	100cc	Five-Speed
KH100-A2	Single cylinder	100cc	Five-Speed
KH100-B8	Single cylinder	100cc	Five-Speed
KH100-C1	Single cylinder	100cc	Five-Speed
KH100-E1	Single cylinder	100cc	Five-Speed
KC125-A6	Single cylinder	125cc	Five-Speed
KD125-A2	Single cylinder	125cc	Six-Speed
KE125-A4	Single cylinder	125cc	Six-Speed
KH125-A1	Single cylinder	125cc	Six-Speed
KD175-A1	Single cylinder	175cc	Five-Speed
KE175-B2	Single cylinder	175cc	Five-Speed
KZ200	Single cylinder	198cc	Five-Speed
KH250-B2 Mach I	Three-cylinder	250cc	Five-Speed
KE250-B1	Single cylinder	250cc	Five-Speed
KH400-A4	Three-cylinder	398cc	Five-Speed
KZ400-A1	Two-cylinder	398cc	Five-Speed
KZ400-D4	Two-cylinder	398cc	Five-Speed
KZ400-S3	Two-cylinder	398cc	Five-Speed
KZ650	Four-cylinder	652cc	Five-Speed
KZ650-B1 Ltd	Four-cylinder	652cc	Five-Speed
KZ750-B2	Two-cylinder	745cc	Five-Speed
KZ900-A5	Four-cylinder	903cc	Five-Speed
KZ1000-A1	Four-cylinder	1015cc	Five-Speed
KZ1000-B1 Ltd	Four-cylinder	1015cc	Five-Speed

KAWASAKI
1978

STANDARD CATALOG OF® JAPANESE Motorcycles

Building on the success of their KZ1000, Kawasaki rolled out the Café styled Z1-R for 1978.

Jim Goebel

In the 1978 model year, Kawasaki trimmed their small models and added several significant big bikes to the catalog. The loss of all but one of their infamous two-stroke models would be quickly eclipsed by a few bikes at the upper end of the stratosphere.

Kawasaki's small cycles now started at 100cc with the elimination of the 90cc bracket. Only the KE100-A7 was left in the sub 125cc group too, making room for more of the larger bikes that were being introduced. The sole remaining two-stroke in 1978 was to be the KH400-A5, and it too would be a memory when the 1979 models were introduced.

The popularity of the 650 models grew and the KZ650 Custom featured a trio of disc brakes, alloy wheels and custom paint. The KZ650 wore wire wheels and fewer discs, but offered great performance at a budget price.

After bumping the bar up a few notches with the KZ1000, the mighty Z-1 was no longer sold in 1978. The big four cylinder had opened lots of doors for Kawasaki, and the larger KZ1000 blew through those openings to find even greener pastures. The KZ1000 was now seen in standard and Limited trim, both with slightly different features.

The Z1-R was introduced for 1978. The R model was much more than a cosmetic upgrade for the KZ, and helped to draw even more attention to the Kawasaki brand. Wanting to create a distinctive model without reinventing the wheel, the Z1-R did employ a chassis that was similar to the other 1015cc machines. Reinforced steering head and bolstered tubes were the biggest difference and brought a new level of rigidity and confidence to the chassis. An 18-inch front tire was fatter than the 19-inch rubber on the KZ1000 for more grip in the corners. A threesome of drill brake rotors help to haul the Z1-R down from speed.

Using the same powerful mill found in the KZ1000, the Z1-R went even further and carried four 28mm Mikuni carburetors for improved intake. Spent fumes made their way through a four-into-one exhaust that was finished in chrome.

Bodywork on the R was the most obvious change, and made a strong statement. Sharply creased lines on the fuel tank were mated to the triangular side covers. This motorcycle was led by a shapely Cafe fairing up front.

The icy blue paint and subtle pinstripes added mystique to this rare and fairly exotic machine from Japan. The front fender and rear tail section were finished in the same color as the sheet metal. A tidy panel of gauges resided behind the nicely sized fairing that actually did a fair job of providing some aerodynamic benefits. The Z1-R package came at a price, and that was $3,695 in 1978.

Kawasaki rolled out one of their most unusual bikes ever in 1978. By combining the race ready traits of the Z1-R and bolting on a turbocharger, the Z1-RTC was born. When it was introduced, the TC was the only production motorcycle to be fitted with a turbo. The '78 TC broke the ice.

About the only difference between the TC and its base model R was the turbo system. The same bodywork and running gear was used but it benefited by the addition of the puffer. After being force-fed into the engine, the exiting exhaust fumes rushed out through an enormous bologna-slice header. The TC ran with less noise then the R since the turbo actually masked some of the exhaust racket.

When this Kawasaki was taken to the local drag strip, period magazine staffers were able to record high 10- and low 11-second runs in stock trim.

With a half a tank of fuel on board, the Z1-RTC weighed in at over 500 lbs., making the radical quarter mile times even more remarkable. Of course all of this speed carried a high price. The TC listed for $4,995, making it a choice of royalty or the payment-happy buyers. The performance delivered made the TC a true collector's machine both then and now.

As if the rakish design and turbocharged motor weren't enough, Kawasaki decided to add a set of attention getting accent stripes to the TC.

Tom Turner

1978 KAWASAKI

Model	Engine	Displacement	Transmission
KE100-A7	Single cylinder	100cc	Five-Speed
KD125-A2	Single cylinder	125cc	Six-Speed
KE125-A5	Single cylinder	125cc	Six-Speed
KH125-A2	Single cylinder	125cc	Six-Speed
KX125-A3	Single cylinder	125cc	Five-Speed
KD175-A1	Single cylinder	175cc	Five-Speed
KE175-B3	Single cylinder	175cc	Five-Speed
KZ200	Single cylinder	198cc	Five-Speed
KE250-B2	Single cylinder	250cc	Five-Speed
KL250-A1	Single cylinder	250cc	Five-Speed
KX250	Single cylinder	250cc	Five-Speed
KH400-A5	Three-cylinder	398cc	Five-Speed
KZ400-A2	Two-cylinder	398cc	Five-Speed
KZ400-B1	Two-cylinder	398cc	Five-Speed
KZ400-C1	Two-cylinder	398cc	Five-Speed
KZ650-B2 Ltd.	Four-cylinder	652cc	Five-Speed
KZ650-C2	Four-cylinder	652cc	Five-Speed
KZ650-D1 SR	Four-cylinder	652cc	Five-Speed
KZ750-B3	Two-cylinder	745cc	Five-Speed
KZ1000-A2	Four-cylinder	1015cc	Five-Speed
KZ1000-D1	Four-cylinder	1015cc	Five-Speed
KZ1000 Z1-R Café styling	Four-cylinder	1015cc	Five-Speed
KZ1000 Z1-RTC Turbocharged	Four-cylinder	1015cc	Five-Speed

KAWASAKI

1979

Kawasaki's 1979 model lineup would remain fairly stable, with only a few alterations found.

The middle ground was still proving to be the most active, with numerous 400cc and 650cc examples being offered. The inline-four KZ650 was seen in Standard, Custom and SR trim, the latter carrying a unique gas tank, fenders and seat. The twin cylinder KZ750 was also back for another year, but was often overlooked as riders selected one of the smoother four-cylinder machines to bring home.

Near the top of the model listings, the big KZ1000 was now available with a shaft drive along with the two returning chain drive versions. The shaft added a new level of convenience to the rider by removing the traditional chain lubrication and maintenance from the equation. Both versions of the Z1-R returned for a second year, but it would be the last appearance for the turbo equipped TC.

Honda released their amazing CBX for 1979, and the six-cylinder motorcycle set new standards for power and sport riding in a massive machine. With that in mind, Kawasaki took another tack when they also rolled out a new six-cylinder motorcycle in 1979. The KZ1300 was instantly the biggest kid on the block.

Displacing 1,286ccs, it dwarfed the CBX by more than 200ccs, and was larger in every dimension. When fully fueled with 5.5 gallons of petrol, the KZ1300 tipped the scales at just over 700 lbs. That made it nearly 150 lbs. heavier than the CBX. These numbers did not really hold the KZ1300 back since Kawasaki positioned it as a touring machine versus a sporting model like the CBX.

The engine of the biggest

The one-lung KZ200 was back for another year, and continued to offer neophyte riders a great way to begin motorcycling.

Moving up one step, the KZ400 provided a slightly larger machine for more advance riders.

When the buyer wanted more style from his machine, the KZ650 Custom often filled the bill.

KZ was a complex maze but worked very well. Obviously it was a bit of a handful when parking or at low speeds.

The monster came into its own when it hit the open road. Its length, girth and weight made this Kawasaki a spectacular long distance mount, and it was capable of carrying riders and passengers with power to spare. The KZ1300 slowly morphed into a more refined touring machine, but the platform it began with was more than up to the task.

1979 KAWASAKI

Model	Engine	Displacement	Transmission
KE100-A8	Single cylinder	100cc	Five-Speed
KM100-A4	Single cylinder	100cc	Five-Speed
KD125-A2	Single cylinder	125cc	Six-Speed
KE125-A6	Single cylinder	125cc	Six-Speed
KX125-A3	Single cylinder	125cc	Five-Speed
KD175-A4	Single cylinder	175cc	Five-Speed
KZ200-A2	Single cylinder	198cc	Five-Speed
KE250-B3	Single cylinder	250cc	Five-Speed
KL250-A2	Single cylinder	250cc	Five-Speed
KX250	Single cylinder	250cc	Five-Speed
KDX400	Single cylinder	398cc	Five-Speed
KZ400-B2	Single cylinder	398cc	Six-Speed
KZ650-B3 Ltd.	Single cylinder	652cc	Five-Speed
KZ650-C3	Four-cylinder	652cc	Five-Speed
KZ650-D2 SR	Four-cylinder	652cc	Five Speed
KZ750-B4	Two-cylinder	745cc	Five-Speed
KZ1000-A3	Four-cylinder	1,015cc	Five-Speed
KZ1000-B3	Four-cylinder	1,015cc	Five-Speed
KZ1000-E1	Four-cylinder	1,015cc	Five-Speed
KZ1000 Z1-R Café styling	Four-cylinder	1,015cc	Five-Speed
KZ1000 Z1-RTC Turbocharged	Four-cylinder	1,015cc	Five-Speed
KZ1300-A1	Six cylinder	1,286cc	Five-Speed

Blending features of the 650 Custom and the standard model, the 650SR delivered the best of both worlds.

KAWASAKI
1980

Of the two variations offered in 1980, the Standard KZ650 was as popular as the Limited version.
National Motorcycle Museum

The brunt of model changes for Kawasaki for 1980 started in mid-pack, leaving the remaining small bikes as they were.

Seeing the value of an entry-level cruiser, the KZ440 was introduced for 1980 in three different trim packages. Regardless of which model was selected, a 443cc, twin-cylinder power plant was found in the frame. The D1 was different with its final drive a polymer belt instead of a chain or shaft. Belt drives were getting installed on a few models in the industry, with more to follow. The belt was cleaner than a chain and avoided the pogo effect of the shaft drive machines. Along with the belt driven KZ440, it was sold in Standard and Limited form. The belt driven D1 was the priciest, coming in at $1,829.

With the popularity of the middle class bikes growing, Kawasaki was the first company to design and deliver a 550cc inline-four to the market. The KZ550 was an instant hit with the media and buyers alike. Powered by a 553cc engine and shifted through a six-speed gearbox, the nimble 550 delivered performance and handling in a package that weighed only 449 lbs. when fully fueled. To cater to both the Standard and Cruiser audiences, the KZ550 was sold in two trim styles. The Ltd. carried the typical "cruiser" trappings including a more deeply contoured saddle and buckhorn bars. The Standard sold for $2,179 while the Limited added a few hundred dollars to the total.

The 650 class was still in session with an Limited and Standard version offered for 1980.

With a long-standing record, the 750 twin was joined by a pair of inline-four models that displaced 738cc compared to the 745cc of the twin. Sold in Standard and Limited trim, the inline-four 750s were favorably received with price tags falling just under the $3,000 mark.

Another variation in the 1000 design was shown for 1980, and had the distinction of being one of the first fuel-injected motorcycles to reach the market. Governmental regulations were getting more stringent every year, and to contend with the new rules, Kawasaki added electronic fuel injection to their KZ1000 Ltd. The system was advanced and complex, but delivered easy warm up and crisp throttle response.

In addition to those traits, the big KZ returned healthy mileage numbers nearing 50 miles per gallon, no mean feat for a 1,015cc engine.

Unique features of the Classic were panels of chrome on the tear drop fuel tank and unique winged logos on the side covers. All of this wonderful technology made the KZ1000 Classic a bit pricey though, carrying an MSRP of $4,199 onto the sales floor.

The KZ1300 also made a second appearance in 1980, and the naked model was joined by a full-blown touring version that featured a large fairing and saddlebags. The frame-mounted fairing was a Vetter Windjammer that wore Kawasaki badges. In addition to hard-sided saddlebags, this Kawasaki had a rack-mounted rear trunk. That added immensely to the carrying capability of the big six.

Selling for $5,699, the touring version was nearly $1,000 more than the base KZ1300, but was well equipped and ready for the open road.

The twin-cylinder KZ440 provided plenty of power and features for both the novice and experienced rider.

Chris Bednas Collection

1980 KAWASAKI

Model	Engine	Displacement	Transmission
KE100-A9	Single cylinder	100cc	Five-Speed
KM100-A6	Single cylinder	100cc	Five-Speed
KE125-A7	Single cylinder	125cc	Six-Speed
KDX175-A1	Single cylinder	175cc	Five-Speed
KE175-D2	Single cylinder	175cc	Five-Speed
KZ200-D1 Ltd	Single cylinder	198cc	Five-Speed
KL250-A3	Single cylinder	250cc	Five-Speed
KLX250-A2	Single cylinder	250cc	Five-Speed
KX250-A6	Single cylinder	250cc	Five-Speed
KDX400-A2	Single cylinder	398cc	Five-Speed
KX400	Single cylinder	398cc	Five-Speed
KZ440-A1 Ltd	Two-cylinder	443cc	Six-Speed
KZ440-B1	Two-cylinder	443cc	Six-Speed
KZ440-D1 Belt Drive	Two-cylinder	443cc	Six-Speed
KZ550-A1	Four-cylinder	553cc	Six-Speed
KZ550-C1 Ltd	Four-cylinder	553cc	Six-Speed
KZ650-E1 Ltd	Four-cylinder	652cc	Five-Speed
KZ650-F1 Custom	Four-cylinder	652cc	Five-Speed
KZ750-G1 Ltd	Two-cylinder	745cc	Five-Speed
KZ750-E1	Four-cylinder	738cc	Five-Speed
KZ750-H1 Ltd	Four-cylinder	738cc	Five-Speed
KZ1000-A4	Four-cylinder	1,015cc	Five-Speed
KZ1000-B4 Ltd	Four-cylinder	1,015cc	Five-Speed
KZ1000-E2 Shaft drive	Four-cylinder	1,015cc	Five-Speed
KZ000-G1	Six-cylinder	1,286cc	Five-Speed
KZ1300-B2 Touring model	Six-cylinder	1,286cc	Five-Speed

KAWASAKI

1981

It was missing a few features of the higher-priced 650s but the CSR still delivered a lot of machine for the money.

Chris Bednas Collection

Growth in the middle and upper end of the market saw Kawasaki's 1981 model mix change again, with a few new faces joining the ranks.

Better suited for use as a pit bike, the AR80 carried only 78cc of displacement but was fairly stylish for a small machine.

Near the bottom end of the Kawasaki spectrum, the KZ200 was replaced with the KZ250 CSR. By adding a bit more power to the diminutive machine, they did little to take away from its amazing fuel sipping nature of 75 miles per gallon. The new KZ305 CSR carried a two-cylinder engine and six-speed gearbox in the frame. The 305 CSR sold for only $200 more than the lowly KZ250, making it a real deal.

Seeing how successful the KZ550 had been, Kawasaki upped the ante and brought out two new models for 1981. The GPz designation was aimed at an ever sportier segment, and the 550 version was the smaller of the two first sold. The GPz family was another blockbuster for Kawasaki. A factory stock bikini fairing only added to the sport bike demeanor of the GPz550.

A few losses in the 650 ranks were seen as the KZ650 Standard and Limited went away leaving only the CSR to carry the flag at that level. The long-running two-cylinder KZ750 also went into retirement, but left the four cylinder models in its wake.

The KZ1000 received several improvements for the latest year and was 15 pounds lighter. The 1015cc engine was reduced to 998cc, but no loss of power was experienced. The reduced weight added to the speed and agility of the liter sized KZ. The higher priced Z1-R was no longer offered. To help heal the pain of the missing R, Kawasaki rolled out the KZ1100-A, the more traditional of two new machines. It carried the latest 1090cc in-line four in its flanks. Fed by four Mikuni carburetors, it was also fairly basic in its mechanical layout. The KZ1100 could be easily equipped with the official line of Kawasaki touring accessories to better suit the long haul rider.

Second in the new 1100 class was the GPz 1100. It held a blacked-out 1090cc motor in its clutches. Not only did the big GPz carry the second biggest power plant motor in Kawasaki's catalog, the engine was fuel injected.

The entire cluster of gauges on the GPz1100 was electronic versus the typical mechanical speedometer and tachometer. The tach and speedometer delivered a full array of information in a large rectangular panel. The bigger GPz lacked the front fairing used on the 550 version but few complaints were voiced.

Even if they were you wouldn't be able to hear them over the screams of fun as the GPz rocketed forward through the five-speed gearbox. The fuel injected GPz required about $300 more to ride home than the KZ1100, but buyers snapped them up. The massive KZ1300 was still sold, but only in the base model trim. Kawasaki offered a complete line of touring components for the serious touring rider, but left the specifics up to each buyer instead of loading the big bike up at the factory as they had in the past.

For 1981, the big KZ1000 was lighter by 15 lbs., adding even more potential to an already stellar performer.

1981 KAWASAKI

Model	Engine	Displacement	Transmission
AR80	Single cylinder	78cc	Six-Speed
KE100-A10	Single cylinder	100cc	Five-Speed
KM100-A7	Single cylinder	100cc	Five-Speed
KE125-A8	Single cylinder	125cc	Six-Speed
KE175-D3	Single cylinder	175cc	Five-Speed
KZ250 CSR	Single cylinder	246cc	Five-Speed
KL250-A4	Single cylinder	250cc	Five-Speed
KZ305A CSR	Two-cylinder	306cc	Six-Speed
KZ440-A2 Ltd	Two-cylinder	443cc	Six-Speed
KZ440-B2	Two-cylinder	443cc	Six-Speed
KZ440-D2 (Belt Drive)	Two-cylinder	443cc	Six-Speed
KZ550-A2	Four-cylinder	553cc	Six-Speed
KZ550-C2 Ltd	Four-cylinder	553cc	Six-Speed
GPz550 (New for 1981)	Four-cylinder	553cc	Six-Speed
KZ650-H1 CSR	Four-cylinder	652cc	Five-Speed
KZ750-E2	Four-cylinder	738cc	Five-Speed
KZ750-H2 Ltd	Four-cylinder	738cc	Five-Speed
KZ1000 CSR	Four-cylinder	998cc	Five-Speed
KZ1000 Ltd	Four-cylinder	998cc	Five-Speed
KZ1000-A (Shaft Drive)	Four-cylinder	998cc	Five-Speed
KZ1000-J	Four-cylinder	998cc	Five-Speed
KZ1100-A (New for 1981 Shaft drive)	Four-cylinder	1090cc	Five-Speed
GPx1100 (New for 1981)	Four-cylinder	1090cc	Five-Speed
KZ1300-A3	Six-cylinder	1286cc	Five-Speed

KAWASAKI
1982

Proudly wearing the official "Team Green" livery, the 1982 KZ1000R was also known as the "Eddie Lawson Replica" or ELR.

Model year 1982 would be a quiet one for Kawasaki with only a few but very significant changes in the catalog as two important models being added to the lineup.

A few small models left the stage as the KM100 and KE175 were no longer available. Even with their dismissal, there were plenty of entry-level motorcycles to fill the gap.

The success of the 1981 GPz group was expanded by one model in 1982 as the 750 iteration joined the ranks. Using the same winning formula that was applied to the 550 and 1100 versions, the GPZ750 met the needs of the more aggressive rider or simply someone who needed a bit more power than the 550 could deliver.

Knowing full well that when winning races, the Kawasaki name became synonymous with victory. To mark the 1981 and 1982 championships, the KZ1000R was born. Designed to mimic the race-ready KZ1000S1 that was piloted by Eddie Lawson, the R carried several cosmetic features onto the street. The most obvious aspect was the Bright Green paint applied to the tank and related bits. Accenting the green was a set of blue and white stripes that adorned the fuel tank, tail section and handlebar fairing. This vivid ensemble looked the part of the track-only version although it lacked the large number plates of Mr. Lawson's machine.

The all-black engine displaced 998cc and drew life through a set of four Mikuni 34mm carburetors. Exhaust duty was handled by an all-black Kerker four-into-one header that carried a street

New for 1981, the KZ1100 was a returning model for the latest year and continued to deliver performance and comfort.

legal baffle in the final port. Continuing the race bike formula, the saddle had been deeply sculpted, placing the rider into a cradle of comfort.

A set of short handlebars were also finished in black and rested behind the tiny fairing. Alloy wheels with gold accents rolled at each end with slightly wider rubber stretched around their form. A small World Championship decal was placed on the top of the fuel tank to advertise Eddie Lawson's winning ways and to make the buyer feel like part of the team.

This raft of cosmetic changes placed the sticker price a bit higher, but for today's collector, the 1982 list of $4,400 sounds like a bargain.

1982 KAWASAKI

Model	Engine	Displacement	Transmission
AR80	Single cylinder	78cc	Six-Speed
KE100-A10	Single cylinder	100cc	Five-Speed
KE125-A8	Single cylinder	125cc	Six-Speed
KZ250 CSR	Single cylinder	246cc	Five-Speed
KL250-A4	Single cylinder	250cc	Five-Speed
KZ305A CSR	Two-cylinder	306cc	Six-Speed
KZ440-A2 Ltd	Two-cylinder	443cc	Six-Speed
KZ440-B2	Two-cylinder	443cc	Six-Speed
KZ440-D4 (Belt Drive)	Two-cylinder	443cc	Six-Speed
KZ550-A2	Four-cylinder	553cc	Six-Speed
KZ550-C2 Ltd	Four-cylinder	553cc	Six-Speed
GPz550	Four-cylinder	553cc	Six-Speed
KZ650-H1 CSR	Four-cylinder	652cc	Five-Speed
GPz750 (New for 1982)	Four-cylinder	738cc	Five-Speed
KZ750-E2	Four-cylinder	738cc	Five-Speed
KZ750-H2 Ltd	Four-cylinder	738cc	Five-Speed
KZ1000 CSR	Four-cylinder	998cc	Five-Speed
KZ1000 Ltd	Four-cylinder	998cc	Five-Speed
KZ1000-A (Shaft drive)	Four-cylinder	998cc	Five-Speed
KZ1000-J	Four-cylinder	998cc	Five-Speed
KZ1000R (Eddie Lawson Replica)	Four-cylinder	998cc	Five-Speed
KZ1100-A	Four-cylinder	1090cc	Five-Speed
GPz1100	Four-cylinder	1090cc	Five-Speed
KZ1300-A3	Six-cylinder	1286cc	Five-Speed

KAWASAKI

1983

Sporting a colorful red, black and silver paint scheme, the GPz550 delivered on its promise to be a sport bike despite its smaller size.
Armand Ciabattari

The 1983 model year was to be a busy time for Kawasaki with the upgrades of several models and the additions of many others. The majority of the transformation was at or near the top end of the line, but even the smaller machines grew some fresh wings.

Joining the fairly new GPz clan was the 305. A higher performance version of the same 306cc inline-four was at the heart of the mini GPz along with the new Uni-Trak rear suspension. Swoopier bodywork, revised graphics and a small bikini fairing finished off the entry level sport bike, bringing the total number of GPz models to four in 1983.

In the middle of the pack, numerous additions were seen in the 550cc models too. A 550 Spectre was added to the bunch, and it carried many of the same features found on the 750 and 1100 versions of the same. These cruiser models wore two-tone paint on their fuel tanks along with alloy wheels. The two-place saddles were deeply sculpted to work better with the buckhorn handlebars that reached back to greet the rider's hands. Truncated exhaust mufflers were another sign of the Spectre and each variation carried them in style.

Only one version of the KZ650 was sold for 1983, and it was the budget-priced CSR model that embodied features of the Custom and Standard editions while carrying a lower sticker price.

The GPz550 was also improved when Kawasaki grafted the single shock Uni-Trak to the rear end of the chassis. Styling on the 550 remained the same with the café fairing and red paint, trimmed with blue and white stripes.

The 750 and 1100 GPz models saw extensive changes implemented, making them better than the examples they replaced. Kawasaki's Uni-Trak suspension was installed on new chassis for both of the bigger GPz models along with anti-dive braking on the front hoops. Three-spoke alloy rims carried the wider rubber on both bikes, adding control and handling to the already competent line. On top of the new chassis and running gear was a sleeker, frame-mounted sport fairing. The 750 and 1100 carried this bit of aerodynamic aid while the 305 and 550 GPz maintained the bikini style windscreen.

Shapely fuel tanks swept into sleek side covers that led the eye to the revised tail sections. The GPz550 was virtually identical to the 1982 model save for the new stripes applied to the bodywork.

Making its debut for Kawasaki as a 1983 model was the lightning-quick 750 Turbo. By adding a turbocharger to an already potent package of handling and speed, the Turbo bested all comers. Carrying a weight of just over 500 lbs., this two-wheeled missile quickly shot to the top of the performance charts.

Sadly, the insurance industry had already begun putting the screws to the blown bikes in general, and being a late entry to the field, the Kawasaki Turbo was not long for this world.

In the 1000c category, only one model remained for 1983. The screaming green KZ1000R was back for a second year and now sported adjustable forks and shocks with revised gauges. This would mark the final year of the ELR, leaving nothing to fill its brightly colored shoes.

Another attempt at selling a fully equipped KZ1300 was made for 1983 as the six-cylinder monster continued to be the flagship for the brand.

The blacked-out engine and exhaust made for a nice contrast to the screaming red paint on the bodywork.

Armand Ciabattari

1983 KAWASAKI

Model	Engine	Displacement	Transmission
AR80	Single cylinder	78cc	Six-Speed
KE100-A10	Single cylinder	100cc	Five-Speed
KE125-A8	Single cylinder	125cc	Six-Speed
KZ250 CSR	Single cylinder	246cc	Five-Speed
KL250-A4	Single cylinder	250cc	Five-Speed
GPz305 (First year of Uni-Trak)	Two-cylinder	306cc	Six-Speed
KZ305A CSR	Two-cylinder	306cc	Six-Speed
KZ440-A2 Ltd	Two-cylinder	443cc	Six-Speed
KZ440-B2	Two-cylinder	443cc	Six-Speed
KZ440-D4	Two-cylinder	443cc	Six-Speed Belt Drive
KZ550-A2	Four-cylinder	553cc	Six-Speed
KZ550-C2 Ltd	Four-cylinder	553cc	Six-Speed
KZ550 Shaft Drive Spectre	Four-cylinder	553cc	Six-Speed
GPz550 Uni-Trak	Four-cylinder	553cc	Six-Speed
KZ650 CSR	Four-cylinder	652cc	Five-Speed
GPz750 Uni-Trak	Four-cylinder	738cc	Five-Speed
KZ750-E2	Four-cylinder	738cc	Five-Speed
KZ750-H4 Ltd	Four-cylinder	738cc	Five-Speed
KZ750 Shaft Drive Spectre	Four-cylinder	738cc	Five-Speed
KZ750 Turbo	Four-cylinder	738cc	Five-Speed
GPz1100 Uni-Trak	Four-cylinder	1090cc	Five-Speed
KZ1000R Eddie Lawson Replica	Four-cylinder	998cc	Five-Speed
KZ1100-A	Four-cylinder	1090cc	Five-Speed
KZ1100 Shaft Drive Spectre	Four-cylinder	1090cc	Five-Speed
KZ1300	Six-cylinder	1286cc	Five-Speed
KZ1300 (Fuel-Injected Touring)	Six-cylinder	1286cc	Five-Speed

KAWASAKI

1984

STANDARD CATALOG OF ® JAPANESE Motorcycles

The new Ninja cut a sleek profile and was treated to a unique red and graphite paint scheme.

Keith Olliges

Kawasaki would experience a year of drastic changes in 1984, along with the other Japanese makers, as they were forced to trim some displacement to meet with governmental tariffs. Kawasaki also introduced a brand new model that would set the stage for sport bikes to come.

A certain Milwaukee builder of motorcycles was claiming they were experiencing unfair competition from the Japanese builders, and that there needed to be a change. A tariff on motorcycles over 750cc was signed into law. In order to get around the new law, all four makers brought out models powered by 700cc motors.

With the 750cc class being the most popular, it would have been too expensive to pay the fine on each bike in that engine category, so the smaller displacement kept them legal and popular. The 1984 model year was the debut for the "tariff beaters." The entire scenario would be over by 1986.

Still perched at the top of the heap was the mighty KZ1300 Voyager. The inline-six engine was still fuel injected and now had a switch that allowed the rider to choose a lean mode, saving fuel in the process. At 840 lbs. before fuel and fluids, it was by far the heaviest touring machine on the market, but was packed with features for comfort and convenience.

Kawasaki's family of GPz models returned in the 305, 550, 750 and 1100 configurations. Having been improved in 1983, most were carried over with few changes. Only the 550 variant received fresher bodywork and a frame-mounted fairing to match the 750 and 1100s. Performance of the 554cc engine was also enhanced with quarter-mile runs attained in the mid 12-second range.

The 750 Turbo model was also back in 1984,

and was the last example of a blown bike on the market. Honda, Suzuki and Yamaha had all produced puffer bikes in the two previous years, but pulled them from the shelves as the insurance industry priced them out of existence.

Left as the only turbo machine sold in 1984, the powerful Kawasaki sat alone in the record books.

With the planned departure of the Turbo imminent, Kawasaki rolled out a new model for 1984 and set the stage for a long line of future product. The Ninja 900 carried a 908cc inline-four engine in its frame and was fuel injected. The Ninja's motor was also liquid cooled and more compact. The overall dimensions of the Ninja were condensed and helped to blast it into record speeds. While many others were spending their days working on the 1000cc motorcycles, the Ninja was smaller, faster and better equipped than some of the larger models on the market.

Kawasaki took their successful 750 format and trimmed it to 694cc to create the return of the KZ700 in 1984. Designed to beat the tariff, the KZ700 was probably 99 percent of the machine it was forced to replace, even while staying within the boundaries. Another entry in the tariff-beater class was the KZ700 Limited model.

Still packed with stylish features and rolling on re-styled alloy hoops, the Limited was a terrific choice among the growing members of the cruiser class.

The KE100 carried on as Kawasaki's smallest model. The tiny KE100 was offered as a dual-purpose motorcycle, and was fitted with attributes for both on- and off-road riding. A bigger KL600 was also introduced, serving the same crowd as the KE100, but with 500cc more displacement and improved amenities.

The biggest of the GPz models was still the 1100, and it wore silver paint with blue and red stripes.

Brad Powell Collection

1984 KAWASAKI

Model	Engine	Displacement	Transmission
KE100-B3	Single cylinder	100cc	Five-Speed
GPz305 First year/Uni-Trak	Two-cylinder	306cc	Six-Speed
KZ305A CSR	Two-cylinder	306cc	Six-Speed
KZ440-A3 Ltd	Two-cylinder	443cc	Six-Speed
KZ440-B2	Two-cylinder	443cc	Six-Speed
KZ440-D4 Belt Drive	Two-cylinder	443cc	Six-Speed
KZ550-A2	Four-cylinder	553cc	Six-Speed
KZ550-C3 Ltd	Four-cylinder	553cc	Six-Speed
GPz550	Four-cylinder	553cc	Six-Speed
KL600-A1 (Dual purpose machine)	Single cylinder	564cc	Five-Speed
KZ700	Four-cylinder	694cc	Five-Speed
KZ700 Ltd	Four-cylinder	694cc	Five-Speed
GPz750 Uni-Trak	Four-cylinder	738cc	Five-Speed
KZ750 Turbo	Four-cylinder	738cc	Five-Speed
Ninja 900 (16-inch front tire)	Four-cylinder	908cc	Six-Speed
GPz1100 Uni-Trak	Four-cylinder	1090cc	Five-Speed
KZ1100-A	Four-cylinder	1090cc	Five-Speed
KZ1100 Ltd	Four-cylinder	1090cc	Five-Speed
KZ1300 (Fuel-Injected Touring)	Six-cylinder	1286cc	Five-Speed

KAWASAKI

1985

STANDARD CATALOG OF ® JAPANESE Motorcycles

Back for another of class dominating fun, the 900 Ninja continued to turn heads and low quarter mile times.

Chris Bednas

Kawasaki had six new faces thrown into the mix for 1985. Taking the KL600 platform and shrinking it down to size, the KL250 was delivered to satisfy the needs of the dual-purpose rider who wished for something smaller. The KL250 weighed a scant 258 lbs. and had a saddle height that was about one-half inch closer to the ground. Plenty of ground clearance for rugged terrain and all the lighting required by law for street use, the KL models served two masters.

The GPz305 had been Kawasaki's way of luring first time riders into the fold, but the sales were not strong. In 1985, the 454 Limited was introduced with hopes of being a starting point for new riders. Powered by a 454cc, two-cylinder mill, the newest Limited also featured liquid cooling and a six-speed gearbox. A final belt drive and front disc brake completed the package.

After being improved for 1984, the GPz550 was back with an identical machine in 1985. Even the list price of $2,899 was left the same.

Slotted in just above the little GPz was a new Ninja for 1985. Its slippery bodywork helped to move the 600 Ninja through the air cleanly as the 592cc, inline-four engine produced better than average power. Feeding the output into a six-speed gearbox allowed the rider to keep the ZX600 in the proper RPM range and a trio of disc brakes slowed the 446-lb. motorcycle efficiently. A price of $3,299 was all it took to take the 1985 ZX600 Ninja home. It provided a high degree of performance for a low entry fee.

Taking up the reins in the mid-range cruiser class was the new ZN700 Ltd. The 694cc mill was used in other Kawasakis, but the new ZN employed shaft drive and great styling to carry the theme. Alloy rims and three disc brakes provided looks and stopping power.

Another cruiser in the 700cc arena was the all new VN700 Vulcan that carried a V-twin engine, a first for Kawasaki. The liquid-cooled engine displaced 699cc and shifted through a five-speed gearbox. Two disc brakes on the front and a drum on the rear slowed the 483 lb. Vulcan with confidence. A total of 3.6 gallons of fuel could be carried in the teardrop tank.

Sport bikes did not go without notice for the 1985 model year, and the GPz750 now featured a more radical front fairing and lower belly pan. The ZX750 Turbo was also back and was the last remaining turbo bike sold at that time.

The others had caved to insurance industry pressure but the lightning-fast 750 from Kawasaki continued on. The ZX900 Ninja was also back in the catalog and was staged to become Kawasaki's best seller for a second year running. The 94 horsepower and crisp styling only added to the terrific handling and competence of the big Ninja.

Joining the newfound class of "power cruiser," Kawasaki rolled out the ZL900 Eliminator for 1985. Yamaha's V-Max may have been the first to create this genre, but the ZL900 fell right in line with its power and drag bike styling.

The extended wheelbase, fat rear tire and low mounted handlebars gave the Eliminator an aggressive stance, but that's just what buyers of these machines were after. The 908cc engine provided the output that kept the ZL's numbers in line with its looks.

Rounding out the 1985 models were the ZN1100 Limited and ZN1300 Voyager. Both models were mostly carry-overs from the previous year. The simplicity of the ZN1100 was a true contrast to the electronic complexity of the big bagger that included cruise-control and an on-board air compressor to alter ride height as needed.

The profile of the Eliminator was long and low as Kawasaki intended the bike to mimic a drag bike in street clothing.

Ray Landy

1985 KAWASAKI

Model	Engine	Displacement	Transmission
KL250 (Dual Purpose)	Single cylinder	249cc	Six-Speed
454 Ltd	Two-cylinder	454cc	Six-Speed
GPz550	Four-cylinder	553cc	Six-Speed
KL600-A1 (Dual Purpose)	Single cylinder	564cc	Five-Speed
Z600 Ninja	Four-cylinder	600cc	Six-Speed
KZ700 Ltd	Four-cylinder	694cc	Five-Speed
VN700 Vulcan	V-Twin	699cc	Five-Speed
GPz750 Uni-Trak	Four-cylinder	738cc	Five-Speed
KZ750 Turbo	Four-cylinder	738cc	Five-Speed
Ninja 900 (16-inch front tire)	Four-cylinder	908cc	Five-Speed
ZL900 Eliminator	Four-cylinder	908cc	Six-Speed
ZN1100 Ltd	Four-cylinder	1089cc	Five-Speed
ZN1300 (Fuel-Injected Touring)	Six-cylinder	1286cc	Five-Speed

KAWASAKI

1986

STANDARD CATALOG OF JAPANESE Motorcycles

Street bikes have never sunk so low.

Kick a leg over Kawasaki's long, low, V-Twin Vulcan. Ease down into the saddle, kick back and let it take you on a V cruise.

Prowl the drive-ins. Haunt the stop lights. And fear no evil from any bike that rides through the valley. For Vulcan is with you.

Vulcan takes to the streets like a panther takes to jungle. With stealth. Grace. And a cool confidence born of its fitness to survive.

The beast growls with anticipation. Big pistons eager to unleash big torque. A full 750cc of liquid-cooled power ready to pounce. Eight valves. Double overhead cams. Twin plugs.

Vulcan has shaft drive and hydraulic valve lash adjusters for low maintenance. And air shocks and air-assisted forks for stalking smoothly.

The way to a city's heart is through its streets. So take the low road on Vulcan. It's an incredible high.

Kawasaki
Let the good times roll.

Always wear a helmet and appropriate apparel. Call 1-800-447-4700 for the Motorcycle Safety Foundation beginner or expert course near you. Specifications subject to change without notice. Availability may be limited.

The Kawasaki Vulcan was depicted in a dark and menacing manner in this 1986 magazine ad.

There were new models added to both ends of the Kawasaki spectrum for 1986, broadening the appeal of the brand.

For the novice sport bike fan, a 250cc Ninja was spotted. The twin-cylinder engine fed a six-speed gearbox and breathed through a set of flat-slide CV carburetors. The single-shock Uni-Trak suspension kept the tail end in order along with an alloy wheel and single disc brake. A second alloy wheel up front was also fitted with a single disc brake. Bodywork on the smallest Ninja included a half fairing and flush mounted headlight.

Based on the success of the ZL900 Eliminator and the 600 Ninja, the ZL600 was the best of both worlds. Using the potent motor of the Ninja and adding a shaft drive placed the reduced Eliminator at the head of middleweight power cruiser class. More midrange power was gained by using carburetors that were 2mm smaller than the ones on the Z600 Ninja.

Moving upscale, two new names were added to the 1000cc yearbook as the ZG1000 and ZX1000R Ninja appeared as 1986 models. The ZG was a sport touring machine complete with a full fairing, saddle bags and more precise handling than the ultra baggers of the day.

Shaft drive kept things smooth and quiet. The ZX1000R Ninja made an immediate impression on the media due to its immense power and terrific balance. A 997cc, inline-four engine was liquid-cooled and fed through a set of Keihin CVK36mm carbs.

A six-speed gearbox gave the rider plenty of choices as he carved through the canyons. The sleek, full-coverage bodywork added to the bullet mystique of the "Master Ninja", and was sold in your choice of Ebony with Pearl, Cosmic Gray or Firecracker Red with Metallic Black paint.

Slotted in just below the behemoth ZN1300 was the all-new ZG1200 XII Voyager. Although it shared the Voyager name with the inline-six model, it was not about to share any of the limelight. The new machine was a svelte shadow of the 1,300cc beast and would begin to put pressure on the elder touring machine as soon as it was released.

The ZG1200 was loaded with every modern convenience and with a fuel storage tank that lived beneath the seat, and the center of gravity was much lower, making for nimbler handling at slow speeds. This class of motorcycle was getting crowded as Honda's Gold Wing continued to mature and Yamaha introduced their own flavor of long distance ride in the super touring market.

1986 KAWASAKI

Model	Engine	Displacement	Transmission
KL250 Dual Purpose	Single cylinder	249cc	Six-Speed
Z250 Ninja	Two-cylinder	248cc	Six-Speed
454 Ltd	Two-cylinder	454cc	Six-Speed
KL600-A1 (Dual Purpose)	Single cylinder	564cc	Five-Speed
Z600 Ninja	Four-cylinder	592cc	Six-Speed
ZL600 (Shaft Drive Eliminator)	Four-cylinder	592cc	Six-speed
KZ700 Ltd	Four-cylinder	694cc	Five-Speed
VN700 Vulcan	V-twin	699cc	Five-Speed
GPz750 Uni-Trak	Four-cylinder	738cc	Five-Speed
KZ750 Turbo	Four-cylinder	738cc	Five-Speed
Ninja 900 (16-inch front tire)	Four-cylinder	908cc	Five-Speed
ZL900 Eliminator	Four-cylinder	908cc	Six-Speed
ZG1000 Concours	Four-cylinder	997cc	Six-Speed
ZX1000R Ninja	Four-cylinder	997cc	Six-Speed
ZN1100 Ltd	Four-cylinder	1089cc	Five-Speed
ZG1200 XII Voyager XII	Four-cylinder	1196cc	Five-Speed
ZN1300 (Fuel-Injected Touring)	Six-cylinder	1286cc	Five-Speed

1987

For 1987, most of the changes to the Kawasaki line would be subtle, but additions continued to fall into place, taking up the spots left by departing machines.

Continuing efforts to attract first-time buyers came in the shape of the KZ305. Taking the now popular cruiser styling and installing a 306cc two-cylinder engine seemed to make sense. Wire wheels and a lack of doo-dads kept the price to within easy access at $1,899. The 454 Limited was still an option for the buyer who sought a bit more from his cruiser and carried on the reputation as solid choice for many levels of rider. The muscle bound ZL600 was also a repeat for 1987 and was unchanged from the debut 1986 model.

KAWASAKI STANDARD CATALOG OF JAPANESE Motorcycles

And only the hungry survive.

Hungry bikes prowl where others fear to tread. So they have to be well equipped to handle themselves. This fearsome foursome is.

The '87 KZ305. Priced and sized for entry level. But it's larger than the 250's and hot enough to give 400's fits.

The 454 LTD. A liquid-cooled, eight-valve sophisticated street stalker. Ready for action.

ZL600. The heart of a superbike, tuned for more bottom end. Liquid-cooled, 16 valves, shaft drive. Basic boulevard brilliance.

The new Vulcan.™ Restyled with a full 750cc. A torquey V-twin with low-end pull. And maintenance-free hydraulic valve lash adjusters. The prince of the city.

If you're ready for some heavy cruising, try the Kawasaki Street Quartet. They play for keeps.

Kawasaki Let the good times roll.

The 1987 Kawasaki KZ-305, 454 Limited, ZL-600 and Vulcan were arrayed in this gritty industrial-looking ad from 1987 captioned "Only the Hungry Survive."

A return of 750cc machines was seen across the board. Kawasaki bumped the Vulcan from 699 to 749cc, but retained the V-twin engine and the distinctive styling of the previous iteration. Making another appearance was the ZL1000, keeping all the same specs as the year before.

The 1500 Vulcan 88 was powered by a 1,470cc V-twin that looked classic but was a fully modern ride. Four-valve heads and hydraulic lash adjusters were found inside the liquid-cooled engine that was mated to a four-speed transmission. Alloy rims and shaft drive were all part of the fun as the Vulcan stormed the cruiser field.

Kawasaki was not about to forgo their sport bike roots. The 250 Ninja returned and continued to offer a great way to enter the world of motorcycling.

Brand new for '87 was the EX500. Although not labeled a Ninja, the EX500 was every bit a sport bike. Using the twin cylinder engine from the 454 Ltd and adding another 44cc to the equation, the 498cc engine was mounted into a perimeter frame. Uni-Trak suspension and 16-inch wheels brought more sporting attitude to the EX and the six-speed gearbox was on tap for flexibility.

The 600 and 1000cc versions of the Ninja were also back for another round, and were joined by a limited edition model of the 600. Using an aluminum frame saved more than 16 lbs. and a dark cloak made the 1,000 copies that came to the USA a hot commodity. The entire package was only $200 more than the base 600 Ninja, adding to the allure.

Offerings in the 750cc sport bike field were reduced with the loss of the GPz and Turbo models. In their stead, Kawasaki finally introduced a 750cc Ninja. The 750R was chock full of Kawasaki technology including a compact, yet very powerful 748cc engine. It quickly rose to the head of the class when compared to other sport bikes. A dry weight of only 430 lbs. was part of the magic, as the 1,000cc Ninja carried almost 100 more lbs. The liter-sized Ninja continued to be one the fastest machines that money could buy.

The dual-purpose arena was joined by the KLR650. Based on the winning Paris to Dakar machine, the KLR had a powerful 651cc engine and street legal lighting all around.

Touring riders still had three Kawasaki models to choose from, including the sporty Concours and the full-blown 1,200 and 1,300cc Voyagers.

Leading the displacement pack was the VN1500 Vulcan. The V-twin machine carried 1,470cc in the frame and featured a shaft drive. Weighing nearly 700 lbs., the Vulcan was not light but fit right in to the market for those seeking a massive V-twin machine.

1987 KAWASAKI

Model	Engine	Displacement	Transmission
KLR250 (Dual Purpose)	Single cylinder	249cc	Six-Speed
Z250 Ninja	Two-cylinder	248cc	Six-Speed
KZ305	Two-cylinder	306cc	Six-Speed
454 Ltd	Two-cylinder	454cc	Six-Speed
EX500	Two-cylinder	498cc	Six-Speed
KLR650 (Dual Purpose)	Single cylinder	651cc	Five-Speed
Z600 Ninja	Four-cylinder	592cc	Six-Speed
Z600RX Ninja (Limited to 1,000 in USA)	Four-cylinder	592cc	Six-Speed
ZL600 Shaft Drive Eliminator	Four-cylinder	592cc	Six-Speed
VN750 Vulcan	V-twin	749cc	Five-Speed
Z750 Ninja Uni-Trak	Four-cylinder	248cc	Six-Speed
ZL1000 Eliminator	Four-cylinder	997cc	Six-Speed
ZG1000 Concours	Four-cylinder	997cc	Six-Speed
ZX1000R Ninja	Four-cylinder	997cc	Six-Speed
ZN1100 Ltd	Four-cylinder	1089cc	Five-Speed
ZG1200 XII Voyager XII	Four-cylinder	1196cc	Five-Speed
ZN1300 (Fuel-Injected Touring)	Six-cylinder	1286cc	Five-Speed
VN1500 Vulcan	V-twin	1470cc	Four-Speed

KAWASAKI

1988

STANDARD CATALOG OF JAPANESE Motorcycles

Returning for 1988, but wearing some fresh skin, was the ZX-10, previously known as the 1000R Ninja.

Atomic Power & Steam

Another year of mostly trivial alterations was seen by Kawasaki for 1988 as the previous year's mix seemed to fill most of the gaps in the existing market. It would mark the final year for one model with a few name changes applied to a few others, leaving 99 percent of the catalog the same.

The GPX250R Ninja was one of the machines now wearing new nomenclature along with a few tweaks to its previous composition. The 600cc version of the same was also sporting new trim and the revised model name.

The ZL1000 Eliminator was in its last year as the muscle bike class failed to get any traction in the market. Only Yamaha's V-Max would carry on the tradition as buyer's demands seemed to shift towards the cruiser segment with growing intensity.

The ZX1000R Ninja was revised to become the ZX-10 in 1988 and carried the tradition of Kawasaki's most super bike to the head of the class.

1988 KAWASAKI

Model	Engine	Displacement	Transmission
KLR250	Single cylinder	249cc	Six-Speed
GPX250R Ninja	Two-cylinder	248cc	Six-Speed
KZ305	Two-cylinder	306cc	Six-Speed
454 Ltd	Two-cylinder	454cc	Six-Speed
EX500	Two-cylinder	498cc	Six-Speed
KLR650 (Dual Purpose)	Single cylinder	651cc	Five-Speed
Z600 Ninja	Four-cylinder	592cc	Six-Speed
GPX600R Ninja	Four-cylinder	592cc	Six-Speed
VN750 Vulcan	V-twin	749cc	Five-Speed
750 Ninja Uni-Trak	Four-cylinder	748cc	Six-Speed
ZL1000 Eliminator	Four-cylinder	997cc	Six-Speed
ZG1000 Concours	Four-cylinder	997cc	Six-Speed
ZX10 Ninja	Four-cylinder	997cc	Six-Speed
ZN1100 Ltd	Four-cylinder	1089cc	Five-Speed
ZG1200 XII Voyager XII	Four-cylinder	1196cc	Five-Speed
ZN1300 (Fuel-Injected Touring)	Six-cylinder	1286cc	Five-Speed
VN1500 Vulcan	V-twin	1470cc	Four-Speed

KAWASAKI 1989

Perhaps the biggest news for 1989 was the debut of the Kawasaki ZX-7. By applying racing technology to the already popular 750cc class, the ZX-7 delivered a new level of performance and handling to the buyer.

The 748cc inline-four engine was rated at 107 hp when spinning at 10,500 rpm. Four Keihin CVK-D36 carburetors doled out the fuel and air mix and a curb weight of 453 lbs. made for spirited riding. Both front and rear wheels were 17 inches in diameter with a front tire of 120/70 and a rear of 170/60. Final drive was via chain with a 46-tooth rear sprocket.

Colorful "Team Green" graphics and paint made the new ZX-7 stand out even when at rest, adding to the allure of the sporting machine.

The bigger ZX-10 was back for another round but little changed from the 1988 debut version. The rumored ZX-11 was still a no-show for 1989, but eager speculators would not have much longer to wait.

The 250 and 500cc versions of the Ninja soldiered on and remained appealing to buyers of smaller, yet still potent sport bikes.

The balance of the 1989 lineup was a repeat of 1988 but Kawasaki had several fresh models in the wings, waiting for their chance to outshine the competition.

1989 KAWASAKI

Model	Engine	Displacement	Transmission
EL250 Eliminator	Two-cylinder	248cc	Six-Speed
KLR250 Dual Purpose	Single cylinder	249cc	Six-Speed
EX250R Ninja	Two-cylinder	248cc	Six-Speed
454 Ltd	Two-cylinder	454cc	Six-Speed
EX500	Two-cylinder	498cc	Six-Speed
KLR650 Dual Purpose	Single cylinder	651cc	Five-Speed
X600C2 Ninja	Four-cylinder	592cc	Six-Speed
VN750 Vulcan	V-twin	749cc	Five-Speed
Z750 Ninja Uni-Trak	Four-cylinder	748cc	Six-Speed
ZX-7	Four-cylinder	748cc	Six-Speed
ZG1000 Concours	Four cylinder	997cc	Six-Speed
ZX10 Ninja	Four-cylinder	997cc	Six-Speed
ZN1100 Ltd	Four-cylinder	1089cc	Five-Speed
ZG1200 XII Voyager XII	Four-cylinder	1196cc	Five-Speed
VN1500 Vulcan	V-twin	1470cc	Four-Speed

KAWASAKI
1990

The ZG1000 Concours was unchanged for 1990 but continued to be a popular choice of sport touring fans. Chris Bednas

The 1990 model year would prove to be interesting for Kawasaki as a few new names were added to the menu. Most of the catalog would simply be a repeat of the previous year, but changes could be found throughout.

Both versions of the Vulcan 1500 returned to maintain Kawasaki's presence in the heavy weight cruiser division. The smaller 750 Vulcan was also retained for the buyer who desired something a bit smaller. First introduced in the late 1980s, the 454 Limited was replaced by the slightly larger Vulcan 500. The cruiser market was hot, but most of Kawasaki's efforts were turned towards the Ninja products.

The big ZG1200 Voyager was offered in an unusual shade of violet for 1990 but was otherwise a carryover model. The ZG1000 Concours was also still listed with no changes.

The Ninja cast grew by one for 1990 and it was

a major addition. For the buyer who wanted more than the ZX-10 could deliver, the ZX-11 rolled out for 1990. A liquid-cooled 1,052cc engine was fed by 40mm carbs and exhaled through a four-into-one-into-two exhaust system.

An alloy perimeter chassis held the blend together and a six-speed gearbox was again included in the mix. A pair of floating rotors on the front hoop was joined by a 250mm disc on the rear for ultra-quick stops. With nearly 150 hp available, the 503-lb. ZX-11 was quick. An MSRP of $7,599 would hasten the pace at which it left dealer's showrooms too.

The ZX-7 returned and was lighter, faster and one step closer to being a true race bike for the street. Part of this racing influence was due to the increased use of bits taken from Kawasaki's racing parts bin. The application of alloy components saved five pounds in the chassis alone, helping to add to the nimble handling.

ZX-6 improvements were also impressive and pushed the middleweight Ninja closer to the top of the heap. A slightly tamer ZX600 Ninja was still sold alongside the racier ZX-6 providing greater variety to the fan base.

Another new entrant was the EN500 Vulcan. Taking the cruiser equation and applying a twin cylinder engine from the EX500, the baby Vulcan filled a void in the category. Long and low, the latest Vulcan carried a retail tag of $3,699 in its debut year.

The 250cc Eliminator was removed from the family as sales of the not so muscular muscle bike had waned to unsustainable levels.

Introducing a standard model for 1990, the 550 Zephyr would satisfy the buyer wanting a great starter bike. The inline-four engine displaced 553cc and was mounted into a traditional chassis with a sleek fuel tank and sweeping side panels. The 392 lb. curb weight added to the appeal of the middleweight "naked" bike.

The Vulcan 1500SE would bow out after the 1990 model year, leaving only the standard version behind.

1990 KAWASAKI

Model	Engine	Displacement	Transmission
KL250D7 Dual Purpose	Single cylinder	249cc	Six-Speed
EX250F4 Ninja	Two-cylinder	248cc	Six-Speed
EN500 Vulcan (Replacement for 454 Ltd.)	Two-cylinder	498cc	Six-Speed
EX500	Two-cylinder	498cc	Six-Speed
ZR550B Zephyr (New for 1990)	Four-cylinder	553cc	Five-Speed
KL650A4 (Dual Purpose)	Single cylinder	651cc	Five-Speed
ZX600 Ninja	Four-cylinder	592cc	Six-Speed
ZX-6 Ninja	Four-cylinder	592cc	Six-Speed
VN750 Vulcan	V-twin	749cc	Five-Speed
ZX750 Ninja Uni-Trak	Four-cylinder	748cc	Six-Speed
ZX-7 Ninja	Four-cylinder	748cc	Six-Speed
ZG1000 Concours	Four-cylinder	996cc	Six-Speed
ZX10 Ninja	Four-cylinder	997cc	Six-Speed
ZX11 Ninja (New for 1990)	Four-cylinder	1052cc	Six-Speed
ZG1200 XII Voyager XII	Four-cylinder	1196cc	Five-Speed
VN1500 Vulcan	V-twin	1470cc	Four-Speed

KAWASAKI

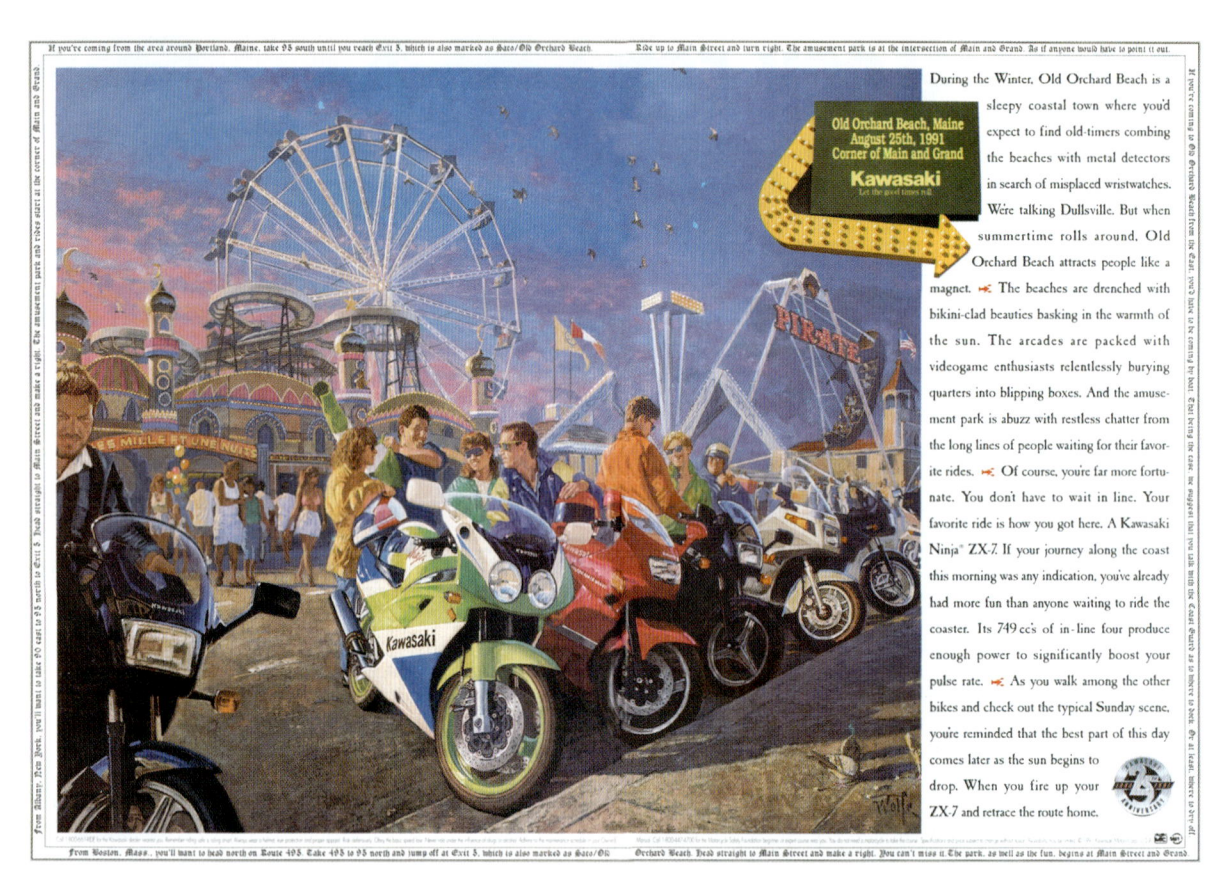

1991

STANDARD CATALOG OF JAPANESE Motorcycles

Kawasaki used this festive ad to show off its 25th anniversary in 1991.

Since the appearance of the 1984 Ninja, the name had become synonymous with sporting motorcycles from Kawasaki. Having set the stage with the 900 Ninja, new models continued to roll off the assembly line, each with a more capable package of handling and performance. The ZX-7 was first sold as a 1989 model, then improved for 1990. Taking the equation one step further, the ZX-7R made its debut for 1991.

The 7R weighed nearly 20 lbs. less than the ZX-7 and produced an additional 10 hp. Magazine reviews saw quarter-mile times as low as 11 seconds—at that time a class-leading number. A calculated top speed of 163 mph in sixth gear was illustrated in period articles as well.

This level of performance did not come cheaply, and the ZX-7R sold for $2,000 more than the ZX-7. For those who had to have the latest and best 750 class machine available, the cost was no barrier.

In its second year of sale, the ZX-11 continued to claim the crown in the liter bike category.

Joining the 550 Zephyr for 1991 was a larger 750 version. Honda still offered their Nighthawk in 250 and 750 guises, so the 750 Zephyr gave Kawasaki buyers an option in the standard bike segment.

The new Zephyr clocked in at 441 lbs. when serviced, putting it on par with the other machines in its class. The larger Zephyr was cloaked in similar bodywork as the 550 version and delivered style and confidence in an uncluttered format. Model year 1991 would be the final year for the 550 Zephyr as a majority of buyers flocked to the more powerful 750 offerings.

The remaining 1991 lineup was mostly the same as the previous year with the exception of minor upgrades and altered hues.

1991 KAWASAKI

Model	Engine	Displacement	Transmission
KL250D7 Dual Purpose	Single cylinder	249cc	Six-Speed
EX250F4 Ninja	Two-cylinder	248cc	Six-Speed
EX500	Two-cylinder	498cc	Six-Speed
EN500 Vulcan (Belt Drive)	Two-cylinder	498cc	Six-Speed
ZR550B Zephyr	Four-cylinder	553cc	Five-Speed
KL650A4 Dual Purpose	Single cylinder	651cc	Five-Speed
ZX600 Ninja	Four-cylinder	592cc	Six-Speed
ZX-6 Ninja	Four-cylinder	592cc	Six-Speed
VN750 Vulcan	V-twin	749cc	Five-Speed
ZR750C Zephyr (New for 1991)	Four-cylinder	738cc	Five-Speed
ZX-7 Ninja	Four-cylinder	748cc	Six-Speed
ZX-7R (New for 1991)	Four-cylinder	749cc	Six-Speed
ZG1000 Concours	Four-cylinder	996cc	Six-Speed
ZX11 Ninja	Four-cylinder	1052cc	Six-Speed
ZG1200 XII Voyager XII	Four-cylinder	1196cc	Five-Speed
VN1500 Vulcan	V-twin	1470cc	Four-Speed

1992

Things would remain on an even keel for the 1992 Kawasaki lineup, with only a few players being affected by the new calendar year.

One such machine was the 250 Ninja that would take a brief vacation from the rest of the family.

The 750 Zephyr, introduced as a 1991 model, would see its final year of sales in 1992. No replacement for the middleweight standard would appear for many years although a larger mount would debut in 1993.

Touring models included the Concours and Voyager with no additions or revisions listed.

The ZX-7R continued to be a dominant player in that segment as other manufacturers did their best to build something comparable. The combination of lighter weight and immense power was not an easy summit to climb, as Kawasaki learned when creating the 7R.

1992 KAWASAKI

Model	Engine	Displacement	Transmission
KL250D7 (Dual Purpose)	Single cylinder	249cc	Six-Speed
EN500 Vulcan	Two-cylinder	498cc	Six-Speed
EX500	Two-cylinder	498cc	Six-Speed
KL650A4 (Dual Purpose)	Single cylinder	651cc	Five-Speed
ZX600 Ninja	Four-cylinder	592cc	Six-Speed
ZX-6 Ninja	Four-cylinder	592cc	Six-Speed
VN750 Vulcan	V-twin	749cc	Five-Speed
ZR750C Zephyr (Final year of sale)	Four-cylinder	738cc	Five-Speed
ZX-7 Ninja	Four-cylinder	748cc	Six-Speed
ZX-7R	Four-cylinder	749cc	Six-Speed
ZG1000 Concours	Four-cylinder	996cc	Six-Speed
ZX11 Ninja	Four-cylinder	1052cc	Six-Speed
ZG1200 XII Voyager XII	Four-cylinder	1196cc	Five-Speed
VN1500 Vulcan	V-twin	1470cc	Four-Speed

KAWASAKI

1993

With the performance genre being Kawasaki's specialty, they turned up the heat on three of their already potent sport bikes in an effort to distance themselves further from the competition.

In the middleweight class, the ZX600 was joined by the ZX600-E1, which delivered enhanced power and handling. The chassis of the E1 was formed using new technology that resulted in a design that was both stronger and lighter than before. The swing arm and sub frame were formed using a hollow-cast process making them more effective while still weighing less. Dual Ram Air Induction was employed on the smaller 600. The 592cc engine was also re-engineered to produce more power with no sacrifice.

The supremacy of the ZX-7R was enhanced further with the addition of the same casting techniques used to create the ZX600-E1. The new frame weighed less but provided more rigidity. Combined with the added power of the engine's improvements meant that amazing leaps were made. Dual Ram Air Induction also found its way into the 7R equation, forcing more air into the engine and delivering even more power. The ZX11 was joined by an even faster ZX1100-D1. It added a second Ram Air opening, the same Dual Ram Air Induction was found on the big Ninja. The added inlet boosted horsepower by four on the bike. Reductions in weight were gained by using the hollow casting process found on the 600 and 750cc variants. The newly formed swing arm had a claimed increase in torsional rigidity of 58 percent. By wrapping all of this technology in a more slippery set of bodywork, speeds and jealous stares were increased.

A new version of the Vulcan 750 called the V-Force Tour Pak set the existing model into a touring configuration with the use of a full fairing, hard-sided saddlebags and floorboards in place of foot pegs. As a bonus, the hardware could be easily mounted to existing machines.

The Concours did not receive any mechanical upgrades for '93 but did get black paint highlighted by gold details. The Voyager II was completely unaltered for the latest year and was still considered a great buy in the full-fledged touring market.

Taking the place of the now departed Zephyr models, Kawasaki released the ZR1100 to satisfy the standard bike audience. Powered by an air-cooled 1062cc, inline-four engine, the ZR1100 was a super bike sans the fancy fairing. The sim-

1993 KAWASAKI

Model	Engine	Displacement	Transmission
EX250F4 Ninja (Returning model)	Two cylinder	248cc	Six-Speed
KL250D7 (Dual Purpose)	Single cylinder	249cc	Six-Speed
EN500 Vulcan	Two-cylinder	498cc	Six-Speed
EX500 Ninja	Two-cylinder	498cc	Six-Speed
KL650A4 (Dual Purpose)	Single cylinder	651cc	Five-Speed
ZX600 Ninja	Four-cylinder	592cc	Six-Speed
ZX600E1 (New for 1993)	Four-cylinder	592cc	Six-Speed
ZX-6 Ninja	Four-cylinder	592cc	Six-Speed
VN750 Vulcan	V-twin	749cc	Five-Speed
VN750 V-Force Vulcan Tour Pak	V-twin	749cc	Five-Speed
ZX-7 Ninja	Four- cylinder	748cc	Six-Speed
ZX-7R Ninja	Four-cylinder	749cc	Six-Speed
ZG1000 Concours	Four-cylinder	996cc	Six-Speed
ZR1100 (New for 1993)	Four-cylinder	1062cc	Five-Speed
ZX11 Ninja (New for 1993)	Four-cylinder	1052cc	Six-Speed
ZG1200 XII Voyager XII	Four-cylinder	1196cc	Five-Speed
VN1500 Vulcan	V-twin	1470cc	Four-Speed

plicity of the design and capability of the engine delivered an unbeatable package.

A threesome of disc brakes helped to slow the 584-lb. machine and an o-ring chain delivered the energy to the rear wheel. Swirling five-spoke cast wheels at both ends added some style to the mostly unadorned 1100.

A chrome four-into-two exhaust was installed to handle the departing fumes and a pair of gauges kept the rider informed as to his progress and rate of speed. A fuel gauge was nested between the primary instruments.

Both brake and clutch levers could be adjusted to better fit the hands of the rider bringing a new level of function to a naked bike. The two-person saddle was nearly flat, but dipped in the front allowing for a 31.3-inch height for the pilot. A list price of $6,999 was in line for liter machines of the day and the ZR provided a lot of bang for the buck.

1994

Only one new model was added to the Kawasaki fold in 1994, while one 1993 cycle would fade from view. Their primary focus remained in the sport bike category, but the cruisers continued to appeal to a segment of the buying public.

The ZR1100, first seen as a new 1993 model, was removed from the catalog for 1994. Despite the performance and price of the standard, it failed to live up to Kawasaki's projections and disappeared as the 550 and 750 had the two years previous. The demand for multiple use standard machines had faded as most manufacturers continued to build and sell cycles that fit into more specific niches.

Whether sport, cruiser or touring, people seemed to gravitate to bikes that fit a certain need versus buying one that could fill all requirements although not being perfect at any.

A new model, the ZX-9R, joined the cadre of Kawasaki sport bikes in 1994. By using the improved frame of the 1993 ZX-7R and bolting in a

By joining the lightweight alloy frame of the ZX-7R and a bigger 899cc engine, Kawasaki trumped the competition again with their new ZX-9R.

Kawasaki Motors Corp.

899cc engine, the new mount was born. The vastly more powerful 9R weighed only 32 lbs. more than the 750, delivering a potent punch upon demand. The race bike ergonomics of the 9R were on par with the 7R and provided immediate feedback to changes in input. The 9R was offered in a Team Green color combination or more subtle Candy Wine Red, Ebony and Pearl Gentry Grey.

ZX-7 and ZX-7R models returned for another round and were little changed for 1994. Only two versions of the 600cc Ninja were seen in the ZX-6 and 600R models. The EX500-D1 Ninja was sold with a wide range of updates that included digital electronic ignition and larger diameter fork tubes that provided better damping. A pair of 17-inch wheels were also added and were wrapped with tires of a wider profile.

Styling and wind protection were improved with the installation of a revised frame-mounted half-fairing. Behind the fairing, additional instrumentation greeted the rider along with bars that put the pilot in a racier stance. Pearl Purplish-Black Mica or Candy Wine Red were the 1994 color choices for the 500cc Ninja. The littlest Ninja still carried a 248cc inline twin engine in its flanks and a retail price of $3299. Ebony was the only hue listed for the 1994 version.

The smaller Vulcan 500 returned to the fray again for 1994 with a revised price tag showing $4,399.

1994 KAWASAKI

Model	Engine	Displacement	Transmission
EX250-F8 Ninja	Two-cylinder	248cc	Six-Speed
KL250D7 (Dual Purpose)	Single cylinder	249cc	Six-Speed
EX500 Ninja	Two-cylinder	498cc	Six-Speed
EN500 Vulcan	Two-cylinder	498cc	Six-Speed
KL650A4 Dual Purpose	Single cylinder	651cc	Five-Speed
ZX600 Ninja	Four-cylinder	592cc	Six-Speed
ZX600-E2 Ninja	Four-cylinder	592cc	Six-Speed
VN750 Vulcan	V-twin	749cc	Five-Speed
VN750 V-Force Vulcan Tour Pak	V-twin	749cc	Five-Speed
ZX-7 Ninja	Four-cylinder	748cc	Six-Speed
ZX-7R Ninja	Four-cylinder	749cc	Six-Speed
ZX-9R-B1 (New for 1994)	Four-cylinder	899cc	Six-Speed
ZG1000 Concours	Four-cylinder	996cc	Six-Speed
ZX11 Ninja	Four-cylinder	1052cc	Six-Speed
ZG1200 XII Voyager XII	Four-cylinder	1196cc	Five-Speed
VN1500 Vulcan	V-twin	1470cc	Four-Speed

1995

Kawasaki continued their winning ways for 1995 by having two new models roll onto the showroom floors. With the cruiser and sport bike segments claiming the lion's share of the market, the new models were designed to satisfy demands of those buyers.

Bolstering the model lineup in the cruiser division, the Vulcan 800 delivered a mix of old and new in a slightly larger version of the remaining Vulcan 750. The classic style of the cruiser was embodied in the bigger Vulcan, but a raft of features would set it apart from the other variations being peddled by Kawasaki. Chrome spoke wheels were found under both fenders, providing one of the classic design elements. A ducktail rear fender was similar to those being used on some U.S. built machines and the front fender was slim.

The heart of the new Vulcan was an 805cc liquid-cooled V-twin that featured a large diameter circular air cleaner. A single 36mm Keihin side draft carburetor lurked behind the chrome housing and was assisted by an accelerator pump to ensure smooth delivery of the fuel upon demand. A pair of staggered exhaust tubes lent their own flair to the Vulcan and when combined with the wide fork legs, created a real stir.

With cost of entry being a consideration on the latest Vulcan, final drive was via chain versus the shaft found on the 750 version. This choice, along with several other factors allowed the 800 model to sell for only $600 more than the 750 Vulcan, making an easy selling point for the 1995 edition. A wide range of factory accessories could easily alter your Vulcan from stock to a personal statement and many buyers did just that.

Second in the new model listing for 1995 was the ZX-6R. Following in the footprints of the bigger 750 and 900 examples offered, the ZX-6R took the base model ZX-6 and benefited from lower weight and increased power.

Claiming a dry weight of 401 lbs. for the 6R, that made the ZX-6 29 pounds heavier. By altering the major components of the engine, 16.5 lbs. were shaved.

Revised exhaust, crank, cam drive and gearbox all played a role in the weight savings in that department. Further poundage was trimmed by using a new one-piece frame that was formed from aluminum. Final losses were earned through altered clutch and shifter assemblies. The wheelbase of the 6R was also shorter than the ZX-6 and measured 55.7 inches, which was a bit more than ½-inch less.

All of this technology came at a price, and the lighter ZX-6R carried a price tag that was $800 heavier than the ZX-6. An MSRP of $7,899 was shown for the 1995 ZX-6R, but buyers responded eagerly to the new middleweight sport bike.

The ZX-9R was enhanced with a better gearbox as well, adding more muscle to the big sport model.

1995 KAWASAKI

Model	Engine	Displacement	Transmission
EX250-F8 Ninja	Two-cylinder	248cc	Six-Speed
KL250D7 Dual Purpose	Single cylinder	249cc	Six-Speed
EX500 Ninja	Two-cylinder	498cc	Six-Speed
EN500 Vulcan (Returning model)	Two-cylinder	498cc	Six-Speed
KL650A4 Dual Purpose	Single cylinder	651cc	Five-Speed
ZX600 Ninja	Four-cylinder	592cc	Six-Speed
ZX-6 Ninja	Four-cylinder	599cc	Six-Speed
ZX-6R Ninja (New for 1995)	Four-cylinder	599cc	Six-Speed
VN750 Vulcan	V-twin	749cc	Five-Speed
VN750 V-Force Vulcan Tour Pak	V-twin	749cc	Five-Speed
ZX-7 Ninja	Four-cylinder	748cc	Six-Speed
ZX-7R Ninja	Four-cylinder	749cc	Six-Speed
VN800 Vulcan (New for 1995)	V-twin	805cc	Five-Speed
ZX-9R	Four-cylinder	899cc	Six-Speed
ZG1000 Concours	Four-cylinder	996cc	Six-Speed
ZX11 Ninja	Four-cylinder	1052cc	Six-Speed
ZG1200 XII Voyager XII	Four-cylinder	1196cc	Five-Speed
VN1500 Vulcan	V-twin	1470cc	Four-Speed

KAWASAKI

1996

Kawasaki continued to play with existing models and add new variations of returning machines for 1996 with intentions of cornering the entire market.

Back for a third year was the mighty ZX-9R, included in the open-class market segment that featured the Ducati 916, Honda CBR900RR and Suzuki's GSXR1100. The ZX-9R often rated as one of the more comfortable sport mounts available. Little, if anything, was changed since the '95 models had their gearboxes revised. Few complaints had been registered about the bike, so why mess with what people loved?

Having been pulled from the catalog nearly a decade earlier, the Eliminator 600 was back to deliver its own blend of muscle and design. Low drag bars were teamed with a low saddle height and the potent 592cc engine from the Ninja. Honda and Yamaha sold "muscle" machines in the same era, but their offerings were fitted with V-four engines, making them a different animal than the inline-four powered Eliminator.

Another version of the 800 Vulcan was introduced in 1996, the 800 Vulcan Classic. Fat tires and taller ratios for first and second gear gave the Classic a different feel than the standard model. The same frame was employed but 16-inch rims dropped the seat height to 27.6 inches from the ground.

When fully prepped to ride, the Vulcan 800 Classic weighed nearly 80 lbs. less than the 1500 Vulcan. The 800 Classic offered the smaller rider a terrific option when it came time to bring a cruiser home. A full range of factory custom accessories allowed the buyer to build a machine to meet with his own specific tastes and needs.

A complete redesign was delivered to dealers for 1996. Realizing the appeal of the cycles being built in Milwaukee, Kawasaki set out to build its own version of the iconic Wisconsin-built craft.

A close examination of the 1500 Vulcan's trim showed only three small Kawasaki logos, thus adding to the confusion when viewed from afar. Several additional styling cues were borrowed from the

1996 KAWASAKI

Model	Engine	Displacement	Transmission
EX250-F8 Ninja	Two-cylinder	248cc	Six-Speed
KL250D7 Dual Purpose	Single cylinder	249cc	Six-Speed
EX500 Ninja	Two-cylinder	498cc	Six-Speed
EN500 Vulcan (Final year of sale)	Two-cylinder	498cc	Six-Speed
EN500 Vulcan Ltd. (New Version of Std. Vulcan 500)	Two-cylinder	498cc	Six-Speed
ZL600 Eliminator (Returning Model)	Four-cylinder	592cc	Six-Speed
ZX600 Ninja	Four-cylinder	592cc	Six-Speed
ZX-6 Ninja	Four-cylinder	599cc	Six-Speed
ZX-6R Ninja	Four-cylinder	599cc	Six-Speed
KL650A4 (Dual Purpose)	Single cylinder	651cc	Five-Speed
VN750 Vulcan	V-twin	749cc	Five-Speed
ZX-7R Ninja	Four-cylinder	749cc	Six-Speed
VN800 Vulcan	V-twin	805cc	Five-Speed
VN800 Vulcan Classic (New for 1996)	V-twin	805cc	Five-Speed
ZX-9R	Four-cylinder	899cc	Six-Speed
ZX11 Ninja	Four-cylinder	1052cc	Six-Speed
ZG1200 XII Voyager XII	Four-cylinder	1196cc	Five-Speed
VN1500 Vulcan	V-twin	1470cc	Four-Speed
VN1500 Vulcan Classic (New for 1996)	V-twin	1470cc	Four-Speed
VN1500L Vulcan (New for 1996)	V-twin	1470cc	Four-Speed

competition drawing new buyers to the showrooms. A large diameter nacelle held the speedometer, which was mounted into the top of the tank.

This addition was a close cousin to the method used by Harley, and that was exactly what Kawasaki had in mind. The staggered exhaust pipes furthered the deception although the 1500 Vulcan had a liquid cooled engine nestled in the frame.

When ready to ride, the 1500 Vulcan tipped the scales at 683 lbs. The saddle's height from the tarmac was the same 27.6 inches, as found on the 800 Classic, helping to make the weight more manageable. The 4.2 gallons of fuel could deliver a range of up to 163 miles depending on riding style and conditions. The deeply sculpted seat made a comfortable perch for much longer distances. The 1500L also joined the team for 1996 and provided slightly different ergonomics and styling than the standard 1500 Vulcan.

Pullback bars of the 1500 were replaced with a flat drag style unit and spoke wheels took over where the cast models were found on the standard 1500 Vulcan. In the sport touring class, the ZG1000 Concours was given a year off but would return for 1997.

1997

Only new color choices were seen on the 1997 ZX-11, but until further notice, it remained the world's fastest production motorcycle.

Kawasaki Motors Corp.

Model year 1997 would prove to be a year of few changes for Kawasaki as most models returned in the same state as they left in 1996.

The baby Ninja 250R was now delivered in Firecracker Red and remained a popular choice for the new rider who wanted a sport machine under their seat. The bigger 500R was back and was offered in Luminous Peacock Blue or Firecracker Red for this season. Three choices were still shown in the 600 Ninja clan with the ZX-6 finished in Luminous Windsor Green or Candy Wine Red. The ZX-7R was still the only flavor sold in the 750 class and it was unchanged after being redesigned for 1996. Lime Green or Ebony were the latest shades.

KAWASAKI

STANDARD CATALOG OF JAPANESE Motorcycles

Now when you purchase a '96 Vulcan™ 1500L, you can get up to $1,000* which you can use toward your choice of cruiser accessories thanks to special factory-to-dealer incentives. There's no better way to go. Because half the fun of owning a cruiser is customizing it to suit your own taste. With the biggest production V-twin available, the Vulcan 1500L gives you a whole lot to work with. Spoke wheels and low-rise handlebars further add to its rakish look. So visit a participating Kawasaki dealer. The Vulcan 1500L with custom accessories. It's just your style.

Vulcan™ 1500L

IT'S NOT REALLY YOURS UNTIL YOU MAKE IT YOURS.
HERE'S $1,000 TO HELP YOU GET STARTED.

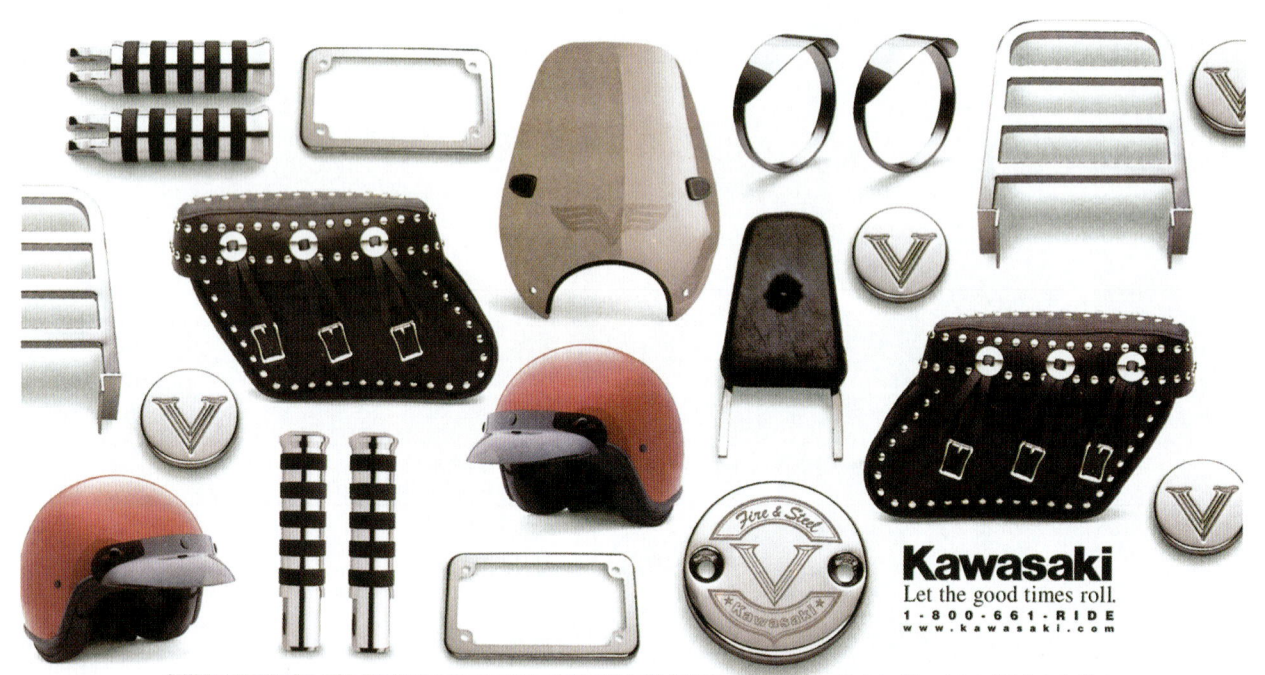

Kawasaki
Let the good times roll.
1-800-661-RIDE
www.kawasaki.com

©1997 Kawasaki Motors Corp., U.S.A. This offer supersedes any previous retail offer on this model. Retail prices of accessories are set by dealer. Offer available April 1 to September 30 at participating dealers only. See dealer for details. Specifications are subject to change without notice. Availability may be limited. Always wear a helmet and appropriate apparel. *Amount of factory-to-dealer incentive up to $1,000 retail value will vary based on dealer participation.

Kawasaki, Circle 47 on Reader Service Card

Kawasaki proudly put its accessories on display in this 1997 ad.

The open class ZX-9R was treated to stiffer springs and improved damping in the forks. Front anchors were enhanced with the use of six-piston calipers that squeezed floating rotors. Rear passengers now had a set of hand holds at their avail helping to keep them on the seat when the rider took the ZX-9R ballistic. Lime Green with Pearl Alpine White or an all Firecracker Red version were sold. The big ZX-11 was back and unchanged with rumors of a replacement being bandied about. The '97 hues included Luminous Windsor Green and Amaranth Red Mica.

The ZG1000 Concours returned to the fray for 1997 after missing 1996 altogether. It remained the same competent sport touring machine as before. Two-tone red paint applied to the Voyager XII was the only alteration listed for '97.

Six different Vulcan models were listed for 1997, but all were carried over from the previous year. The duo-tones of the Vulcan 1500 were now Ebony and Candy Persimmon Red. The Vulcan 750 had Ebony with Galaxy Silver or Candy Cardinal Red with Cosmic Splendor Red as color choices, but was otherwise the same mount as in 1996. The Vulcan 500 Limited made its debut in 1996 and was now the only model in that range having replaced the standard version versus being sold side by side.

The Eliminator 600 was another returning member that was unchanged, save the Firecracker Red color for 1997.

The popular Ninja profile was offered for viewing courtesy of Kawasaki.

1997 KAWASAKI

Model	Engine	Displacement	Transmission
250R Ninja	Two-cylinder	248cc	Six-Speed
KL250D7 (Dual Purpose)	Single cylinder	249cc	Six-Speed
500R Ninja	Two-cylinder	498cc	Six-Speed
EN500 Vulcan Ltd.	Two-cylinder	498cc	Six-Speed
ZL600 Eliminator (Returning Model)	Four-cylinder	592cc	Six-Speed
600R Ninja	Four-cylinder	592cc	Six-Speed
ZX-6 Ninja	Four-cylinder	599cc	Six-Speed
ZX-6R Ninja	Four-cylinder	599cc	Six-Speed
KL650A4 Dual Purpose	Single cylinder	651cc	Five-Speed
VN750 Vulcan	V-twin	749cc	Five-Speed
ZX-7R Ninja	Four-cylinder	749cc	Six-Speed
VN800 Vulcan	V-twin	805cc	Five-Speed
VN800 Vulcan Classic	V-twin	805cc	Five-Speed
ZX-9R	Four-cylinder	899cc	Six-Speed
ZG1000 Concours (Returning Model)	Four-cylinder	996cc	Six-Speed
ZX11 Ninja	Four-cylinder	1052cc	Six-Speed
ZG1200 Voyager XII	Four-cylinder	1196cc	Five-Speed
VN1500 Vulcan	V-twin	1470cc	Four-Speed
VN1500 Vulcan Classic	V-twin	1470cc	Four-Speed
VN1500L Vulcan	V-twin	1470cc	Four-Speed

KAWASAKI

1998

STANDARD CATALOG OF® JAPANESE Motorcycles

Adding a lot of spice to the lives of riders and anyone who enjoyed motorcycles was the 1998 Kawasaki Ninja ZX-9R.

The Kawasaki Vulcan 1500 Classic was prominently featured in this 1998 magazine ad.

The 1997 model year had offered few changes from the year before, but in 1998 Kawasaki introduced a few improved sport bikes and a new variant in the growing cruiser segment.

Joining the Vulcan 1500 crew was the Nomad. Still powered by the same 1470cc V-twin engine, the Nomad featured a frame that delivered more strength with altered steering geometry. Gear changes were now smoother due to an improved gearbox and a bigger radiator provided added cooling to the engine. Since the big Vulcan was being pressed into more serious touring duties, extra energy was delivered through the use of a higher output alternator. Flat floorboards remained but were relocated rearward of the 1997 mounting spots. A factory windshield and saddlebags were added to the equation and the answer was the 1998 Nomad.

As good as the ZX-9R was, Kawasaki found itself getting spanked by Honda's CBR900RR once too often. To rectify the situation, a stronger and lighter 9R was rolled out for 1998. While the '97 9R was hardly tubby, the '98 edition was 70 lbs. lighter. This new mass equaled that of the rival Honda, thus helping to put them on an even playing field.

The engine was greatly improved and the output of 130 hp seemed to be the result of the changes. Very few features of the 1998 9R were the same as the previous version, and every step was taken to add fuel to the fire. Weight savings were realized by casting oil passages inside the engine, eliminating the need for externally mounted lines.

Smaller clutch plates and a lightened crankshaft also did their part in dropping the weight. California spec bikes were fitted with stainless steel mufflers while the other 49 states received titanium canisters. A truncated wheelbase of 55.2 inches was achieved when using a newly formed pressed-and-welded chassis. Alloy rims remained the same size as before but featured thinner walls, shaving a few precious ounces from each. Smaller front disc brakes now measured 296mm and were halted by six-piston calipers from Tokico.

The latest ZX-7R was virtually the same bike from the 1996 version, but the 6R was another animal altogether. Kawasaki claimed a weight of 12 lbs. fewer than the 1997 model with nearly half of that figure coming from the engine. The oil cooler was ditched and the radiator was now curved with a larger surface area. Engine covers were formed from magnesium in their quest to carve every available ounce of weight from the new ZX-6R. The 1998 chassis looked much the same as the '97 edition but had a 13mm shorter wheelbase. A rake of 23.5 degrees was half a degree more aggressive and one mm of trail was also trimmed from the geometry. Stauncher 46mm fork tubes took the place of the 41mm units and a fully adjustable rear shock added control and adaptability to the overall mix. Dual 300mm brake rotors were matched with six-piston calipers up front for race quality braking.

Kawasaki used an ad called "Don't Stop" to promote the 1998 Vulcan 1500 Classic cycle.

1998 KAWASAKI

Model	Engine	Displacement	Transmission
250R Ninja	Two-cylinder	248cc	Six-Speed
KL250D7 Dual Purpose	Single cylinder	249cc	Six-Speed
500R Ninja	Two-cylinder	498cc	Six-Speed
EN500 Vulcan Ltd.	Two-cylinder	498cc	Six-Speed
ZL600 Eliminator	Four-cylinder	592cc	Six-Speed
600R Ninja	Four-cylinder	592cc	Six-Speed
ZX-6 Ninja	Four-cylinder	599cc	Six-Speed
ZX-6R Ninja	Four-cylinder	599cc	Six-Speed
KL650A4 (Dual Purpose)	Single cylinder	651cc	Five-Speed
VN750 Vulcan	V-twin	749cc	Five-Speed
ZX-7R Ninja	Four-cylinder	749cc	Six-Speed
VN800 Vulcan	V-twin	805cc	Five-Speed
VN800 Vulcan Classic	V-twin	805cc	Five-Speed
ZX-9R	Four-cylinder	899cc	Six-Speed
ZG1000 Concours	Four-cylinder	996cc	Six-Speed
ZX11 Ninja	Four-cylinder	1052cc	Six-Speed
ZG1200 Voyager XII	Four-cylinder	1196cc	Five-Speed
VN1500 Vulcan	V-twin	1470cc	Four-Speed
VN1500 Vulcan Classic	V-twin	1470cc	Four-Speed
VN1500L Vulcan	V-twin	1470cc	Four-Speed
VN1500 Nomad (New for 1998)	V-twin	1470cc	Four-Speed

KAWASAKI 1999

STANDARD CATALOG OF JAPANESE MOTORCYCLES

By adding 16-inch tires, chrome spokes and a different attitude to the Vulcan 800, the Classic version of this famed Kawasaki was created.

Kawasaki Motors Corp.

Model year 1999 would find a few fresh faces in the yearbook photo. Many 1999 Kawasakis were carried over, but had received extensive revisions from their 1998 presentation.

One model missing from the new catalog was the on-again, off-again 600 Eliminator. The demand for a middleweight muscle bike never lived up to the expectations of the sales team, so it was gone again from the lineup.

The Vulcan 1500L was also taken away, leaving three versions of the big Vulcan to carry on the classic theme. Joining the crew for 1999 was an all-new version of the Vulcan, the Drifter. Instead of trying to emulate the motorcycles being built in Milwaukee, Kawasaki went back in time for another subject of adoration.

The Drifter took in the styling of the legendary but defunct Indian Chief and blended modern design and hardware. With a fully valanced front fender and full coverage sheet metal over

The 248cc Ninja was a great place to start your motorcycling experience. It still delivered plenty of fun for those with some experience under their helmets.

Kawasaki Motors Corp.

the rear tire, it didn't take too much imagination to see the old Chief pass before your eyes.

The elongated saddle stretched out over the rear fender in cantilever fashion, much like the sprung seta of the original Chief. Nestled into the top of the 4.2-gallon fuel tank was an instrument panel reminiscent of the early Indian.

A black headlight bucket and matching side covers continued the Indian theme as did the fishtail two-into-one exhaust. Deep Red paint was slathered over every inch of the fenders and tank with only a subtle pinstripe gave any contrast to the hue.

Gleaming spoke wheels were visible under each fender and the entire package weighed a sturdy 668 lbs. Modern disc brakes at each end indicated we were viewing a freshly minted machine and the electronic fuel injection made the Drifter run like a contemporary offering.

The second all-new machine from Kawasaki was the ZRX1100. Its looks were based on the successful KZ1000R, Eddie Lawson Replicas of 1983. In the 1980s, Mr. Lawson could be seen strafing the racing circuits around the USA aboard his Screaming Green KZ1000. To mark his on-track success, Kawasaki built a replica for the street.

Although there is no longer a racing class that catered to the Standard models, the new ZRX could play the part. A 1052cc, inline-four engine was liquid cooled and shifted through a five-speed gearbox. A satin black, four-into-one exhaust was capped with an aluminum canister. Adjustable front forks and piggyback shocks on the rear carried the 1983 motif to the end. The bikini fairing and two-person saddle made a comfortable perch whether heading down to the corner store of blasting across state lines.

The 600R Ninja was pulled from the ranks as well for 1999, but the ZX-6 and ZX-6R remained to carry the flag. Additional sport bike offerings for 1999 included the ZX-7R, ZX-9R and ZX-11. The big ZX would be overshadowed by a new machine for 2000, but had provided years of service for the company and anyone who owned one.

Later dubbed the "Z-Rex" the ZRX-1100 reminded many older generation riders of the original ZX1000R piloted by the factory team in 1984.

Kawasaki Motors Corp.

1999 KAWASAKI

Model	Engine	Displacement	Transmission
KLR250 (Dual Purpose)	Single cylinder	249cc	Six-Speed
250R Ninja	Two-cylinder	248cc	Six-Speed
500R Ninja	Two-cylinder	498cc	Six-Speed
EN500 Vulcan Ltd.	Two-cylinder	498cc	Six-Speed
ZX-6 Ninja	Four-cylinder	599cc	Six-Speed
ZX-6R Ninja	Four-cylinder	599cc	Six-Speed
KLR650 (Dual Purpose)	Single cylinder	651cc	Five-Speed
VN750 Vulcan	V-twin	749cc	Five-Speed
ZX-7R Ninja	Four-cylinder	749cc	Six-Speed
VN800 Vulcan	V-twin	805cc	Five-Speed
VN800 Vulcan Classic	V-twin	805cc	Five-Speed
ZX-9R	Four-cylinder	899cc	Six-Speed
ZG1000 Concours	Four-cylinder	996cc	Six-Speed
ZRX1100 (New for 1999)	Four-cylinder	1052cc	Five-Speed
ZX11 Ninja	Four-cylinder	1052cc	Six-Speed
ZG1200 Voyager XII	Four-cylinder	1196cc	Five-Speed
VN1500 Vulcan	V-twin	1470cc	Four-Speed
VN1500 Vulcan Classic	V-twin	1470cc	Four-Speed
VN1500 Vulcan Drifter (New for 1999)	V-twin	1470cc	Four-Speed
VN1500 Nomad	V-twin	1470cc	Four-Speed

The biggest cruiser in Kawasaki's pen was the Vulcan 1500 and it was a favorite of buyers seeking style and power.

Kawasaki Motors Corp.

The Vulcan by Kawasaki was displayed in all its glory in this 1999 magazine ad.

KAWASAKI 2000

One of the new models for 2000 was the ZX-7. Devoid of any fairings or complications, the 750cc machine met almost any rider's needs.

Kawasaki Motors Corp.

The 2000 model year was one of Kawasaki's most exciting as new machines found their way onto the showroom floors. With hopes of regaining the crown as the fastest production motorcycle, Kawasaki introduced the ZX-12R. Until 1999, when the Suzuki Hayabusa swooped in and stole the prize, the ZX-11 had been the fastest motorcycle that money could buy. Kawasaki hoped to regain the throne with the ZX-12R.

Their efforts started with the world's first aluminum monocoque backbone chassis. An 1199cc, DOHC engine with liquid cooling was hung from the ultra-rigid frame, a compact mill that would either make or break Kawasaki's speed rating.

Cloaking the speed gear was a sleek aerodynamic fairing with a Twin Ram Air system that literally force-fed oxygen to the waiting engine. The design of the ZX-12R was meant to offer the best power-to-weight ratio of any motorcycle on earth. It had a dry weight of only 463 lbs. and a price of $11,999. The release of the ZX-12R put the ZX-11 on a deathwatch, and it would not live beyond the 2001 model year.

A newly re-vamped ZX-9R struggled to keep pace with new entries in the open class segment. The engineers went back to the drawing board to find a few more ponies for the 2000 9R. Its reduced weight made for the best ratio ever on the 899cc machine.

The 2000 ZX-7R was about as close to a street legal racing bike as anyone could buy. Adding to the luster of the Kawasaki trophy case was the victory by Doug Chandler in the final round of AMA Superbike competition in 1999.

KAWASAKI

The 2000 ZX-6R now had a sleeker fairing along with a ram air system that was similar to that used on the ZX-12R. Revised combustion chambers increased compression to 12.8:1 and the all-aluminum cylinder block had electro-plated bores to do away with steel liners. A dry weight of 377 lbs. was listed keeping it on par with its contemporaries.

Both 250R and 500R Ninjas remained on the scene and helped to wet the feet of beginning riders while providing plenty of fun for more experienced pilots. The ZRX-1100 returned wearing altered graphics.

New in the standard legion was the ZR-7. A true naked bike, it sported no fairings or aerodynamic trickery. A 738cc, inline-four engine inhaled through two valves per pot and sent fumes on their way via the four-into-two exhaust. Simplicity and power were the keywords when searching for the ZR-7.

The W650 looked every bit an early W-1 with fully modern running gear. The original W-1 resembled the best that Britain had to offer and the W650 carries on that tradition. A parallel twin engine displaced 676cc and was held in a double-cradle frame of steel. A five-speed gearbox sent the selected ratio to a final drive chain, with a 300mm disc brake at the front wheel. Everything from the flat, two-person saddle to the rubber kneepads on the fuel tank screamed vintage.

A smaller version of the Drifter joined the tribe in 2000. Using the same power plant and running gear of the 800 Vulcan, the baby Drifter wore the same Indian-esque fenders and seat. The bigger 1500 Drifter was seen alongside the junior version wearing only new colors from the 1999 debut.

Two versions of the Vulcan 1500 were available with either carburetors or the latest in fuel injection. The Classic FI and Nomad FI were the same machines as before, with the exception of the new fuel management system. Four-speed gearboxes had been bumped to five-gear units on the Vulcans for 2000.

The Concours and Voyager XII were still on the docket and did their best to hold their place in a world of growing competition from other makers.

2000 KAWASAKI

Model	Engine	Displacement	Transmission
KLR250 (Dual Purpose)	Single cylinder	249cc	Six-Speed
250R Ninja	Two-cylinder	248cc	Six-Speed
500R Ninja	Two-cylinder	498cc	Six-Speed
EN500 Vulcan Ltd.	Two-cylinder	498cc	Six-Speed
ZX-6 Ninja	Four-cylinder	599cc	Six-Speed
ZX-6R Ninja	Four-cylinder	599cc	Six-Speed
KLR650 (Dual Purpose)	Single cylinder	651cc	Five-Speed
W650	Two-cylinder	676cc	Five-Speed
VN750 Vulcan	V-twin	749cc	Five-Speed
ZR-7	Four-cylinder	738cc	Five-Speed
ZX-7R Ninja	Four-cylinder	749cc	Six-Speed
VN800 Vulcan	V-twin	805cc	Five-Speed
VN800 Vulcan Classic	V-twin	805cc	Five-Speed
VN800 Vulcan Drifter	V-twin	805cc	Five-Speed
ZX-9R	Four-cylinder	899cc	Six-Speed
ZG1000 Concours	Four-cylinder	996cc	Six-Speed
ZRX1100	Four-cylinder	1052cc	Five-Speed
ZX11 Ninja	Four-cylinder	1052cc	Six-Speed
ZG1200 Voyager XII	Four cylinder	1196cc	Five-Speed
VN1500 Vulcan	V-twin	1470cc	Five-Speed
VN1500 Vulcan Classic	V-twin	1470cc	Five-Speed
VN1500 Vulcan Classic FI Fuel Injection (New for 2000)	V-twin	1470cc	Five-Speed
VN1500 Vulcan Drifter	V-twin	1470cc	Five-Speed
VN1500 Nomad	V-twin	1470cc	Five-Speed
VN1500 Nomad FI Fuel Injection (New for 2000)	V-twin	1470cc	Five-Speed

KAWASAKI

2001

The 2001 Vulcan by Kawasaki was shown in profile in this ad with a good looking green and cream paint scheme.

Changes in the 2001 lineup were mild as Kawasaki settled into a mix that suited every facet of the market.

One new entrant in the race was the Eliminator 125. It was not quite the raucous brawler that the ZL1000 had been but the latest Eliminator was powered by a 124cc engine with a single cylinder. A five-speed gearbox let the rider keep the engine in the proper rev range for power. A long wheelbase of 57.9 inches stretched the diminutive machine out nicely and a low saddle height of only 26.8 inches made it a great ride for shorter cyclists. The dry weight of only 282 lbs. was also a benefit to smaller riders and gave the Eliminator a nimble feel. A meaty 15-inch rear tire was mated with a bigger hoop up front for the ultimate in cruiser style. Adjustable rear shocks and a front disc brake helped to keep the ride safe and comfortable.

The recently added ZX-7 was upgraded to the ZX-7S and carried fresh styling and a frame mounted half-fairing. The combination of style, speed and comfort remained the strong suits of the all around ZX-7S. Only Candy Persimmon Red was shown on the sales sheet.

Kawasaki's other naked bike, the ZRX-1100, was bumped to a ZRX-1200R listing and carried a bigger engine in the frame. The 1164cc mill featured linerless cylinders that functioned without steel sleeves, saving weight. The chassis was also revised for more rigidity and the rear mounted piggyback shocks also received some changes. The diagonal stripes were still in place but they colors were reversed. In addition to the Lime Green ensemble, you could get a more ominous Black Pearl with Metallic Blue Violet colored Z-Rex for 2001.

Both versions of the Drifter returned, but were wearing new clothes. A thickly padded solo saddle was now installed, replacing the elongated two-person version used before. As an accessory, you could get a two-up seat for the new models if you had a passenger to haul around. Along with the new saddles, both 800 and 1500 Drifters were trimmed with chrome packages to add some dazzle to the design.

The big Drifter was fitted with electronic fuel injection and dual 36mm throttle bodies while the smaller version wore a single 36mm carburetor. Even with their new wardrobe, the Drifters carried on the Indian motorcycle impression well.

The W650 used a redesigned fuel tank and trimmer kneepads as well as a fresh saddle. These alterations did nothing to take away the old world look of the modern W650.

The remaining catalog for 2001 was the same as the year before. The sport bike class contained the ZX-6R, 7R, 9R and 12R as well as a slightly milder ZX-6. Both small Ninjas were still shown as well, and continued to bring new riders to the fold.

2001 KAWASAKI

Model	Engine	Displacement	Transmission
BN125 Eliminator (New for 2001)	Single cylinder	124cc	Five-Speed
KLR250 (Dual Purpose)	Single cylinder	249cc	Six-Speed
250R Ninja	Two-cylinder	248cc	Six-Speed
500R Ninja	Two-cylinder	498cc	Six-Speed
EN500 Vulcan Ltd.	Two-cylinder	498cc	Six-Speed
ZX-6 Ninja	Four-cylinder	599cc	Six-Speed
ZX-6R Ninja	Four-cylinder	599cc	Six-Speed
LR650 Dual Purpose	Single cylinder	651cc	Five-Speed
W650	Two-cylinder	676cc	Five-Speed
VN750 Vulcan	V-twin	749cc	Five-Speed
ZR-7S (New fairing and styling)	Four-cylinder	738cc	Five-Speed
ZX-7R Ninja	Four-cylinder	749cc	Six-Speed
VN800 Vulcan	V-twin	805cc	Five-Speed
VN800 Vulcan Classic	V-twin	805cc	Five-Speed
VN800 Vulcan Drifter (Newly styled for 2001)	V-twin	805cc	Five-Speed
ZX-9R	Four-cylinder	899cc	Six-Speed
ZG1000 Concours	Four-cylinder	996cc	Six-Speed
ZRX1200R (Bigger engine)	Four-cylinder	1164cc	Five-Speed
ZX11 Ninja	Four-cylinder	1052cc	Six-Speed
ZG1200 Voyager XII	Four-cylinder	1196cc	Five-Speed
VN1500 Vulcan	V-twin	1470cc	Five-Speed
VN1500 Vulcan Classic	V-twin	1470cc	Five-Speed
VN1500 Vulcan Classic FI Fuel Injection	V-twin	1470cc	Five-Speed
VN1500 Vulcan Drifter (New style and fuel injection)	V-twin	1470cc	Five-Speed
VN1500 Nomad	V-twin	1470cc	Five-Speed
VN1500 Nomad FI Fuel Injection	V-twin	1470cc	Five-Speed

KAWASAKI 2002

Another round of subtle changes was in store for 2002 with only a few new faces and a few more leaving the herd.

First of the departed was the long running ZX-11. The king of speed had been rolling around since 1990 and had served Kawasaki and its owners well in that time. Motorcycles from the competing brands as well as from within Kawasaki's own farm were now cutting into the ZX-11's sales, so the time was here to retire it from the team.

The non-fuel injected Vulcan 1500 Nomad was also pulled as the popularity and efficiency of the fuel injected models took control.

The W650 would not be sold in 2002, and would never return to the stage. Although it provided the rider with a rewarding and fully modern experience, there were other machines on the market that captured the old world essence even better. People seemed to turn to Kawasaki for powerful sport bikes and cruisers, leaving the retro W650 out in the cold.

Making their debut for 2002 were two new models, or at least one new and one fresh flavor in the Vulcan parlor.

Joining the boisterous Vulcan 1500 gang was the Mean Streak. By blending features of some sportier machines with the aggressive cruiser styling a new niche was formed. Up front, a set of stout 43mm inverted cartridge forks led the way and enhanced handling and ride comfort. Held between the robust fork legs were an alloy rim and a pair of brakes borrowed from the ZX-9R.

2002 KAWASAKI

Model	Engine	Displacement	Transmission
BN125 Eliminator	Single cylinder	124cc	Five-Speed
KLR250 (Dual Purpose)	Single cylinder	249cc	Six-Speed
250R Ninja	Two-cylinder	248cc	Six-Speed
500R Ninja	Two-cylinder	498cc	Six-Speed
EN500 Vulcan Ltd.	Two-cylinder	498cc	Six-Speed
ZX-6 Ninja	Four-cylinder	599cc	Six-Speed
ZX-6R Ninja	Four-cylinder	599cc	Six-Speed
KLR650 Dual Purpose	Single cylinder	651cc	Five-Speed
VN750 Vulcan	V-twin	749cc	Five-Speed
ZR-7S	Four-cylinder	738cc	Five-Speed
ZX-7R Ninja	Four-cylinder	749cc	Six-Speed
VN800 Vulcan	V-twin	805cc	Five-Speed
VN800 Vulcan Classic	V-twin	805cc	Five-Speed
VN800 Vulcan Drifter	V-twin	805cc	Five-Speed
ZX-9R	Four-cylinder	899cc	Six-Speed
ZG1000 Concours	Four-cylinder	996cc	Six-Speed
ZG1200 Voyager XII	Four-cylinder	1196cc	Five-Speed
ZRX1200R	Four-cylinder	1164cc	Five-Speed
ZZ-R1200 (New for 2002)	Four cylinder	1164cc	Five-Speed
VN1500 Vulcan	V-twin	1470cc	Five-Speed
VN1500 Vulcan Classic	V-twin	1470cc	Five-Speed
VN1500 Vulcan Classic FI Fuel Injection	V-twin	1470cc	Five-Speed
VN1500 Vulcan Drifter Fuel Injection	V-twin	1470cc	Five-Speed
VN1500 Vulcan Mean Streak (New for 2002)	V-twin	1470cc	Five-Speed
VN1500 Nomad FI Fuel Injection	V-twin	1470cc	Five-Speed

KAWASAKI

The use of the staunch forks and amazing anchors brought a new level of handling to the playing field. Inside the V-twin engine, hydraulic valve adjusters that were self-adjusting were the first in their class. A flowing fuel tank and a set of dual exhaust pipes completed the new painting that was used on the Mean Streak.

Another fresh model for Kawasaki was the ZZ-R1200. By melding components from their dearly departed ZX-11 and up to date ZRX-1200R, a new class of sport touring machine was created. Taking the successful frame from the ZX-11 and revising it for the new power plant was the first step. Once girded, the 1164cc, inline-four of the ZRX-1200R was bolted in place.

Twin Ram Air ducts helped to keep the big lump breathing clearly and integrated turn signals kept the flow of air around the newly designed fairing clean. A comfortable perch and hard saddlebags provided ample space for two people and their travel needs. Larger and more powerful than the carryover Concours and sleeker than the returning Voyager XII the ZZ-R1200 created its own market niche and filled it nicely. Priced in between the other two touring machines gave the space age ZZ-R1200 an advantage it could call its own.

Every other model from the Eliminator 125 to the Vulcan 1500 Nomad FI were back for a new year, but carried much the same regarding hardware and features.

2003

Designed to be taken to the track, the ZX-6RR was fitted with a smaller engine than the ZX-6R but could easily be hot-rodded for greater racing performance.
Kawasaki Motors Corp.

Model year 2003 would see the entrance of several new models for Kawasaki bringing fresh blood into the family. The Eliminator 125 was stricken from the catalog after a brief ride.

Kawasaki's sport bike regime was mostly the same for 2003 with the ZX-12R, 9R and 7R still listed. Galaxy Silver for the 9R and Pearl Blazing Orange for the 7R were new hues on unchanged machines. The ZX-6R came in four colors, and the standard issue ZX-6 was removed from the field.

For 2003, the ZX-6R received a bump in displacement to 636cc. In addition to the bigger engine, the ZX-6R was vastly improved over the 2002 edition and set new standards for the class. A redline of 15,500 rpm was one indicator of the 6R's potential and the altered ergonomics was another. The new mount was more aggressive and seemed destined for the track. Oddly enough, the racing class was limited to 600cc or less and kept the 6R on the streets.

To compete on the racing circuits, Kawasaki

Playing the role of Indian imitator, the Drifter was again offered in 2003. It was sold in 1500cc and 800cc trim with matching sheet metal and style.

Kawasaki Motors Corp.

Back for another round was the Mean Streak version of the Vulcan. New colors were the only alteration from 2002.

Kawasaki Motors Corp.

rolled out their ZX-6RR. This machine was a virtual clone of the 6R but carried an engine that fell within one cc of the racing limit. The 6R was actually a better performing bike while the 6RR was designed for track use and was easily modified to conquer.

Physical differences in stock trim were the adjustable swingarm pivot and torque-limiting clutch of the 6RR. These two factors would make a world of difference when taken to the track and dialed in for maximum results. Unlike the wide range of hues sold on the 6R the RR was only offered in Lime Green and would set the buyer back an additional $400.

Slotted in where the ZX-6 had been seen, the ZZ-R600 was added for 2003. Basically a tamer version of the 6R and 6RR, the ZZ-R featured a full fairing and was sold in Pearl Mystic Black.

The bigger ZZ-R1200 returned without changes, as did the ZRX-1200R. New paint on the Z-Rex was available in the Candy Lightning Blue with Galaxy Silver trim.

Entering to compete in the expanding naked bike category, the Z1000 was introduced in 2003. As Yamaha's FZ1 and Honda's 919 made great strides in that direction, Kawasaki needed something to take them on. Aggressively styled and fitted with an angular, bikini fairing, the Z1000 was certainly not boring

All new for 2003 was the Z1000. When pitted against the machines sold by Honda and Yamaha, the Z1000's appearance and performance held up well.

Kawasaki Motors Corp.

KAWASAKI

STANDARD CATALOG OF JAPANESE MOTORCYCLES

For the rider who demanded speed and comfort in his full size mount, the ZZ-R1200 delivered on both fronts and was a stylish option for the sport touring rider.

Kawasaki Motors Corp.

to look at. The liquid-cooled 953cc four-cylinder engine exhaled through an unusual array of four-into-two-into-four exhausts that fit the theme of the Z perfectly. Digital fuel injection and a six-speed gearbox ensured consistent performance regardless of what was demanded.

Sold in Black Pearl or Pearl Blazing Orange, the Z1000 was a worthy opponent to the competition's offerings.

The ZR-7S was also a rerun for 2003 but now wore a coat of Pearl Chrome Yellow.

Moving to the cruiser listings, very few changes were found. The Drifter was back in 800 and 1500 sizes but the model was unchanged from its 2002 specs. The Mean Streak was another machine that returned in the same guise as before, save the new hues listed.

The Vulcan Classic was treated to an increase in displacement, growing from 1500 to 1600cc. The chassis was also extended and lowered for a more ground-hugging stance and revised fuel injection delivered the required mix with higher efficiency. Fresh 16-inch alloy hoops were also new as the cruiser segment continued to flux and grow.

2003 KAWASAKI

Model	Engine	Displacement	Transmission
KLR250 (Dual Purpose)	Single cylinder	249cc	Six-Speed
250R Ninja	Two-cylinder	248cc	Six-Speed
500R Ninja	Two-cylinder	498cc	Six-Speed
EN500 Vulcan Ltd.	Two-cylinder	498cc	Six-Speed
ZX-6R Ninja (Increased displacement)	Four-cylinder	636cc	Six-Speed
ZX-6RR Ninja (New for 2003)	Four-cylinder	599cc	Six-Speed
ZZ-R600 (New for 2003)	Four-cylinder	599cc	Six-Speed
KLR650 (Dual Purpose)	Single cylinder	651cc	Five-Speed
VN750 Vulcan	V-twin	749cc	Five-Speed
ZR-7S	Four-cylinder	738cc	Five-Speed
ZX-7R Ninja	Four-cylinder	749cc	Six-Speed
VN800 Vulcan	V-twin	805cc	Five-Speed
VN800 Vulcan Classic	V-twin	805cc	Five-Speed
VN800 Vulcan Drifter	V-twin	805cc	Five-Speed
ZX-9R	Four-cylinder	899cc	Six-Speed
Z1000 (New for 2003)	Four-cylinder	953cc	Six-Speed
ZG1000 Concours	Four-cylinder	996cc	Six-Speed
ZG1200 Voyager XII	Four-cylinder	1196cc	Five-Speed
ZRX1200R	Four-cylinder	1164cc	Five-Speed
ZZ-R1200	Four-cylinder	1164cc	Five-Speed
VN1500 Vulcan	V-twin	1470cc	Five-Speed
VN1500 Vulcan Classic FI Fuel Injection	V-twin	1470cc	Five-Speed
VN1500 Vulcan Drifter Fuel Injection	V-twin	1470cc	Five-Speed
VN1500 Vulcan Mean Streak	V-twin	1470cc	Five-Speed
VN1500 Nomad FI Fuel Injection	V-twin	1470cc	Five-Speed
VN1600 Vulcan Classic	V-twin	1552cc	Five-Speed

KAWASAKI 2004

Kawasaki made some bold moves for the 2004 model year as they bumped a few sport bikes from the line and injected some fresh blood into the clan.

Missing for 2003, the Eliminator 125 returned for 2004. The latest version of the small cruiser was finished in Metallic Phantom Silver without additional revisions.

The long running Voyager XII was a no show for 2004 as the touring market grew more populated by better performing sport mounts that were capable of devouring great distances in a single bound.

In the cruiser department, the Mean Streak was enhanced with the installation of a larger 1552cc engine. The bigger V-twin was fed by 40mm throttle bodies and electronic fuel injection. The teardrop tank was also stretched to hold 4.5 gallons of fuel in greater style. Metallic Spark Black, Candy Thunder Blue or Candy Lime Green were shown as the choices for 2004.

Taking the V-twin format to a new level, the Vulcan 2000 carried the largest displacement engine ever produced in its frame. The 2053cc mill delivered 141 lbs.-ft. of torque and was fed by 46mm throttle bodies and fuel injection. A low 27-inch seat height was joined by a massive 5.6 gallon fuel tank and an adjustable rear shock. Belt drive motivated the 200mm rear tire that was wrapped around a 16-inch alloy hoop. A matching alloy rim was used up front as was a triple projector lens headlight. Triple disc brakes were used to slow the big Vulcan. Large-diameter exhaust tubes rode prominently on the Vulcan and were dipped in chrome. Three hues were shown in Pearl Glacier Blue, Metallic Dark Purple Prism and Pearl Majestic Red.

Also gone from the 2004 play list were the ZX-7R and ZX-9R. Stepping in to fill the wake was the new ZX-10R. By creating a liter class

Hoping to fill the void left by the missing ZX-7R and ZX-9R, the ZX-10R embodied the best that Kawasaki had to offer in a lightweight, liter-sized machine.

Kawasaki Motors Corp.

Taking a styling cue from Kawasaki's past, the 2004 ZRX-1200R was draped in red, black and silver, much like the previous GPz models had been.

Kawasaki Motors Corp.

Getting a bit more ornery for 2004, the Mean Streak gained 100cc of displacement to keep the competition at bay in this energetic segment of the market.

Kawasaki Motors Corp.

KAWASAKI

Taking the cruiser definition to new levels was the Vulcan 2000, powered by the biggest V-twin engine in production.

Kawasaki Motors Corp.

sport bike that weighed little more than a 600cc machine, Kawasaki had a winning formula. The 998cc ZX-10R weighed a scat 409 lbs. dry—less than all three of the competitors' attempts.

Central ram air was in charge of delivering adequate oxygen to the engine and 43mm throttle bodies transferred the fuel on demand. A slipper clutch fed the six-speed gearbox without fuss and the Positive Neutral Finder helped when coming to a stop. Helping to bring the ZX-10R down from speed was a set of 300 mm wave-pattern brake rotors on the front wheel that were grasped by radial mount four-piston calipers. An ultra rigid swingarm held the 190 series rear tire in check as well as Kawasaki's fully adjustable Uni-Trak suspension. Forks were inverted 43mm in the front and delivered both control and stability regardless of the riding surface. Saving more weight was the all titanium, four-into-one exhaust system with its high-mounted canister.

The new ZX-10R was available in Lime Green, Candy Thunder Blue, Pearl Blazing Orange or Metallic Spark Black. At just under $11,000, it was priced well within the range of the rival machines of 2004.

The ZX-6RR was the recipient of an improved 599cc engine that delivered more peak horsepower and torque while maintaining durability and staying within the racing rules. Lime Green remained the only available hue.

Offered up in Passion Red with contrasting stripes, the ZRX-1200R looked every inch the GPz of Kawasaki's past. Only the modern power plant and current technology would set the two generations apart.

After sitting 2003 out, the Eliminator 125 returned as a 2004 model, but was unchanged from its last appearance.

Kawasaki Motors Corp.

2004 KAWASAKI

Model	Engine	Displacement	Transmission
Eliminator 125 (Returning model)	Single cylinder	124cc	Five-Speed
KLR250 Dual Purpose	Single cylinder	249cc	Six-Speed
250R Ninja	Two-cylinder	248cc	Six-Speed
500R Ninja	Two-cylinder	498cc	Six-Speed
EN500 Vulcan Ltd.	Two-cylinder	498cc	Six-Speed
ZX-6R Ninja	Four-cylinder	636cc	Six-Speed
ZX-6RR Ninja	Four-cylinder	599cc	Six-Speed
ZZ-R600	Four-cylinder	599cc	Six-Speed
KLR650 (Dual Purpose)	Single cylinder	651cc	Five-Speed
VN750 Vulcan	V-twin	749cc	Five-Speed
ZR-7S	Four-cylinder	738cc	Five-Speed
VN800 Vulcan	V-twin	805cc	Five-Speed
VN800 Vulcan Classic	V-twin	805cc	Five-Speed
VN800 Vulcan Drifter	V-twin	805cc	Five-Speed
Z1000	Four-cylinder	953cc	Six-Speed
ZG1000 Concours	Four-cylinder	996cc	Six-Speed
ZX-10R (New for 2004)	Four-cylinder	998cc	Six-Speed
ZRX1200R	Four-cylinder	1164cc	Five-Speed
ZZ-R1200	Four-cylinder	1164cc	Five-Speed
VN1500 Vulcan	V-twin	1470cc	Five-Speed
VN1500 Vulcan Drifter (Fuel Injection)	V-twin	1470cc	Five-Speed
VN1500 Nomad (Fuel Injection)	V-twin	1470cc	Five-Speed
VN1600 Vulcan Classic	V-twin	1552cc	Five-Speed
VN1600 Vulcan Mean Streak (More displacement)	V-twin	1552cc	Five-Speed
VN2000 Vulcan (New for 2004)	V-twin	2053cc	Five-Speed

KAWASAKI

2005

STANDARD CATALOG OF JAPANESE Motorcycles

The 2005 Kawasaki Ninja ZX-6R offered excitement as well as thoroughly modern styling.

After shaking up several divisions for 2004, Kawasaki would introduce a far more subtle catalog for 2005.

Replacing the ZR-7 was the Z750S. The latest version of their naked bike included a 748cc engine in a steel frame, helping to keep the sale price low. By sleeving down the inline-four of the Z1000, they avoided the need for a fresh design. Like the machine it supplanted, the Z750S provided a great all around machine at a price that added to its popularity.

With an AMA Supersport title from 2004 in the trophy case, the plan to sell two versions of their 600cc machine was becoming more obvious. When fully prepped for the track, the ZX-6RR was hard to beat, and the street bound ZX-6R was no slouch either. Even with these accolades in hand, Kawasaki revamped both machines for 2005 in their effort to stay on top of the middleweight division.

The ZX-6R was created with an all-new chassis that shortened the wheelbase and increased cornering clearance. The aluminum swingarm was stronger and lighter than the 2004 unit and was mated to a bottom-link Uni-Trak suspension from Kawasaki. A newly installed exhaust valve was controlled by a servo and helped to monitor the internal pressure and paved the way for a smooth exit regardless of RPM.

The new exhaust also swept upward and made its exit beneath the seat much like many of the

KAWASAKI

modern GP bikes. A slipper clutch was installed to deliver smooth acceleration and deceleration at speed. A dual fuel injector system also improved delivery of the "go juice" both at idle and at redline. Larger 300mm front brake discs were of the wave configuration making them the same weight as the smaller 280mm units they replaced. Radial calipers also boosted braking on the 2005 ZX-6R.

ZX-10R revisions were also added to boost the behavior of the big sport bike. A re-worked gearbox improved shifting under racing conditions.

Based on their success with the powerful Vulcan 1600 Classic, the same principles were applied the Nomad for 2005. Bumping the displacement to 1552cc had proven to be a powerful step in improving the breed. More subtle changes in the 2005 version included a 16-bit ECU and 36mm throttle bodies in the fuel injection array. Additional torque and crisper response were the benefits of the adjustments.

Fresh contours on the fuel tank and re-shaped chrome dash add to the visual appeal of the big cruiser. Fuel capacity also grew to 5.3 gallons with the new shape. Even adding all of these changes failed to add to the cost of the 2005 Nomad, making it a better deal than before.

The balance of the 2005 catalog looked much the same as the year before with completely new models still one model year away.

Many people probably saw the rear view of the Vulcan 2000 by Kawasaki. This cycle looked great from any angle.

2005 KAWASAKI

Model	Engine	Displacement	Transmission
Eliminator 125 (Returning model)	Single cylinder	124cc	Five-Speed
KLR250 (Dual Purpose)	Single cylinder	249cc	Six-Speed
250R Ninja	Two-cylinder	248cc	Six-Speed
500R Ninja	Two-cylinder	498cc	Six-Speed
EN500 Vulcan Ltd.	Two-cylinder	498cc	Six-Speed
ZX-6R Ninja	Four-cylinder	636cc	Six-Speed
ZX-6RR Ninja	Four-cylinder	599cc	Six-Speed
ZZ-R600	Four-cylinder	599cc	Six-Speed
KLR650 (Dual Purpose)	Single cylinder	651cc	Five-Speed
VN750 Vulcan	V-twin	749cc	Five-Speed
Z750S (New for 2005)	Four-cylinder	748cc	Six-Speed
VN800 Vulcan	V-twin	805cc	Five-Speed
VN800 Vulcan Classic	V-twin	805cc	Five-Speed
VN800 Vulcan Drifter	V-twin	805cc	Five-Speed
Z1000	Four-cylinder	953cc	Six-Speed
ZG1000 Concours	Four-cylinder	996cc	Six-Speed
ZX-10R (New for 2004)	Four-cylinder	998cc	Six-Speed
ZRX1200R	Four-cylinder	1164cc	Five-Speed
ZZ-R1200	Four-cylinder	1164cc	Five-Speed
VN1500 Vulcan	V-twin	1470cc	Five-Speed
VN1500 Vulcan Drifter (Fuel Injection)	V-twin	1470cc	Five-Speed
VN1600 Nomad (More displacement)	V-twin	1552cc	Five-Speed
VN1600 Vulcan Classic	V-twin	1552cc	Five-Speed
VN1600 Vulcan Mean Streak (More displacement)	V-twin	1552cc	Five-Speed
VN2000 Vulcan	V-twin	2053cc	Five-Speed

KAWASAKI 2006

While a few familiar faces were erased from the 2006 parade, there was a raft of new additions to fill their shoes.

The massive Vulcan 2000 was back, but now offered in several variations. The original, bare bones version was offered alongside a Limited, Classic and LT version. The Limited will be just that, with so few copies being built that not every dealer got one to sell. Two-tone paint adorned with extra chrome will set it apart from the standard issue 2000. The new Classic version carries a less unique headlight than used on the base and Limited. Different, handlebars a revised speedometer and reshaped passenger saddle are part of the Classic theme. Rounding out the new 2000 models is the LT. Basically a touring edition, the LT came with an adjustable windshield floorboards for the passenger and leather saddlebags.

Taking the place of the new defunct Vulcan 800 was a 900 and 900 LT variant. The only 800 Vulcan left behind was the Drifter and it was the only Drifter still sold for 2006. The new 900s were 1.4-inches longer than the 800s and featured belt drive. As with the 2000 LT, the 900 LT was equipped with a windshield, leather bags and a backrest for the passenger.

When they introduced the ZX-12R, Kawasaki's intention was to trump all comers with a new king of horsepower. Sadly it was not to be, and the Green Team wanted to try again for 2006. Taking power to the next level was the all-new ZX-14. A 1,352cc, inline-four, the new engine was the most powerful ever created by Kawasaki. The new mill was wrapped in sleek new bodywork that included strangely shaped headlights that lurked from the beak-like nose of the fairing. Ram air was employed to en-

Taking the reins with hopes of regaining the crown as the planet's fastest machine, the ZX-14 was powered by the most powerful engine ever created by Kawasaki. Kawasaki Motors Corp.

The ZX-10R received another round of changes for 2006 and was even lighter than before. Kawasaki Motors Corp.

KAWASAKI

sure adequate breathing and the ZX-14 quickly vaulted its way back to the top of the performance heap.

Only released two years before, the ZX-10R fell under the knife and was completely overhauled for '06. Carrying a bit less weight than the '05 version, the latest ZX-10R was also down on the delivery of power but was more useable as a result.

Both versions of the ZX-6 returned unchanged after experiencing makeovers in 2005. The Ninja 250R and 500R were also back for yet another year of never ending sales.

Joining the ranks of the other basic Ninjas was the new 650R. A parallel twin engine, displacing 649cc was nestled into the frame tubes and

A new entrant in the Ninja clan was the 650R, making its debut for 2006. The simple design and pleasant characteristics appealed to riders of all stripes.

Kawasaki Motors Corp.

2006 KAWASAKI

Model	Engine	Displacement	Transmission
Eliminator 125 (Returning Model)	Single cylinder	124cc	Five-Speed
KLR250 (Dual Purpose)	Single cylinder	249cc	Six-Speed
250R Ninja	Two-cylinder	248cc	Six-Speed
500R Ninja	Two-cylinder	498cc	Six-Speed
ZX-6R Ninja	Four-cylinder	636cc	Six-Speed
X-6RR Ninja	Four-cylinder	599cc	Six-Speed
ZZ-R600	Four-cylinder	599cc	Six-Speed
KLR650 (Dual Purpose)	Single cylinder	651cc	Five-Speed
650R Ninja (New for 2006)	Two-cylinder	649cc	Six-Speed
VN750 Vulcan	V-twin	749cc	Five-Speed
Z750S (New for 2006)	Four-cylinder	748cc	Six-Speed
VN800 Vulcan	V-twin	805cc	Five-Speed
VN800 Vulcan Classic	V-twin	805cc	Five-Speed
VN800 Vulcan Drifter	V-twin	805cc	Five-Speed
VN900 Vulcan Classic (New for 2006)	V-twin	903cc	Five-Speed
VN900 Vulcan Classic LT (New for 2006)	V-twin	903cc	Five-Speed
Z1000	Four-cylinder	953cc	Six-Speed
ZG1000 Concours	Four-cylinder	996cc	Six-Speed
ZX-10R (New for 2006)	Four-cylinder	998cc	Six-Speed
ZX-14 (New for 2006)	Four-cylinder	1352cc	Six-Speed
VN1500 Vulcan	V-twin	1470cc	Five-Speed
VN1500 Vulcan Classic	V-twin	1470cc	Five-Speed
VN1600 Nomad (More displacement)	V-twin	1552cc	Five-Speed
VN1600 Vulcan Classic	V-twin	1552cc	Five-Speed
VN1600 Vulcan Mean Streak (More displacement)	V-twin	1552cc	Five-Speed
VN2000 Vulcan	V-twin	2053cc	Five-Speed
VN2000 Vulcan Classic (New for 2006)	V-twin	2053cc	Five-Speed
VN2000 Vulcan 2000 Classic LT (New for 2006)	V-twin	2053cc	Five-Speed
VN2000 Vulcan Limited (New for 2006)	V-twin	2053cc	Five-Speed

delivered entertainment for all. Wrapped with a full set of slippery bodywork, the 650R played the role of superbike to a T. The dry weight of only 416 lbs. assured nimble handling and ease of operation at slow speeds.

Chain drive and a simple design kept the price of entry low with an MSRP of only $6,299 whether you chose the Galaxy Silver with Metallic Graystone or Ebony with Galaxy Silver paint. Red swingarms, frames and forks helped to color the 650R different.

Both of Kawasaki's naked bikes returned for 2006 with no changes seen. The Z1000 could be had in an interesting Candy Flat Raw Plasma Blue paint while the Z750S came in any color you wanted as long as that was Metallic Spark Black.

With the ZX-14 aimed squarely at the pure performance slice of the buying audience, and the ZZ-1200R gone, the long-in-the-tooth Concours was left to carry the sport touring torch for Kawasaki.

The Concours was the only machine left in Kawasaki's sport touring stable and carried on with no changes for 2006. Kawasaki Motors Corp.

The Ninja-Style Kawasaki ZZ-R600 was shaped for speed.

Kawasaki Motors Corp.

The LT versions of the Vulcan included adjustable windshields, passenger backrests and leather saddlebags.

Kawasaki Motors Corp.

KAWASAKI
2007

STANDARD CATALOG OF® JAPANESE Motorcycles

Belt drive, a 903cc V-twin engine and a five-speed transmission all were part of the Kawasaki Vulcan 900 Custom.

The Vulcan 2000 Classic LT added an adjustable windshield, studded seats and other pieces of comfort in addition to having spacious saddlebags.

The Kawasaki KLR 650 for 2007 used a 651cc engine and five-speed transmission.

KAWASAKI

Red accents were available on the flat-black Kawasaki gas tank. It offered a custom look to the 2007 Vulcan 1600 Mean Streak.

The 2007 Kawasaki Z1000 Sport used a 935cc inline-four engine, a six-speed transmission and had a dry weight of 452 lbs.

SUZUKI

Introduction

As happened with the other manufacturers of Japanese motorcycles we know today, Suzuki began as a simple and completely different business before the company turned to making motorcycles.

Suzuki's humble beginnings were known as the Suzuki Loom Works, a company noted as early as 1909. Suzuki Loom Works continued to expand and, by 1939, they had constructed a fully modern facility to take their concern to the next level.

As history shows us, World War II ended or diverted the efforts of most Japanese companies until the conflict was resolved. This applied to Suzuki as well, and after the dust had cleared, Shunzo Suzuki began to search for another venue in which to build a business.

On a bicycle trip in 1951, Mr. Suzuki had the idea of adding a small motor to a motorcycle to create an economical form of motorized transportation. He was not alone in his vision as there were already 100 other Japanese companies using the same equation to satisfy demand. As luck would have it, the state of the union at the time made it very difficult for most Japanese companies to produce such a device. Technical and financial limitations constrained what could be achieved, and most of the eager builders dropped out of the race.

Of the many names that were initially involved in the effort to mobilize Japan, only five would remain. At the time, the Emperor of Japan awarded Michio Suzuki and his son Shunzo with a rare Blue Ribbon Medal for their contributions to the growing country. With this honor in hand, Shunzo again turned his attentions to building a reliable yet inexpensive form of motorized bicycle.

His 36cc "Power Free" was quickly followed by the larger 50cc "Mini Free." Suzuki's creations proved to be durable and economical, his goals from the beginning. Continuing to develop the line, he renamed the company the Suzuki Motor Company Ltd. in 1954 and pushed on with his research. The production year of 1955 saw the debut of the "Porter Free" which was powered by a 100cc motor, making it the first true motorcycle built by Suzuki. The Porter Free used a hand clutch and foot shift to select from the two ratios installed. Weighing 187 lbs., the machine was hardly a speed demon, but provided the rider with power to get around in most conditions. By 1958, mass production had taken over at Suzuki and assembly line techniques helped to increase the number and quality of Suzuki motorbikes being built.

By 1961, an office in London was opened to expand the availability of their product and 1963 saw them land in the USA. Entering their motorcycles in racing events helped to improve the breed and increased worldwide exposure to the brand. Until the 1960s, very few people outside of Japan had ever heard the name "Suzuki." Racing would break that barrier in a hurry.

From their humble beginnings, the Suzuki brand went on to become one of the four major Japanese marques in the world. From a rickety, motorized bicycle in the early 1950s to some of the world's finest and fastest motorcycles today, Suzuki has made the long journey to success.

SUZUKI
1963

The first lineup of motorcycles sold in the USA included three street machines and two racing models. The smallest of the road-ready Suzukis was the S31. Powered by a 124cc, twin-cylinder motor, it looked like a typical machine of the day. High mounted exhaust tubes were covered with horizontally-slotted heat shields that covered the central section of the chrome pipe. An enclosed chain drive and spoke wheels were also a standard protocol for a motorcycle of the early 1960s. A rounded fuel tank, complete with the ubiquitous rubber kneepads, completed the overall picture of the S31. Climbing up the social ladder, the S250 Colleda was fitted with a 248cc, twin-cylinder engine of the two-stoke variety. The air-cooled engine produced 20 hp at 8000 rpm and the curb weight was listed as 308 lbs.

"Colleda" was roughly translated as "this is it." This Suzuki wasn't "it" to look at or ride on. The Colleda was fitted with a squarish, solo saddle. A small luggage rack was mounted atop the rear fender and a semi-valanced fender was seen over the front tire. White wall tires and chrome spoke wheels completed the ensemble. The exhaust of the Colleda ran low on the chassis and was not adorned with any form of heat shield. Although first offered in the states in 1963, it had been sold in Japan since 1954 in a variety of iterations. The TC250 El Camino appeared to be the sportier machine in the 1963 catalog. Fitted with a two-person saddle and less decorative fenders, it was still powered by a 248cc, twin cylinder engine. It featured an electric starter that was part of the 12-volt electrical system.

An hydraulic rear brake and another on the front wheel brought the 315-lb. El Camino to a stop. Chrome panels on the fuel tank were also fitted with rubber kneepads and a fuel gauge was included. A small luggage rack extended from the rear of the seat that placed the rider 28.2 inches from the ground.

Of the two 248cc models that Suzuki sold in the U.S. in 1963, the Colleda was a simpler machine but provided dependable transportation.
Suzuki Motors Corporation.

The El Camino was equipped with a two-person saddle and an electric start, making it a more useful motorcycle than other 1963 Suzukis
Suzuki Motors Corporation.

1963 SUZUKI

Model	Engine	Displacement	Transmission
S31	Two-cylinder	124cc	–
S250 Colleda	Two-cylinder	248cc	–
TC250 El Camino	Two cylinder	248cc	–

SUZUKI

1964

Of the three machines Suzuki offered for 1964, two of them were actually the same chassis with some engine choices. The M12 Sport 50 and K11 Sport 80 used the same pressed steel frame and suspension. The M12 was powered by a 50cc, two-stoke engine while the K11 carried 80cc of displacement in the same configuration. Both engines were fitted with a mid-level mounted exhaust that featured a slotted heat shield.

The fuel tank's side panels were chrome with rubber kneepads and a portion of the side panels was finished in white. The frame, headlight housing and rear fender were almost a single component and were delivered in the base color selected.

Both engines were started with a kick lever. The M12 version delivered 4.5 hp, while the K11 edition offered 7.3 hp. The smaller model could attain a top speed of 53 mph and the larger machine could reach 59 mph. A two-place saddle was found on both versions as was a rear-mounted luggage rack. Coil springs were used to suspend the front forks and rear section, bringing a modicum of comfort to the table.

The M12 Sport 50 was the smaller of the two Sport models in 1964 and it used a 50cc, single-cylinder engine to propel the machine and rider along.

Suzuki Motors Corporation.

With a 246cc, two cylinder power plant, the T10 provided far more comfort, speed and carrying capacity than the sport models and did so with a higher degree of style.

Suzuki Motors Corporation.

Moving upscale to the next 1964 model we find the 246cc T10. First sold in 1962 in other countries, the T10 made its USA debut in 1964. The T10 was really an extension of the Colleda line but was built around an improved chassis that delivered better handling and comfort.

The two-stroke engine used in the T10 provided 21 hp at 8,000 rpm and weighed 308 lbs. before adding fuel and fluids. Additional style was also a part of the T10's intentions, and white wall tires added a bit of class to the small cycle. Chrome fenders matched the side panels of the fuel tank and side covers. Rubber kneepads continued to be used almost universally and a spacious saddle had room for two and included a grab strap for the passenger. The frame, forks and headlight bucket were delivered in whichever color the bike was ordered in, with black or blue being shown as the paint choices.

A variety of accessories could be added to the T10 and some of the more popular choices were the clear windshield and lower leg shrouds. An enlarged luggage rack could also be bolted to the rear of the T10, greatly increasing carrying capacity and usefulness.

1964 SUZUKI

Model	Engine	Displacement	Transmission
T10	Single cylinder	50cc	–
K11	Single cylinder	80cc	–
T10	Two-cylinder	246cc	Four-Speed

SUZUKI 1965

Only one model from the 1964 catalog would reappear for 1965, but the lineup now totaled five Suzukis. The larger 79cc K11 Sports 80 was back with no changes from the previous year. The smaller M12 was pulled for 1965 but another 49cc model would be introduced the following year.

First of the new entries for 1965 was the B100, powered by a single cylinder engine that displaced 118cc. The two-stroke engine delivered 9 hp at 7,000 rpm and shifted through a four-speed gearbox. The S10 was also new and featured a slightly larger 124cc engine but still used only a single lung. The added displacement provided more power with 10.5 ponies on tap at 7,000 rpm. The exhaust ports were teamed with matching exhausts to provide improved breathing. Weighing 257 lbs. dry, the S10 also carried curvaceous fenders and an amply-padded pillion for the rider.

Moving to the twin cylinder listings, the S32 was powered by a 149cc mill that supplied 16 hp. Weighing in at only a few pounds more than the S10, this twin cylinder machine was much quicker yet remained nimble. Overall dimensions of the S32 matched the S10 as well, putting them on par as far as size went, but the S32 won out in the speed category.

The next new face for Suzuki was the X-6 Hustler, also known as the T20. With a 247cc, twin-cylinder engine in its frame, the X-6 pumped out 29 hp at only 7,500 rpm. A dry weight of 316 lbs. was still fairly light despite the more spacious accommodations and bigger motor. A real two-person saddle was part of the plan and the ubiquitous chrome fuel tank sides were still adorned with rubber kneepads.

The K11 was the smallest Suzuki sold for 1965 with a 79cc, single-cylinder engine in charge of moving the lightweight model along.
Suzuki Motors Corporation.

New for 1965 was the X-6 Hustler. Also known as the T20, it carried a 247cc twin-cylinder engine and comfortable seating for two.
Suzuki Motors Corporation.

1965 SUZUKI

Model	Engine	Displacement	Transmission
K11 Sports 80	Single cylinder	79cc	–
B100 (New for 1965)	Single cylinder	118cc	Four-speed
S10 (New for 1965)	Two-cylinder	124cc	–
S32 (New for 1965)	Two-cylinder	149cc	–
X-6 Super Six (New for 1965)	Two-cylinder	247cc	Four-Speed

SUZUKI
1966

The X-6 Hustler returned for more fun in 1966 but was basically the same machine that was introduced the year before.

Owner/Photo: Roger Smith

A few smaller models made their way into the 1966 Suzuki catalog while most of the bigger machines carried on as before.

The M15 was first sold as a 1965 edition and was motivated by a 49cc, two-stroke engine. For a small machine, it was well dressed with a valanced front fender and two-person saddle. White wall tires brought a level of sophistication to the entry-level crew and the rubber kneepads were still in use against chrome side panels on the fuel tank.

The A100 was also a new entry and was slotted in between the returning K11 and B100, now called the B120. The A100 was fairly typical of the machines in that class and used a 98cc engine to move it along producing 9.5 hp at 5000 RPM. A single exhaust pipe led spent fumes away.

The previously named B100 returned wearing a B120 badge. The same 118cc engine was used, as was the rest of the 1965 hardware. The S32 and T20 (X-6) also returned in 1966 with few if any alterations from the previous versions.

The 1966 model year would be a fairly quiet one, but 1967 would see a raft of new models being introduced to the US market by Suzuki.

1966 SUZUKI

Model	Engine	Displacement	Transmission
M15 (New for 1966)	Single cylinder	49cc	–
K11 Sports 80	Single cylinder	79cc	–
A100 (New for 1966)	Single cylinder	98cc	–
B120 (New for 1966)	Single cylinder	118cc	Four-Speed
S32	Two-cylinder	149cc	–
X-6 Super Six	Two-cylinder	247cc	Four-Speed

SUZUKI
1967

After a year of mild revisions, 1967 would deliver a bountiful model range with fresh blood at both ends of the displacement rainbow.

The K10P Corsair was the smallest of the new street legal machines. The 167 lb. model was fitted with a single cylinder engine that produced 7.5 hp at 6,500 rpm. A two-person saddle sat atop the pressed steel frame. The chassis, fenders and swing arm were all finished in the color of choice. Chrome panels on the fuel tank contours continued to be accented by chrome panels and rubber kneepads. The K15P Hillbilly featured a revised fuel tank and luggage rack. Chrome trim finished off the bottom edge of the saddle and rubber fork gaiters replaced the metal versions of the 1966 models. Suzuki introduced their automatic lubrication system, dubbing it "Posi-Force." A decal claiming the addition to the K15P was found on the side cover. With a dry weight of only 176 lbs., the 8-hp ride was entertaining.

The A100 Charger was joined by a more rugged AS100 Sierra variation as well, bringing another option to the scrambler market. Two new models were powered by the same 118cc engine, but were designed to take on different roles. The B100P Magnum was bent on street riding while the B105P Bearcat set its sights on off-road adventures. Both variants included the new Posi-Force oiling and the Bearcat added a dual-range, four-speed gearbox. This feature doubled the choices of gear ratios to better meet with the demands of off-street riding.

The Bearcat's exhaust pipe was also mounted high on the chassis, unlike the low-mounted tube

The K10 Corsair was another new model for 1967 and featured a 79cc, single-cylinder engine and was a light, 167-lbs. dry weight.
Suzuki Motors Corporation.

The K15P was altered from the K15 it replaced. A new fuel tank, luggage rack and chrome trim set it apart from the 1966 version.
Suzuki Motors Corporation.

Designed for purely off-road riding, the TC120 had a high-mounted exhaust and its front fender provided the clearance needed for rugged terrain.
Suzuki Motors Corporation.

Destined for street legal riding was the T125, new for 1967.
Suzuki Motors Corporation.

| SUZUKI | STANDARD CATALOG OF JAPANESE Motorcycles |

Switch craft.

For more facts on the X-6 Hustler and other models write: U. S. Suzuki Motor Corp., P.O. Box 2967, Dept. 656, Santa Fe Springs, Calif. 96070.

Why is everyone switching to bewitching Suzuki?

Is it the kicky X-6 Hustler, the bike that set a world land speed record for 250cc machines at Bonneville.

Is it the Suzuki Dual-Stroke engine; the spirited master-stroke that brews up more response, more usable hp than a 4-stroke—with less urging. (Hup, two. Not Hup, two, three, four.)

Is it Posi-Force lubrication that ends oil-gas mixing for good.

Is it Suzuki's noticeably mellower pitch (so she can hear yours).

Is it the amazing comfort and safety Suzuki alone has achieved by designing for America's longer roads and riders.

Or is it the extra run—and fun—for the money the Suzuki 12 month/12,000 mile Warranty guarantees.

It's longest of the leading sportcycles and the only one with valuable trade-in provisions.

Just ask a nearby Suzuki dealer.

With fifteen beguiling models, you are bound to get caught up in the spell.

solo SUZUKI
You won't be alone!

of the Magnum. Knobby tires and a high-mounted front fender played a role in the Bearcat's more rugged personality. Both machines weighed in at just under 200 lbs. when dry and produced nearly the same amount of power. The Bearcat claimed 11 hp at 7,500 rpm while the Magnum's chart showed 10 hp at 7,000 rpm. The Magnum was shifted through a traditional four-speed box.

Suzuki was developing a habit of selling many of their machines in two variations, one for the street and one for dual-purpose riding. The T200 and TC200 Stingray were included in these Jekyll and Hyde teams. The "TC" denomination referred to the dual purpose or Scrambler flavor. Both T200 and TC200 were powered by a 196cc, twin-cylinder engine that cranked out 23 hp when spun at 7,500 rpm.

Both machines fired up quickly and fed their power to the chain-driven rear wheel via a five-speed gearbox. Two people could be carried on either version and each had a fuel tank of slightly different contours. The TC200 wore a high-mounted exhaust that was covered with a chrome heat shield. No extra clearance was gained at the front fender of the TC. It only required $575 to ride home a brand new 1967 T200 from the dealer. There were three variations powered by the same 247cc, parallel twin engine. The T21 version shifted through a six-speed gearbox. The X6, T21 and TC250 all filled different needs by adapting the same drive train to the required audience.

The X6 was a returning model while the T21 was an improved version of the T20. The TC250 Hustler was the latest iteration—the "TC" meant on and off-road use.

High-mounted exhausts protected the rider's legs from heat with slotted shields. The high performance T21 also carried a twin-shoe front brake and tachometer, both exotic in the day. The 33 hp reading made the T21 one of the quickest machines of the period and it was quite popular among buyers.

Available in street or scrambler formats, the TC200 was geared for riding on both paved and unpaved surfaces.
Suzuki Motors Corporation.

In 1967, Suzuki positioned its X-5 Invader as a motorcycle that realized its place in the pecking order, a smaller version of the successful X-6 Hustler.
Suzuki Motors Corporation

1967 SUZUKI

Model	Engine	Displacement	Transmission
K10P Corsair (New for 1967)	Single cylinder	79cc	–
K11P Challenger	Single cylinder	79cc	–
K15P Hillbilly Revised K15 Model	Single cylinder	79cc	–
A90 (New for 1967)	Single cylinder	86cc	–
A100 Charger	Single cylinder	98cc	–
AS100 Sierra (New for 1967)	Single cylinder	118cc	Four-Speed
B100P Magnum (New for 1967)	Single cylinder	118cc	Four-Speed
B105P Bearcat (New for 1967)	Single cylinder	118cc	Dual-Range Four-Speed
B120	Single cylinder	118cc	Four-Speed
TC120 (New for 1967)	Single cylinder	118cc	–
T125 (New for 1967)	Two-cylinder	124cc	–
T200 (New for 1967)	Two-cylinder	196cc	Five-Speed
TC200 Stingray (New for 1967)	Two-cylinder	196cc	Five-Speed
X-6 Super Six	Two-cylinder	247cc	Four-Speed
T21 Super (New for 1967)	Two-cylinder	247cc	Six-Speed
TC250 Hustler (New for 1967)	Two-cylinder	247cc	Four-speed

SUZUKI
1968

Replacing the chrome-sided storage cell of the standard X6 was this shapely fiberglass tank which added some real zest to the model.
Vintage Memories, Inc.

Bringing up the lower end of the spectrum was the 50cc AS50 for 1968. After a blockbuster year of new model releases, Suzuki culled the herd in 1968, leaving fewer models behind than they pulled. Among the new names, their T500/Five would set the stage for changes at Suzuki.

In a market that was mostly filled with smaller machines, Suzuki rolled out their big 492cc, five-speed model for 1968. The twin-cylinder motor claimed a "cool 46 horses" at only 7,000 rpm and a top speed of 110 to 120 mph. Brakes and tires were closer to racing machines than to street-legal craft and the 34mm Mikuni carburetors compensated for changes in altitude automatically. Period magazine reviews were mostly positive about the big Suzuki, with a few nagging complaints offered as well. Overall it was considered to be a worthy competitor to Honda's Black Bomber. Posi-Force lubrication remained a primary feature, but on the 500/Five it almost got lost in the blend of outstanding features.

The next new notch in the Suzuki belt was the 305 Raider. A twin-cylinder mill displaced exactly 305cc and was shifted with the class leading six-speed gearbox. With a half a tank of fuel on board, the Raider was a reasonably svelte 332 lbs. A seat height of only 30.7 inches made it more attractive to riders who lacked in stature but still enjoyed the fun of riding. An MSRP of $609 was shown for the new middleweight machine and it proved to be a popular choice among buyers.

"Suzuki makes it" was shouted from the rooftops, or at least from the pages of period magazines. Suzuki Motors Corporation.

The biggest 1968 Suzuki was the new 500/Five. Its 492cc engine was tamed by a five-speed gearbox and a top speed of 110 mph was touted.
Suzuki Motors Corporation.

Another fresh entry in the 1968 lineup was the T305. A six-speed gearbox made it unique among other machines of the same class.
Suzuki Motors Corporation.

The TM250 was a pure Moto-cross machine, and was powered with a 250cc aluminum Dual-Stroke engine that sent 32 horsepower to the rear wheel. Both the X-6 Scrambler and Hustler received cosmetic alterations, turning them into sleek, European race machines. In place of the standard fuel tanks, a molded fiberglass unit led directly to the rear of the machine in an under-seat fashion. The taillight was also housed in a racy enclosure, giving the X-6 a brand new look while still delivering the same performance as before.

It motored along with only 50cc of displacement. The AS50 featured a five-speed gearbox to enhance the experience. The diminutive machine could reach a top speed of 60 miles per hour and the racing-style fuel tank did nothing to dispel the notion of speed.

The T200 and TC200 both returned for 198 as well but offered nothing new to the buyer.

1968 SUZUKI

Model	Engine	Displacement	Transmission
AS50 Colt (New for 1968)	Single cylinder	49cc	Five-Speed
AC90	Single cylinder	86cc	–
AS100 Sierra	Single cylinder	98cc	–
T200	Two-cylinder	196cc	Five-speed
TC200 Stingray	Two-cylinder	196cc	Five-Speed
TC250 Hustler	Two-cylinder	247cc	Four-Speed
TM250 (New for 1968)	Single cylinder	249cc	–
TC305 Raider (New for 1968)	Two-cylinder	305cc	Six-speed
TC305 (New for 1968)	Two-cylinder	305cc	Six-speed
T500/Five (New for 1968)	Two-cylinder	492cc	Five-speed

SUZUKI
1969

The 1969 Titan was actually a 500/Five wearing new clothes for the latest model year.

Suzuki Motors Corporation

Eight models comprised the entire 1969 Suzuki catalog as they wrestled with product mix and changing market demands. Honda had already fired their mighty CB750 across the bow of every other manufacturer, sending them running to the drawing boards in an effort to keep up.

Even with a relatively low quantity of models offered, there were numerous changes to the faces seen on the showroom floors.

The AC100 Wolf was the smallest of the new street models and was assembled using a "Flying-Wedge" frame and 14 horsepower motor. Suzuki flaunted its "Grand Prix" design and turn signals as major selling points of the Wolf. The smaller AS50 remained in the catalog as well.

Taking a small step forward was the T125 Stinger. Also built for riding on the street, the Stinger used a two-cylinder, 124cc engine to propel itself to a top speed that was claimed to be 120 mph. For a machine that weighed only 211 lbs. dry, that's quite a handful at speed. Roman Red adorned the fuel tank for 1969 and was the only color listed for the Stinger.

The X6R Hustler returned and was now stopped with the help of a double-leading-shoe front brake. Morro Green or Mesa Orange was topped off with a black stripe across the top of the fuel tanks. One all=new model for 1969 was the T-350 Rebel. A 315cc parallel twin engine hung in its frame and a six-speed transmission was on hand for gear selection. Some 39 hp was listed along with a dry weight of 328 lbs. for the Rebel. The 1969 hues were Cape Ivory or Redondo Blue with a white racing stripe. The retail prices were listed as $749 for the Rebel regardless of color.

Suzuki's 500/Five returned as the T500 II Titan for 1969 and was the recipient of several revisions. A redesigned fuel tank was the most obvious change and it gave the Titan a sleeker profile. Beneath the tank resided the 492cc Dual-Stroke engine that put 47 hp in the rider's hands.

Posi-Force lubrication and Vol-U-Matic Induction helped the big two-stroke to breath and stay slippery. Red line tires added a bit of flair to the Titan's looks as well and Colorado Gold or Mesa Orange was accented with a black stripe. For the buyer looking at the Scrambler range, the TC-120 Cat was another new selection. The 210-

New for 1969 was the T-350 Rebel. A 315cc, twin-cylinder engine and six-speed gearbox delivered ample fun for any rider.

Suzuki Motors Corporation.

lb. machine featured a 118cc, single-cylinder engine and could hit 55 mph when it was prompted. Nearly eight inches of ground clearance proved to be adequate under most conditions the Cat would approach. A Tri-Form frame was utilized to carry the remaining hardware with all the required clearance and rigidity an off-road machine would need. The motorcycle's 12 hp was also enough to move the rider and his machine over rugged terrain without a hitch. A dual-range gearbox provided six ratios to the rider and a simple flip of a switch was all it took to go from low to high range. The Cat was sold in your choice of Aspen Yellow with a red stripe or Mesa Orange with white accent stripe.

For the more aggressive Enduro rider, the TS-250 Savage was right up their alley. Powered by a 246cc single-lung engine, the Savage was Suzuki's most powerful Dual-Stroke motor in 1969. A competition power-pipe exhaust boosted output while keeping things quiet. Both the Cat and Savage included flip-top seats that provided easy access to the necessary tool kit and for easier maintenance. Whether the choice was a Savage in Roman Red or Monterey Green, silver accent stripes dolled up the finish.

1969 SUZUKI

Model	Engine	Displacement	Transmission
AS50 Maverick	Single cylinder	49cc	Five-Speed
AC100 Wolf	Single cylinder	100cc	Five-Speed
TC120 Cat	Single cylinder	118cc	Dual Range Three-Speed
T125 Stinger	Two-cylinder	124cc	Five-Speed
TC250 Hustler	Two-cylinder	247cc	Four-Speed
TS250 Savage	Single cylinder	246cc	Four-Speed
TC350 Rebel (New for 1969)	Two-cylinder	315cc	Six-speed
T500 II Titan (Revised for 1969)	Two-cylinder	492cc	Five-speed

1970

Another year of quiet fell over the Suzuki catalog as most models returned with few changes. A pair of 89cc models joined the ranks of the multi-purpose machines as people continued to embrace that segment of the market. The AC50 Maverick was back in Pop Green with chrome fenders. The upswept exhaust was matte black with a chrome heat shield with no other alterations listed.

The first of the new 89cc models was the TC90 Blazer. A two-stroke, 89cc engine was fitted with a chrome exhaust and heat shield and featured a dual range, four-speed transmission. An oversized trail saddle provided plenty of comfort whether on- or off-road riding. Ascot Red or Monterey Green paint was used on the tank and front fender with an accent stripe of white along the bottom edge of the fuel tank. The front fender of the Blazer was mounted high above the tire, providing extra clearance needed when riding in the rough. Powered by the same 89cc engine, the TS90 Honcho featured a low mounted, chrome fender up front and a blacked-out exhaust. A chrome heat shield was added for protection. Strip Orange or Aspen Yellow was accented by a Suzuki "S" and white stripe on the fuel tank.

The TC120 Cat was back for 1970 and wore grab of Pop Green or Baja Gold with black stripes on the tank. The three-speed, dual range transmission was still in place. The TC125 Stinger was now designated with a "II" and carried a few minor changes. Pop Green paint was trimmed with a black stripe and white "Suzuki" name on the tank. The high mounted exhaust was black with chrome

Whether you chose the Ascot Red or Monterey Green, the fuel tank and front fender received the same treatment.

Suzuki Motors Corporation.

SUZUKI

Chrome fenders offset the Pop Green hue of the 1970 Maverick but little else was different from the 1969 edition.

Suzuki Motors Corporation.

heat shield and silencer. The torque link for the rear brake was moved and now mounted below the swing arm.

Another model to be upgraded to level two status was the T250 Hustler. Black exhaust now ran higher on the frame and was guarded by a chrome shield and complimented with a matching silencer. Redondo Blue and Aspen Yellow were listed as the available hues. Continuing with their application, the TS250 Savage was also now named the TS250 II. Strip Orange or Aspen Yellow were used on the fuel tank while the high-mounted front fender was finished in chrome. The T350 II Rebel returned and provided many riders with a stable machine in the middleweight class. Both tank and side covers wore Sophia Green or Scarlet Medium paint with white accent stripes.

Having been upgraded to a level II in 1969, the T500 Titan received a grade III title in 1970. A chrome luggage rack was added to the top of the fuel tank and Corporate Blue or Lime Green could be selected to cover the sheet metal and side covers.

1970 SUZUKI

Model	Engine	Displacement	Transmission
AC50 Maverick	Single cylinder	49cc	Five-Speed
TC90 Blazer (New for 1970)	Single cylinder	89cc	Dual Range Four-Speed
TS90 Honcho (New for 1970)	Single cylinder	89cc	Five-Speed
TC120 II Cat	Single cylinder	118cc	Dual Range Three-Speed
T125 II Stinger	Two-cylinder	124cc	Five-Speed
TC250 Hustler	Two-cylinder	247cc	Four-Speed
TS250 II Savage	Single cylinder	249cc	Five-Speed
TC350 Rebel	Two-cylinder	315cc	Six-speed
T500 II Titan	Two-cylinder	492cc	Five-speed

1971

Suzuki continued to retain its composure as the market tried to respond to Honda's trendsetting CB750 of 1969. One model was pulled from the 1971 Suzuki catalog while three new names were chiseled in.

The AC50 Maverick rode off into the sunset and was replaced by a different 49cc machine. The TS50R Gaucho was similar to the Maverick in that it still incorporated a close-fitting chrome fender over the rear wheel. Where the Maverick had a matching rear wheel cover, the Gaucho had none. The bezel of

Suzuki reused the Sierra name on the 1971 T185R. They applied silver side covers with both the Aspen Yellow or Daytona Blue versions.

Suzuki Motors Corporation.

the Gaucho's headlight featured a flat bottom and the exhaust was found on the right side, finished in black and trimmed with a chrome heat shield. Ascot Red was applied to the fuel tank and side covers and was the only hue listed for 1971.

As a rule, any of the 1970 Suzukis that had been labeled with a "II" designation were now shown with an "R" instead. The Titan III also earned the new "R" label in place of the previous identifier. The TS125R Duster was the next new family member to play in the on- and off-road segment of the Suzuki line. With

The 1971 Suzuki T-500 Titan was posed by a drag strip in this magazine ad, ready to "take on the country."

Strip Orange or Hawaii Green. Side covers were finished in silver. Added durability came from using steel for the lower sections of the front forks.

The T250R Hustler featured low pipes finished in chrome and a selection of Hawaii Green or Mojave Copper paint. 1971 saw the side covers of the T350R Rebel extended to hide the airbox with Candy Yellow or Lime Green covering the bodywork.

Besides gaining the latest "R" designation, the T500R Titan now wore a flat-bottom headlight bezel and the added convenience of a flip-up fuel cap. White stripes on the fuel tank offset the California Burgundy or Newport Blue paint nicely.

a 123cc, single-cylinder engine in the frame, the Duster carried its front fender high. The blacked-out exhaust pipe was adorned with a stylishly perforated heat shield of chrome. A flat-bottom headlight bezel was again seen, and the gauges included a wide swath of chrome across their lower flank.

Daytona Blue or Aspen Yellow was applied to the front fender and fuel tank while the side covers were silver. The Sierra name was re-applied to a new TS185R for 1971. A single lung, 183cc two-stroke engine drove the Sierra and a high-mounted exhaust was again black with a chrome heat guard. A circular headlight and chrome fenders were complimented by a fuel tank of either

Suzuki promoted the TS-185 Sierra as a new class of off-road machine in its 1971 advertising.

1971 SUZUKI

Model	Engine	Displacement	Transmission
TS50R Gaucho (New for 1971)	Single cylinder	49cc	Five-Speed
TC90R Blazer	Single cylinder	89cc	Dual Range Four-Speed
TS90R Honcho (New for 1971)	Single cylinder	89cc	Five-Speed
TC120R Cat	Single cylinder	118cc	Dual Range Three-Speed
T125R Stinger	Two cylinder	124cc	Five-Speed
TS125R Duster (New for 1971)	Single cylinder	123cc	Five-Speed
TS185R Sierra (New for 1971)	Single cylinder	183cc	Five-Speed
TC250R Hustler	Two-cylinder	247cc	Four-Speed
TS250R Savage	Single cylinder	249cc	Five-Speed
T350R Rebel	Two-cylinder	315cc	Six-Speed
T500R Titan	Two-cylinder	492cc	Five-Speed

SUZUKI

STANDARD CATALOG OF ® JAPANESE Motorcycles

MT-50R Trailhopper
Anyone can ride it. 3 hp. engine. 3 speed automatic. Full suspension, handbrakes. Adjustable seat, handlebars. CCI automatic lube.

TC-120R Cat
Ride it on street or trail. Dual-range trans. — changes with a kick. CCI automatic lube. Chrome luggage carrier.

T-250R Hustler
The fastest 250cc street bike made! 15.1 quarter, 100 mph. 6 speeds. CCI automatic lube. 6 port power. Double leading shoe front brakes.

F-50R Cutlass
"Step-through" frame. 3 speed automatic. 50cc reed-valve engine. 45 mph. CCI automatic lube. Nearly 200 mile per gallon economy.

T-125R Stinger
125 cc's of quickness. 70 mph. Parallel twin carbs & pipes. Tach & Speedo. Competition styling. CCI automatic lube. 5 speeds.

T-350R Rebel
Outrides any 350 made. 13.8 quarter. 40 hp. 6 speeds. CCI automatic lube. 6 port power. Double leading shoe front brakes.

TS-50R Gaucho
The only 50 built like a real motorcycle. 5 speeds. Enduro-styling. 60 mph. CCI automatic lube. Rotary-valve engine.

TS-125R Duster
The 125 enduro machine. 13 hp/7000 rpm. Bead stoppers. Primary kick. 5-way adjustable rear shocks. CCI automatic lube. 5 speeds.

TM-400R Cyclone
Complete moto-cross competition racer. 40 hp. Alum. alloy rims. Competition muffler. 5 speeds. Single leading shoe front brakes. CCI automatic lube. PEI ignition.

TS-90R Honcho
The "king" of the lightweight enduros! 65 mph. Alum. rotary-valve engine. 5 speeds. Tube frame. CCI automatic lube.

TS-185R Sierra
Outperforms anything in its class. 17.5 hp. 5-way adj. rear shocks. 3-way adjustable front forks. 5 speeds. CCI automatic lube.

TC-90R Blazer
Ride it on street or trail. 8 spd. dual-range trans. Tube frame. CCI automatic lube. Dual passenger seat. Alum. rotary-valve engine.

TS-250R Savage
Built like the world champion motocross Suzuki. 23 hp @ 6500 rpm. Alum. engine. PEI ignition. CCI automatic lube. 5-way adjustable rear shocks. 5 speeds. Single leading shoe front brakes.

T-500R Titan
Championship performance. 13.2 quarter. 47 hp. 5 speeds. CCI automatic lube. Deep cushion dual saddle. Double leading shoe front brakes.

Suzuki
U.S Suzuki Motor Corp. Santa Fe Springs, Calif. 90670

The complete Suzuki lineup was shown in this 1971 ad from the tiny Trailhopper to the T-500R Titan.

STANDARD CATALOG OF® JAPANESE MOTORCYCLES

SUZUKI
1972

The three-cylinder engine was wrapped in a jacket that circulated fluids to keep things cool, even under extreme conditions.

Vintage Memories, Inc.

The 1972 model year saw Suzuki sticking to its two-stroke regimen and the company even added new models to the fray. Every model was powered by a two-stroke engine, but growing US government scrutiny put the smoky machines to the test. All the Suzuki "R" designations from 1971 were supplanted by "J" in the Suzuki line for 1972.

Missing from the 1972 lineup were the TC120R Cat and T125R Stinger. A solitary new model, the TC125J Prospector, filled their shoes in the Scrambler category. Chrome fenders over both wheels and a matching luggage rack added some flash. Another application of the rakishly perforated heat guard was seen over the black exhaust that led spent fumes from the 123cc engine. Adding useful ratios to the rider's tool box was the four-speed, dual-range transmission. A bigger bike for the Scrambler class arrived with the TS400J Apache. A single cylinder engine that displaced 386cc hung from the frame and was finished in black. A black exhaust dropped low

209

The GT550J Indy was a new model for 1972 and produced 12 more horsepower than its smaller sibling, the GT380.

Owner/Photo: Philip A. Koenen

before swinging north and was treated to the same perforated heat shield as seen on other Suzukis of the period. Suzuki chose to introduce a line of street machines that were powered by larger two-stroke engines. The bikes were named for fabled racing courses around the world.

First in the pits was the GT380J Sebring. Adding a third cylinder to the two-stroke equation produced more power with little in the way of weight penalties. The 371cc engine featured Suzuki's latest Ram-Air cooling for the engine and their unique three-into-four exhaust system. A drum brake on the front wheel helped to slow the Sebring and rubber fork boots were found on the debut model. With half a tank of fuel onboard, the Sebring weighed just under 400 lbs. and could return mileage up to 46 miles per gallon. A top speed that fell just short of 100 mph was attainable on the $925 Sebring.

The GT550J Indy was also released for 1972. Sharing much of the same architecture as its smaller Sebring sibling, the Indy was rated at 50 hp, a gain of 12 over the 380. The same three-into-four chrome exhaust was used to quiet the two-stroke roar. A dual, twin-leading brake shoe was found on the front wheel of the 550, helping to slow the slightly heavier machine. Starting the 550 was much easier with its new electric mechanism, a feature not found on the 380. The chosen color was also applied to the side covers and headlight mounting ears.

Perhaps the biggest news in the triple-cylinder entries was the GT750J Le Mans, also known as the Water Buffalo. The water-jacketed engine was blamed for the unusual nickname, but has become synonymous with the Le Mans today. Although fairly heavy, weighing 535 lbs. when it was fueled, the 738cc, three-cylinder engine produced 67 hp—big enough to push it along with decent swiftness.

Electric start made bringing the big triple to life a breeze and a five-speed gearbox was on hand. Drum brakes on the front wheel made stopping confident. A large radiator was hung from the frames, down tubes and was a big part of the Le Mans cooling system. The temperature-controlled fluid was sent swirling around the trio of pots to keep things within range. The system worked well but was a unusual for the period. Carrying a retail tag of $1,575, the Le Mans fell in line with competitors' machines of the same period. The radiator cover, headlight mounts and side covers also received the chosen color.

1972 SUZUKI

Model	Engine	Displacement	Transmission
TS50J Gaucho	Single cylinder	49cc	Five-Speed
TC90J Blazer	Single cylinder	89cc	Dual Range Four-Speed
TS90J Honcho (New for 1972)	Single cylinder	89cc	Five-Speed
TC125J Prospector (New for 1972)	Single cylinder	123cc	Dual Range Four-Speed
TS125J Duster	Single cylinder	123cc	Five-Speed
TS185J Sierra	Single cylinder	183cc	Five-Speed
TC250J Hustler	Two-cylinder	247cc	Four-Speed
TS250J Savage	Single cylinder	249cc	Five-Speed
T350J Rebel	Two-cylinder	315cc	Six-Speed
GT380J Sebring (New for 1972)	Three-cylinder	371cc	Six-Speed
TS400J Apache (New for 1972)	Single cylinder	386cc	Five-Speed
T500J Titan	Two-cylinder	492cc	Five-speed
GT550J Indy (New for 1972)	Three-cylinder	543cc	Five-Speed
GT750J Le Mans (New for 1972)	Three-cylinder	738cc	Five-Speed

1973

Having introduced their new line of road-going two-strokes for 1972, only minor changes would grace the 1973 team of Suzukis.

The TC90J Blazer was replaced with a slightly larger TC100K Blazer, just as the TS90J Honcho saw a bigger TS100K Honcho ride in to take the reins. The 1972 T250J Hustler was pulled from the bench only to be supplanted by the 1973 GT250K Hustler. Ram Air cooling was added to the engine and the exhaust canisters bore a new profile. The fuel tank and side covers also carried new contours and a chrome headlight bucket was held in position by equally chromed ears. Wine Red and Rally Blue were listed for color options.

Although not in keeping with the race track-inspired series of 1972, the GT185K Adventurer was a smaller version of a similar machine. Powered by a twin-cylinder, 184cc engine, it differed from other models by having vertical cylinder orientation versus the angled versions used on all other Suzuki models.

A lighter alloy was used for the jugs and cast-in liners provided a long life. The engine produced 21 hp at 7,500 rpm with the lat-

Shown as a new model for 1973, the GT185K Adventurer carried a twin-cylinder engine in its flanks and shifted through a five-speed gearbox.
Suzuki Motors Corporation

SUZUKI

The Water Buffalo was back in 1973 and was seen with a set of disc brakes on the front wheel and chrome trim on the radiator shroud.
Suzuki Motors Corporation

The T250J of 1972 became the GT250K Hustler in 1973, although changes were made in the engine and with related hardware.
Suzuki Motors Corporation

The GT380K Sebring received several upgrades for the latest year including a hydraulic front disc brake. A gas cap that was locked when not in use and a circular headlight set the 1973 models apart from the earlier versions. Canyon Red and Coronado Blue were the new shades for 1973. The slightly larger GT550K Indy also got the hydraulic front disc brake and Lime Green or Hermosa Blue as hues.

After its 1972 debut, the GT750K Le Mans was back for another round of liquid cooled fun. The big triple now sported a pair of disc brakes on the front wheel, greatly improving the rider's ability to stop the heavyweight machine. Color matched radiator covers were swapped for chrome versions and the gas cap now flipped open and could be locked. Royal Red or Royal Blue were trimmed by a top stripe of white on the fuel tank.

est power plant. The kick-start lever was found on the right side of the chassis and a five-speed gearbox was installed. A tubular steel frame was typical of the period and did a fine job of keeping the GT185K together.

Remaining in the family photo for 1973 was the GT380K Sebring and it now carried a disc brake on its front wheel.
Suzuki Motors Corporation

1973 SUZUKI

Model	Engine	Displacement	Transmission
TS50K Gaucho	Single cylinder	49cc	Five-Speed
TS100K Blazer (New for 1973)	Single cylinder	97cc	Dual Range Four-Speed
TS100K Honcho (New for 1973)	Single cylinder	89cc	Five-Speed
TC125K Prospector	Single cylinder	123cc	Dual Range Four-Speed
TS125K Duster	Single cylinder	123cc	Five-Speed
GT185K Adventurer (New for 1973)	Two-cylinder	184cc	Five-Speed
TS185K Sierra	Single cylinder	183cc	Five-Speed
GT250K Hustler (Revised for 1973)	Two-cylinder	247cc	Four-Speed
TS250K Savage	Single cylinder	249cc	Five-Speed
GT380K Sebring	Three-cylinder	371cc	Six-Speed
TS400K Apache	Single cylinder	396cc	Five-Speed
T500K Titan	Two-cylinder	492cc	Five-Speed
GT550K Indy	Three-cylinder	543cc	Five-Speed
GT750K Le Mans	Three-cylinder	738cc	Five-Speed

STANDARD CATALOG OF ® JAPANESE MOTORCYCLES   SUZUKI

1974

Changes to the 1974 Suzuki catalog were sparse although the "K" designation was changed to "L" for the 1974 models.

A front disc brake was added to the GT185L Adventurer, making the small machine more capable than before.

The only new model to join Suzuki for 1974 was the TC185L Ranger. Yet another variation in their on- and off-road lineup, the Ranger could be started with the push of a button. A kick-start leg was still in place to bring the 183cc, two-stroke engine to life. Chrome fenders, both fore and aft, were joined by headlight mounts to match. Candy Gold paint was highlighted by red and white stripes on the fuel tank.

A factory luggage rack was added to this 1974 Water Buffalo to enhance its ability to tote bulkier objects.
Bill Abdou

SUZUKI

The water jackets of the GT750's engine lacked any form of cooling fins since that chore was tackled by the circulating fluid.

Bill Abdou

The GT250L Hustler received the bonus of Ram Air cooling for its motor, helping to maintain the proper temperature and add some power.

New technology saw the addition of a digital gear indicator being added to the GT380L Sebring, GT550L Indy and GT750L Le Mans. With the exception of new colors on all models, no additiona; modifications were seen for 1974.

1974 SUZUKI

Model	Engine	Displacement	Transmission
TS50L Gaucho	Single cylinder	49cc	Five-Speed
TC100L Blazer	Single cylinder	97cc	Dual Range Four-Speed
TS100L Honcho	Single cylinder	89cc	Five-Speed
TC125L Prospector	Single cylinder	123cc	Dual Range Four-Speed
TS125L Duster	Single cylinder	123cc	Five-Speed
GT185L Adventurer (Front disc brakes)	Two-cylinder	184cc	Five-Speed
TC185L Ranger Electric Start (New for 1974)	Single cylinder	183cc	Five-Speed
TS185L Sierra	Single cylinder	183cc	Five-Speed
GT250L Hustler (Ram Air cooling)	Two-cylinder	247cc	Four-Speed
TS250L Savage	Single cylinder	249cc	Five-Speed
GT380L Sebring (Digital Gear Indicator)	Three-cylinder	371cc	Six-Speed
TS400L Apache	Single cylinder	396cc	Five-Speed
T500L Titan	Two-cylinder	492cc	Five-Speed
GT550L Indy (Digital Gear Indicator)	Three-cylinder	543cc	Five-Speed
GT750L Le Mans (Digital Gear Indicator)	Three-cylinder	738cc	Five-Speed

STANDARD CATALOG OF ® JAPANESE Motorcycles

SUZUKI
1975

Powered by an unusual, yet exceptionally smooth rotary motor, the RE5 caused quite a stir when it was released to the public.

Bill Abdou

The 1975 model year would prove to be another quiet one on the Suzuki front with the exception of one radical new machine designed for the street. The TS50L Gaucho was removed from the corral but the TS75M Colt was saddled up to take its place. Motivated by a 72cc engine that was finished in natural silver, the Colt had a bit more power than the departing Gaucho. Orange paint on the fuel tank was spruced up with silver stripes that matched the headlight support brackets.

The GT250M Hustler was seen in only Aztec Gold and a revised brake hose made its way to the front caliper. The T500M Titan was another model to be sold in only one color for 1975 and that was Coronado Blue with gold pinstripes on the fuel tank.

Still shying away from the four-stroke revolution applied elsewhere, Suzuki took the two-stroke design in a new direction when they introduced the RE5M, a Wankel-powered motorcycle for 1975.

The principal behind the rotary was that by avoiding the usual thrust and parry of a reciprocating piston, the engine would be far smoother

SUZUKI

Suzuki saw no sense in using a typical set of gauges on their unusual RE5, and instead chose this tubular panel with a retractable front cover of translucent blue plastic.

Bill Abdou

in its operation. On paper the design was flawless, but as with many plans of mice and men, complexity quickly became an issue. A solitary triangular "piston" rotated within the walls of the "cylinder" creating the usual compression and release without the usual stops and starts. The thought process made a great argument. When it was applied to a motorcycle engine things became complicated fast. The physical layout of the engine was a cause of concern and the end result was a frame that was literally jam-packed with motor and its related hardware. Once underway the RE5M did deliver a fairly seamless power band, helping to offset the rest of the confusion.

Period magazine reviews liked the RE5, but their resulting numbers didn't bear any great gain over more traditional machines. The smoothness of the rotary motor was almost perfect once revved higher than idle with an exhaust note that's hard to explain.

Perhaps even harder to explain was the unique, tubular instrument panel used on the 1975 RE5. Hiding behind a blue plastic lens were the gauges that could be revealed by rolling the cover open like a roll top desk. Like the motor itself, the pod was like nothing seen before or since.

The rest of the RE5's design was typical with a fully padded saddle that easily held two adults and spoke wheels. A duo of disc brakes graced the front wheel while a drum was found at the rear. With a claimed weight of 507 lbs. to deal with, the disc brakes were the least that could be expected. Décor on the RE5 was Firemist Blue or Firemist Orange with white accents on the tank and chrome fenders at both ends. The appearance of the RE5 caused quite a stir when first rolled onto the showroom floors, but things got quiet too quickly to ensure a long life for the Wankel-powered craft.

Carrying a massive radiator up front and a single rotary piston engine in its frame, the RE5 was an entirely new species.

Bill Abdou

1975 SUZUKI

Model	Engine	Displacement	Transmission
TS75M Colt (New for 1975)	Single cylinder	72cc	Five-Speed
TC100M Blazer	Single cylinder	97cc	Dual Range Four-Speed
TS100M Honcho	Single cylinder	89cc	Five-Speed
TC125M Prospector	Single cylinder	123cc	Dual Range Four-Speed
TS125M Duster	Single cylinder	123cc	Five-Speed
GT185M Adventurer	Two-cylinder	184cc	Five-Speed
TC185M Ranger (Electric Start)	Single cylinder	183cc	Five-Speed
TS185M Sierra	Single cylinder	183cc	Five-Speed
GT250M Hustler (Ram Air cooling)	Two-cylinder	247cc	Four-Speed
TS250M Savage	Single cylinder	249cc	Five-Speed
GT380M Sebring (Digital Gear Indicator)	Three-cylinder	371cc	Six-Speed
TS400M Apache	Single cylinder	396cc	Five-Speed
T500M Titan	Two-cylinder	492cc	Five-Speed
RE5M (New for 1975)	Rotary	497cc	Five-Speed
GT550M Indy (Digital Gear Indicator)	Three-cylinder	543cc	Five-Speed
GT750M Le Mans (Digital Gear Indicator)	Three-cylinder	738cc	Five-Speed

SUZUKI
1976

With plans to roll out a new series of machines the following year, 1976 would remain very quiet for Suzuki, with only one new face joining the team. The "M" designation of 1975 was changed to "A" for 1976 and a few models lost their names while still carrying the same alpha-numerical listings.

The A100A Go-Fer was a brand new entry for 1976. Weighing only 183 lbs. dry, the A100A didn't need much power to get itself going, so the 98cc engine worked just fine. The engine had 9.3 hp on tap and a four-speed, constant mesh gearbox kept the nimble machine in the power band. Drum brakes on both wheels ensured safe stops to compliment the forward motion available. A two-person saddle and basic instrument panel delivered on the Go-Fer's promise of being easy to ride. Black, Maui Blue Metallic or Lip Maroon Metallic were shown as available hues.

The 1976 GT250A no longer carried the "Hustler" name and also lost its Ram Air cooling feature. As with several of the 1976 Suzuki street machines, the front fender would now be supported by a single rear support. Ontario Orange was the solitary color shown.

GT500A Titan models were given lower fork legs of aluminum and the added stopping power of a front disc brake. Daytona Blue or Targa Red were listed as paint options.

Returning for a second year was the RE5A. The rotary-powered cycle still carried a 497cc engine in its frame, but the space age instrument pod was replaced with a set of traditional gauges. The headlight housing was now finished in chrome versus the body color of 1975 and Black was the only shade the "Water Buffalo" was sold in.

The 1976 model year would prove to be the final one for the RE5 as the rotary concept failed to catch on with buyers. The 1976 Le Mans was now only labeled the GT750A but featured revised tank art and a locking gas cap cover. Coronado Blue and Ontario Orange were the colors of the year.

The rotary-powered RE5 was back in 1976. It was having trouble gaining respect with buyers and was pulled from the catalog at the end of the model year.
Suzuki Motors Corporation

1976 SUZUKI

Model	Engine	Displacement	Transmission
TS75A Colt	Single cylinder	72cc	Five-Speed
A100A Go-Fer (New for 1976)	Single cylinder	98cc	Four-Speed
TC100A Blazer	Single cylinder	97cc	Dual Range Four-Speed
TC100A	Single cylinder	97cc	Five-Speed
TC125A Prospector	Single cylinder	123cc	Dual Range Four-Speed
TS125A Duster	Single cylinder	123cc	Five-Speed
GT185A Adventurer	Two-cylinder	184cc	Five-Speed
TC185A Ranger (Electric Start)	Single cylinder	183cc	Five-Speed
TS185A Sierra	Single cylinder	183cc	Five-Speed
GT250A (Ram Air cooling)	Two-cylinder	247cc	Four-Speed
TS250A	Single cylinder	249cc	Five-Speed
GT380A Sebring (Digital Gear Indicator)	Three-cylinder	371cc	Six-Speed
TS400A Apache	Single cylinder	396cc	Five-Speed
GT500A Titan	Two-cylinder	492cc	Five-Speed
RE5A	Rotary	497cc	Five-Speed
GT550A Indy (Digital Gear Indicator)	Three-cylinder	543cc	Five-Speed
GT750A Le Mans (Digital Gear Indicator)	Three-cylinder	738cc	Five-Speed

SUZUKI
1977

STANDARD CATALOG OF® JAPANESE Motorcycles

After a few mostly peaceful years at Suzuki, 1977 would see the introduction of their first ever four-stroke powered motorcycles. Honda had rolled out their CB750 in 1968 and Kawasaki their Z-1 in 1972. Although not the first one out of the blocks, Suzuki created a great line of new machines in their first attempt. For 1977, a "B" took the place of the previous "A" in listing each model for the year.

The rotary RE5 was no longer offered and was the only model de-listed for 1977. Several others lost their names but kept the same product listing. In the exciting world of four-stroke machines, the GS400B was the first entry for Suzuki. The twin-cylinder mill displaced 398cc and featured a six-speed transmission. A Suzuki exclusive was the "Posi-Tension" cam chain adjuster that maintained the proper tension on the critical component. The use of the "Vibro-Balancer" helped to quell vibrations and delivered a much smoother ride. Suzuki also touted that the configuration of the exhaust allowed a 45-degree lean angle in both directions. A single disc brake on the front wheel was joined by a drum on the rear and storage compartment

The biggest and brightest of the new four-strokes was the GS750B which carried 748cc in its frame.

Bill Abdou

was found beneath the tail section. A digital gear indicator was a part of the instrument cluster and "Astro-Lighting" provided glare-free illumination when taking to the streets after dark. For the bargain-minded buyer, Suzuki offered up the GS400XB. It was identical to the GS400B but lacked the electric start feature, and carried a drum brake on the front wheel.

New in the new four-stroke category was Suzuki's first four-cylinder machine, the GS550B. By combining four-stroke technology with a total of four cylinders, a new level of smoothness was achieved. Dual overhead camshafts played their part in making the GS550B as quick as it was smooth. A six-speed gearbox allowed the rider to keep the GS550 in the sweet spot of rpms when turning the throttle of the 549cc engine. Exhaust was handled by a four-into-two system that was all chrome and whisper quiet.

A single disc brake on the front wheel delivered sure stops. Spoke wheels were still the status quo for the period as was the comfortable two-person saddle. Sitting at the top of the heap was the all-new GS750B. Fitted with a 748cc, dual overhead valve engine, the GS750B was fast and smooth. A five-speed transmission was used on the biggest of the Suzuki four-stroke machines in place of the six-speed found on the other two. A pair of disc brakes, one fore and another aft, brought the heavier GS to a halt without a fuss. The four-into-two exhaust kept the powerful engine quiet and provided the same 45-degree lean angle as the smaller machines. The fuel tank and tail section were offered in red or blue with black side covers. "Astro-Lighting" was again found along with the digital gear indicator that was nestled between the speedometer and tach. The use of four-stroke engines would usher in a new era for Suzuki with a long string of fresh models entering the fray each year.

A dual-overhead cam engine and four-into-two exhaust made the GS750 quiet and powerful, achieving new levels of speed and comfort for Suzuki.

Bill Abdou

1977 SUZUKI

Model	Engine	Displacement	Transmission
TS75B	Single cylinder	72cc	Five-Speed
A100A Go-Fer (New for 1976)	Single cylinder	98cc	Four-Speed
TC100B	Single cylinder	97cc	Dual Range Four-Speed
TS100B	Single cylinder	97cc	Five-Speed
TC125B	Single cylinder	123cc	Dual Range Four-Speed
TS125B	Single cylinder	123cc	Five-Speed
GT185B	Two-cylinder	184cc	Five-Speed
TC185B (Electric Start)	Single cylinder	183cc	Five-Speed
TS185B	Single cylinder	183cc	Five-Speed
GT250B	Two-cylinder	247cc	Four-Speed
TS250B	Single cylinder	249cc	Five-Speed
GT380B Gear Indicator	Three-cylinder	371cc	Six-Speed
GS400B (First Year for Suzuki Four-Stroke)	Two-cylinder	398cc	Six-Speed
GS400XB (Kick Start Only)	Two-cylinder	398cc	Six-Speed
TS400B	Single cylinder	396cc	Five-Speed
GT500B (Final Year of Sale)	Two-cylinder	492cc	Five-Speed
GT550B Indy (Final Year of Sale)	Three-cylinder	543cc	Five-Speed
GS550B (First Year for Suzuki Four-Stroke)	Four-cylinder	549cc	Six-Speed
GT750B (Final Year of Sale)	Three-cylinder	738cc	Five-Speed
GS750B (First Year for Suzuki Four-Stroke)	Four-cylinder	748cc	Five-Speed

The four-stroke, two-cylinder GS400B engine was smoother and more powerful than the two-stroke variants. It also was sold in a GS400XB version.

Suzuki Motors Corporation

SUZUKI

1978

Adding more power to the new four-stroke family was the 1978 GS1000EC that included cast wheels, a trio of disc brakes and upgraded graphics.

Jeff Kalin

Having introduced their first line of four-stroke machines in 1977, the 1978 catalog would be a mere shadow of the previous edition. Many of their two-stroke models had been pulled and a pair of even bigger four-stroke machines joined the fun.

Eleven different models were yanked off the floor for 1978 including the A100B, TS75B, TC100B and the TC125B. Further losses were felt by the GT185B, GT250B, GT380B and GT500B. The big thumper TS400B was another goner, as were the GT550B Indy and GT750B models. The crackdown on two-stroke power plants was the primary reason for the loss of these models, as the government placed strict restrictions on pollution controls and emission levels. Of the 10 remaining models for 1978, only four were of the Scrambler variation, leaving the rest of the crew to hit the streets. The only revisions seen on the

GS400 models were the use of color matched side covers taking over where black units had been for 1977. The GS400C was offered in Blue or Burgundy and the bargain model GS400XC was sold in Red only.

The bigger GS550C was also fitted with side covers to match the chosen color with Midnight Blue and Midnight Burgundy on the menu. The GS750C now had a chrome strip that ran along the bottom edge of its saddle and side covers that mirrored the base color of the tank. A second version of the GS750 was the GS750EC.

By taking the same platform and adding cast wheels and a third disc brake, the EC was born. A more steeply contoured saddle was also a part of the GS750EC's parts list, but Black was the only hue offered.

The success of their four-stroke machines was underway and Suzuki added a bigger version of the same for 1978. The GS1000C and GS1000EC were both built with a 997cc, inline-four engine in the frame and a five-speed gearbox. Four-into-two exhaust handled the exited fumes and chrome was applied to the entire system. The GS1000C rolled on wire wheels and was sold in Midnight Blue or Burgundy. The GS1000EC featured cast wheels, and extra brake disc and self-canceling turn-signals. The solid black paint was offset with a horizontal panel of white and contrasting stripes of gold.

1978 SUZUKI

Model	Engine	Displacement	Transmission
TS100C	Single cylinder	97cc	Five-Speed
TS125C	Single cylinder	123cc	Five-Speed
TS185C	Single cylinder	183cc	Five-Speed
TS250C	Two-cylinder	249cc	Four-Speed
TS250B	Single cylinder	249cc	Five-Speed
GS400C	Two-cylinder	398cc	Six-Speed
GS400XC (Kick Start Only)	Two-cylinder	398cc	Six-Speed
GS550C	Four-cylinder	549cc	Six-Speed
GS750C (Final Year of Sale)	Four-cylinder	748cc	Five-Speed
GS750EC (New for 1978)	Four-cylinder	748cc	Five-Speed
GS1000C (New for 1978)	Four-cylinder	997cc	Five-Speed
GS1000EC (New for 1978)	Four-cylinder	997cc	Five-Speed

SUZUKI
1979

STANDARD CATALOG OF® JAPANESE Motorcycles

Looking a lot like the machine campaigned by Wes Cooley on the tracks across the USA, the 1979 GS1000S was built in limited numbers and is a rare find today.

Vintage Memories, Inc.

After purging the catalog of their two-strokes for the 1978 model year, 1979 would prove to be fairly quiet by comparison.

The two versions of the GS400C were removed for 1979 to make room for the newly designed GS425N series. The "N" designation would apply to all 1979 models in place of the "C." The GS425 line of three motorcycles was powered by a 423cc, twin-cylinder engine that shifted through a five-speed gearbox. The GS425N had spoke wheels and was the basic edition done in the classic Suzuki style. The next version was the GS425EN and it differentiated by having cast wheels and a stepped saddle. Third in the lineup and the first of the "L" models was the GS425LN. The entire series of L models from Suzuki would do their best to capture the feeling of the more relaxed cruiser models being sold elsewhere. A set of pullback handlebars and stubby megaphone exhaust mufflers helped to set the stage. A deeply contoured saddle and teardrop tank completed the cosmetic alterations.

The GS550 family album had a new member included in the GS550LN. Like the GS425 LN, the 550 wore a set of buckhorn handlebars, a deeply sculpted saddle and a chrome grab rail at the rear of the seat. The front forks were also delivered with a leading axle design that altered the geometry of the chassis. Chrome exhaust mufflers were again chopped off in a truncated fashion that was true to the cruiser class. The motor and transmission were unchanged from the previous year's models.

A 750 version of the "L" models was also introduced for 1979. The GS750LN sported the same pullback bars, steeped saddle and shortened mufflers as the other smaller variations. A leading axle fork was incorporated on the 750 as well. Airbox covers were added to the chrome rear fender and were also finished in the gleaming silver finish.

Fourth in the series of Suzuki's "Low Slingers" was the GS1000LN. All the same elements of style were applied to the big liter bike including the stepped saddle and abbreviated mufflers.

Perhaps the biggest news for 1979 was the debut of the GS1000SN, otherwise known as the Wes Cooley Replica. By taking the GS1000 and adding a raft of performance upgrades, the GS1000SN was created. On top of the performance enhancements, the "S" wore a unique paint scheme that was white with accenting stripes of blue. A sporty bikini fairing hid an expanded set of gauges and was also found only on the "S." Lower handlebars added to the racing image of the GS1000SN, and the saddle featured only a minor step between the rider and passenger sections. Only 700 copies of this machine were sent to the USA for 1979, making it a true collectible among today's enthusiasts.

Hidden behind the sport fairing of the GS1000S was this complete bank of gauges, unique to this model.

Vintage Memories, Inc.

1979 SUZUKI

Model	Engine	Displacement	Transmission
TS100N	Single cylinder	97cc	Five-Speed
TS125N	Single cylinder	123cc	Five-Speed
TS185N	Single cylinder	183cc	Five-Speed
TS250N	Single cylinder	249cc	Five-Speed
GS425N (New for 1979)	Two-cylinder	423cc	Five-Speed
GS425EN (New for 1979)	Two-cylinder	423cc	Five-Speed
GS425LN (New for 1979)	Two-cylinder	423cc	Five-Speed
GS550N	Four-cylinder	549cc	Six-Speed
GS550EN	Four-cylinder	549cc	Six-Speed
GS550LN (New for 1979)	Four-cylinder	549cc	Six-Speed
GS750N	Four-cylinder	748cc	Five-Speed
GS750EN	Four-cylinder	748cc	Five-Speed
GS750LN (New for 1979)	Four-cylinder	748cc	Five-Speed
GS1000N	Four-cylinder	997cc	Five-Speed
GS1000EN	Four-cylinder	997cc	Five-Speed
GS1000LN	Four-cylinder	997cc	Five-Speed
GS1000SN (New for 1979)	Four-cylinder	997cc	Five-Speed

The paint scheme, bikini fairing and enhanced instrument panel all help to set the 700 copies of the GS1000S apart from the crowd.

Vintage Memories, Inc.

SUZUKI
1980

Created with balanced lines and a powerful 997cc motor, there was little left to change on the now classic GS1000ET.

Owner/Photo: Floyd Webb

Suzuki added 13 models to their 1980 catalog. Standard models of the GS550, 750 and 1000 were discontinued in favor of more creature comforts and features. The 1980 models earned a "T" designation.

The new OR50T was powered by a single-cylinder 49cc engine and carried a back rest on a miniature sissy bar and tall pullback bars. The GS250T was a more powerful 249cc, twin-cylinder engine that got the GS down the road. Wire wheels were matched by dazzling chrome fenders.

The single-cylinder GN400T and GN400XT were new. Both models featured the same 397cc one-lung, four-stroke engine and tubular steel chassis. The T included cast-alloy wheels, chrome fenders and a set of pullback bars. The less expensive XT used spoke wheels and traditional handlebars.

Suzuki pulled the trio of GS425 machines for 1980 and a triple play of new GS450 models stepped in. The GS450ET and ST shared the same

The 1980 GS1000ET remained true to its original form and continued to be a popular choice among buyers of liter-sized standard models.

Owner/Photo: Floyd Webb

fuel tank and side covers while the GS450LT was done in the lowrider genre. All three found a new 448cc, two-cylinder engine in their frames with matching chrome exhaust. The GS450LT package featured a more actively stepped saddle and pullback bars.

The ET and ST carried more muscular fuel tanks and seats that were nearly flat, yet tapered upwards toward the rear. The ST was unique in the application of the small sport fairing that was attached to the bars and gold colored cast wheels.

Suzuki rolled out the first of their Twin Swirl Combustion Chamber (TSCC) machines in the GS750ET. The 16-valve engine of the GS750ET was fitted improved heads that put the TSCC technology to use.

Suzuki motorcycles had all been fitted with a chain as their final drive method. Several shaft drive models appeared in the 1980 Suzuki catalogs. The first of these were the new GS850GT and GLT models. The "G" in the designation denoted shaft drive while the "L" indicated the cruiser models. The GS850GLT was the first to incorporate both trends into a single machine.

Both of the new 850s were powered by an 843cc, inline-four engine with dual overhead cams. Three slotted disc brakes were aboard to haul the big bikes down and the GLT also used a leading-axle fork in its design. The GT steered with mid-rise bars and offered a fairly flat pillion for the rider and passenger. The GLT had bars that reached back to the rider's hands and a more aggressively stepped saddle.

Two chain-driven GS1000 models remained for 1980 but two shaft-driven models were added. The GS1000ET and GS1000ST still used the standard chain for their final drive while the new GS1000GT and GLT had their shaft drive fitted. The ET and GT 850 were built in a traditional format with mid-level bars and flat saddles. The GLT was the cruiser of the bunch. Cast wheels were found on all four variations.

Suzuki entered two new machines into the contest for 1980. Both the GS1100ET and GS1100LT had 1074cc, inline-four engines in their frames that provided new levels of smoothness and power. Final chain drive made sure none of the power was lost in a shaft-drive translation.

The sporty ET had the TSCC engine joined by the same rectangular headlight wrapped in a close-fitting nacelle as was used on the GS750ET. Leading axle forks and aluminum lower legs added to the racing nature of the GS1100ET and it could be had in silver or red with contrasting stripes. The GS1100LT was created to fill the needs of the bigger cruiser buyer and was replete with taller bars and a two-level saddle.

1980 SUZUKI

Model	Engine	Displacement	Transmission
OR50T (New for 1980)	Single cylinder	49cc	Five-Speed
TS100T	Single cylinder	97cc	Five-Speed
TS125T	Single cylinder	123cc	Four-Speed
TS185T	Single cylinder	183cc	Five-Speed
GS250T (New for 1980)	Two-cylinder	249cc	Five-Speed
TS250T	Single cylinder	249cc	Five-Speed
GN400T (New for 1980)	Single cylinder	397cc	Five-Speed
GN400XT (New for 1980)	Single cylinder	397cc	Five-Speed
GS450ET (New for 1980)	Two-cylinder	448cc	Five-Speed
GS450LT (New for 1980)	Two-cylinder	448cc	Five-Speed
GS450ST (New for 1980)	Two-cylinder	448cc	Five-Speed
GS550ET	Four-cylinder	549cc	Six-Speed
GS550LT	Four-cylinder	549cc	Six-Speed
GS750ET	Four-cylinder	748cc	Five-Speed
GS750LT	Four-cylinder	748cc	Five-Speed
GS850GT (New for 1980)	Four-cylinder	843cc	Five-Speed
GS850GLT (New for 1980)	Four-cylinder	843cc	Five-Speed
GS1000N	Four cylinder	997cc	Five-Speed
GS1000ET	Four-cylinder	997cc	Five-Speed
GS1000GT (New for 1980)	Four-cylinder	997cc	Five-Speed
GS1000GLT (New for 1980)	Four-cylinder	997cc	Five-Speed
GS1000ST (Final Year of Sale)	Four-cylinder	997cc	Five-Speed
GS1100ET (New for 1980)	Four-cylinder	1074cc	Five-Speed
GS1100LT (New for 1980)	Four-cylinder	1074cc	Five-Speed

SUZUKI
1981

The battle between new and old models was nearly a wash for 1981 as four machines left the picture and three new entered. The tiny OR50T was the first to go, and had only proved to be a one-year model.

Climbing the scale, the next changes were the addition of the three new GS650 machines. Typical for Suzuki, the GS650 was offered in three versions to appeal to different segments of the market. The EX was at the base with cast wheels and a front fender that matched the red or silver paint chosen for the fuel tank and side covers. The same 673cc, four-cylinder engine was applied to all three versions. The EX was the only chain-drive while the other two carried shaft-drive propulsion. The GS650GX was sold in black or maroon and had black turn signal shafts replacing the standard issue chrome units. The GS650GLX included leading axle forks, shaft-drive and chrome fenders in its array. Being slotted as the cruiser of the bunch, it also had taller pullback bars and a more contoured saddle.

For the liter class, two models were gone from the scene. The standard GS1000ET and race inspired GS1000ST had gone missing for 1981. The "S" model was destined to be a limited production run from the beginning and the base GS1000 was simply overshadowed by other Suzuki offerings in the same arena. The last big bruiser to be taken off of life support was the GS1100LT. The cruiser genre had become quite crowded in the years since it was created, and few saw the benefit of a cruiser of that dimension.

1981 SUZUKI

Model	Engine	Displacement	Transmission
TS100X	Single cylinder	97cc	Five-Speed
TS125X	Single cylinder	123cc	Four-Speed
TS185X	Single cylinder	183cc	Five-Speed
GS250X	Two-cylinder	249cc	Five-Speed
TS250X	Single cylinder	249cc	Five-Speed
GN400TX	Single cylinder	397cc	Five-Speed
GN400XX	Single cylinder	397cc	Five-Speed
GS450EX	Two-cylinder	448cc	Five-Speed
GS450TX	Two-cylinder	448cc	Five-Speed
GS450LX	Two-cylinder	448cc	Five-Speed
GS450SX	Two-cylinder	448cc	Five-Speed
GS550TX	Four-cylinder	549cc	Six-Speed
GS550LX	Four-cylinder	549cc	Six-Speed
GS650EX (New for 1981)	Four-cylinder	673cc	Six-Speed
GS650GX (New for 1981)	Four-cylinder	673cc	Six-Speed
GS650GLX (New for 1981)	Four-cylinder	673cc	Six-Speed
GS750EX	Four-cylinder	748cc	Five-Speed
GS750LX	Four-cylinder	748cc	Five-Speed
GS750GX	Four-cylinder	843cc	Five-Speed
GS1000GX	Four-cylinder	997cc	Five-Speed
GS1000GLX	Four-cylinder	997cc	Five-Speed
GS1100EX	Four-cylinder	1074cc	Five-Speed

SUZUKI
1982

Subtle two-tone paint, offset with gold pinstripes, made a good match for the deeply contoured saddle and handlebars that reached back to the rider's hands.

Larry Barasch

Suzuki's 1982 model year would be another tumultuous one, with numerous machines deleted and nearly as many being introduced.

At the bottom of the new model list was the GN125Z. The miniature cruiser held a 124cc engine in its frame and was built to mimic the larger machines in the same genre. The GN125Z used taller handlebars and a two-tier saddle. The teardrop tank added the needed curves to carry the style. Chrome fenders and spoke wheels were part of the plan. A slightly larger version of the same machine was found in the new GN250Z. The engine displaced 249cc while the rest of the details were the same as on the GN125Z. Taking a small step forward we find the GS300LZ for 1982. Powered by a 299cc twin-cylinder engine, the 300LZ was still created in the cruiser mold. Cast wheels were used in place of the smaller models' wire spokes, but all else was a repeat.

The GN400TZ returned for 1982 wearing newly styled cast wheels and a black headlight housing. The GS450SX was no longer an option but a new GS450GAZ was entered into the race. The 448cc engine was the same as in the other GS450 models but the GAZ was fitted with shaft-drive and created in the cruiser motif. In addition to the shaft drive, the GAZ featured a two-speed semi-automatic transmission.

Joining the 550 class was the oddly-styled GS550MZ. Taking some fashion cues from its bigger brother the Katana, the GS550MZ bore a mild resemblance in the contours of the sheet metal. An orange and black, two-tone saddle was accented by brightly colored front brake calipers of orange. The 549cc, inline-four engine was used. The GS750TZ was another new entry for 1982. Chrome fenders, a polished alloy grab rail at the rear of the saddle and a rear drum brake helped to keep the cost of entry low.

Taking avant-garde design to the masses was the GS1000SZ Katana. Penned by Hans Muth, the Katana featured sheet metal like nothing ever seen before.

Flowing contours and a two-tone saddle set the stage. A 998cc engine was called upon when the rider grasped the clip-on handlebars. A tiny windscreen rose over the pointed frame mounted fairing up front and an unusual instrument pod resided behind the clear screen.

The 1982 version was done in all silver, including the motor. Cast wheels had black highlights and the four-into-two exhaust was black from start to finish. Disc brakes on the front wheel were assisted by anti-dive forks that delivered better handling in panic situations. The saddle dipped low in the frame, making the Katana a motorcycle you sat in versus on. Very few of these machines were exported to the USA, making them a rare sight today. The GS1100EX of 1981 was back, but now sported revised sheet metal and a more traditional round headlight. Anti-dive forks were also employed to improve handling under hard braking. A GS1100GZ was also new and used shaft drive and mag wheels to help distinguish itself from other Suzuki models of the day. For the long distance rider, Suzuki rolled out the GS1100GKZ that came complete with a full coverage fairing, hard sided saddlebags and tour trunk. It offered loyal Suzuki buyers an option when choosing a machine to tackle the open road. The final new model for 1982 was the latest version of their big cruiser, the GS1100GLZ. The low-rider style was complimented by low maintenance shaft drive and a powerful 1074cc engine.

The 1982 GS850GLZ was a stylish machine that came complete with a shaft drive and a smooth 843cc engine.

Larry Barasch

1982 SUZUKI

Model	Engine	Displacement	Transmission
GN125Z (New for 1982)	Single cylinder	124cc	Four-Speed
GN250Z (New for 1982)	Single cylinder	249cc	Five-Speed
GS300LZ	Two-cylinder	299cc	Five-Speed
GN400TZ	Single cylinder	397cc	Five-Speed
GS450EZ	Two-cylinder	448cc	Five-Speed
GS450GAZ (New for 1982)	Two-cylinder	448cc	Five-Speed
GS450LZ	Two-cylinder	448cc	Five-Speed
GS450TXZ (New for 1982)	Two-cylinder	448cc	Five-Speed
GS450TZ	Two-cylinder	448cc	Five-Speed
GS550LZ	Four-cylinder	549cc	Six-Speed
GS550MZ (New for 1982)	Four-cylinder	549cc	Five-Speed
GS650EZ	Four-cylinder	673cc	Six-Speed
GS650GZ	Four-cylinder	673cc	Six-Speed
GS650GLZ	Four-cylinder	673cc	Six-Speed
GS750EZ	Four-cylinder	748cc	Five-Speed
GS750TZ (New for 1982)	Four-cylinder	747cc	Five-Speed
GS850GZ	Four-cylinder	843cc	Five-Speed
GS850GLZ	Four-cylinder	843cc	Five-Speed
GS1000SZ Katana (New for 1982)	Four-cylinder	998cc	Five-Speed
GS1100EZ	Four-cylinder	1074cc	Five-Speed
GS1100GZ (New for 1982)	Four-cylinder	1074cc	Five-Speed
GS1100GKZ (New for 1982)	Four-cylinder	1074cc	Five-Speed
GS1100GLZ (New for 1982)	Four-cylinder	1074cc	Five-Speed

SUZUKI
1983

Carrying the same artistic lines as the missing GS1000S Katana of 1982, the 750 version was trimmed in silver and maroon paint with a black engine and exhaust.
Suzuki Motors Corporation

A few new 1983 machines found their way onto the showroom floors. A trio of previous models was sent out to pasture in the GN400TZ, GS550MZ and GS650EZ.

Fresh examples began at the 550cc level with the new GS550ED and ESD models. Both sporty bikes were fairly similar with a 16-inch front wheel and full floater rear suspensions. The sharply creased bodywork of both was the same and the ED carried a small, handlebar mounted fairing while the ESD had a larger, frame-mounted half-fairing. Blacked-out, 572cc inline-four motors were found in both examples and they provided a great way for riders to join the sport bike crowd.

Two versions of the all-new GR650 Tempter were seen in D and XD trim. The GR650D was trimmed with two-tone paint and cast wheels. The GR650XD carried a smaller price tag as well as wire wheels and solid Red paint. A twin cylinder 651cc motor was used in both styles along with dual exhaust finished in chrome.

A slightly larger, shaft driven GS650MD Katana was seen. Mostly a copy of its former self,

The larger of the two Katanas for 1983 sported an 1100cc engine and was finished in blue and silver along with the blacked-out engine and exhaust system.

Suzuki Motors Corporation

the new model had 100cc more displacement and a final shaft drive in place of the chain used on the GS550M. The bigger 650 also had a black motor and two-tone red and silver paint on the tank to go along with the duo-tone saddle.

Joining the huffer bike parade a bit late, Suzuki introduced their XN85D Turbo for 1983. By taking the same 673cc engine that was used in their other machines and adding a turbocharger, vast increases in power were achieved. The XN85D was also draped in a rakishly designed half fairing with bold use of the "Turbo" identification. A full floater rear suspension was also added to the chassis and a wicked black exhaust carried away the fumes. When riding the XN85D at typical speeds, the rider barely noticed the effects of the blower. When additional throttle was applied, the bike reached ultra-legal speeds without a fuss. Sadly for all versions of the blown bikes, the insurance industry slapped huge rate increases, taking away from the fun of riding them.

The GS750ED and ESD were a pair of sporty entries. Each was powered by a 747cc inline-four engine that exhaled through an all-black exhaust. The 16-inch front tires were installed on both as well as anti-dive forks. The ED was complete with a handlebar mounted bikini fairing and the ESD had a larger frame mounted half-fairing installed. Two iterations

Included in the sweeping panels of the Katana were a rotary choke lever and two accessory switches, keeping the design clean and efficient.

SUZUKI

of the now departed GS1000SZ Katana were sold for 1983. The GS750SD and GS1100SD were built with the same unusual styling as the previous version, but carried black motors in their frames. The 750 version was painted in a silver and maroon while the 1100 carried a blue and silver livery. It was to be the final year for the unique Katana designs.

Adding some muscle to the upper end of the rainbow was the new GS1150ES3. Power for the big sport bike came in the form of an 1135cc four-cylinder engine with dual-overhead cams. A wind cheating half-fairing was bolted to the frame and added some style to the lumbering machine. Choices of Blue and White or Red and White were on tap with both paint schemes carrying an all-black engine in the frame. The size and capabilities of the GS1150 put it firmly into the sport touring class and suited the needs of the rider who rode long distances while enjoying a spirited ride.

Located behind the tiny windshield of the Katana was an unusual speedometer/tachometer combination that shared the same space and was nestled between the clip-on bars.

1983 SUZUKI

Model	Engine	Displacement	Transmission
GN125D	Single cylinder	124cc	Four-Speed
GN250D	Single cylinder	249cc	Five-Speed
GS300LD	Two cylinder	299cc	Five-Speed
GS450ED	Two cylinder	448cc	Five-Speed
GS450GAD	Two cylinder	448cc	Five-Speed
GS450LD	Two cylinder	448cc	Five-Speed
GS450TXD	Two cylinder	448cc	Five-Speed
GS550ED (New for 1983)	Four cylinder	572cc	Five-Speed
GS550ESD (New for 1983)	Four cylinder	572cc	Five-Speed
GS550LD	Four cylinder	549cc	Six-Speed
GR650D Tempter (New for 1983)	Two cylinder	651cc	Five-Speed
GR650XD Tempter (New for 1983)	Two cylinder	651cc	Five-Speed
GS650GD	Four cylinder	673cc	Six-Speed
GS650GLD	Four cylinder	673cc	Six-Speed
GS650MD Katana (New for 1983)	Four cylinder	673cc	Five-Speed
XN85D Turbo (New for 1983)	Four cylinder	673cc	Five-Speed
GS750ED Sport Fairing	Four cylinder	748cc	Five-Speed
GS750ESD (New for 1983)	Four cylinder	747cc	Five-Speed
GS750SD Katana (New for 1983)	Four cylinder	747cc	Five-Speed
GS750TD	Four cylinder	747cc	Five-Speed
GS850GD	Four cylinder	843cc	Five-Speed
GS850GLD	Four cylinder	843cc	Five-Speed
GS1100ED	Four cylinder	1074cc	Five-Speed
GS1100GD	Four cylinder	1074cc	Five-Speed
GS1100GKD	Four cylinder	1074cc	Five-Speed
GS1100GLD	Four cylinder	1074cc	Five-Speed
GS1100SD Katana (New for 1983)	Four cylinder	1074cc	Five-Speed
GS1150ES3 (New for 1983)	Four cylinder	1135cc	Five-Speed

SUZUKI

1984

Although I can find no explanation, any written history for Suzuki lists only three street machines for 1984. When compared to the previous years, this paltry catalog seems rather unusual. Even the Motorcycle and ATV Identification Guide, printed and compiled by Suzuki, lists only three street machines, so one has to believe it to be true, no matter how bizarre. Many of the units shown in 1983 returned in 1985 but were not listed in 1984. Motorcyclist magazine produced an annual buyers guide, and even it only included the three 1984 Suzuki models shown in this book.

At the upper end was the GS1100GKE. The big touring mount was still fully-equipped with fairing bags and touring trunk and powered by the 1074cc four-cylinder as before. Two-tone Gray and Silver paint was applied for this year of sale.

Next on the agenda was the sporty GS1150ES. Holding an 1135cc power plant in its frame, the 1150ES was more than capable of swallowing long stretches of highway in comfort while maintaining the ability to handle sweeping curves with ease.

Rounding out the truncated parade for 1984 was the GS550ES. The middleweight entry continued to provide riders of all skill levels with a confident and energetic performance with plenty of style.

1984 SUZUKI

Model	Engine	Displacement	Transmission
GS550ES	Four cylinder	572cc	Five-Speed
GS1100GKE	Four cylinder	1074cc	Five-Speed
GS1150ES	Four cylinder	1135cc	Five-Speed

1985

The 1985 Suzuki catalog was beefier than the mysterious three-bike 1984 edition. Yet more of the previous models were missing than new models added in 1985. The beginning of governmental tariffs on motorcycles over 750cc eliminated many previous units from the plan, though a few 700cc "tariff beaters" were sold by the big four Japanese manufacturers. First of the new under-700cc machines was the GS700EF and ESF. Carrying a 699cc inline four in its flanks skirted the new law and still delivered plenty of power for most riding needs. Both versions carried Suzuki's full-floater rear suspension under the bodywork along with a black engine highlighted with polished case covers.

The four-into-two exhaust was also finished in chrome on the EF and ESF. The ES wore no fairing at all while the ESF included a frame-mounted half-fairing. When buying the new GS700 from Suzuki, the choices were white with red or blue scallops.

Next in the line of tariff beaters was the all-new Madura GV700GLF. The Madura carried the smooth lines of the cruiser to a new extreme and held a 698cc liquid cooled V-four engine beneath the swept back fuel tank.

A two-position saddle that extended upwards to form a passenger backrest helped to accentuate the lines of the swooping panels. Spoke wheels were used at both ends and a shaft drive sent the power to the rear wheel on demand. Black or Maroon were available and the fuel tank was adorned with a simple badge to signify the maker. Side covers bore additional details of the model. Losses were heavy in the middle of the range and included models ranging from 125 to 850cc. All varieties of the Katana were banished as were the 750cc machines to meet with the new governmental limitations. Four of the biggest 1100cc bikes were also de-listed as Suzuki pared their offerings down to better suit existing market demands.

The big GS1150ESF was back but little changed from 1984. Joining the sport fairing model was the GS1150EF that was delivered to showrooms with no fairing at all. The running gear was the same as on the ESF but appealed to the all around rider due to the naked design.

One additional model made its debut for 1985. Sitting alongside the GV700GLF was the GV1200GLF Madura. Taking the same equation to the next degree, the 1200 Madura carried an 1165cc V-four in the frame. It was also liquid cooled and included Suzuki's TSCC, 16 valve heads for improved performance. Hydraulic valve adjusters reduced maintenance as did the shaft drive. A five-speed gearbox was also built with an overdrive gear to lower engine revs at speed. Each side of the big Madura carried a pair of staggered shotgun exhaust pipes that were sliced at a diagonal for added drama.

Spoke wheels and a chrome fender added to the custom style and the saddle was built to include a rear backrest for the passenger, much like the one seen on the 700 Madura. A mostly black engine did have polished cooling fins and matching engine covers. A trio of disc brakes hauled the Madura down from speed with no trouble.

1985 SUZUKI

Model	Engine	Displacement	Transmission
GN250F	Single cylinder	249cc	Five-Speed
GS300LF	Two cylinder	299cc	Five-Speed
GS450GAF	Two cylinder	448cc	Five-Speed
GS450LF	Two cylinder	448cc	Five-Speed
GS550EF	Four cylinder	572cc	Five-Speed
GS550ESF	Four cylinder	572cc	Five-Speed
GS550LF	Four cylinder	549cc	Six-Speed
GS700EF (New for 1985)	Four cylinder	699cc	Five-Speed
GS700ESF (New for 1985)	Four cylinder	699cc	Five-Speed
GV700GLF Madura (New for 1985)	Four cylinder	698cc	Five-Speed
GS1150EF (New for 1985)	Four cylinder	1135cc	Five-Speed
GVS1200GLF Madura (New for 1985)	Four cylinder	1135cc	Five-Speed with Overdrive

SUZUKI
1986

Suzuki continued to trim the herd for 1986 as a raft of old models were pulled from the catalogs. The GN250, GS300, 450 and 550 were some of the lost machines, as were both versions of the GS700. The 700 Madura was a one-year machine but the 1200 stayed on. The sport touring GS1100ESF was also a goner for 1986 but the unfaired model remained. Suzuki entered the sport bike and touring mount categories.

Two new LS650 Savage editions were powered by the same single-cylinder 652cc engine. The FG design had flat handlebars and the PG had taller, pullback bars. The seating, sheet metal, belt drives and spoke wheels were the same for both machines.

There were four versions of the new VS700 Intruder. All four variants carried a 699cc V-twin engine in their frames. Two editions wore spoke wheels, one with flat bars and the other with pullback units. The other Intruders sported cast wheels. The engines were finished in plain silver with a chrome exhaust tube. Suzuki joined the performance sport bike fray in a big way for 1986.

The GSX-R750, GSX-R750R and GSX-R1100 were little more than race bikes in street clothing. At the heart of the new machines were 16-valve engines with the Suzuki TSCC technology. Their unique Direct Air System enhanced the intake of oxygen and therefore helped the new engines breath better than ever. Oil cooling aided in

The GS450L was the smallest model in the 1986 Suzuki catalog but offered comfort and style for the budget-minded rider.
Suzuki Motors Corporation

For the mid-range sport rider, the GS550ES provided a great platform for days in the canyons or simply tooling around town. Suzuki Motors Corporation

SUZUKI STANDARD CATALOG OF ® JAPANESE Motorcycles

START A RUMBLE.

Intruder

It all begins the first time you press the starter button.

The rumble of the exhaust. The power of the liquid-cooled V-twin engine. The way you seem to fit into the machine.

It's the one bike that's customized exactly the way you want it. Because *you* customized it.

It's up to you whether it comes with traditional pullback bars or low-profile drag bars. Wire spoke wheels or optional mag-type wheels. Deep maroon or midnight black lacquer finish.

And once it's just the way you want it, you're ready for the streets. Now. Go out and start something.

MAN AND MACHINE WORK LIKE A SINGLE MOVING PART. SUZUKI®

Be safe. Always wear a helmet, eye protection and protective riding apparel. For riding courses, call the Motorcycle Safety Foundation at 1-800-447-4700.

In 1986, a magazine ad with a close-up image of the engine and two Intruder cycles invited potential Suzuki owners to "Start a Rumble."

keeping operating temperatures in line despite the tremendous power being generated.

Six-speed, close-ratio gearboxes delivered clean shifts between gears. A factory installed, four-into-one exhaust made quick work of any departing gases. All of the hardware was held together by a lightweight aluminum chassis.

The GSX-R750 wore a pair of 11.8-inch front disc brakes with a set of dual puck calipers. The 1100 had even bigger 12.2-inch discs that were designed with the latest in floating rotor technology. A full fairing was borrowed off of the track. The GSX-R750R was sold in only a red, white and blue motif and featured blue alloy rims, a racing style seat with rear seat cowl and a dry clutch.

Some riders wanted to see how many miles they could ride in a day versus how quickly they could turn a lap. Suzuki introduced their own line of luxury touring mounts and called them

A late entry in the sport bike market, Suzuki made up the ground it had lost with the GSX-R750. The GSX-R was at the top of the radar for all others to catch.
Suzuki Motors Corporation.

Perhaps not quite as svelte as the 750 version, the GSX-R1100 delivered even more power while maintaining the terrific strengths of the 3/4 machine.
Suzuki Motors Corporation.

SUZUKI

STANDARD CATALOG OF JAPANESE Motorcycles

Taking the cruiser theme a notch higher, the GS550L provided a slightly larger and more powerful platform than what the GS450L Suzuki offered.

Suzuki Motors Corporation

the Cavalcade. The Honda Gold Wing had already been around for more than a decade, so Suzuki had a great target to aim for when they released their own luxury barge on two wheels. Three versions of the new Cavalcade appeared for 1986, the standard, LX and top of the line LXE. Each unit carried a 1360cc, V-four motor under the sleek bodywork along with liquid cooling and shaft drive. A full protection front fairing, hard saddlebags and tail trunk were also a part of all three versions. An AM/FM/cassette audio system and pneumatically inflatable passenger pillion were also included in the LX. The top model was the LXE that also had a pneumatic saddle for the rider. Audio speakers were incorporated into the rear backrest and an adjustable headrest was also included for the passenger's comfort.

1986 SUZUKI

Model	Engine	Displacement	Transmission
GN450LG	Two cylinder	448cc	Five-Speed
GS550ESG	Four cylinder	572cc	Five-Speed
GS550LG	Four cylinder	549cc	Six-Speed
LS650FG Savage (New for 1986)	Single cylinder	652cc	Four-Speed
LS650PG Savage (New for 1986)	Single cylinder	652cc	Five-Speed
VS700GLFG Intruder (New for 1986)	Two cylinder	699cc	Five-Speed
VS700GLPG Intruder (New for 1986)	Two cylinder	699cc	Five-Speed
VS700LEFG Intruder (New for 1986)	Two cylinder	699cc	Five-Speed
VS700GLEPG Intruder (New for 1986)	Two cylinder	699cc	Five-Speed
GSX-R750G (New for 1986)	Four cylinder	749cc	Six-Speed
GSX-R750RG (New for 1986)	Four cylinder	749cc	Six-Speed
GSX-R1100G (New for 1986)	Four cylinder	1052cc	Six-Speed
GS1150EG	Four cylinder	1135cc	Five-Speed
GVS1200GLG Madura (New for 1986)	Four cylinder	1165cc	Five-Speed with Overdrive
GV1400GCG Cavalcade (New for 1986)	Four cylinder	1360cc	Five-Speed
GV1400GDG Cavalcade LX (New for 1986)	Four cylinder	1360cc	Five-Speed
GV1400GTG Cavalcade (New for 1986)	Four cylinder	1360cc	Five-Speed

SUZUKI 1987

Suzuki continued to trim the fat for 1987 as seven 1986 models were removed from the listings. Two new machines entered the rank and file, but it was otherwise a quiet year.

At the bottom of the ranking was the new RB50H. Looking like a shrunken GSX-R, the RB was often pressed into duty as a pit bike at the race track since it was not street legal everywhere. A 49cc engine propelled the tiny cycle and a racing-style fairing enveloped the chassis. The sporty GS550ES and cruiser GS550LG were both no-shows for 1987 as was the VS700 Intruder. The race-track-only GSX-R750R was also pulled along with the GS1150E. Buyers were beginning to gravitate towards true sport bikes or more heavily designed cruisers, leaving some of the older all-around models in the lurch. The GV1200 Madura was another unit removed from the 1987 roster joining the base model Cavalcade.

New for 1987 were two versions of the biggest cruiser Suzuki had to offer. Powered by the same 1360cc, V-four engine used in the Cavalcade, the VS1400 Intruder made a bold statement. Sold in one of two versions, both carried teardrop fuel tanks, king and queen saddles that included a rear passenger backrest and aggressive bologna sliced mufflers.

The new Suzuki VS1400 Intruder raised the bar in the cruiser market. The 1360cc Cavalcade engine was implanted in the Intruder, the biggest Suzuki cycle.
Suzuki Motors Corporation

With many buyers leaning toward more radically styled cruisers, the GS450L found a dwindling audience even though it still provided a great deal for the price. Suzuki Motors Corporation

SUZUKI

STANDARD CATALOG of® JAPANESE MOTORCYCLES

Perhaps not quite as svelte as the 750 version, the GSX-R1100 delivered even more power while maintaining the terrific strengths of the 3/4 machine.

Suzuki Motors Corporation.

The GSX-R750 was only sold in one level for 1987 but continued to dominate that segment of the market.

Suzuki Motors Corporation.

One version wore flat drag style bars while the other the tall buckhorn style. A ducktail rear fender completed the cosmetics of Suzuki's new cruiser. Spoke wheels were used and Blue, Black and Maroon were listed as available hues.

1987 SUZUKI

Model	Engine	Displacement	Transmission
RB50H (New for 1987)	Single cylinder	49cc	–
GS450LH	Two cylinder	448cc	Five-Speed
LS650FH Savage	Single cylinder	652cc	Four-Speed
LS650PH Savage	Single cylinder	652cc	Five-Speed
VS700GLFH Intruder	Two cylinder	699cc	Five-Speed
VS700GLPH Intruder	Two cylinder	699cc	Five-Speed
VS700GLEPH Intruder	Two cylinder	699cc	Five-Speed
GSX-R750H	Four cylinder	749cc	Six-Speed
GSX-R1100H	Four cylinder	1052cc	Six-Speed
GV1400GCH Cavalcade LXE	Four cylinder	1360cc	Five-Speed
GV1400GDH Cavalcade LX	Four cylinder	1360cc	Five-Speed
VS1400GLFH Intruder (New for 1987)	Four cylinder	1360cc	Five-Speed
VS1400GLPH Intruder (New for 1987)	Four cylinder	1360cc	Five-Speed

SUZUKI
1988

Wrapped in a set of curvaceous body work, the new Katana 600 provided a great all around mount for the sport-minded rider.

Kawasaki Motors Corp.

The 1988 model year saw Suzuki remove twice as many listings as they added, shrinking their catalog further, but expanding the scope of their machines. Gone were both the Lilliputian RB50H and the stylish LS650 Savage. Also taken off life support were two versions of the VS700 Intruder, leaving one example behind. The Cavalcade family also shrunk to a single LX model. Only one version of the VS1400 Intruder was seen for 1988.

A returning model was the GN250J. It had last been seen for 1986, and would again be taken away after the 1988 model year. As much as Suzuki hoped the small cruiser would be accepted, the numbers never reached their goals. The dominance of the GSX-R was raging strong, but there were some buyers who sought a sport bike that wasn't quite as radical for more all around use. While the GSX-R's were fully capable of being ridden all day long, their ergonomics were better suited to a track day than an interstate jaunt. Responding to the demands of the sport minded buyer, two motorcycles carrying the Katana name were again seen in the catalog. The GSX600 and GSX1100 were distant cousins to the unusual styling of the 1982/'83 models, but were considered far better at being a universal machine that could do it all. Beneath the all-encompassing bodywork of each new Katana was an inline-four engine complete with dual-overhead cams and Suzuki's TSCC technology. The Katana 600 held a 599cc mill while the 1100 was

SUZUKI

The rider who wanted some sport touring could choose the bigger Katana 1100. It provided comfort and performance to travel long distances without pain.

Suzuki Motors Corporation.

at 1127cc. Both versions used a four-into-two exhaust to send the gases packing. The 600 was finished in gloss black from stem to stern while the 1100 had black tubing with silver canisters at the end.

With the exception of some oddly-shaped openings in their bodywork, the entire chassis and motor were hidden from view. The 600 was sold in White with Red or Blue topside paint and a lower section of black. White alloy wheels were used on both variants. The 1100 was seen in Maroon or Dark Blue with again, a lower section of black. The cast wheels on the 1100 were silver but detailed with black accents. The 600 version weighed 429 lbs. when dry and the larger Katana tipped the scales at 537 lbs. The smaller Katana included six gears in the transmission while the 1100 had the standard five. The windscreen of the 600 Katana was fixed, but the unit on the bigger model was electrically operated and could be adjusted for height depending on the rider's needs and preferences.

With the tariffs on larger machines now over, Suzuki bumped the remaining Intruder to 747cc for 1988. The pullback bar model also carried the control wiring inside the bars for a neater appearance and rolled on a taller 21-inch front hoop. Spoke wheels were the only choice but Black or Maroon were listed as optional colors.

Only the mid-level Cavalcade LX was seen for 1988 but it provided a high level of luxury and comfort features to the long distance rider. A computerized cruise control offered more demands and flexibility while the AM/FM/cassette audio system could be enhanced with a CB radio. The Cavalcade weighed in at 768 lbs. before fuel and fluids were added, and the tank could store 6.1 gallons of "go juice" when topped off. Two-tone ensembles of Maroon or Silver were sold.

1988 SUZUKI

Model	Engine	Displacement	Transmission
GN250J Returning for 1988	Single cylinder	249cc	Five-Speed
GS450LJ	Two cylinder	448cc	Five-Speed
GSX600FJ Katana (New for 1988)	Four cylinder	448cc	Six-Speed
LS650PJ Savage	Single cylinder	652cc	Four-Speed
GSX-R750J	Four cylinder	749cc	Six-Speed
VS750GLPJ Intruder 750cc for 1988	Two cylinder	747cc	Five-Speed
GSX-R1100J	Four cylinder	1052cc	Six-Speed
GSX1100FJ Katana (New for 1988)	Four cylinder	1127cc	Five-Speed
GV1400GDJ Cavalcade LX	Four cylinder	1360cc	Five-Speed
VS1400GLPJ Intruder	Four cylinder	1360cc	Five-Speed

SUZUKI
1989

Suzuki continued to trim the fat for 1989 as three models were taken off the menu. Missing were the GN250, GS450L and LS650 Savage. All three machines had been crafted in the mild cruiser motif that continued to lose ground to the more dramatically styled offerings of the same bent.

The only new entry in the 1989 catalog was the GS500E. Positioned as a sporty naked bike, the exposed aluminum frame showed us the 487cc, twin-cylinder engine and all of its related hardware. A darkened two-into-one exhaust system was dressed up with a stainless steel sleeve over the canister.

Disc brakes ensured confident braking on the lightweight bike and Suzuki's full-floater rear suspension provided both handling and comfort. Taking the place of the ubiquitous tubular handlebar were forged aluminum units, one for each set of hand controls. The GS500E was sold in Black or White and rolled on cast wheels.

The 600 Katana was back and also carried the stainless steel trim on the exhaust canisters and featured an adjustable front brake lever. Three-spoke cast wheels replaced the six-spoke variants of 1988 and Red, or a Black and Blue paint scheme were sold. The GSX-R750 was also the recipient of the steel exhaust covers and adjustable front brake lever. In its final year of sale, the VS750 Intruder was unchanged except for the Purple hue.

The big GSX-R received an all-new four-into-two exhaust that was stainless steel, replacing the four-into-one unit of the previous year. Front brake rotors were now grooved and activated by an adjustable lever at the handgrip. This new lever was also used on the 1100 Katana, which was sold in only Black for the 1989 season.

Neither the VS1400 or Cavalcade saw any alterations for 1989.

1989 SUZUKI

Model	Engine	Displacement	Transmission
GS500EK (New for 1989)	Two cylinder	487cc	Five-Speed
GSX600FK Katana	Four cylinder	599cc	Six-Speed
GSX-R750K	Four cylinder	749cc	Six-Speed
VS750GLPK Intruder 750cc for 1988	Two cylinder	747cc	Five-Speed
GSX-R1100K	Four cylinder	1052cc	Six-Speed
GSX1100FK Katana	Four cylinder	1127cc	Five-Speed
GV1400GDK Cavalcade LX	Four cylinder	1360cc	Five-Speed
VS1400GLPK Intruder	Four cylinder	1360cc	Five-Speed

SUZUKI

1990

Suzuki decided to pull their Cavalcade off the sales floor for 1990, but it was the only loss for the latest model year.

Two fresh faces were seen, one of which was the middle-class Katana 750. Joining its smaller and larger siblings, the 750 Katana wore the same sleek bodywork but carried a 748cc motor under its garb. Alloy wheels at both ends and an exhaust that included the stainless wrap on the canister were also carried over to the new Katana. Silver with Black trim or Black with Silver trim were listed as color options.

The second new model was the VX800L. Designed as an all around machine, the VX800 was powered by an 805cc, V-twin engine that sent the drive to the rear wheel via shaft. A five-speed gearbox was part of the layout as was liquid cooling for the engine. A fairly long wheelbase and 31-degree rake at the front end made the VX800 a stable machine but not as nimble as sport minded machines. The 494-lbs. at dry weight was typical and carried low due to the V-twin configuration. Separate exhaust pipes handled the exiting fumes and their entire lengths were covered in chrome. Five-spoke alloy rims held the rubber in check and choices of Blue or Maroon was on tap. A retail price tag of $4,599 hung from the adjustable front brake lever when displayed at the local dealer. The GS500E was back in the lineup for 1990 but the alloy handlebars of 1989 were supplanted with a more traditional tubular steel unit. This change allowed the rider to install bars of different configurations and saved him money if they were bent in a collision or simple tip-over. Two-tone choices included Black and Silver or Red and White. The adjustable front brake lever found its way onto the GS500E too.

Although the touring Cavalcade was plucked from the family tree, there was talk of a replacement in the wind. Even with Honda's Gold Wing commanding most of the touring machine market, Suzuki hated to miss out on an opportunity to provide their own version of an ultra-luxury motorcycle to its audience.

1990 SUZUKI

Model	Engine	Displacement	Transmission
GS500EL	Two cylinder	487cc	Five-Speed
GSX600FL Katana	Four cylinder	599cc	Six-Speed
GSX750FL Katana (New for 1990)	Four cylinder	748cc	Five-Speed
GSX-R750L	Four cylinder	749cc	Six-Speed
VS750GLPL Intruder	Two cylinder	747cc	Five-Speed
VX800L (New for 1990)	Two cylinder	805cc	Five-Speed
GSX-R1100L	Four cylinder	1052cc	Six-Speed
GSX1100FL Katana	Four cylinder	1127cc	Five-Speed
VS1400GLPL Intruder	Four cylinder	1360cc	Five-Speed

SUZUKI
1991

No models were lost from the previous year, but one returned from the past and two new entries were made in the captain's log. Despite rumors, the Cavalcade did not yet show its face as a 1991.

Last seen as a 1983 model, the GN125 was back for 1991. The same 124cc, single cylinder engine powered the tiny cruiser and Suzuki hoped to entice beginning riders to the fold with the lightweight machine.

The popularity of standard or "naked" bikes continued to flourish as riders could more easily adapt these undressed machines to their personal taste. Joining the crew for '91 was the GSF400 Bandit. The smoothness of the four-cylinder 399cc engine added some appeal, and dual-overhead cams and TSCC provided plenty of power. A six-speed gearbox allowed the rider to keep the one-lung engine in the proper rev range for optimum performance. Slowing the 364-lb. machine was the duty of the disc brakes, one on each three-spoke cast wheel. Red or Black were the color choices leaving the rest of the added features and accessories up to the buyer. A silver frame was used regardless of the body panel color chosen.

Next up was the GS500E, back for another round of naked bike fun. To better make the 487cc machine your own, a small sport fairing and chin spoiler could be selected from the Suzuki catalog. Still using a six-speed gearbox and with a weight of only 373 lb., the GS500E was a strong buy for the beginner or intermediate rider.

The factory accessories for the GS500E included the handlebar-mounted sport fairing and lower chin spoiler.

Suzuki Motors Corporation

SUZUKI

STANDARD CATALOG OF® JAPANESE Motorcycles

Inverted forks were also installed on the larger 1991 GSX-R1100, bringing better handling to the liter-sized sport machine.

Suzuki Motors Corporation

After its debut in 1990, the 1991 VX800 returned and remained a popular selection for buyers who liked the V-twin torque wrapped in a useful configuration. Suzuki Motors Corporation

STANDARD CATALOG OF JAPANESE MOTORCYCLES   SUZUKI

Filling the top slot in the Katana hierarchy was still the 1100 version, delivering potent power in a multi-purpose machine.

Suzuki Motors Corporation

Taking the naked-bike equation to new heights, Suzuki introduced the GSX1100G for '91 and allowed a new group of riders a great platform to build on.   Suzuki Motors Corporation

SUZUKI
STANDARD CATALOG OF JAPANESE Motorcycles

All three variants of the Katana were back for 1991 and the 600 remained the baby of the family unit.

Suzuki Motors Corporation

Staking out the middle ground for the Katana clan was the 750 version.

Suzuki Motors Corporation

The true sport-bike nature of the GSX-R750 was enhanced with the addition of the inverted forks for 1991.

Suzuki Motors Corporation

The 1991 editions of the GSX-R750 and 1100 now steered with inverted front forks, a trick taken straight from the track to the street. The GSX-R's retained a dominant position in the pure sport bike arena, but other makers were growing nearer to offering similarly equipped motorcycles. All three levels of the Katana were sold for 1991, with different colors being the only change from the previous year. Joining Suzuki's naked bike regime was the mighty GSX1100G. By taking the liquid cooled motor from the GSX-R1100, adding shaft drive and eliminating the racer's bodywork, the GSX1100G was born. The motor of the G was actually detuned for better multi-purpose applications, and a four-into-two exhaust was employed along with a five-speed gearbox.

Lacking some of the GSX-R race bred tricks, the G weighed almost 70 lbs. more, but still handled well for a large bike.

For the buyer wanting to spend more time on the open road, a full coverage fairing and hard-sided saddlebags could be added to your GSX1100G. Cast aluminum wheels featured six spokes and were wider to allow for larger tires to be spooned on. Disc brakes helped to slow the big naked bike to a halt and a full compliment of gauges kept the rider informed as to his machines vital functions. Tasteful hues of Gray or Maroon were offered and brought a level of refinement to the powerful GSX1100G.

1991 SUZUKI

Model	Engine	Displacement	Transmission
GN125M Returning Model	Single cylinder	124cc	Five-Speed
GSF400M Bandit (New for 1991)	Four cylinder	398cc	Six-Speed
GS500EM	Two cylinder	487cc	Five-Speed
GSX600FM Katana	Four cylinder	599cc	Six-Speed
GSX750FM Katana	Four cylinder	748cc	Five-Speed
GSX-R750M	Four cylinder	749cc	Six-Speed
VS750GLPM Intruder	Two cylinder	747cc	Five-Speed
VX800M	Two cylinder	805cc	Five-Speed
GSX1100GM (New for 1991)	Four cylinder	1127cc	Five-Speed
GSX-R1100M	Four cylinder	1127cc	Six-Speed
GSX1100FM Katana	Four cylinder	1127cc	Five-Speed
VS1400GLPM Intruder	Four cylinder	1360cc	Five-Speed

SUZUKI

1992

STANDARD CATALOG OF JAPANESE Motorcycles

With race-inspired styling and a liquid-cooled four-cylinder for power, the 1992 Suzuki GSX-R1100 was one fun ride.

Suzuki Motors Corporation

Only a single new model was added to the 1992 roster, but none of the 1991 machines were deleted. It appeared that Suzuki was growing content with their product mix for now, although changes were still afoot for future listings. Joining the ranks of the GSX-R brigade was a smaller 600cc edition. This class of sport bike had become wildly popular, especially with the Honda CBR600F2 as a front runner. In order to keep up with the Jones' Suzuki delivered their own version of 600cc sport bike justice for the new year. Like its bigger brothers, the GSX-R600 used inverted front forks to enhance handling at speed. Liquid cooling for the motor was another carry-over feature from the 750 and 1100 variants and the race inspired bodywork did little to dispel the intentions of the GSX-R600. Dry weight of 458 lbs. was in line with other machines

The Suzuki sport touring machine was the GSX1100G. It was capable of traveling long distances without breaking a sweat and could be outfitted for added capacity.

Suzuki Motors Corporation

Positioned as a perfect machine for beginning riders, the GN125 provided adequate power for highway use while keeping its weight and mass to a minimum.

Suzuki Motors Corporation

Displacement for the smaller Intruder was increased from 750 to 800 for 1991, adding even more desirability to the low-saddled cruiser.

Suzuki Motors Corporation

For the buyer who wanted the most power and style, the Intruder 1400 provided plenty of both.

Suzuki Motors Corporation

The four-cylinder Bandit continued to be a common purchase for riders wanting a nimble yet powerful cycle for daily use.

Suzuki Motors Corporation

The VX800 was turning out to be a common selection for buyers who sought something a little different in their two-wheeled transportation.

Suzuki Motors Corporation

The larger displacement and added simplicity of the twin-cylinder engine still made the GS500E an appealing choice for many riders.

Suzuki Motors Corporation

of the day. The VS800 Intruder was an upgrade of the previous 750 version and was still created in the classic cruiser form. A 61.4-inch wheelbase and low 27-inch seat height gave the Intruder its long and low profile, appealing to large audience of buyers.

The rest of the Suzuki catalog was a re-run of the year before, albeit with new colors and graphics used to spice up the cosmetics. Still no sign of the Cavalcade's return, but the newly crafted GSX1100G was doing its best to fill those shoes as a long distance touring machine.

1992 SUZUKI

Model	Engine	Displacement	Transmission
GN125	Single cylinder	124cc	Five-Speed
GSF400 Bandit	Four cylinder	398cc	Six-Speed
GS500E	Two cylinder	487cc	Five-Speed
GSX600F Katana	Four cylinder	599cc	Six-Speed
GSX-R600 (New for 1992)	Four cylinder	600cc	Six-Speed
GSX750F Katana	Four cylinder	748cc	Five-Speed
GSX-R750	Four cylinder	749cc	Six-Speed
VS800GLP Intruder Bumped to 805cc	Two cylinder	805cc	Five-Speed
VX800	Two cylinder	805cc	Five-Speed
GSX1100G	Four cylinder	1127cc	Five-Speed
GSX-R1100	Four cylinder	1127cc	Six-Speed
GSX1100F Katana	Four cylinder	1360cc	Five-Speed
VS1400GLP Intruder	Four cylinder	1360cc	Five-Speed

SUZUKI 1993

There was only one change made to the 1993 catalog for Suzuki. The latest mix of beginner, sport and cruiser machines was viewed as a perfect balance for now, and only revised hues were seen on most of the 1993 offerings. Having had a two-year run under its belt, the GS400 Bandit was a no-show for 1993. The slightly larger GS500E carried on as Suzuki's starter bike for the sport riding enthusiast.

All three of the GSX-R models had revised engines that now used water cooling for parts of the operation versus the oil cooled variations of the early models. A different valve angle and thinner stems allowed the latest range of GSX-R motors to be narrower than those they replaced. The same amazing power band was retained as was the knife-edge handling.

The GN125 continued its reign as the class leading starter bike and both the 800 and 1400cc versions of the Intruder remained on the sales floors.

1993 SUZUKI

Model	Engine	Displacement	Transmission
GN125	Single cylinder	124cc	Five-Speed
GS500E	Two cylinder	487cc	Five-Speed
GSX600F Katana	Four cylinder	599cc	Six-Speed
GSX-R600	Four cylinder	600cc	Six-Speed
GSX750F Katana	Four cylinder	748cc	Five-Speed
GSX-R750	Four cylinder	749cc	Six-Speed
VS800GLP Intruder Bumped to 805cc	Two cylinder	805cc	Five-Speed
VX800	Two cylinder	805cc	Five-Speed
GSX1100G	Four cylinder	1127cc	Five-Speed
GSX-R1000	Four cylinder	1127cc	Six-Speed
GSX1100F Katana	Four cylinder	1360cc	Five-Speed
VS1400GLP Intruder	Four cylinder	1360cc	Five-Speed

SUZUKI

1994

Another downsizing at Suzuki left fewer models behind, but as was typical, a few new names were thrown into the hat for the latest year of sale. The starter bikes, the GN125 and GS500 were left unharmed for another year as they continued to provide terrific places for new riders to get their boots wet. Buyers would be excited to see the introduction of two new sport bikes for 1994. The RF600R and RF900R were designed in the same theme as the Katanas with sport inspired, inline-four engines and sexy bodywork to cover the mechanics beneath.

The RF600R weighed only 429 lbs. when dry and shifted through a six-speed gearbox. The all-encompassing bodywork included some sharper lines than were used on the Katanas and included two pair of diagonal vents to cover openings in the fairings. The RF900R featured a 937cc inline-four mill and weighed a total of 447 lbs. before fuel was added.

The same artistic body panels were used to wrap the RF900R and the fuel tank held one gallon more than the RF600R at 5.5 gallons. Only a five-speed gearbox was found on the RF900R versus the six of the RF600R.

The crew of the GSX-R found their 600cc model missing for 1994, leaving only the 750 and 1100 versions in its wake. The 750 model lost 24 lbs. due to a stringent diet of alloy bits and weight saving techniques.

The V-twin Intruder was offered in two flavors with an 800 and 1400 still on the menu. The 1100cc Katana was also pulled as Suzuki planned the new RF900 to take over in the large sport touring class.

The ultra small size of the GN125 made it a great starting point for many riders.
Suzuki Motors Corporation

With the departure of the GS400 Bandit, the GS500E was left behind as Suzuki's smaller naked- bike offering.
Suzuki Motors Corporation

Bumped into the 800cc class in 1992, the 1993 VS800 Intruder carried Suzuki's legacy of building middleweight cruisers.
Suzuki Motors Corporation

Still carrying the torch for Suzuki as their biggest cruiser, the VS1400 Intruder maintained a solid reputation.
Suzuki Motors Corporation

1994 SUZUKI

Model	Engine	Displacement	Transmission
GN125	Single cylinder	124cc	Five-Speed
GS500E	Two cylinder	487cc	Five-Speed
GSX600F Katana	Four cylinder	599cc	Six-Speed
RF600R (New for 1994)	Four cylinder	599cc	Six-Speed
RF600R	Four cylinder	699cc	Five-Speed
GSX750F Katana	Four cylinder	748cc	Five-Speed
GSX-R750	Four cylinder	749cc	Six-Speed
VS800GLP Intruder Bumped to 805cc	Two cylinder	805cc	Five-Speed
RF900R (New for 1994)	Four cylinder	937cc	Five-Speed
GSX-R1000	Four cylinder	1127cc	Six-Speed
VS1400GLP Intruder	Four cylinder	1360cc	Five-Speed

SUZUKI
1995

Suzuki pulled their LS650 Savage out of mothballs for 1995 where it had taken roost since 1988. The single-cylinder cruiser was still belt driven and powered by 652cc of displacement. The same four-speed gearbox was on hand and all that had changed were the new colors, Black or Maroon. A price tag of $3,999 was all it took to ride the Savage home.

Still carrying the flag for eager beginners were the GN125E and GS500E. No changes were listed for the carry-over machines but buyers weren't crying for any.

The Intruder was also back for 1995 and sold in either the 800 or 1400 guise. The liquid-cooled cruisers continued to earn a solid audience despite the few changes made in their production runs.

Only two Katanas were still shown for 1995 with the bigger 1100 still gone. The 600 and 750 were still draped in their curvaceous body panels but fresh graphics graced the contours for 1995.

The RF600R and RF900R were also back for 1995 and the 600 was treated to some upgrades for its latest year. By revising the cam timing and changing the muffler to a bolt-on aluminum can, midrange power was enhanced,

Beginning riders still bought the GN125E to use as a starter on their two-wheel riding experience. Many continued to ride them for years.

Suzuki Motors Corporation

The GS500E was still a terrific platform for riders who wanted to create a sport bike to fit their own needs.

Suzuki Motors Corporation

After shedding 24 lbs. for 1994, the GSX-R750 only received a new speedometer assembly and revised throttle grip for 1995.

Suzuki Motors Corporation

Removed from the lineup in 1988, the 650 Savage returned to the playing field for 1995 and was unchanged from its last appearance.

Suzuki Motors Corporation

SUZUKI

STANDARD CATALOG OF JAPANESE Motorcycles

It was the GSX-R1100's turn to lose some weight. For 1995, 16 lbs. was sheared off by using lightweight materials.

Suzuki Motors Corporation

Of the two remaining Katanas, the 600 was the smaller, yet it was still plenty powerful for almost any rider.

Suzuki Motors Corporation

With the 1100 version gone, the 750 Katana was the biggest version sold in 1995.

Suzuki Motors Corporation

Filling the shoes of the de-listed Katana 1100, the RF900R was unchanged for 1995.
Suzuki Motors Corporation

making the RF600R even better than before. The RF900R was the same as the previous year and sold at a price that was akin to most 750cc machines of the day. After shedding 24 lbs. for 1994, the GSX-R750 returned for 1995 with only minor alterations. A modified speedometer and new throttle grip were all the differences to be found, and the machine continued to awe riders of all skill levels with its stiff chassis and terrific handling.

For 1995, it was the turn of the GSX-R1100 to shed some excess poundage and the latest model weighed in with 16 lbs. less than the one it replaced. A new headlight assembly, magnesium cam cover and aluminum mufflers all did their part in the weight loss program. The new model rode in at 493 lbs. and lost none of the legendary power in the process.

1995 SUZUKI

Model	Engine	Displacement	Transmission
GN125E	Single cylinder	124cc	Five-Speed
GS500E	Two cylinder	487cc	Five-Speed
GSX600F Katana	Four cylinder	599cc	Six-Speed
RF600R	Four cylinder	599cc	Six-Speed
LS650 Savage (Returning for 1995)	Single cylinder	652cc	Four-Speed
GSX750F Katana	Four cylinder	748cc	Five-Speed
GSX-R750	Four cylinder	749cc	Six-Speed
VS800GLP Intruder	Two cylinder	805cc	Five-Speed
RF900R	Four cylinder	937cc	Five-Speed
GSX-R1100	Four cylinder	1127cc	Six-Speed
VS1400GLP Intruder	Four cylinder	1360cc	Five-Speed

SUZUKI
1996

STANDARD CATALOG OF JAPANESE Motorcycles

Call 1-800-828-RIDE for the name of your nearest Suzuki motorcycle dealer. Suzuki firmly believes racing belongs in one place - on the racetrack. We want every ride to be safe and enjoyable. So always wear a helmet, eye protection and protective clothing. Never ride under the influence of alcohol or other drugs. Study your owner's manual and always inspect your Suzuki before riding. Take a riding skills course. For the course nearest you, call the Motorcycle Safety Foundation at 1-800-447-4700. The Suzuki GSX-Rs are engineered for experienced riders. *396 lbs. CA model

The 1996 Suzuki GSX-R 750 looked like it was in motion even when it was standing still.

Suzuki Motors Corporation

The bulk of the 1996 roster remained unchanged for Suzuki with the exception of alterations in the 600cc class.

Speaking of bulk, for 1996 the GSX-R750 was completely retooled, losing 50 lbs. in the process. The Suzuki engineers had already trimmed 24 lbs. off of the race-inspired sport bike a few years back, so to locate and trim twice that amount was truly remarkable. Every facet of the 750's design was reviewed with precious ounces shaved wherever they were found. Improved engine breathing was also achieved by adding their SRAD (Suzuki Ram Air Direct) ductwork that more efficiently fed the hungry motor with the required oxygen. The dry weight of the GSX-R750 was now an incredible 394 lbs. while the rear wheel horsepower rating was nearing 118. It was no wonder why Suzuki was always on the podium when they wasted no time in recreating a winning bike time and time again. The Katana listing remained at two, with 750 and 600 versions offered, but the RF900R was now alone as the RF600R was removed from the plan.

In its stead was the new GSF600S Bandit. Considered more of a naked bike than the RF it replaced, the Bandit lacked nothing in appeal of middleweight performance. The 599cc engine was fed with a set of four 33mm carburetors and shifted through a six-speed gearbox. The stainless steel exhaust collected all four outlets into a single muffler and helped to raise the Bandit's rated horsepower to 74. A frame-mounted sport fairing helped ease through the wind and upright ergonomics delivered plenty of comfort. Triple disc brakes were joined by V-rated rubber to provide sure-footing and confident stopping power. A 4.8-gallon fuel tank provided ample nourishment for decent stretches between fill-ups and when dry the 600 Bandit weighed only 438 lbs.

Carry-over models included the tiny GN125E and the sporty GS500E for yet another year of entry-level fun. The 800 and 1400 versions of the Intruder still held their own in the cruiser class while the single cylinder Savage put great value under the rider for another season. The RF900R continued to do what it could to fill the roles of sport touring riders while the big GSX-R1100 retained the crown of power and speed.

The Suzuki RF-900R had the modern look in 1996, complete with decorative flame-like striping. Suzuki Motors Corporation

The 1996 Suzuki Intruder had the classic look of motorcycles from the past, yet still had all the modern amenities. Suzuki Motors Corporation

1996 SUZUKI

Model	Engine	Displacement	Transmission
GN125E	Single cylinder	124cc	Five-Speed
GS500E	Two cylinder	487cc	Five-Speed
GSF600SBandit (New for 1996)	Four cylinder	599cc	Six-Speed
GSX600F Katana	Four cylinder	599cc	Six-Speed
LS650 Savage	Single cylinder	652cc	Four-Speed
GSX750F Katana	Four cylinder	748cc	Five-Speed
GSX-R750	Four cylinder	749cc	Six-Speed
VS800GLP Intruder	Two cylinder	805cc	Five-Speed
RF900R	Four cylinder	937cc	Five-Speed
GSX-R1100	Four cylinder	1127cc	Six-Speed
VS1400GLP Intruder	Four cylinder	1360cc	Five-Speed

SUZUKI
1997

THE MARAUDER CAN SET YOU FREE FOR AS LITTLE AS $139 A MONTH*

BORN FREE.

A profile of the 1997 Marauder 800 was advertised with the sub heading "Born Free."

Suzuki Motors Corporation

Suzuki transfused some new blood into the 1997 lineup, adding machines at different ends of the scale as they attempted to rein in a larger crowd of buyers. The majority of the catalog returned from 1996 with only minor changes. Feeling they were missing out on the rush to the middleweight sport bikes, Suzuki rolled out a 600cc version of their race-bike-for-the-street GSX-R. Looking every inch the true GSX-R the baby Gixxer sported a 599cc engine in its frame and was fed through a quadrant of 36mm Mikuni carburetors. Suzuki's own SRAD technology aided in the free-breathing 600 and helped to raise the output of the compact engine to new heights.

The six-speed gearbox sent the power to a chain drive although the GSX-R600 lacked the braced swing arm of its bigger sibling. A 4.8-gallon fuel storage tank rode on the aluminum frame and before being filled the 600 weighed a scant 384 lbs.

The GSX-R750 and 1100 were also sold in 1997 but showed us nothing new over the previous year's editions. Suzuki has never been a company afraid of taking chances, and for 1997 they introduced an entirely new flavor of sporting machine in their TL1000S. In place of the traditional inline-four engine, the TL carried a 996cc V-twin that was fed by fuel injection. The 90- degree spread of the cylinders and two-into-two exhaust produced a distinct sound that helped to set it apart from other sporting machines on the market. A European style trellis chassis was formed from aluminum and carried a matching alloy swing arm at the rear. Three-spoke alloy rims were equipped with a trio of disc brakes

ENGINE:
805cc, 45 degree V-twin,
SOHC, 8-valve, liquid-cooled

INDUCTION:
Dual 36mm carburetors

TRANSMISSION:
5-speed

WHEELBASE:
64.8" (1,645mm)

DRY WEIGHT:
456 lbs. (207kg)

Marauder **$ SUZUKI.**

We didn't just build a new motorcycle. We created a whole new category of bikes. *ready* or not, here comes the Marauder 800. The first cruiser to combine classic hot-rod styling with modern technology for surprising performance. If you love muscular V-twin engines, you're all *set.* But this torque monster also boasts overhead cams, four valves per cylinder and our heavy-breathing Twin Swirl Combustion Chambers. Its style is a combination of classic touches like a contoured fender with a removable rear seat, drag-style handlebars and so much chrome you hardly need the rearview mirrors. Plus custom features like a massive inverted front fork, billet-style cast-aluminum wheels and the throaty rumble of a dual exhaust. All you need is one look and you'll *go change everything you* ever believed or *thought about cruisers.* The Marauder 800. Contemporary performance, classic style and a price that won't make you sweat. One ride and you'll never stop.

CALL 1-800-828-RIDE OR VISIT US ON THE WEB AT WWW.SUZUKI.COM FOR MORE INFORMATION.
At Suzuki, we want every ride to be safe and enjoyable. So always wear a helmet, eye protection and protective clothing. Never ride under the influence of alcohol or other drugs. Study your owner's manual and always inspect your Suzuki before riding. Take a riding skills course. For the course nearest you, call the Motorcycle Safety Foundation at 1-800-446-9227.

American Suzuki, Circle 28 on Reader Service Card

The unique paint scheme, bikini fairing and enhanced instrument panel all help to set the 700 copies of the GS1000S apart from the crowd.

SUZUKI

The Suzuki Fest '97 offered the Savage and Intruder models and asked prospective buyers to "Do the Math."

with inverted forks to provide crisp handling. Six forward speeds and a chain drive were included to maintain the true nature of the TL and the 4.8-gallon fuel tank provided hours of fun between stops. When dry, the liter-sized twin weighed 412 lbs., making it a potent performer that carried a retail price tag of $8,999.

The debut of the GSF600S Bandit had proven to a successful move, so Suzuki followed up with a pair of GSF1200S Bandits for 1997. By doubling the displacement of the baby Bandit, Suzuki doubled the fun in their full-sized naked bike. Power for the big Bandit was earned by using the 1157cc inline-four from the GSX-R, and we all know what fun that unit is. A simple steel-tube frame held the Bandit's components in place including the frame mounted half-fairing. The 471-lb. (dry) Bandit rowed through a five-speed transmission and rode on radial rubber.

Adding a new measure of safety to the equation, the Bandit could be purchased with ABS braking. This system prevented the wheels from locking up and sliding under extreme use, thus bringing the machine to a halt with little fuss. The ABS was applied to both wheels and took very little practice to get used to. This system did add $1500 to the base model's $7,099 price, but many considered that a bargain.

Everything else for 1997 was a re-run of 1996 as buyers still enjoyed a wide variety of models and styles shown in the Suzuki showrooms.

1997 SUZUKI

Model	Engine	Displacement	Transmission
GN125E	Single cylinder	124cc	Five-Speed
GS500E	Two cylinder	487cc	Five-Speed
GSF600S Bandit	Four cylinder	599cc	Six-Speed
GSX600F Katana	Four cylinder	599cc	Six-Speed
GSX-R600 (New for 1997)	Four cylinder	599cc	Six-Speed
LS650 Savage	Single cylinder	652cc	Four-Speed
GSX750F Katana	Four cylinder	748cc	Five-Speed
GSX-R750	Four cylinder	749cc	Six-Speed
VS800GLP Intruder	Two cylinder	805cc	Five-Speed
RF900R	Four cylinder	937cc	Five-Speed
TL1100S (New for 1997)	Two cylinder	996cc	Six-Speed
GSX-R1100	Four cylinder	1127cc	Six-Speed
GSF1200S Bandit (New for 1997)	Four cylinder	1157cc	Five-Speed
GSF1200SA Bandit (New for 1997)	Four cylinder	1157cc	Five-Speed
VS1400GLP Intruder	Four cylinder	1360cc	Five-Speed

SUZUKI
1998

Another year of mostly carry-over machines lay in store for buyers in 1998, but Suzuki still had some magic to work.

Having introduced their fuel-injected TL1000S for 1995 it seemed only fitting that the same fuel delivery system be added to the GSX-R750. Along with the fresh delivery system, engine modifications brought the power up to 135 for 1998, putting it on par with their latest liter machine.

The ABS equipped Bandit 1200 was not offered but the standard issue remained in force. The 600cc version also stayed on with a growing fan base.

The trellis-framed TL1000S was joined by a racier TL1000R for 1998. Lurking behind the full race fairing was a chassis much like the one used on the GSX-R models. Using the added strength of the aluminum spar design, Suzuki hung the 996cc V-twin engine for added results. Helping to boost the power of the R was a new airbox that raised the rating by seven over the S version. The latest frame decision lowered the seat height to 32.6 inches and placed the rider in a more aggressive posture. The 43mm

Both size and style marked the 1998 Suzuki TL 1000R—a self-labeled "super bike."
Suzuki Motors Corporation

The 1998 Intruder VL 1500 was all about classic styling with no sacrifice of creature comforts.
Suzuki Motors Corporation

SUZUKI   STANDARD CATALOG OF JAPANESE Motorcycles

Never before has there been a cruiser as smooth and comfortable as the Intruder 1500LC. We gave it an extra long wheelbase for easy cruising. An under-the-seat fuel tank for a lower center of gravity. And a powerful V-twin for loafing down the highway or rushing forward at the twist of the throttle. From this moment forward, what used to be considered the end of the ride will, in fact, be just the beginning.

Accessories shown are optional. See dealer for details.

CALL 1-800-828-RIDE OR VISIT US ON THE WEB AT WWW.SUZUKI.COM FOR MORE INFORMATION. At Suzuki, we want every ride to be safe and enjoyable. So always wear a helmet, eye protection and protective clothing. Never ride under the influence of alcohol or other drugs. Study your owner's manual and always inspect your Suzuki before riding. Take a riding skills course. For the course nearest you call the Motorcycle Safety Foundation at 1-800-446-9227.

The 1998 Suzuki Intruder 1500 LC suggested the ability to cruise wherever the rider dreamed of traveling.

When one looked at the 1998 Suzuki Intruder, there was an eyeful of raw power along with its unique style.

Suzuki Motors Corporation

The 1998 Suzuki Marauder 800 was both heavily classic and pleasantly modern.

Suzuki Motors Corporation

The Suzuki Intruder 800 for 1998 had a V-twin engine as its power plant.

Suzuki Motors Corporation

The 1998 Suzuki Savage 650 offered a sporty profile in this magazine ad.

Suzuki Motors Corporation

SUZUKI

The ultra-modern and smooth-styled '98 Suzuki 750 Katana stood out in this magazine ad.

Suzuki Motors Corporation

powerful and racier R was sold alongside the S offering two distinct twists on a similar theme.

Both the 600 and 750 Katanas received some internal changes to their motors to deliver quieter operation and additional power. Wrapped around the new motors was sleeker bodywork that still retained the DNA of the previous examples of the popular multi-purpose machines.

The 800 and 1400cc versions of the Intruder were joined by a bigger brother in the VS1500LC Intruder. Displacing more than 100cc over the 1400 version, the new Intruder was serious about putting power to the ground. No matter what the power, the latest Intruder was draped with bigger fenders, alloy wheels and more chrome than you could shake a pushrod at. Long, low the 1500LC weighed in at 120 more than the 1400, a testament to all the added styling and bigger engine.

inverted forks were still in place as were a pair of 320mm brakes on the front wheel. Overall, the new chassis configuration placed more weight on the front end of the TL1000R with hopes of adding some stability to the platform. Some riders complained of instability in the TL1000S, and Suzuki hoped to cure those random ills with the R's layout. The more

Additional applications of Suzuki's cruiser know-how would appear in 1999, but for now the rest of the line carried on as before.

1998 SUZUKI

Model	Engine	Displacement	Transmission
GN125E	Single cylinder	124cc	Five-Speed
GS500E	Two cylinder	487cc	Five-Speed
GSF600S Bandit	Four cylinder	599cc	Six-Speed
GSX600F Katana	Four cylinder	599cc	Six-Speed
GSX-R600	Four cylinder	599cc	Six-Speed
LS650 Savage	Single cylinder	652cc	Four-Speed
GSX750F Katana	Four cylinder	748cc	Five-Speed
GSX-R750	Four cylinder	749cc	Six-Speed
VS800GLP Intruder	Two cylinder	805cc	Five-Speed
RF900R	Four cylinder	937cc	Five-Speed
TL1000R (New for 1998)	Two cylinder	996cc	Six-Speed
TL1000S	Two cylinder	996cc	Six-Speed
GSX-R1100	Four cylinder	1127cc	Six-Speed
GSF1200S Bandit	Four cylinder	1157cc	Five-Speed
VS1400GLP Intruder	Four cylinder	1360cc	Five-Speed
VS1500LC Intruder (New for 1998)	Two cylinder	1462cc	Five-Speed

SUZUKI
1999

Bumping their minimum displacement model to 249cc, the GZ250 stepped in during 1999 to take over where the GN125 had left off.

Suzuki Motors Corporation

Several important changes were afoot for the 1999 Suzuki family as a few familiar faces left the flock and some fresh blood entered. The tiny GN125 had enjoyed a long run, but was losing ground to some slightly larger and more powerful models. Suzuki introduced the GZ250. Still fairly light at 302 lbs., the GZ250 used a 249cc, single cylinder engine for motivation. Classic cruiser styling remained and the GZ featured ducktail front and rear fenders and an ample dose of chrome. Wire wheels and a disc brake up front completed the picture and the bigger entry-level machine was a welcome boost. The RF models were now missing from the lineup but the 600 and 750 Katana models stayed on for another round. The big GSX-R1100 was another no-show for 1999 but Suzuki had even bigger things planned for the sport bike community.

Helping to fill the void left by the smaller Katana, the SV650 debuted. A 645cc, V-twin engine hung from the exposed trellis frame and liquid cooling kept things under control. A six-speed gearbox gave the compact SV650 plenty of options for the rider as he powered the 364-lb. machine down the road. Three-spoke cast wheels helped to keep the weight down and disc brakes slowed the SV650. Sold in Red or Blue, the SV650 had a blacked-out motor and natural silver frame. Another new entry expanded the scope of Suzuki's range. The 800 Marauder used the same 805cc V-twin engine as the Intruder,

The SV650 was another new model for 1999 and was a terrific platform to build a weekend racer around.

Suzuki Motors Corporation

267

SUZUKI

STANDARD CATALOG OF® JAPANESE Motorcycles

A large chrome air cleaner cover and dual shotgun exhaust added some flash to the blacked-out engine and enhanced the stylings of the newest 800.

Both the 600 and 1200 Bandits were back for another year and grew in popularity among buyers of adaptable naked bikes.

In a move that placed Suzuki firmly at the top of the performance heap, the release of the GSX1300R Hayabusa sent the motorcycle world into a tailspin. Named for a Japanese falcon considered one of the fastest birds on earth, the Hayabusa hid a 1,298cc engine within its aluminum frame and delivered unheard of horsepower. The GSX1300R could routinely measure 150 rear wheel ponies, a number never before recorded on a street legal machine.

The Hayabusa weighed 474 lbs., but the sleekly draped monster could reach 187 mph without a single alteration from its stock trim. A six-speed gearbox gave the rider one additional ratio when blasting around town. Three massive disc brakes were on hand to bring the Hayabusa down from warp speed and the four-into-two exhaust kept things quiet, despite the raucous performance being meted out.

Of the two color choices for its debut year, the copper and gold hinted at the natural coloration of the winged Hayabusa while the black and silver simply looked menacing. Within a year, gov-

The TL1000R carried on and was still sold alongside its sibling the TL1000S.
Suzuki Motors Corporation

but carried itself in a huskier chassis with altered sheet metal. Fat tires rolled under each of the Marauder's fenders and the rear unit had an exaggerated duck tail flip. A slightly larger fuel tank was used. Its contours were nothing like those of the Intruder.

The TL1000S came first and featured an alloy trellis frame in place of the aluminum structure found on the more powerful TL1000R.
Suzuki Motors Corporation

Putting other performance machines on notice, the GSX1300R produced power and speed that hadn't been recorded from a street-legal motorcycle before.
Suzuki Motors Corporation

erning bodies would slap restrictions on the top velocity allowed for these bikes, making the 1999 Hayabusa the fastest of the breed. Speed shops quickly turned their attentions to the GSX1300R and pushed the amazing machine to stratospheric levels of velocity.

Making its debut in 1998, the Intruder 1500 took Suzuki to a new level of cruiser power and wrapped it in stylish garb to boot.

Suzuki Motors Corporation

The new Marauder 800 used the 805cc engine from the Intruder and wrapped it in fatter trim, along with more chrome and attitude.

Suzuki Motors Corporation

1999 SUZUKI

Model	Engine	Displacement	Transmission
GZ250 (New for 1999)	Single cylinder	249cc	Five-Speed
GS500E	Two cylinder	487cc	Five-Speed
GSF600S Bandit	Four cylinder	599cc	Six-Speed
GSX600 Katana	Four cylinder	599cc	Six-Speed
GSX-R600	Four cylinder	599cc	Six-Speed
LS650 Savage	Single cylinder	652cc	Four-Speed
SV650 (New for 1999)	Two cylinder	645cc	Six-Speed
GSX750F Katana	Four cylinder	748cc	Five-Speed
GSX-R750	Four cylinder	749cc	Six-Speed
VS800GLP Intruder	Two cylinder	805cc	Five-Speed
800 Marauder (New for 1999)	Two cylinder	805cc	Five-Speed
TL1000R	Two cylinder	996cc	Six-Speed
TL1000S	Two cylinder	996cc	Six-Speed
GSF1200S Bandit	Four cylinder	1157cc	Five-Speed
GSX1300R Hayabusa (New for 1999)	Four cylinder	1298cc	Six-Speed
VS1400GLP Intruder	Four cylinder	1360cc	Five-Speed
VS1500LC Intruder	Two cylinder	1462cc	Five-Speed

SUZUKI 2000

STANDARD CATALOG OF JAPANESE Motorcycles

Although powered by a 650cc engine like the Savage, the SV650 fit a completely different profile and provided riders of all levels a terrific platform.

Suzuki Motors Corporation

There was not a single change to the lineup for 2000 although several tweaks were applied to the returning models for the latest sales year. The GSX-R750 was again a complete re-design in Suzuki's ongoing race to stay at the top of that class.

The VS1400 Intruder wore a set of wider handlebars for the 2000 season but no additional alterations were listed. The VS800 Intruder rolled on a different 19-inch spoke front wheel and also carried the wider bars. The VZ800 Marauder carried on as the price point leader and was still driven by belt versus shaft. The 650 Savage sported revised paint schemes for 2000 but was unaltered beyond that. The GZ250 carried the torch as Suzuki's bargain basement cruiser and rode in with no listed changes.

Moving to the sport bike category, similar subtle revisions were seen here and there with

The 1400 Intruder rolled on a new 19-inch front hoop and carried wider handlebars for the latest year but was otherwise unaltered.

Suzuki Motors Corporation

Continuing sales, despite the lack of changes, proved the value of the 650 Savage to the cruiser market.

Suzuki Motors Corporation

Even being number one wasn't enough to keep Suzuki from revamping the GSX-R750, shaving 30 lbs. from the '99 model and gaining five more horses.

Suzuki Motors Corporation

After its debut year in 1999, the speed demon Hayabusa was back for 2000, yet unchanged mechanically. Only new color choices set the '00 apart from the '99s.

Suzuki Motors Corporation

most of them being cosmetic in nature. The record-slashing Hayabusa was back but was unchanged for 2000. Both versions of the TL1000 were on the roster even though Suzuki had abandoned their racing efforts using the R version on the track. Having been largely recreated in 1999, the only change on the Katana 600 was a new clock and the 750 carried nothing in revisions. The GSX-R750 continued to shed weight as another all new iteration took to the streets. Now claiming a feathery dry weight of only 366 lbs., the 750 earned even more respect

SUZUKI

Revised heavily for 1999, the only change found on the 2000 Katana 600 was a new speedometer.

Suzuki Motors Corporation

Cloaked in all-new bodywork for 2000, the 600 Bandit was still a popular choice for those who wanted a naked bike..

Suzuki Motors Corporation

from riders. Not only was the 2000 GSX-R750 lighter but carried five additional horsepower. The aluminum frame was more compact and used a longer swing arm to improve handling as well. The GSX-R600 returned for was the same as in 1999.

The GSF600S Bandit carried the same motor as before but was clothed in all new bodywork and a revised fairing. Frame geometry was altered for sharper steering and wider rims now held radial rubber for better handling. The SV650 and GS500E remained unaltered.

2000 SUZUKI

Model	Engine	Displacement	Transmission
GZ250	Single cylinder	249cc	Five-Speed
GS500E	Two cylinder	487cc	Five-Speed
GSF600S Bandit	Four cylinder	599cc	Six-Speed
GSX600 Katana	Four cylinder	599cc	Six-Speed
GSX-R600	Four cylinder	599cc	Six-Speed
LS650 Savage	Single cylinder	652cc	Four-Speed
SV650	Two cylinder	645cc	Six-Speed
GSX750 Katana	Four cylinder	748cc	Five-Speed
GSX-R750	Four cylinder	749cc	Six-Speed
VS800GLP Intruder	Two cylinder	805cc	Five-Speed
VZ800 Marauder	Two cylinder	805cc	Five-Speed
TL1000R	Two cylinder	996cc	Six-Speed
TL1000S	Two cylinder	996cc	Six-Speed
GSF1200S Bandit	Four cylinder	1157cc	Five-Speed
GSX1300R Hayabusa	Four cylinder	1298cc	Six-Speed
VS1400GLP Intruder	Four cylinder	1360cc	Five-Speed
VS1500LC Intruder	Two cylinder	1462cc	Five-Speed

STANDARD CATALOG OF® JAPANESE Motorcycles

SUZUKI

2001

The GSX-R600 was a re-do for 2001, with less weight and fuel injection appearing for the latest model year.

Suzuki Motors Corporation

With the exception of the all-new GSX-R750 in 2000, the year had been rather uneventful. The 2001 catalog revealed several new versions of previous machines as well as two brand new offerings.

The GSXR-R600 was re-done and the latest version was lighter, more powerful and featured fuel injection for the first time. The GSXR-R750 was untouched but had been all-new for 2000, leaving no stones to be turned.

Joining the Gixxer ranks for 2001 was a bigger GSX-R1000. By using the same formula as with the two smaller versions and bolting in a 988cc engine, a class-leading machine was born. Power from the latest power plant was awe-inspiring and the liter-sized GSX-R weighed a scant 375 lbs., only a handful more than the 750. Styling on the GSX-R1000 was typical for the breed and dominance at racing events followed soon after the big Gixxer took to the track. On the street, the competition was also feeling the heat from the new Suzuki sending them back to the respective drawing boards to catch up.

In the naked bike category, a half-faired SV650S was released and a completely naked GSF1200 Bandit was provided. The running

Adding to the dominant nature of the GSX-R family, the all-new 1000 set standards for sport bikes that hadn't been comprehended a few years earlier.

Suzuki Motors Corporation

By using retro styling and the existing 805cc V-twin engine, the Intruder Volusia rolled in to start a new trend for Suzuki cruisers.

Suzuki Motors Corporation

By adding a small sport-fairing to the already popular SV650, the SV650S was born.

Suzuki Motors Corporation

gear and drive trains remained the same, only the level of trim had changed. The new additions meant that either size of the Bandit could be had with or without a fairing, expanding the audience drawn to the multi-purpose machines.

New in the cruiser division was the Intruder Volusia. With an 805cc V-twin in its flanks, and retro-styling all around, the new Intruder upped the ante for Suzuki. Looking much like a downsized VL1500, the Volusia featured the full fenders, shotgun exhaust and low-slung nature of its bigger sibling. Black with White insets or Black with Red details were offered on the debut versions.

The remaining cruiser catalog returned for the latest year with no changes save fresh hues.

2001 SUZUKI

Model	Engine	Displacement	Transmission
GZ250	Single cylinder	249cc	Five-Speed
GS500E	Two cylinder	487cc	Five-Speed
GSF600S Bandit	Four cylinder	599cc	Six-Speed
GSX600 Katana	Four cylinder	599cc	Six-Speed
GSX-R600	Four cylinder	599cc	Six-Speed
LS650 Savage	Single cylinder	652cc	Four-Speed
SV650	Two cylinder	645cc	Six-Speed
SV650S (New for 2001)	Two cylinder	645cc	Six-Speed
GSX750 Katana	Four cylinder	748cc	Five-Speed
GSX-R750	Four cylinder	749cc	Six-Speed
VL800 Intruder Volusia (New for 2001)	Two cylinder	805cc	Five-Speed
VS800GLP Intruder	Two cylinder	805cc	Five-Speed
VZ800 Marauder	Two cylinder	805cc	Five-Speed
GSX-R1000 (New for 2001)	Four cylinder	988cc	Six-Speed
TL1000R	Two cylinder	996cc	Six-Speed
TL1000S	Two cylinder	996cc	Six-Speed
GSF1200S Bandit	Four cylinder	1157cc	Five-Speed
GSF 1200 Bandit (New for 2001)	Four cylinder	1157cc	Five-Speed
GSX1300R Hayabusa	Four cylinder	1298cc	Six-Speed
VS1400GLP Intruder	Four cylinder	1360cc	Five-Speed
VS1500LC Intruder	Two cylinder	1462cc	Five-Speed

SUZUKI 2002

The final tally of 2002 model would remain the same with one Suzuki departing and another being added.

Gone for 2002 was the TL1000S, leaving only the TL1000R in its wake. The sometimes quirky handling of the S variation forced its removal, leaving the better equipped TL1000R as the only twin cylinder sport bike in the collection. One of the strengths of the TL1000 platform was the V-twin motor, and even though the S had been discontinued, Suzuki used the engine to power their latest entry. The DL1000 carried the 996cc, V-twin engine in a chassis that was penned to be used as a big dual-purpose cycle. Several other cycles were found in this market segment so Suzuki created the DL to compete. A six-speed gearbox and final chain drive ensured the DL had plenty of ratios and a dependable drive train when taken to the rugged terrain. The chain drive was also lighter than a shaft helping to keep the weight of the DL1000 to 456 lbs. A half-fairing was attached to the frame and the exhaust ran high under the tail section to complete the form and function issues. A price of $8,899 was required to put you in the fairly tall saddle that stood 32.7 inches from the pavement.

All three versions of the Bandit were back but unchanged from their 2001 trim. The same pair of Katana models were also repeats for 2002 with only new hues listed for the sporting machines. The three models in the GSX-R family gained new exhaust systems and the 750 received fuel injection bits that weighed less and a modified swing arm pivot that provided better adjustability. The GSX1300R Hayabusa was another 2002 model that rolled into view carrying all the same specs as in 2001, but still wore the speed crown.

The Intruder department was given numerous alterations on their growing clan. The big LC1500 tooled around on wheels that showed us a new finish as well as new brakes. Both 800cc variants

2002 SUZUKI

Model	Engine	Displacement	Transmission
GZ250	Single cylinder	249cc	Five-Speed
GS500E	Two cylinder	487cc	Five-Speed
GSF600S Bandit	Four cylinder	599cc	Six-Speed
GSX600 Katana	Four cylinder	599cc	Six-Speed
GSX-R600	Four cylinder	599cc	Six-Speed
LS650 Savage	Single cylinder	652cc	Four-Speed
SV650	Two cylinder	645cc	Six-Speed
SV650S	Two cylinder	645cc	Six-Speed
GSX750 Katana	Four cylinder	748cc	Five-Speed
GSX-R750	Four cylinder	749cc	Six-Speed
VL800 Intruder Volusia	Two cylinder	805cc	Five-Speed
VS800GLP Intruder	Two cylinder	805cc	Five-Speed
VZ800 Marauder	Two cylinder	805cc	Five-Speed
DL 1000 (New for 2002)	Two cylinder	996cc	Six-Speed
GSX-R1000	Four cylinder	988cc	Six-Speed
TL1000R	Two cylinder	996cc	Six-Speed
GSF1200S Bandit	Four cylinder	1157cc	Five-Speed
GSF 1200 Bandit	Four cylinder	1157cc	Five-Speed
GSX1300R Hayabusa	Four cylinder	1298cc	Six-Speed
VS1400GLP Intruder	Four cylinder	1360cc	Five-Speed
VS1500LC Intruder	Two cylinder	1462cc	Five-Speed

SUZUKI

STANDARD CATALOG OF JAPANESE MOTORCYCLES

The 2002 Suzuki Intruder 1500 LC took riders to wide-open spaces in style.

(Intruder and Volusia) were carried over with no new revisions for 2002 as was the 1400 version. The Marauder was fitted with a final chain drive in place of the belt used on previous versions and the inverted forks and cast alloy wheels delivered a dose of sport bike performance to the elegant cruiser. With their low-slung saddles, light weight and simple operation, both the Savage and GZ250 continued to carry the torch for Suzuki at the low end of the displacement ladder. Only colors were different on the efficient and still popular entry-level cruisers.

SUZUKI 2003

Still perched at the top of the Suzuki cruiser hierarchy was the 1500cc Intruder, complete with retro styling and a powerful V-twin engine.

Suzuki Motors Corporation

It had been a long run for the Suzuki GS500E, but all good things must come to an end and 2003 was the year that claimed the life of the perky, entry-level sport machine. The continuing growth in the SV650s also put some heat on the smaller Suzuki, and for some riders, its loss would be missed. With the popularity of the SV650 models still expanding, Suzuki did the same to the breed and introduced two versions of a new SV1000 for 2003. Sold in naked or half-fairing guise, the bigger SV embodied what was great about the 650 variants and brought more power to the table. By using a fuel-injected version of the TL1000S motor and adding fully adjustable suspension, the new SV1000 and SV1000S made a great combination. An entry fee of just under $8,000 for the SV1000 drew a new crowd to the fold. The frame mounted fairing SV1000S went for an additional $600 but was still a terrific bargain for the gear you acquired.

Not to be outdone by their new rivals, the SV650s were also treated to a major facelift. All new trellis frames were used to haul the now fuel-injected, 645cc engines around, and dramatic new sheet

Joining its naked brother for 2003 was the SV1000S, carrying a frame-mounted fairing along with the rest of the same great features of the standard SV1000.

Suzuki Motors Corporation

SUZUKI

STANDARD CATALOG OF JAPANESE MOTORCYCLES

The GZ250 was still the smallest Suzuki and provided beginning riders with a nice place to get started.

Suzuki Motors Corporation

Like its bigger brother the SV1000S, the SV650S sported a frame-mounted fairing along with the rest of new class-leading features found on the SV.

Suzuki Motors Corporation

Using an all-new chassis and improved engine, the SV650 still featured the same nomenclature as the 2002 model it superseded.

Suzuki Motors Corporation

A new listing for 2003 was the SV1000. It used the TL1000S engine and added fuel injection and fully adjustable suspension for a great all-around package.

Suzuki Motors Corporation

metal added some excitement to the package. Sold in un-faired or half-faired versions, the SV650 was getting closer to true sport bike statistics with every passing year of upgrades. The $5,899 and $6,299 price tags were attached to the SV650 and SV650S, respectively, for 2003.

Although a new model in 2001, the GSX-R1000 was also given a dose of added features for 2003. A new frame carried the engine that now produced five additional horsepower while saving weight in the process.

Radial-mount calipers helped to slow the big Gixxer down from speed and an LED taillight assembly showed your competition your plans to stop. Front forks were finished with a new Diamond Like Carbon product for a different look. New skin was draped over the latest frame and engine to make sure the 2003 GSX-R1000 didn't look the same as the class leading model it replaced.

The balance of the 2003 Suzuki catalog was the same as the year before, except for course for new paint colors and combinations on the cruiser models.

Five additional horsepower and fewer pounds were two of the newly added traits of the 2003 GSX-R1000. New bodywork dressed the latest version in style.

Suzuki Motors Corporation

2003 SUZUKI

Model	Engine	Displacement	Transmission
GZ250	Single cylinder	249cc	Five-Speed
GSF600S Bandit	Four cylinder	599cc	Six-Speed
GSX600 Katana	Four cylinder	599cc	Six-Speed
GSX-R600	Four cylinder	599cc	Six-Speed
LS650 Savage	Single cylinder	652cc	Four-Speed
SV650	Two cylinder	645cc	Six-Speed
SV650S	Two cylinder	645cc	Six-Speed
GSX750 Katana	Four cylinder	748cc	Five-Speed
GSX-R750	Four cylinder	749cc	Six-Speed
VL800 Intruder Volusia	Two cylinder	805cc	Five-Speed
VS800GLP Intruder	Two cylinder	805cc	Five-Speed
VZ800 Marauder	Two cylinder	805cc	Five-Speed
DL 1000 V-Strom	Two cylinder	996cc	Six-Speed
GSX-R1000	Four cylinder	988cc	Six Speed
SV1000 (New for 2003)	Two cylinder	996cc	Six-Speed
SV1000S (New for 2003)	Two cylinder	996cc	Six-Speed
TL1000R	Two cylinder	996cc	Six-Speed
GSF1200S Bandit	Four cylinder	1157cc	Five-Speed
GSF 1200 Bandit	Four cylinder	1157cc	Five-Speed
GSX1300R Hayabusa	Four cylinder	1298cc	Six-Speed
VS1400GLP Intruder	Four cylinder	1360cc	Five-Speed
VS1500LC Intruder	Two cylinder	1462cc	Five-Speed

SUZUKI   STANDARD CATALOG OF JAPANESE Motorcycles

IF YOU'VE NEVER USED A TANKER TRUCK AS A VANITY MIRROR
IF YOUR DINING GUIDE ISN'T A GAS-FOOD-LODGING SIGN
IF YOU THINK A HOME HAS TO HAVE FOUR WALLS
GET GET OUT OF THE WAY

45-DEGREE 805CC V-TWIN • LOW-MAINTENANCE SHAFT DRIVE • LACED WHEELS
DEEP, RICH PAINT AND CHROME • TRADITIONAL STYLING • MODERN ENGINEERING

The Suzuki Intruder® Volusia™ 800.

$SUZUKI.$
www.suzuki.com

CALL 1-800-828-RIDE OR VISIT US ON THE WEB AT SUZUKI.COM FOR MORE INFORMATION. At Suzuki, we want every ride to be safe and enjoyable. So always wear a helmet, eye protection and protective clothing. Never ride under the influence of alcohol or other drugs. Study your owner's manual and always inspect your Suzuki before riding. Take a riding skills course. For the course nearest you call the Motorcycle Safety Foundation at 1-800-446-9227. ©2003 American Suzuki Motor Corporation.

Coming at you was the 2003 Suzuki Intruder Volusia 800, featured in this magazine ad.

SUZUKI
2004

Improvements to the engine, suspension and braking made the 2004 GSX-R600 the best one ever.

Suzuki Motors Corporation.

A raft of modifications to existing and a few new models graced the 2004 Suzuki lineup.

In the ultra-sport GSX-R division, Suzuki delivered two all-new versions of their 600 and 750cc offerings. Both sizes of the engines now featured Suzuki's Dual Throttle Valve (SDTV) with race tested titanium valves. Rigid 43mm inverted front forks delivered tremendous handling and control adding to the magic of the Gixxer. A pair of 300mm full-floating front rotors were each clamped by Tokico four-puck calipers, stopping the revised GSX-R in record time. A third, 220mm rear rotor was seized by a two-puck caliper for greater control. The newest 600 weighed 355 lbs. while the 750 only added four lbs. to that number for an unequaled power-to-weight ratio.

The long running GS500E had been pulled from the 2003 catalog, but an ever better machine made its debut for 2004. The GS500F was still powered by a 487cc, V-twin mill but an oil cooler was added to maintain a consistent operating temperature. Unlike the naked design of the GS500E the F was draped in a full coverage fairing putting it on par with the GSX-R crew. At 396 lbs., it was also fairly light in weight making it a terrific entry point for sport minded buyers.

Taking the place of the now departed GS500E was the new GS500F, complete with its racy full fairing.

Suzuki Motors Corporation

For fans of the cruiser genre, the new Marauder 1600 delivered more power and style with a V-twin engine.

Suzuki Motors Corporation.

All four variations of the SV offerings returned and were unchanged from 2003. The cruiser district was populated with new multi-reflector turn signals for brighter output and fresh appearance. The Intruder 800 now featured a

281

SUZUKI

The 750 version of the GSX-R was also treated to an enhanced engine plus new brakes and suspension. It weighed only four lbs. more than the 600 variant.

Suzuki Motors Corporation

four-way emergency flasher system and a switch that allowed the rider to use the high beam as a passing indicator.

Brand new for 2004 was the Marauder 1600. The new model rose above the Intruder 1500 as Suzuki's biggest machine and held a 1552cc, V-twin engine in its frame. The 45-degree twin also was fed via fuel injection and included electronic instrumentation as a plus. A low-fuel light was added to notify the rider when he needed to start looking for a station seeing as to how the fuel injection system lacked the reserve position of a traditional petcock. Dressed as a muscle bike, the new Marauder was less retro than its smaller floor mate and weighed 639 lbs., a substantial bump over the returning Marauder 800. The DL1000 V-Strom stayed on for another year and was joined by a smaller 650cc variant for 2004. The DL650 V-Strom was moved by a 645cc, V-twin engine that was liquid cooled and fuel injected. The lower saddle height made the reduced V-Strom more appealing to shorter riders who still sought off-road adventures as a part of their routine. An adjustable windscreen allowed the rider to compensate for height and preferences by raising or lowering the shield with ease. Like the bigger V-Strom, the 650 also provided a rear-mounted luggage rack with rubber padding for a non-skid surface.

The 650 V-Strom tipped the scales at 418 lbs., a savings of 40 lbs. over the bigger version. The DL1000 was seen with revised hand guards for greater protection from off-road scrapes and the height adjustable windshield was added to it as well. Easier to view gauges included larger speedometer and tach along with an LCD readout for fuel usage and a clock.

The dual-purpose DL1000 V-Strom was joined by a smaller 650 version for 2004 and the reduced V-Strom was still a multi-purpose machine.

Suzuki Motors Corporation

2004 SUZUKI

Model	Engine	Displacement	Transmission
GZ250	Single cylinder	249cc	Five-Speed
GS500F (New for 2004)	Two cylinder	487cc	Six-Speed
GSF600S Bandit	Four cylinder	599cc	Six-Speed
GSX600 Katana	Four cylinder	599cc	Six-Speed
GSX-R600	Four cylinder	599cc	Six-Speed
DL650 V-Strom (New for 2004)	Two cylinder	645cc	Six-Speed
LS650 Savage	Single cylinder	652cc	Four-Speed
SV650	Two cylinder	645cc	Six-Speed
SV650S	Two cylinder	645cc	Six-Speed
GSX750 Katana	Four cylinder	748cc	Five-Speed
GSX-R750	Four cylinder	749cc	Six-Speed
VL800 Intruder Volusia	Two cylinder	805cc	Five-Speed
VS800GLP Intruder	Two cylinder	805cc	Five-Speed
VZ800 Marauder	Two cylinder	805cc	Five-Speed
DL 1000 V-Strom	Two cylinder	996cc	Six-Speed
GSX-R1000	Four cylinder	988cc	Six-Speed
SV1000 (New for 2004)	Two cylinder	996cc	Six-Speed
SV1000S (New for 2004)	Two cylinder	996cc	Six-Speed
TL1000R	Two cylinder	996cc	Six-Speed
GSF1200S Bandit	Four cylinder	1157cc	Five-Speed
GSF 1200 Bandit	Four cylinder	1157cc	Five-Speed
GSX1300R Hayabusa	Four cylinder	1298cc	Six-Speed
VS1400GLP Intruder	Four cylinder	1360cc	Five-Speed
VS1500LC Intruder	Two cylinder	1462cc	Five-Speed
VZ1600 Marauder (New for 2004)	Two cylinder	1552cc	Five-Speed

SUZUKI
2005

At the top of the SV hierarchy was the SV1000S that also sported the new black frame and enjoyed more horsepower due to a modified engine.

Suzuki Motors Corporation

The Suzuki class of 2005 saw numerous changes in the group photo with may students failing to make the grade for the latest year. Several other names were replaced with new nomenclature as well as some fresh duds and hardware. As their efforts on the race track continued to flourish they had a hard time keeping the GSX-R on the top step of the podium. In an effort to stay on top, the GSX-R1000 was again completely new for 2005. It seemed difficult to surpass the previous edition, but the '05 bristled with new technology while staying thin and trim. Increasing the displacement of the engine to 998cc produced more power and torque partially in part to the enhanced fuel injection that now included two injectors per jug.

A slipper clutch allowed the rider to make smoother downshifts regardless of RPM, and a rack and pinion mechanism assisted in that effort. Chassis dimensions were reduced overall to produce the most compact 1000 ever. The seat height was also 20mm closer to the ground aiding shorter sport bike fans. A narrower fuel tank and closer spacing between the saddle and bars also helped riders get a better grasp on the amazing power the GSX-R1000 could deliver. A bevy of machines were trimmed from the faculty including the standard SV1000, both versions of the Bandit and the TL1000R. The SV650, SV650S and SV1200S all had black-coated

Designed from the ground up again for 2005, the GSX-R1000 continued its dominance on race tracks and streets all across the USA.

Suzuki Motors Corporation

SUZUKI

Taking over where the Marauder 1600 left off was the latest Boulevard M95. Fuel injection moved the 540-lb. cruiser with added efficiency.

Suzuki Motors Corporation

frames, wheels and swing arms. The SV1000S also found new levels of power delivered upon the twist of the throttle due to increased compression and larger, 54mm throttle bodies in the fuel injection equation. Other modifications to operation of the motor were made as they delivered the best SV1000S ever.

Joining the departing machines were the GZ250 and 800 Marauder. Suzuki was however releasing a new series of cruisers, many of which used the 2004 platforms and applied new nomenclature and revised trim. The smallest of new cruiser listings was the S40, previously known as the 650 Savage. The same terrific package of motor, trans and belt drive were in place all with a new name. The previously named 800 Intruder was now the S50 and was sold in your choice of Black or Gray. No other revisions were listed for that model. The Intruder 1400 became the S83, the 1500 the C90 and the 1600 Marauder the M95.

Although looking every inch the same bikes that they replaced, Suzuki added the C90, C90T, C50 and C50T to the team. All four now featured fuel injection systems that were borrowed from the GSX-R's bag of tricks, making them more efficient and easier to operate in cold temperatures. The "T" designations related to the touring equipped versions which cam complete with windshield, saddlebags and passenger backrest. White wall tires also dressed up the C50T and C90T and staggered, shotgun pipes were fitted to all variants. In addition to the new hardware, the "Boulevard" name was applied to the entire series, further helping to set them apart from the models they replaced.

All three of the 2005 SV models were equipped with frames, wheels and swing arms finished in black. The SV650 was seated at the bottom of the listings.

Suzuki Motors Corporation

2005 SUZUKI

Model	Engine	Displacement	Transmission
GS500F	Two cylinder	487cc	Six-Speed
GSX600 Katana	Four cylinder	599cc	Six-Speed
GSX-R600	Four cylinder	599cc	Six-Speed
DL650 V-Strom	Two cylinder	645cc	Six-Speed
SV650	Two cylinder	645cc	Six-Speed
SV650S	Two cylinder	645cc	Six-Speed
S40 Savage Replaced the 650	Single cylinder	652cc	Five-Speed
GSX750 Katana	Four cylinder	748cc	Five-Speed
GSX-R750	Four cylinder	749cc	Six-Speed
S50 Replaced 800 Intruder	Two cylinder	805cc	Five-Speed
DL 1000 V-Strom	Two cylinder	996cc	Six-Speed
GSX-R1000	Four cylinder	988cc	Six-Speed
SV1000S	Two cylinder	996cc	Six-Speed
GSF1200S Bandit	Four cylinder	1157cc	Five-Speed
GSX1300R Hayabusa	Four cylinder	1298cc	Six-Speed
S83 Replaced 1400 Intruder	Four cylinder	1360cc	Five-Speed
C90 Replaced 1500 Intruder	Two cylinder	1462cc	Five-Speed
M95 Replaced 1600 Marauder	Two cylinder	1552cc	Five-Speed

The exotic 2005 Suzuki Boulevard lineup was arranged on a colorful city street for this ad.

SUZUKI

2006

STANDARD CATALOG OF ® JAPANESE Motorcycles

Missing for one model year, the entry level GZ250 returned for 2006, making all kinds of new riders happy.

Suzuki Motors Corporation

Adding some muscle to their already wide range of cruisers, the Boulevard M109R brought a new level of power and style to the field.

Suzuki Motors Corporation

By adding the Boulevard series for 2005, Suzuki had created a new breed of cruisers that grew by one new model for 2006. The GZ250 made a return to the fold after being away for a year in 2005. No changes were seen on the latest version of the diminutive cruiser, but allowed new riders to expose themselves to the joy of riding.

Boosting the Boulevard's reputation was the massive M109R. Poised as a muscle cruiser, the M109R carried a huge 1783cc V-twin in its low slung frame and used fuel injection to feed the beast. A five-speed gearbox was tied to final shaft drive along with spiral cast wheels under both fenders. An inverted front fork and radial mount brakes joined the hunt up front adding to the sporting nature of the big cruiser. A small handlebar mounted fairing was wrapped around the multi-reflector headlight for another dose of style and attitude. Checking in at 695 lbs., the Boulevard M109R was no lightweight but wasn't posed to be one. A hefty $12,399 was the cost

The Hayabusa was sold in a special edition paint job of all-white with silver graphics.

Suzuki Motors Corporation

Unlike the earlier versions of the GS500, the newest models wore racy fairings and graphics that closely mimicked the GSX-R series.

Suzuki Motors Corporation

of entry. The rest of the 2005 Boulevard line returned with no changes for 2006, proving that Suzuki had done well in their first makeover of the breed.

After trouncing all comers in its 1999 debut, the Hayabusa was scheduled to be retired after 2006. Adding a bit of sunshine to an otherwise sad event, Suzuki released a special edition Hayabusa that was treated to an all white with silver highlights ensemble. The special edition would set the buyer back and extra $200 but many knew it was worth the added tariff to get a copy of the special edition. Rumors of the Hayabusa's death were not to become true as it returned for 2007.

2006 SUZUKI

Model	Engine	Displacement	Transmission
GZ250 (Back for 2006)	Single cylinder	249cc	Five-Speed
GS500F	Two cylinder	487cc	Six-Speed
GSX600 Katana	Four cylinder	599cc	Six-Speed
GSX-R600	Four cylinder	599cc	Six-Speed
DL650 V-Strom	Two cylinder	645cc	Six-Speed
SV650	Two cylinder	645cc	Six-Speed
SV650S	Two cylinder	645cc	Six-Speed
S40	Single cylinder	652cc	Five-Speed
GSX750 Katana	Four cylinder	748cc	Five-Speed
GSX-R750	Four cylinder	749cc	Six-Speed
M50	Two cylinder	805cc	Five-Speed
S50	Two cylinder	805cc	Five-Speed
DL 1000 V-Strom	Two cylinder	996cc	Six-Speed
GSX-R1000	Four cylinder	988cc	Six-Speed
SV1000S	Two cylinder	996cc	Six-Speed
GSF1200S Bandit	Four cylinder	1157cc	Five-Speed
GSX1300R Hayabusa	Four cylinder	1298cc	Six-Speed
S83	Four cylinder	1360cc	Five-Speed
C90	Two cylinder	1462cc	Five-Speed
M95	Two cylinder	1552cc	Five-Speed
M109R (New for 2006)	Two cylinder	1783cc	Five-Speed

Designed to tackle both on- and off-road duties, the V-Strom was sold in 650 (seen here) or 1000cc variations.

Suzuki Motors Corporation

SUZUKI
2007

The 2007 Suzuki GSX-R1000 was captured in action. It used a 999cc four-cylinder DOHC engine coupled to a six-speed transmission.

The 2007 Suzuki Boulevard M50 showed off its aircraft-quality aluminum accessory pieces.

The 2007 Suzuki Boulevard C50 had a head-turning, street-wise presence.

STANDARD CATALOG OF® JAPANESE MOTORCYCLES SUZUKI

BLUE/WHITE

WHITE

RED

BLACK

The M109R was a limited edition motorcycle by Suzuki with special paint and a 1783cc V-twin engine. Paint colors included Blue and White, Red and White or Black.

The 1462cc SOHC 2007 Suzuki Boulevard C90 series was shown as it cruised down the highway.

The 2007 Suzuki S50 cycle in the Boulevard series had a classic look with modern, lightweight features.

YAMAHA

Introduction

As we have learned from the history of Honda, Kawasaki and Suzuki, motorcycles were not the initial products offered by those Japanese manufacturers and Yamaha is no different in that respect.

In the latter part of the 1800s, the Yamaha name was affixed to musical instruments, primarily organs. Their reputation for quality kept the factories busy building and selling their products under the name of Nippon Gakki.

It was not until the middle of the 1950s that the decision to turn toward motorcycle production was made. Kaichi Kawakami, who had long stood as the president of Nippon Gakki and had led it through amazing periods of expansion, suffered from poor health in 1950. Kawakami chose to retire from the company and hand the reins over to his son, Gen-Ichi, who had been working closely with his father for many years and was in a prime position to step in.

Once he had gained control of the company, the choice was made to begin a second firm to design and produce motorcycles. Gen-Ichi was acting president for the parent company and the newly-founded Yamaha Motors.

By 1954, the Yamaha flavor of two-wheeled transportation was rolling off of the assembly lines and being sold in Japan. As with the other makers, it took time to grow the company to the point of exporting their efficient machines to the USA. In 1961, they took their first foray across the pond. This was actually a few years prior to the arrival of Kawasaki and Suzuki, giving Yamaha a few extra years to learn the ways of the American market and its diverse audience. A total of seven different motorcycles were offered in their first year of U.S. sales, and that figure would quickly expand as technology, development and mastering the selling techniques required to move product in the states increased. The first mailing address for the Yamaha International Corporation was 1300 S. Pedro Street in Los Angeles, California.

Their innocent beginnings have led them on a long journey that continues today. Yamaha also continues to build and sell a line of fine pianos and musical instruments, but our focus will stay on the line of terrific motorcycles that have graced our shores for more than four decades. The logo of the three crossed tuning forks remind us of their musical interest and suggest precision in their two-wheeled creations as well.

YAMAHA
1961

Typical for the period, the 1961 Yamahas were simplistic in design, but well built and highly efficient. The MF1 and MF2 were step-through models that used 50cc engines to push them along the street. Luggage racks were found over the rear fenders, allowing for the transportation of worldly goods.

Taking the middle road, the 125cc YA2 and YA3 models by Yamaha provided a bit more power and could more easily be put to use in a variety of activities. The YC1 went one step further and used a 175cc engine to propel itself down the road. All of these models featured single-cylinder engines, but the last two in the 1961 catalog included two lungs.

Both the YD2 and YDS1 were fitted with 250cc twin-cylinder mills, and looked much more like actual motorcycles than their smaller siblings. Two-person saddles and the ubiquitous chrome-sided fuel tank included the equally common rubber kneepads. Chrome exhausts led the spent fumes away. As far as early Japanese motorcycles went, the Yamaha offerings were off to a good start.

1961 YAMAHA

Model	Engine	Displacement	Transmission
MF1	Single cylinder	50cc	–
MF2	Single cylinder	50cc	–
YA2	Single cylinder	125cc	–
YA3	Single cylinder	125cc	–
YC1	Single cylinder	175cc	–
YD2	Two-cylinder	250cc	–
YDS1	Two-cylinder	250cc	–

YAMAHA

1962

Changes were afoot early in the Yamaha plans and only four models were seen in the catalog for 1962. The 175cc YC1 and 50cc MF2 were pulled as the company trimmed the excess weight in hopes of turning a profit with their new venture in the USA.

Advertising in an August 1962 issue of Cycle World, Yamaha claimed that the 50cc "Omaha Trail" was the first rotary valve engine in the USA. "Fun in '62" was also a part of their pitch and the step-through machine was the "answer to the hunter's and fisherman's dream!" The small machine extolled the virtues of its 5 hp engine, big knobby tires and a climbing ability that exceeded 45 degrees. A quick-change rear end was also shouted from the rooftops as a potential benefit to the rider. Carrying a list price of $285 in 1962, it offered a lot of cycle for the money. A rack on the rear fender gave the Yamaha owner a solid place to carry gear as well.

"Brand new 25 hp fun" was the claim of the new YDS2. The 250cc sport machine touted Daytona-type brakes, a five-speed gearbox and dual carburetion. Monitoring top speed, which was listed as 90 mph plus, was achieved by using the tach-speedometer combination of gauges. The twin-cylinder machine sold for $599.50 and included the two-person pillion and close-fitting fenders. The rating of 25 hp was earned at 7,500 rpm, according to the ad.

This full-page ad told the story of Yamaha's latest 1962 models.

Yamaha International Corp.

1962 YAMAHA

Model	Engine	Displacement	Transmission
MF1 Omaha Trail	Single cylinder	50cc	–
YA5 Electric Starter	Single cylinder	125cc	–
YD3 Electric Starter	Two-cylinder	250cc	Four-Speed
YDS2 Sport Model	Two-cylinder	250cc	Five-Speed

YAMAHA 1963

Further cuts in the 1963 lineup resulted in only three models being listed and one of them a carry-over from 1962.

The YG1 and YG1T were both shown as having 73cc, single-cylinder engines in their frame. The YG1T was destined for on- and off-street use while the YG1 was geared strictly for pavement riding.

The YDS2 returned and was seen with no alterations from the previous year. The same five-speed gearbox churned the 25 hp and provided ample energy for a motorcycle of that period.

1963 YAMAHA

Model	Engine	Displacement	Transmission
YG1	Single cylinder	73cc	–
YG1T	Single cylinder	73cc	–
YDS2	Two-cylinder	250cc	Five-Speed

YAMAHA

1964

STANDARD CATALOG OF ® JAPANESE MOTORCYCLES

New models were abundant for 1964 as Yamaha expanded their scope of motorcycles to reach a wider audience. A full-page ad taken out in the January 1964 issue of *Floyd Clymer's Motor Cycle* magazine told of the complete line in great detail.

The MJ2SA was meant for street use only and included front and rear fenders to keep the rider clean and dry. The 55cc engine was linked to a three-speed gearbox with an automatic clutch. When "fully equipped," it sold for $285. For those who wanted to be able to ride on paved and more rugged terrain, the MJ2TH filled the bill. Powered by the same 55cc engine as the MJ2SA, the TH used knobby tires and an oversized sprocket to provide ample traction. Listed as being "sweet and saucy," the 80cc YG-1S returned a claimed 160 miles per gallon and could reach a top speed of 50 to 60 mph. The cost of admission for all the fun was $340.

Next in the 80cc division was the YG-1T. It was better equipped for riding on or off the streets. The knobby tires and an oversized sprocket were joined by a four-speed gearbox for plenty of choices whether on the trail or on the street. Moving up a notch was the 125cc YA5 that averaged 145 miles per gallon and started electrically, all for only $454. The rotary-valve engine offered the torque and power of larger machines while remaining fuel efficient.

"Nine ways that beat walking" was the headline in this 1964 ad touting the lineup of Yamaha machines for that year.

Yamaha International Corp.

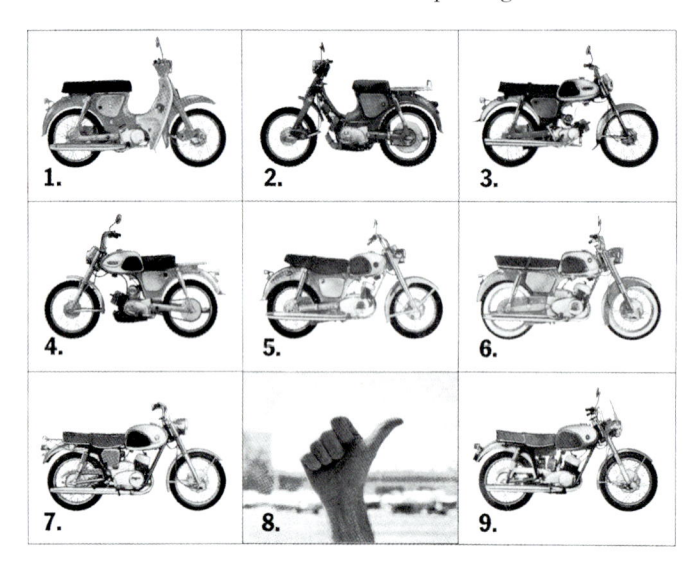

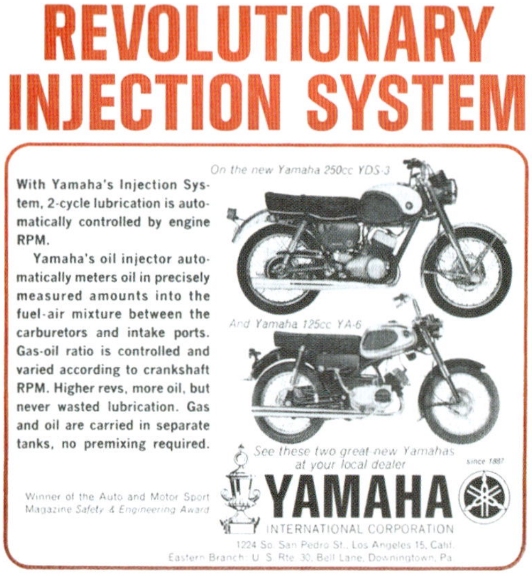

Yamaha promoted its injection system as well as the new YDS-3 and YA-6 models in this 1964 ad.

Adding a second cylinder and another 125cc equaled the YDT-1. A tubular frame held the engine, a four-speed gearbox and an electric starter in place. Chrome fenders brought some flash to the table. Seated on the throne was the YDS2. Drawing breath through a pair of carburetors, the twin cylinder, five-speed sport model had it all. Capable of reaching 100 mph, the $615 Yamaha could carry two adults in comfort courtesy of the well-padded saddle.

Yet another model in the 250cc class was the YD3. Adding whitewall tires to the four-speed, single-carb equation, meant a price tag of only $549. A more stylish front fender was part of the overall design and 19 hp moved two people along smartly. An electric starter got things going without any effort.

This 1964 Yamaha ad showed a drag strip star and a very street-worthy Yamaha YG-1 cycle.

They may not have been slingshot drag racers but Yamaha cycles got people where they wanted to go.

1964 YAMAHA

Model	Engine	Displacement	Transmission
MJ2SA	Single cylinder	55cc	Three-Speed
MJ2TH Dual Purpose	Single cylinder	55cc	Three-Speed
YG-1S	Single cylinder	80cc	Four-Speed
YG-1T	Single cylinder	80cc	Four-Speed
YA5	Single cylinder	125cc	Four-Speed
YD3	Two-cylinder	250cc	Four-Speed
YDT-1	Two-cylinder	250cc	Four-Speed
YDS2	Two-cylinder	250cc	Five-Speed

YAMAHA

1965

STANDARD CATALOG OF ® JAPANESE MOTORCYCLES

It takes one to know one

... And men who really know performance know Yamaha. That's because all Yamahas are race-bred; offsprings of the Yamaha 250cc World Grand Prix Champion. There's a bit of checkered flag in every Yamaha built.

The Cobra pictured above, and the Yamaha Rotary Jet 80 are both born of competition and built for safety. Couple this performance with Yamaha's new oil injection system, big dust and waterproof brakes, big bike styling, and you've got a real champion.

The price is a winner, too. Only $350 POE, Los Angeles, plus modest set-up and destination charges.

For 2-wheel performance, the Cobra Teams choose Yamaha.

YAMAHA INTERNATIONAL CORPORATION
since 1887
Winner of Auto & Motor Sport Magazines Safety and Engineering award
1964 250cc Grand Prix Champion
P.O. Box 54540, Los Angeles, Calif. 90054
Eastern Branch: U.S. Rte. 30, Bell Lane, Downingtown, Pa.
Canada: Pacific Seaboard B.C. Limited
1961 West 4th Ave., Vancouver 9, B.C.

A 1965 ad combined a Yamaha Rotary Jet 80 and a Grand Prix roadster.

Many of Yamaha's 1964 models migrated into 1965 and there were two new models that brought some fresh excitement to the field. The first of these new machines was the YDS-3C, otherwise known as the Big Bear Scrambler. A two-stroke, 250cc, twin-cylinder engine produced 27 hp, making the 349-lb. model fairly responsive.

A kick-start was used to bring the Big Bear to life and five-speeds were on tap. A suggested top speed of 85 to 90 mph seemed within reason for the street tire shod cycle. Close fitting fenders and high mounted exhaust contradicted each other when it came to any off-road abilities, but it was still positioned as a scrambler. Extensive application of heat shields on the twin exhaust tubes kept the rider's and passenger's legs safe from burns

The Excitement's Mutual

Yamahas and Cobras are both champions: Grand Prix winners born of competition and built for maximum safety.

The Yamaha Rotary Jet 80, shown above, gives you big-bike styling, Yamaha's new Oil Injection System, and hot Rotary Valve Engine.

And, it takes a champion to know one. That's why the Cobra* racing teams choose Yamaha for 2-wheel performance.

Yamaha's Rotary Jet 80 is a real winner — with a price to match... only $350, POE Los Angeles, plus modest set-up and destination charges.

YAMAHA INTERNATIONAL CORPORATION
Winner of the Auto and Motor Sport Magazine Safety and Engineering Award.
250cc World Grand Prix Champion
P.O. Box 54540, Los Angeles, California 90054
Eastern Branch: U.S. Rte. 30 Bell Lane, Downingtown, Pa.
Northwest Branch: Morrow Bldg., Room 117 811 E. Burnside, Portland, Oregon
Canada: Pacific Seaboard Ltd. 1961 W. 4th Ave., Vancouver 9, B.C., Canada

No less than a Shelby Cobra coupe was juxtaposed with a Yamaha Rotary Jet 80 in this 1965 ad.

when under way. Large rubber kneepads were used on the sides of the two-tone fuel tank and an expansive two-person saddle was included in the Big Bear Scrambler's DNA. A single instrument face carried the needles for the speedometer and tach, with both swinging to the right, in concert, when throttle was applied. A retail tag of $690 hung from the YDS-3C for 1965.

The second new model was the slightly larger YM1 that carried a 305cc engine in its frame. The rest of the machine was similar to the Big Bear, although it carried the exhaust low on the chassis and lacked the system of heat shields found on the YDS-3C.

1965 YAMAHA

Model	Engine	Displacement	Transmission
MJ2SA	Single cylinder	55cc	Three-Speed
MJ2T Dual Purpose	Single cylinder	55cc	Three-Speed
YG-1S	Single cylinder	80cc	Four-Speed
YG-1T	Single cylinder	80cc	Four-Speed
YA5	Single cylinder	125cc	Four-Speed
YD3	Two-cylinder	250cc	Four-Speed
YDT-1	Two-cylinder	250cc	Four-Speed
YDS-3C Big Bear Scrambler (New for 1965)	Two-cylinder	250cc	Five-Speed

YAMAHA
1966

STANDARD CATALOG OF® JAPANESE Motorcycles

Still powered by the same 250cc twin engine, the YDS-3C was now called only the Big Bear.

Vintage Memories, Inc.

Yamaha began to apply names to their previous alpha-numeric designations, making it more pleasant to keep track of new faces. Some old models were simply given names while some fresh entries had both applied right out of the gate.

The YJ2 Riverside remained near the bottom of the displacement range with a 60cc single in the frame, and was found in between the 55cc Omaha Trail and 73cc Rotary Jet. The Trailmaster was another entry powered by a 73cc single, followed closely by the bigger 80cc Omaha Trail.

Moving to the twin cylinder realm, the YL1 only displaced 98cc into its two jugs but delivered smoother output having a second cylinder added to the equation.

The Yamaha Twin Jet 100 offered a colorful window on fun with a motorcycle in 1966.

YAMAHA

STANDARD CATALOG OF® JAPANESE Motorcycles

DISCOVER THE SWINGING WORLD OF YAMAHA

When was the last time you were on two wheels? Whatever your answer, it's time you entered the Swinging World of Yamaha on a Twin Jet 100. This is something new...a small displacement twin-cylinder sportcycle. 2 cylinders, 2 carburetors, 2 exhaust pipes...on the road for the first time in the oil-injected Twin Jet 100. Try it out for yourself. You'll like the performance, handling, style and price...$409.* You'll discover that you can get twice as much fun. Try it and see if we're not right. **Make this your year to Yamaha. It's America's top-selling 2-stroke sportcycle.**

*SUGGESTED RETAIL PRICE P.O.E. WEST COAST, PLUS MODEST SET-UP AND DESTINATION CHARGES.

since 1887 YAMAHA INTERNATIONAL CORPORATION

Winner of the Auto and Motor Sport Magazine Safety and Engineering Award

1964 & 1965 250cc World Grand Prix Champion

P.O. Box 54540, Los Angeles, California 90054 · Eastern Branch: U.S. Rte. 30, Bell Lane, Downingtown, Pa. · Northwest Branch: Morrow Bldg., Room 117, 811 East Burnside, Portland, Oregon · Midwest Branch: 1440 W. North Avenue, Melrose Park, Ill. · Available in Canada

The Yamaha Twin Jet 100 was ready to show riders the world, as portrayed in this 1966 ad.

Discover the SWINGING WORLD of Yamaha

If you get a charge out of a four-wheel drift...or if you get a boot out of turning a top time in the quarter...here's just the swing for you. It's a thrill called Twin Jet 100. Here's the first small-displacement twin-cylinder bike on the road...and nothing in its class can come near it. It handles like a 250cc World Grand Prix Champion Yamaha. Goes and looks fast. Yet the price is an easy $409.* Get one and find out why Yamaha, with proven oil injection, is the top-selling 2-stroke in the U.S.

*P.O.E. LOS ANGELES, PLUS MODEST SET-UP AND DESTINATION CHARGES

since 1887 YAMAHA INTERNATIONAL CORPORATION

Winner of the Auto and Motor Sport Magazine Safety and Engineering Award

1964 & 1965 250cc World Grand Prix Champion

P.O. Box 54540, Los Angeles, California 90054
Eastern Branch: U.S. Route 30, Bell Lane, Downingtown, Pa.
Midwest Branch: 1440 W. North Ave., Melrose Park, Illinois
Northwest Branch: Morrow Bldg., Room 117, 811 E. Burnside, Portland, Oregon.
Available in Canada.

A Yamaha and a brand new Mustang fastback were two keys to an active world in 1966.

The Santa Barbara, also known as the YA6, carried 125cc in its set of jugs and was the sole Yamaha with a 125cc mill.

The next rung on the ladder found two machines fitted with 250cc engines. The YDS-3C Big Bear and YDSM Ascot Scrambler both found their power from twin-cylinder, 250cc engines tied to five-speed transmissions. Rounding out the 1966 catalog was the YM1 that was powered by a 305cc engine. The bigger displacement was achieved by adding length to the stroke of the 250cc variant, thus saving the cost and trouble of creating an entirely new motor.

The yin and yang paint scheme used on the Big Bear was only complete when adding the rubber knee pads, a common feature for the period.

Vintage Memories, Inc.

1966 YAMAHA

Model	Engine	Displacement	Transmission
MJ2T Omaha Trail Dual Purpose	Single cylinder	55cc	Three-Speed
YJ2 Riverside (New for 1966)	Single cylinder	60cc	Three-Speed
YGK Rotary Jet (New for 1966)	Single cylinder	73cc	Three-Speed
YGTK Trailmaster (New for 1966)	Single cylinder	73cc	Three-Speed
MJ1T Omaha Trail	Single cylinder	80cc	Four-Speed
YL1	Two-cylinder	98cc	Four-Speed
YA6 Santa Barbara	Single cylinder	125cc	Four-Speed
YDS-3C Big Bear	Two-cylinder	250cc	Five-Speed
YDSM Ascot Scrambler	Two-cylinder	250cc	Five-Speed
YM1 Big Bear Scrambler (Added Displacement)	Two cylinder	305cc	Five-Speed

Fun scenes offered glimpses into the Yamaha version of a "swinging world" in this 1966 ad.

YAMAHA
1967

One of the fresh faces for 1967 was the Bonanza. It featured big-bike styling and a 180cc engine.
Owner/Photo: Chris Bednas

Yamaha pulled out all the stops for their 1967 catalog and we find a bevy of new models scattered amongst returning faces.

The step-through Newport 50 was offered with an optional electric start and promised up to 200 miles per gallon, even with its automatic clutch. The YJ2 Campus was new for 1967 and claimed to have "Big bike style" based on the features on the 60cc machine that were borrowed from larger cycles. An upswept exhaust with a horizontally slotted heat shield brought the feel of a bigger unit as well as the mostly chrome fuel tank. The YL2C Twin Jet displaced only 98cc, but featured twin carburetors and exhaust, a first for a motorcycle in that range.

Making its debut for 1967 was the 180cc Bonanza. Started with an electric leg and shifting through a five-speed gearbox proved that small can be big when it came to features. Rated at 21 hp at 8,000 rpm, the Bonanza could achieve a top speed of nearly 90 mph. "Waterproof and dustproof" brakes were installed to deliver safe stops no matter what the conditions. Brand new candy-tone paint added some more luster to the line.

Two versions of the new Catalina were listed—one with electric start and the other with kick start only. The Electra was the sleeker of the two versions and was complete with chrome fenders and candy-tone paint. On tap was 29.5 hp with a claimed top speed of 105 mph. Yamaha's oil-injection system made operation of their two-stroke motors a breeze with no need to manually mix oil and gas in the proper ratio.

Big news for 1967 was the introduction of

Start something new! Yamaha 350

Start something powerful, something exciting, something really **new** — Yamaha's Grand Prix 350 — the ultimate in high performance motorcycles. Developed and engineered for discerning enthusiasts who demand the absolute in performance coupled with maximum reliability.

This twin cylinder 5-speed charger unleashes 36 horses at 7500 RPM — takes you through the quarter mile in 14 seconds flat. Cruises effortlessly at 80 mph... top speed 100 to 110 mph.

It features Yamaha's famous oil injection system and big, safe, waterproof-dustproof brakes ...plus deep lustrous chrome fenders and brilliant candy tone paint. It looks and runs like the biggest, hottest bikes on the market but it's priced much lower. 7 new models...17 in all, make Yamaha the most complete line in cycling. If it's really new it's Yamaha.

For additional information write:
YAMAHA
INTERNATIONAL CORPORATION
P.O. Box 54540, Los Angeles,
Calif. 90054, Dept. HR-4-7

A Yamaha Grand Prix rider was getting to know a pretty Mustang GT 350 driver in this 1967 ad.

Start something new!

You'll discover fun, excitement and pure go in the Swinging World of Yamaha. And here's a great new way to get there. TRAILMASTER 100 (YL2-C) The tough one! Goes where the goin's rough! Greatest off-the-road bike ever. What's it got for you? Plenty! Full trail gear. Electric starter. Spark arrester. Quick change dual sprocket. 3-position adjustable rear shocks. Clearance 8.7". Rugged 4-speed box. 18-inch wheels. Winds up 9.5 BHP at 8000 RPM. Powerful performance plus Yamaha's total Safety Engineered Concept. Your Yamaha Dealer has the biggest line-up in Sportcycling. From 50 to 350. See all 17!

YAMAHA
INTERNATIONAL CORPORATION

A beach, a dune buggy, a young couple and the Yamaha Trailmaster 100 presented a portrait of fun 1967-style.

YAMAHA

Start something new! You'll discover fun, excitement and pure go in the Swinging World of Yamaha. And here's a great new way to get there! Yamaha Big Bear 305 (YM2-C). ZAP! It moves you up and out. It runs with just about everything. Race-bred from Champions. Develops maximum horsepower at lower RPM to give you real low end acceleration and lugging power. Big 5-speed box with an engine that winds up 30.5 BHP at 7000 RPM. Top speed range 90-100. It comes with Yamaha's famous waterproof and dustproof brakes, proven oil injection and Yamaha's total Safety Engineered Concept. Your Yamaha Dealer has the biggest line-up in Sportcycling. From 50 to 350. See all 17!

YAMAHA SINCE 1887
INTERNATIONAL CORPORATION
CANADIAN DISTR.: YAMAHA DIVISION OF
FRED DEELEY LTD., VANCOUVER, B.C.

FOR ADDITIONAL INFORMATION OR "COMMON SENSE TIPS FOR SAFE SPORTCYCLING" WRITE: P. O. BOX 54540, LOS ANGELES, CALIFORNIA 90054, DEPT. HR-6-7

Finished with a jaunt in the old slingshot dragster? Then it's time to cruise away on the '67 Yamaha Big Bear 305!

the 350cc Grand Prix. A 348cc twin-cylinder engine shifted through a five-speed gearbox and produced 36 hp, a number typically found on bigger machines of the day. A terminal velocity of 110 mph was claimed for the 371 lb. Grand Prix—that was with a half-tank of fuel! Brakes that were listed as being waterproof and dust- proof were included in Yamaha's list of six safety zones on the YR1. As with most machines of the period, chrome panels on the fuel tank were accented with rubber kneepads and a center section painted in one of Yamaha's new candy-tone hues. The YR1 retailed for $800 in 1967 and offered a lot of motorcycle for the money.

1967 YAMAHA

Model	Engine	Displacement	Transmission
U5 Newport	Single cylinder	50cc	–
YJ2 Campus (New for 1967)	Single cylinder	60cc	Three-Speed
YGK Rotary Jet	Single cylinder	73cc	Three-Speed
MJ1T Omaha Trail	Single cylinder	80cc	Four-Speed
YL1	Two cylinder	98cc	Four-Speed
YL2C Twin Jet (New for 1967)	Two cylinder	98cc	Four-Speed
YA6 Santa Barbara	Single cylinder	125cc	Four-Speed
YCS1 Bonanza (New for 1967)	Two cylinder	180cc	Five-Speed
YDS3 Catalina (New for 1967)	Two cylinder	250cc	Five-Speed
YDS5 Catalina Electra (New for 1967)	Two cylinder	250cc	Five-Speed
YDS-3C Big Bear	Two cylinder	250cc	Five-Speed
YDSM Ascot Scambler	Two cylinder	250cc	Five-Speed
YM1 Cross Country	Two cylinder	305cc	Five-Speed
YM2C	Two cylinder	305cc	Five-Speed
YR1 Grand Prix (New for 1967)	Two cylinder	348cc	Five-Speed

YAMAHA 1968

The DT1 Enduro was destined for more off-road use than street riding, but was equipped to do either task quite well. Brad Powell Collection

Following a year that saw numerous new models being added to the roster, 1968 would be fairly quiet. Most of the period advertising extolled the virtues of Yamaha's extensive winning record at venues like Daytona. Hoping the "Win on Sunday sell on Monday" idiom applied, very little was printed about their existing lineup.

For those wanting to boost the power of their DT1, Yamaha created a GYT kit to provide a bolt-on method of achieving that goal. The kit included a new cylinder, piston and cylinder head along with enhanced piston rings for added durability. The installation of the kit brought instant improvement to the already spunky DT1.

A single-cylinder engine displacing 250cc powered the DT1 and Yamaha's own GYT kit could easily bring new levels of power to the table. Brad Powell Collection

YAMAHA

STANDARD CATALOG OF JAPANESE Motorcycles

The YM1 Cross Country of 1968 carried a 305cc engine and offered plenty of style for the rider who wanted it all.

Owner/Photo: Chris Bednas

The YG5T only had a 73cc engine in its frame, but the diminutive machine still delivered plenty of fun, both on road and off.

Brad Powell Collection

1968 YAMAHA

Model	Engine	Displacement	Transmission
U5 Newport	Single cylinder	50cc	–
YJ2 Campus	Single cylinder	60cc	Three-Speed
YG5T	Single cylinder	73cc	Three-Speed
YL1 Trailmaster	Two-cylinder	98cc	Four-Speed
YL2 Rotary Jet	Two-cylinder	98cc	Four-Speed
YL2C Trailmaster	Two-cylinder	98cc	Four-Speed
YA6 Santa Barbara	Single cylinder	125cc	Four-Speed
YCS1 Bonanza	Two-cylinder	180cc	Five-Speed
YCS1C Bonanza Scrambler	Two-cylinder	180cc	Five-Speed
DT1 Enduro	Single cylinder	250cc	Five-Speed
YDS3 Catalina	Two-cylinder	250cc	Five-Speed
YDS5 Catalina Electra	Two-cylinder	250cc	Five-Speed
YDS-3C Big Bear	Two-cylinder	250cc	Five-Speed
YDSM Ascot Scrambler	Two-cylinder	250cc	Five-Speed
YM1 Cross Country	Two-cylinder	305cc	Five-Speed
YM2C	Two-cylinder	305cc	Five-Speed
YR2 Grand Prix	Two-cylinder	348cc	Five-Speed
YR2C Grand Prix Scrambler	Two-cylinder	348cc	Five-Speed

YAMAHA
1969

The 1969 Yamaha 125 Single Enduro AT-1 was shown in action in this ad.

Model year 1969 was a time of drastic changes for Yamaha as they found themselves struggling against the tide of bigger machines being sold elsewhere, especially by Honda. The CB750 made its debut and sent everyone running to the R&D departments to find a way to battle the four-cylinder beast. Some trimming of models also took place, but the remaining mix covered nearly all the bases.

For the street rider, four models were shown. The smallest was the GS5 that used an 80cc single to propel the sport mount along. A high mounted exhaust was teamed with chrome fenders. The GS5 had a rating of 5 hp. Next up was the new AS2C Street Scrambler. A 125cc power plant was mated to a five-speed gearbox that was activated by the Easy-Toe shift lever. The 250cc DS6C was the third largest street machine for the

YAMAHA

DISCOVER PERFORMANCE
Climb on cold metal and get a jump on the asphalt.
Skim the concrete.
Kick it down through a corner.
Dig your knees in and turn it loose.
Even a trip to the store has its moments.
This 250cc comes on like twice its size.
5-port power does it. (2 extra ports
in the cylinder for better combustion,
more power.) Nobody else has it.
Add a 5-speed, no-grind transmission.
An automatic oil injection system.
(Autolube.) It moves.
It's the same engine
that swept Daytona last year.
And the year before.

250 Street Scrambler DS6-C
Yamaha International Corporation,
P.O. Box 54540, Los Angeles, California 90054

YAMAHA
It's a better machine

The Yamaha 250 Street Scrambler DS6-C was featured in this 1969 ad.

year and the motor included Yamaha's five-port design on the engine.

A five-speed gearbox and Autolube injection completed the package. The 350cc Grand Prix was still around and wore revised bodywork adding to the graceful nature of the top of the line Yamaha.

For riders who would divide their riding time between street and trail, there were four models listed. The YG5T Trailmaster sported an 80cc displacement, an electric starter and a top speed of 40 mph. The L5T Trailmaster claimed 100cc and Yamaha's Trailmatic transmission, that featured three gears and two ranges, gave the rider a total of six ratios to play with. Electric start got the whole thing moving with ease.

Two new Enduro models were also shown. One of them was the CT1 that held a 175cc, single-cylinder engine in its frame. Five speeds in the gearbox, spring-loaded foot pegs and detachable lights made an adaptable cycle for on- or off-road riding. Those who sought more power turned to the DT1B with its 250cc motor and 70-mph top speed.

The 1969 Yamaha Trailmaster YG5-T, 100 Trailmaster L5-T and 175 Single Enduro CT-1 were called the "better machines."

Nearly six inches of travel were available in the front forks and spring-loaded pegs, and removable lighting was included in this deal as well.

The DT1B was joined by a smaller version of itself in the AT1. The AT1 used a 125cc engine instead of the DT1B's 250cc engine. Electric start, adjustable rear shocks and a speedometer that registered miles by the tenth made the little Enduro machine feel like a much bigger model. A true racing version was also sold which was stripped of its un-needed accessories and already included the GYT performance upgrade.

1969 YAMAHA

Model	Engine	Displacement	Transmission
GS5	Single cylinder	80cc	Three-Speed
YG5T Trailmaster	Single cylinder	80cc	Three-Speed
L5T Trailmaster	Two-cylinder	98cc	Three-Speed
AT1 Enduro (New for 1969)	Single cylinder	125cc	Four-Speed
AS2C Street Scrambler (New for 1969)	Single cylinder	125cc	Four-Speed
CT1 Enduro (New for 1969)	Single cylinder	175cc	Five-Speed
DT1B Enduro	Single cylinder	250cc	Five-Speed
DS6C Street Scrambler (New for 1969)	Two-cylinder	250cc	Five-Speed
R3 Grand Prix	Two-cylinder	348cc	Five-Speed

YAMAHA
1970

Yamaha's 360 RT-1 Enduro was shown in action and in profile in this 1970 magazine ad.

Only one machine was pulled off the stage for 1970 but four new players stepped into the limelight. The 80cc YG5T was no longer a member of the staff, but a slightly stronger replacement filled its shoes.

The HT1 featured a 90cc engine and included five-speeds in its gearbox. Yamaha's Autolube system and Enduro-style forks provided convenience and plenty of suspension for off-road adventures. At the top of the Enduro category were two examples of the new RT1. Both models featured single-cylinder, 360cc engines and five-speed gearboxes. A single exhaust tube was used for both, but the civilian model RT1 included a chrome heat shield. The RT1M was considered the racing model and lacked lighting and gauges, but included the GYT performance upgrade as part of its basic package. Autolube kept both motors filled with the proper blend of fuel and oil.

Yamaha introduced several new models for 1970, including the 200cc CS3C which featured electric start and a five-speed gearbox.

Yamaha International Corporation

Catch 8,000 rpm, fifth gear and a look of envy, all at the same time. Yeeeeeehaaaaaa!

The 350 street R-5 is that kind of bike: a very sanitary looker with a heart of solid dynamite. Take a look at it. Then take a look at the specs. It's got a 36-horse twin pulling around just 310 pounds of beautiful machinery.

It's also got a five-speed gearbox, separate instruments, waterproof brakes and a new frame patterned after our RD-56 road racer. That means the R-5 has handling to match the power and the looks. So turn one on and go see what all the excitement is about.

Yamaha International Corporation
P.O. Box 54540, Los Angeles, Calif. 90054
In Canada: Fred Deeley, Ltd., Vancouver, B.C.

YAMAHA It's a better machine

The 1970 Yamaha R-5 was a street version of the Yamaha RD-56 road racer.

YAMAHA

With a displacement of 653cc and four-stroke operation, the motor of the new XS1 was the smoothest ever for a Yamaha.

Yamaha International Corporation

For the street riding crowd, two new models could be found at the local drive-in. A 195cc CS3C featured a five-speed transmission and electric starting. Chrome fenders and a flat, two-person saddle made the accommodations adequate for grown adults and the twin-cylinder motor provided the power.

The R5 was designed with a 348cc, twin-cylinder engine and ranked high when tested against other machines in its class. The style was fairly mundane but typical for the period with chrome trim on the side covers and a wide white stripe across the top of the fuel tank.

The biggest news for 1970 was the debut of the 650cc XS1. Not only did it have the largest displacement in Yamaha's history, but it was a four-stroke motor. Two cylinders displaced a total of 653cc between them and air cooling kept things under control. Some 50 hp was at the rider's beck and call at 7,200 rpm and a five-speed gearbox offered plenty of selections. When dry, the XS1 weighed 435 lbs. and the fuel tank could hold 3.7 gallons.

A saddle height of 31.9 inches was typical of the period when steel tubes were used to create the frame. Drum brakes and chain drive completed the ensemble. Cosmetically the XS1 featured an upside down "Nike" stripe on the tank and small chrome trim pieces on the side covers. Wire wheels, chrome fenders and a passenger grab rail were also parts of the design.

1970 YAMAHA

Model	Engine	Displacement	Transmission
G6S	Single cylinder	80cc	Three-Speed
HT1	Single cylinder	90cc	Five-Speed
L5TA (New for 1970)	Single cylinder	98cc	Three-Speed
AT1B Enduro	Single cylinder	125cc	Four-Speed
AS2C Street Scrambler	Single cylinder	125cc	Four-Speed
CT1B Enduro	Single cylinder	175cc	Five-Speed
CS3C (New for 1970)	Two cylinder	195cc	Five-Speed
DT1M Enduro	Single cylinder	250cc	Five-Speed
DS6B Street Scrambler	Two-cylinder	250cc	Five-Speed
R3 Grand Prix	Two-cylinder	348cc	Five-Speed
R5 (New for 1970)	Two-cylinder	348cc	Five-Speed
RT1 (New for 1970)	Single cylinder	360cc	Five-Speed
RT1M (New for 1970)	Single cylinder	360cc	Five-Speed
XS1 (New for 1970)	Two-cylinder	650cc	Five-Speed

STANDARD CATALOG OF® JAPANESE MOTORCYCLES

YAMAHA
1971

In its second year of sale, the R5 continued to impress both the motorcycle media and consumers with its nimble package and 348cc engine.

Rick Youngblood

With the debut of the 650 XS1 still fresh in the minds of the cycle world, the 1971 model year was fairly anticlimactic for Yamaha. Two models were pulled from the floor and revisions to remaining models were few, if any, were made at all.

The L5TA and AS2C were both casualties in 1971 as the market seemed to embrace larger motorcycles with ease, leaving the less powerful to wilt. A stauncher set of forks were installed on the CT1C with larger diameter tubes and a pair of piston rings improved dampening. Ten percent more travel was also included in the new design, allowing the 175cc machine to traverse more rugged terrain than before. Increased strength in the handlebar mounting delivered a safer place to hold on when things got rough. The CT1C weighed 233 lbs. and carried a price tag of $625.

The 1971 Yamaha 250 Enduro DT1-E was shown in cutaway and in profile in this ad.

313

The 1971 Yamaha 650 XS-1B engine was front and center in this ad that also showed the motorcycle in profile.

Yamaha's CS3B returned for 1971 but was unchanged. The small twin-cylinder engine continued to impress the media, but, as expected, it did not make the best highway machine. When filled with half a tank of fuel the 195cc twin only weighed 264 lbs. and had a range of 100 miles. The 2.4-gallon tank kept it close to home. Despite these small complaints, the $619 Yamaha CS3B offered the beginning street rider a great way to get some experience.

The R5 made its entrance as a 1970 model and won rave reviews the instant it was tested. The 1971 version was little changed except for color, front and rear turn signals and a larger brake light that produced more illumination. The XS1B was another returning model but saw only new hues being added to the sales sheet.

1971 YAMAHA

Model	Engine	Displacement	Transmission
G6SB	Single cylinder	80cc	Three-Speed
HS1B	Single cylinder	90cc	Five-Speed
AT1C Enduro	Single cylinder	125cc	Four-Speed
CT1C Enduro	Single cylinder	175cc	Five-Speed
CS3B	Two-cylinder	195cc	Five-Speed
DT1E Enduro	Single cylinder	250cc	Five-Speed
DS6B Street Scrambler	Two-cylinder	250cc	Five-Speed
R3 Grand Prix	Two-cylinder	348cc	Five-Speed
R5B	Two-cylinder	348cc	Five-Speed
RT1	Single cylinder	360cc	Five-Speed
RT1B	Single cylinder	360cc	Five-Speed
XS1B	Two-cylinder	650cc	Five-Speed

When you're up to your skidplate in mud, the last thing you need is a gearbox designed to win Daytona.

We've got a gearbox that has beaten Daytona, six years in a row, but we'd no more send you into the boonies with that gearbox than we'd send you into Baja with a Ferrari. All the things that make our close ratio five-speed a jewel on a racing bike make it a roving disaster on a dirt bike.

So for our Enduros® we've put together a super boondock beater—a wide ratio five-speed that puts the power where you need it. The difference is this:

Racing machines do most of their traveling at relatively high speeds, so they're geared for top speed. In the dirt, the going is much slower and tougher. You need a gearbox which gives low end performance. Ours does.

You could solve it by putting a larger rear sprocket on the bike. But that would effectively lower *all* the ratios and leave you with a pretty slow top gear.

That's why we spread our ratios out. Our Enduro low gear is a stump puller that'll take you right up a wall if you can get the traction. Top gear, on the other hand, is right where it ought to be for covering a lot of flat ground in a hurry. Second, third and fourth sort of split the difference. You can see what we mean from the diagram here.

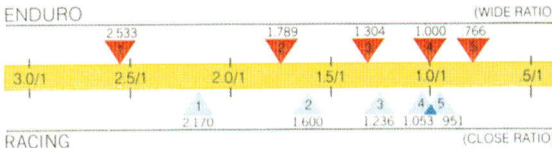

This way, when you're up to your skidplate in mud and hoping for a lot of torque, you've got it. And when there's nothing but open field in front of you, you can fly like the wind. It's a crucial difference, but one that a lot of other dirt bikes seem to have missed. You'll find this type gearbox on all the Yamaha Enduros, including the 125 AT1-C shown here. The AT1-C has a lot of other differences, too. Like high performance Enduro forks that can take a 10-foot plunge without putting an abrupt end to the day's riding. Five-port power to make the most out of every cc in the engine. Dustfree, waterproof brakes, separate instruments and a lot of other niceties that all add up to one thing: a better machine.

Yamaha International Corporation • P.O. Box 54540, Los Angeles, California 90054/In Canada: Fred Deeley, Ltd., Vancouver, B.C.

YAMAHA It's a better machine

Yamaha explained its transmission and showed off its 125 AT1-C for 1971.

YAMAHA
1972

STANDARD CATALOG OF JAPANESE Motorcycles

A fresh face in the 1972 yearbook was the 250cc DS7. It embodied the thrills of its larger sibling, the R5C, but provided a little less performance.

Owner/Photo: Chris Bednas

An all-new LT2 led the way in the Enduro class for Yamaha with its 98cc engine and redesigned frame. Alloy steel was employed to reduce weight without sacrificing strength. Seven ports were found inside the engine making it smoother and more powerful than before. Ten hp was at hand, pushing the tiny machine along the trails with ease. Autolube kept the motor properly fed and the five-speed constant-mesh gearbox gave the needed power to the rear wheel. Turn signals were found at all four corners as well as a headlight for riding the LT2 on the streets at night.

A new feature found on all the 1972 Enduro machines was torque induction. The stainless steel valve responded to demand, delivered more power when required and adjusted the incoming air and fuel mix for peak performance. The seven-

Cycles like this Yamaha were compact and rider friendly . . . closer to bicycle than heavy iron.

Owner/Photo: Chris Bednas

port design was also applied to the entire Enduro lineup in 1972.

Street fans would still find their flickable LS2 in 1972 with no revisions from the previous edition. The parallel twin engine displaced only 98cc but delivered 10.5 hp of fun. Oversized brakes on both wheels ensured safe stops. The speedometer and tachometer were individual gauges and the ignition was located between them. Autolube was still used to maintain the proper blend of oil and gas. All it took to own one in 1972 was $435.

Yamaha offered riders a machine for their needs, including those just starting out. Several models carried engines with less than 100cc in their frames.

Owner/Photo: Chris Bednas

There were plenty of Yamaha Enduro motorcycles to choose from in this 1972 ad, including the AT2-125, the DT2-250, the CT2-175, the JT2-L Mini Enduro and the RT2-360.

YAMAHA

The Yamaha 100cc LT-2 Enduro was called the "green machine" in 1972 advertising.

A slightly larger and better all around choice for the street-bound rider was the CS5. The more powerful 195cc engine started with the touch of a button or the kick of the leg and the engine was nimble once you were moving. Coming in at 281 lbs. with a one-half tank of gas, the CS5 made slow-speed maneuvers and parking a breeze. The CS2 was restyled for 1972 bringing a fresh look to the popular twin. A total of $649 put riders in the saddle and the efficient twin-cylinder engine didn't cost much to keep on the road.

New for 1972 was the DS7, powered by a 250cc twin-cylinder engine that looked a lot like the one found in the class-leading R5. Enduro-style forks and five-way adjustable rear shocks delivered comfort to one or two riders. Five-port power and a matching five-speed gearbox provided the energy needed. The Autolube system was on board for convenience, just as it was in two-stroke Yamahas.

The R5C was back to continue earning kudos from nearly all comers as it put its 350cc motor and stable chassis to great use. No changes were shown for the third-year student but none were needed, at least according to period magazine reviews and buyers alike.

The big XS2 was also a repeat model, but sported many significant upgrades for 1972. The most obvious was the application of a disc brake on the front wheel. The addition of the solitary rotor, formed from stainless steel alloy, brought a new level of stopping power to the 455-lb. XS2—weighed with the tank half filled. A rear drum brake remained on duty to assist the disc up front. Another benefit of the 1972 XS2 was the electric starting system.

While kick starting the XS1 was never a real chore, this new design eliminated the need unless the battery went flat. In fifth gear, the XS2 could reach a velocity of 113 mph, putting it near some of its bigger competitors. A quarter-mile time of just over 14 seconds was available when the XS2 was in the hands of a capable rider. At $1,295, it wasn't the cheapest machine in 1972, but provided a terrific package of style and power all with the added safety of that disc brake.

1972 YAMAHA

Model	Engine	Displacement	Transmission
G7S	Single cylinder	73cc	Three-Speed
U7E	Single cylinder	75cc	Three-Speed
LS2	Two-cylinder	98cc	Five-Speed
LT2 Enduro	Single cylinder	98cc	Five-Speed
LT2M	Single cylinder	98cc	Five-Speed
AT2 Enduro	Single cylinder	125cc	Four-Speed
AT2M	Single cylinder	125cc	Four-Speed
CT2 Enduro	Single cylinder	175cc	Five-Speed
CS5	Two-cylinder	195cc	Five-Speed
DS7 (New for 1972)	Two-cylinder	247cc	Five-Speed
DT2 Enduro	Single cylinder	250cc	Five-Speed
R5C	Two-cylinder	348cc	Five-Speed
RT2	Single cylinder	360cc	Five-Speed
XS2 (Disc Brake)	Two-cylinder	650cc	Five-Speed

YAMAHA
1973

The 1973 TX650 was really the previous year's XS2, but it still provided a smooth and powerful motorcycle that rivaled many of the four-cylinder machines.

Owner/Photo: Chris Bednas

The 1973 model lineup for Yamaha was quite diverse and full of new blood. Several previous models departed to make way for the latest creations. The first of the 1973s was the RD60. The smallest member of the new RD family, it was powered by a 60cc, seven-port engine with Yamaha's own Torque Induction. This system used a valve to better control the flow of fuel and air while not sacrificing any power. A five-speed transmission brought big bike selection to the street bound craft. Telescopic forks up front and coil-over shocks in the rear provided comfort and control whether solo or two-up. The introduction of the RD line would prove to be one of Yamaha's greatest moves as the RD350 and later RD400 would become cult classics among those who rode for fun or in competition.

The RD250 was next, and carried the look of a full-sized bike to the forefront of small bike riders. A 247cc, seven-port engine, also with Torque Induction, was mated to a six-speed gearbox, making it very grown up indeed. The RD250 was kick-start only but included a steering damper to keep things under control when the situation arose.

An indicator light that told the rider when the brake light had failed was a new touch and really helped keep the rider informed. Next in the RD clan was the 350. The bigger machine carried an extra 100cc in the frame and used a disc brake on the front wheel for improved stopping power. Autolube was seen as well as Torque Induction, but only kick starting was used to get the package rolling. Six speeds in the gearbox let the rider

319

YAMAHA

TX 750

743cc, 4 stroke, twin, SOHC, air-cooled engine. Electric and primary kick starter. 5 speed constant mesh transmission. Net weight 485 pounds. Omni-Phase balancing system. Dry sump, trochoid pump lubrication system.

RD 350

347cc, 2 stroke, twin, 7-port engine with Torque Induction. Autolube lubrication system. Primary kick starter. 6 speed constant mesh transmission. Steering damper. Stop lamp outage indicator. Panel type instrumentation. Front wheel disc brake.

TX 650

653cc, 4 stroke, twin, SOHC engine. Wet sump, trochoid pump lubrication system. Electric (with compression release) and primary kick starter. 5 speed constant mesh transmission. Net weight 427 pounds.

RD 250

247cc, 2 stroke, twin, 7-port engine with Torque Induction. Autolube lubrication system. Primary kick starter. 6 speed constant mesh transmission. Steering damper. Stop lamp outage indicator. Panel type instrumentation.

TX 500

500cc, 4 stroke, twin, DOHC engine. 4 valves per cylinder. Wet sump, trochoid pump lubrication system. Electric and primary kick starter. 5 speed constant mesh transmission. Omni-Phase balancing system.

RD 60

60cc, 2 stroke, single, 7-port engine with Torque Induction. Autolube lubrication system. Primary kick starter. 5 speed constant mesh transmission. Double cradle, tube frame. Telescopic fork front suspension. Swing arm rear suspension.

The Yamaha two- and four-stroke cycles were clearly advertised in 1973, including the TX-750, the RD-350, the TX-650, the RD-250, the TX-500 and the RD-60.

keep the bike in the right RPM range for optimum performance.

While the trio of RD models used two-stroke motors, a second triplicate of cycles found four-stroke power plants in their frames. The TX500 displaced 500cc into a pair of cylinders and shifted through a five-speed gearbox. Electric and kick-start were aboard and once running, Yamaha's Omni-Phase balancing made the motor a smooth operator.

The XS650 became the TX650. The 653cc engine and the bike it motivated were basically the same as the previous year. Joining the four-stroke parade was the all-new TX750. The SOHC engine featured a 743cc displacement and was a four-stroke. Omni-Phase balancing made it one of the market's smoothest running twins, keeping pace with the bigger four-cylinder variants sold elsewhere. A five-speed transmission was put into action once the TX750 was started using the electric or kick-start systems included. At 485 lbs., it was not a feather-light, but the performance of the big 750 engine held its own on the open road. A front wheel disc brake and rear-mounted drum brake hauled the TX750 down from speeds that could reach 105 mph. Zero-to-60 times of six seconds were recorded by magazines in the day, making the TX750 a potent choice in the growing large bike market.

For the rider who sought riding time off the beaten path, Yamaha listed six different Enduro machines for 1973. Ranging from 73 to 360cc, each of them offered a different level of power while maintaining the same reliable machine and lighting that allowed them to be taken to the streets when the mood struck. The RT3 and DT3 had new 21-inch diameter front wheels installed, an increase over the 1972 versions. Five of the six shifted through a five-speed gearbox while the smallest GT1 used only four.

The 1973 Yamaha TX 650 was a part of a colorful visual about Australia in this unique ad.

1973 YAMAHA

Model	Engine	Displacement	Transmission
RD60 (New for 1973)	Single cylinder	55cc	Five-Speed
GT1 Enduro	Single cylinder	73cc	Four-Speed
LT3 Enduro	Single cylinder	98cc	Five-Speed
AT3 Enduro	Single cylinder	125cc	Four-Speed
CT3 Enduro	Single cylinder	175cc	Five-Speed
DT3 Enduro	Single cylinder	250cc	Five-Speed
RD250A (New for 1973)	Two-cylinder	247cc	Six-Speed
RD350 (New for 1973)	Two-cylinder	347cc	Six-Speed
RT3 Enduro	Single cylinder	360cc	Five-Speed
TX500	Two-cylinder	500cc	Five-Speed
TX650	Two-cylinder	653cc	Five-Speed
TX750	Two-cylinder	743cc	Five-Speed

"Yama Claus" and his many "Yelves" were preparing for Christmas with all the 1974 Yamaha parts and accessories in this ad.

STANDARD CATALOG OF JAPANESE Motorcycles

YAMAHA
1974

In its second year, the TX-500 saw no revisions over its debut edition. It was a potent choice for riders who journeyed across town and across state lines.

Owner/Photo: Chris Bednas

After their big year of introductory models in 1973, 1974 would give buyers a calendar of carry-over machines with fresh nomenclature. Yamaha rolled out their new line of Trials bikes and the Enduro models could be ridden on- or off-road but carried the required lighting for that purpose. The MX and TY models were designed for purely off-road use. Their descriptions are not included here. Revised nomenclature on the 1974 models included the change from using DT1, DT3 etc., to using the DT prefix followed by the displacement of the machine it was being applied to. This system seems to make more sense, at least to me. The newly released RD 250 and 350 were joined by a smaller RD200. Using styling cues from its larger siblings, the RD200 used a 195cc, parallel twin engine to produce a top speed of 90 mph. Starting the baby RD was achieved by button or kick-lever, a nice feature on such a small cycle.

A five-speed transmission, Autolube and Torque-Induction were all included in the RD200 chemistry. The 250 and especially the RD350 were quickly gaining acceptance from buyers that were previously not interested in riding smaller machines.

Although small in size, the RD-350 had already earned a place in the hearts of sport-bike riders who appreciated its nimble handling and responsive, two-stroke engine. Steve Searles

323

YAMAHA

STANDARD CATALOG OF JAPANESE MOTORCYCLES

Yamaha showed off its championship race riders in this 1974 ad—a board game for selected players.

While some of the smaller variations would eventually be removed from the catalog, the RD350 would grow into bigger models that were transformed into race bikes with headlights by eager riders all around the world.

1974 YAMAHA

Model	Engine	Displacement	Transmission
RD60	Single cylinder	55cc	Five-Speed
GT80	Single cylinder	73cc	Four-Speed
DT100A	Single cylinder	98cc	Five-Speed
DT125A	Single cylinder	125cc	Four-Speed
DT175A	Single cylinder	175cc	Five-Speed
RD200A (New for 1974)	Two-cylinder	195cc	Five-Speed
DT250A	Single cylinder	250cc	Five-Speed
RD250A	Two-cylinder	247cc	Six-Speed
RD350A	Two-cylinder	347cc	Six-Speed
DT360A	Single cylinder	360cc	Five-Speed
TX500A	Two-cylinder	500cc	Five-Speed
TX650A	Two-cylinder	653cc	Five-Speed
TX750A	Two-cylinder	743cc	Five-Speed

YAMAHA
1975

Not the smallest RD in the 1975 Yamaha family, the RD-250 was capable of delivering the rider and a passenger to almost anywhere they needed to go.

David Lucas

Model year 1975 would see a few more new faces join the team at Yamaha as they expanded their road machine listings by going small. No mention of the TX750 was seen in factory literature for 1975, even though it had only been introduced a year before. A three-cylinder model would appear the following year, but the 750 seemed to be devoid of the TX750 machine's listing. To better combat the rising cost of fuel, the RS100 made its debut for 1975. The single-cylinder engine was hung from a double-cradle tubular chassis and displaced 97cc. The two-stroke operation was monitored and kept properly lubricated by the Autolube system and started with a leg kick.

When clicked into the top gear of five, 68 mph was achievable. Next up the daisy chain was the all-new RD125. Now the smallest member of the RD clan, a 124cc parallel-twin engine was at the helm for power. A top speed of 81 mph could be reached aboard the 76.2-inch-long motorcycle. Only kick starting was on hand to get things mov-

YAMAHA

STANDARD CATALOG OF JAPANESE MOTORCYCLES

For 1975, the RD-350 was the biggest version sold, and its list of loyal riders grew with every passing sales year.

Donald R. McCullough

ing and a five-speed gearbox delivered plenty of ratios.

As with the entire Yamaha two-stroke regime, Autolube and Torque-Induction were designed into the blend of the RD125. The RD60, 200, 250 and 350 were repeats for 1975 drawing bigger and bigger crowds as the fuel prices rose. The TX500 and 650 were now known as the XS500 and XS650, with no additional changes made. Both were still using parallel-twin engines, five-speed gearboxes and could exceed 110 mph.

Starting either of the big four-strokes was possible with either the electric button or kick lever. The XS500 featured a dual-overhead-cam engine while the bigger XS650 operated with only one cam.

A different set of accent stripes adorned the fuel tank of the RD-350, but still carried the sport bike theme.

Donald R. McCullough

1975 YAMAHA

Model	Engine	Displacement	Transmission
RD60B	Single cylinder	55cc	Five-Speed
RS100B (New for 1975)	Single cylinder	97cc	Five-Speed
DT100B	Single cylinder	98cc	Five-Speed
DT125B	Single cylinder	125cc	Four-Speed
RD125B (New for 1975)	Two-cylinder	124cc	Five-Speed
DT175B	Single cylinder	175cc	Five-Speed
RD200B	Two-cylinder	195cc	Five-Speed
DT250B	Single cylinder	250cc	Five-Speed
RD250B	Two-cylinder	247cc	Six-Speed
RD350B	Two-cylinder	347cc	Six-Speed
DT400B	Single cylinder	360cc	Five-Speed
XS500B	Two-cylinder	500cc	Five-Speed
XS650B	Two-cylinder	653cc	Five-Speed

YAMAHA
1976

The 1976 model year was to be another fairly uneventful year for the Yamaha catalog, yet a few big changes were found. Two of their legendary RD models were stricken from the field, but a slightly bigger machine would step in to take over and continue the fervor.

Yamaha introduces a production motorcycle no one else is prepared to produce.

The new Yamaha RD400. Right now, there is no other motorcycle like it.

The cast aluminum wheels are an obvious innovation. They're easier to maintain than traditional spoke wheels. Certainly, they're more stylish. And on the RD400, cast aluminum wheels are standard equipment.

Another innovation is the self-cancelling turn signal. This is a Yamaha exclusive that's both a safety feature and a convenience all motorcyclists will appreciate.

Then there's the RD400's engine. A two-stroke, twin 400cc engine that's a direct descendant of the 350 Yamaha world champion road racer. A motorcycle with legendary power.

Yet, for all that power, stopping will be quick and sure. Fade resistant disc brakes are the reason, and the RD400 has a disc brake on the rear, as well as the front. And that's another innovation.

Right now, no one else is prepared to produce a motorcycle like the RD400.

Right now, you could be on it.

Someday, you'll own a Yamaha.

Maybe it was the performance of his RD400 that took his attention from his Ferrari.

YAMAHA

Both the RD250 and RD350 were removed from the floor at the end of the 1975 model year, but Yamaha was scheming to lessen the pain of their loss by bringing in a bigger RD400 for 1976. Instead of re-creating the wheel, Yamaha increased the stroke of the previous engine to reach 399cc. Although the boom was dropping on two-stroke machines due to pollution issues, Yamaha chose to move ahead with the bigger RD400 anyway.

With the previous cases at their limit already, the RD400 required all new tooling to gain the size desired. The newly cast cases were mounted to the frame with vibration reducing rubber attachment points, bringing more smoothness to the "torquey" two-stroke. In an effort to quell the RD400's tendency to do wheelies excessively, the engine was moved forward in the tube frame, shifting the weight closer to the front wheel.

With a weight of only 355 lbs. when topped off with fuel and fluids, and producing lots of torque-ridden horsepower, the Yamaha efforts to squelch front-wheel lift were for naught. This fact hardly scared buyers away as bigger numbers flocked to the showrooms to get their hands on the grips of the latest RD400.

Another missing model for 1976 was the big DT400. Having been increased to 400cc over the previous 360 did little to enhance sales, so the big DT was pulled. Joining the ranks of Yamaha's four-stroke brigade was the XS360. Placed just below the returning XS500, the 358cc edition made a more comfortable home for smaller riders, or for those just getting their first taste of big bike riding. The parallel twin engine was suspended from a tubular steel frame. In 1976, the styling was nothing out of the ordinary for Yamaha.

Seeing Honda and Kawasaki introducing their own versions of inline-four machines, and having their own TX750 fall flat, Yamaha took the middle road when they rolled out the XS750 for 1976. Splitting the difference between the two and four cylinder offerings, the XS750 carried a trio of cylinders that displaced a total of 747cc. The four-stroke design delivered smooth, progressive power with much less noise and vibration than the previous XT750 twin had. This revised delivery of power was a boon to long-distance riders who embraced the triple from Yamaha for being slightly different.

Not only did the XS750 carry three cylinders, but final drive was via shaft, setting it apart in another dimension from the CB750 and Z-1. Disc brakes on both wheels helped to slow the 550 lb. XS750 without fanfare, and two of the rotors were found on the front wheel. A 4.5-gallon fuel tank provided ample storage required for longer rides, and that's the duty the XS750 assumed.

In the convenience column, the XS750 featured cast wheels and self-canceling turn signals, eliminating the time-consuming task of cleaning chrome spokes and remembering to shut off the blinker after a turn was complete. The XS750 was an immediate hit with the media who extolled its smoothness and ride quality, often comparing it to the machines being produced by the big Bavarian maker.

1976 YAMAHA

Model	Engine	Displacement	Transmission
RD60C	Single cylinder	55cc	Five-Speed
RS100C	Single cylinder	97cc	Five-Speed
DT100C	Single cylinder	98cc	Five-Speed
DT125C	Single cylinder	125cc	Four-Speed
RD125C	Two-cylinder	124cc	Five-Speed
DT175C	Single cylinder	175cc	Five-Speed
RD200C	Two-cylinder	195cc	Five-Speed
DT250C	Single cylinder	250cc	Five-Speed
XS360C (New for 1976)	Two-cylinder	358cc	Five-Speed
RD400C (New for 1976)	Two-cylinder	399cc	Six-Speed
XS500C	Two-cylinder	500cc	Five-Speed
XS650C	Two-cylinder	653cc	Five-Speed
XS750C (New for 1976)	Three-cylinder	747cc	Five-Speed

YAMAHA
1977

Almost every model in the 1977 book was the same as in 1976, but some of the smaller machines were no longer offered. The RD60 and RD200 were removed from the model lineup as was the DS100.

The mighty RD400 was back for its second year and was virtually identical to the 1976 edition but wore new colors. It seemed like the RD400 was more accepted than its previous siblings, and they had quickly earned cult status after being introduced. Tightening pollution controls continued to loom large on the horizon, but the RD400 carried on, growing more popular as time went by. The XS650 was still in the game plan and received a few tweaks for 1977. Still suspended from the steel-tubular frame was a parallel-twin engine that made the XS650 big enough for many without being too big for the rest. New for 1977 was an aluminum front brake caliper that grabbed a bigger section of the rotor when pressure was applied to the lever. "Automotive style" instruments were also new and were easier to read at a glance. Self-canceling turn signals rounded up the alterations on the 1977 XS650.

The new for 1976 XS750 was also a repeat for the latest year, bringing nothing new to the table. Its design and construction continued to earn it solid reviews from the motorcycle press, despite the fact that it lacked a cylinder when compared to the Honda and Kawasaki offerings. Suzuki also introduced their first four-cylinder, four-stroke models for 1977, adding to pressures already present for the triple-lunged XS750.

1977 YAMAHA

Model	Engine	Displacement	Transmission
DT100D	Single cylinder	98cc	Five-Speed
DT125D	Single cylinder	125cc	Four-Speed
DT175D	Single cylinder	175cc	Five-Speed
DT250D	Single cylinder	250cc	Five-Speed
XS360D	Two-cylinder	358cc	Five-Speed
RD400D	Two-cylinder	398cc	Six-Speed
XS500D	Two-cylinder	500cc	Five-Speed
XS650D	Two-cylinder	653cc	Five-Speed
XS750D	Three-cylinder	747cc	Five-Speed

YAMAHA
1978

Overshadowed by the debut of the XS Eleven, the RD-400 provided fun in a great-handling, two-stroke design that drew scads of buyers each year.

Yamaha Motors

A new face was added to the 1978 Yamaha lineup and two new versions of returning models made their debut. The XS750, XS650 and RD400 would be recalled in 1980 for a variety of safety-related issues in the fuel and transmission departments. Yamaha would also trump Kawasaki as king of the performance world with their all-new XS Eleven.

The XS360 was replaced by a slightly larger XS400. The new offering was powered by a parallel-twin engine displacing 399cc. The small XS wore fresh sheet metal.

The newly styled XS400 would carry the theme into the Special Edition XS650 and XS750 models, providing Yamaha buyers with a few more selections. Also sold was the reduced-feature XS400 2E. This model rode on wire wheels instead of cast, and drum brakes replacing discs. Kick-start was the only way to get the single cylinder firing. Only one color was offered for the 2E.

The Special Edition XS650 wore a fuel tank, seat and side covers that were similar to the new XS400. A more teardrop shaped tank was mated to a deeply sculpted, two-person saddle and each side cover bore the "Special 650" badge. Cruiser inspired pullback bars were also a part of the Special's composition. There were some who continued to use the XS650 as a smaller touring machine, and the standard garb was better suited to that task. A Special II was also offered and it featured one disc and one drum, wire wheels and again, only one hue from the paint department.

The XS750 also sold in standard and Special Edition trim and it was upgraded with numerous changes to the already solid, reliable platform. Modifications to the airbox, jets in the carburetors and cam timing resulted in more performance from the same 747cc engines. Their Transistor Controlled Ignition eliminated mechanical breakers, one piece of the reliability woes from earlier machines.

Adjustable front forks and rear shocks that could be set to fit riding needs delivered better comfort on the open road. A two-page ad in the

September 1977 *Cycle* showed a fully-dressed XS750, complete with fairing, backrest and hard-sided saddlebags. There was no mention of what this touring-equipped model was called. The XS750 could be purchased in Special Edition trim, and the same teardrop tank, king and queen saddle, and pullback bars were found. The black paint was accented by Special badges on the side covers, too.

The SR500 carried only a single cylinder engine in its frame, and used kick-start. The SR500 was narrow and less daunting at slower speeds due to a lower center of gravity. Cast wheels at both ends, with a disc brake on each, added style and safety to the thumper. The lubricant was stored in the tubes of the frame, saving weight.

Biggest news of all in the 1978 lineup was the massive XS Eleven. By installing an inline-four engine that displaced 1101cc, Yamaha also displaced Kawasaki as the king of power. The double-overhead cam engine was fed with a set of four 34mm Mikuni "Type II" carburetors and sent its power to the rear wheel via shaft drive. The bone stock XS Eleven could turn the quarter mile at under 12 seconds, a new Japanese motorcycle record. The only thing quicker was the turbocharged Kawasaki Z-1R TC but it was not an actual factory-built entry.

Eleven spoke alloy wheels at both ends held a trio of disc brakes in check and an adjustable front fork allowed the ride to be custom tailored. A full bank of electronic gauges kept the rider up to date including one of the earliest fuel gauges used.

Bodywork was done in the standard form with a long and comfortable seat and spacious fuel tank. The XS Eleven could run with the big dogs at the drag strip or tour the country in style without breaking a sweat.

The rock-solid XS-750 gained a bevy of small improvements for 1978 and continued to be admired by a large audience of buyers.

1978 YAMAHA

Model	Engine	Displacement	Transmission
DT100E	Single cylinder	98cc	Five-Speed
DT125F	Single cylinder	125cc	Four-Speed
DT175E	Single cylinder	175cc	Five-Speed
DT250E	Single cylinder	250cc	Five-Speed
XS400E (New for 1978)	Two-cylinder	391cc	Five-Speed
XS400 2E (Reduced Features)	Two-cylinder	399cc	Five-Speed
RD400E	Two-cylinder	399cc	Six-Speed
SR500E (New for 1978)	Single cylinder	499cc	Five-Speed
XS500E	Two-cylinder	500cc	Five-Speed
XS650E	Two-cylinder	653cc	Five-Speed
XS650SE (New for 1978)	Two-cylinder	653cc	Five-Speed
XS650E II (New for 1978)	Two-cylinder	653cc	Five-Speed
XS750E	Three-cylinder	747cc	Five-Speed
XS750SE (New for 1978)	Three-cylinder	747cc	Five-Speed
XS Eleven (New for 1978)	Four-cylinder	1101cc	Five-Speed

YAMAHA
1979

For its final year of production and sale, the RD-400 was sold in a limited Daytona Special edition.

Governmental restrictions would finally catch up with the two-stroke world, and 1979 would be the final year for the street legal motorcycles powered by the sometimes smoky power plants. The biggest casualty of this change would be the loss of the beloved RD400, so Yamaha produced a special edition model to mark its passing.

As the rules of the EPA grew more fervent, it cost Yamaha more and more to keep the RD within the guidelines. By 1979, Yamaha guessed the cost added up to several hundred dollars per unit, and it was time to throw in the towel. Along with the added costs for producing a cleaner running RD, the weight was creeping up as more hardware was used to meet the rules. The difference between the 1977 and 1979 versions was a whopping eight pounds, with every ounce taking its toll on the fun.

Still no slouch, the RD400 Daytona Special recorded a quarter mile time of only 14.03 seconds when tested by *Motorcyclist* magazine in the April 1979 issue. To dress up the Daytona Special for its swan song, Yamaha painted it in all-white then added a stripe of bright red along the top of the front fender, fuel tank and rear seat cowling. Unique "Daytona Special 400" badges adorned the side covers. The MSRP of the 1979 RD400 Daytona Special was listed as $1,694, and may have seemed steep in the day, but would be a bargain for a clean example today.

The XS400, 650 and 750 all returned for another year and were sold in standard or Special trim. The 400 and 650 were also sold in de-contented versions that saved the buyer some money while offering fewer bits of chrome and creature comforts.

For the riders who had chosen the big XS

Eleven for touring, a turn-key package of accessories was sold directly through your Yamaha dealer. The kit included a full coverage fairing, hard-sided bags, chrome case guards and heavier duty suspension. If the whole enchilada was more than you needed or desired, you could pick the bits a la carte to meet your specific needs. Sold in color-matched hues of Magenta Red or Indigo Blue, the bolt-on touring gear put the XS Eleven into Gold Wing territory, albeit four years after the Wing had been introduced.

The XS Eleven was also offered in the custom cruiser "S" variation for 1979 and used a teardrop tank, stepped seat and pullback bars, just like the rest of the Yamaha models created in that vein.

1979 YAMAHA

Model	Engine	Displacement	Transmission
DT100F	Single cylinder	98cc	Five-Speed
DT125F	Single cylinder	125cc	Four-Speed
DT175F	Single cylinder	175cc	Five-Speed
DT250F	Single cylinder	250cc	Five-Speed
XS400 2F	Two-cylinder	358cc	Five-Speed
RD400F (Final Year of Sale)	Two-cylinder	399cc	Six-Speed
RD400F Daytona Special (Special Edition)	Two-cylinder	399cc	Six-Speed
SR500F	Single cylinder	499cc	Five-Speed
XT500F	Two-cylinder	499cc	Five-Speed
XJ650 II F	Two-cylinder	653cc	Five-Speed
XS650SF	Two-cylinder	653cc	Five-Speed
XS750F	Three-cylinder	747cc	Five-Speed
XS750SF	Three-cylinder	747cc	Five-Speed
XS Eleven F	Four-cylinder	1101cc	Five-Speed
XS Eleven SF (New for 1979)	Four-cylinder	1101cc	Five-Speed

YAMAHA

1980

STANDARD CATALOG OF JAPANESE Motorcycles

The one-lunged SR-250G was new for 1980 and offered light weight and terrific fuel economy for the beginning or frugal rider.

Yamaha Motors

Model year 1980 saw the addition of some enhanced motorcycles in the Yamaha line as well as fresh editions of some carry-over machines, but little was changed outside of those alterations. The RD400 had been pulled from the catalog after a successful life and would be missed almost immediately.

Ringing in the New Year of 1980 was the all-new SR250G and SR250SG. These new machines were both powered by a single lung engine that listed 249cc and shifted through a five-speed transmission. A low saddle height and reduced cost made the SR250 variants a great starter machine for new riders. The economy of the single cylinder engine made it appealing to commuters looking to save some money at the gas pumps. Drum brakes and spoke wheels did their part in keeping the weight and cost of entry low.

The second new model listed for 1980 was the

A new theme for two of the 1980 models from Yamaha was the Midnight Special, that cloaked the bikes in mostly black, and accented them with bits of gold.

Yamaha Motors

XJ650. The XJ650 listed a displacement of 653cc just like the XS, but divided its number among four cylinders versus two. The inline-four offered the rider a choice of five speeds and sent the selected ration through a shaft drive to the rear wheel. Spiral cast wheels were fitted with a disc brake up front and a drum brake on the rear wheel. The

YAMAHA

Yamaha's biggest machine remained the XS-1100, sold in three editions for 1980. This was the standard model.

Yamaha Motors

The second Yamaha to be sold in the blacked-out garb of the Midnight Special was the XS-1100LG.

Yamaha Motors

Only one variation was seen for the XS-400 and that was the Special. It used a stepped saddle, pullback bars and badges to set itself apart.

Yamaha Motors

YAMAHA

STANDARD CATALOG OF ® JAPANESE Motorcycles

The XJ-650 was new for 1980 too, and used an inline four-cylinder motor in place of the XS-650's parallel-twin, and included shaft drive.

Yamaha Motors

XJ650 was only seen in one trim level and that was similar to the Special models found elsewhere in the catalog. A two-tier saddle, buckhorn bars and teardrop tank all played a role in the overall design of the latest four cylinder from Yamaha.

Taking the triple cylinder equation to the next level was the increased displacement XS850. Adding 100cc helped the Yamaha to keep pace with the newly offered GS850 from Suzuki, and kept the unique triple up to date. The more powerful XS850 was sold in three levels of trim, one of which was the new Midnight Special. This cosmetic treatment cloaked the bike in black, including both fenders.

Gold highlights were applied to add some flair to the otherwise darkened hues. Cast wheels were also finished in gold to continue the theme. A heavily tufted saddle added to the unique nature of the LG variation as did the blacked-out exhaust system. The new Midnight Specials were identical in the mechanical department, but offered a whole new look for the rider who desired something a little different. The MSRP of the 1980 XS850LG was $3,348, or a premium of $350 over the XS850SG. The limited availability of the Midnight Specials was due partly to the fact that each of them was hand assembled and was lavished with extra care during the process. Tasks like welding and painting were completed by a skilled person rather than on a mechanical basis. That added to the special nature of these rare models.

The big XS1100G was also seen in all three levels of trim including the ominous Midnight Special. The XS1100LG set the buyer back an extra $370 over the price of the SG, and used the same trick book of disguises as was found on the XS850LG.

1980 YAMAHA

Model	Engine	Displacement	Transmission
DT100G	Single cylinder	98cc	Five-Speed
DT125G	Single cylinder	125cc	Four-Speed
DT175G	Single cylinder	175cc	Five-Speed
DT250G	Single cylinder	250cc	Five-Speed
SR250G (New for 1980)	Single cylinder	249cc	Five-Speed
SR250SG (New for 1980)	Single cylinder	249cc	Five-Speed
XS400G	Two-cylinder	358cc	Five-Speed
XS400SG	Two-cylinder	358cc	Five-Speed
SR500G	Single cylinder	499cc	Five-Speed
XT500G	Two-cylinder	499cc	Five-Speed
XJ650 (New for 1980)	Four-cylinder	653cc	Five-Speed
XS650G	Two-cylinder	653cc	Five-Speed
XS650SG	Two-cylinder	653cc	Five-Speed
XS850G (New for 1980)	Three-cylinder	826cc	Five-Speed
XS850LG Midnight Special	Three-cylinder	826cc	Five-Speed
XS850SG	Three-cylinder	826cc	Five-Speed
XS1100G	Four-cylinder	1101cc	Five-Speed
XS1100LG Midnight Special	Four-cylinder	1101cc	Five-Speed
XS1100SG	Four-cylinder	1101cc	Five-Speed

STANDARD CATALOG OF ® JAPANESE MOTORCYCLES

YAMAHA
1981

The 1981 Yamaha Seca 750 was placed in profile against the sun in this 1981 ad.

When compared to some recent years, 1981 would be one of the more active with a variety of new models showing up on the sales floors.

Yamaha rolled out two middle weight versions of their XJ550 for 1981. Both variants were powered by a 528cc inline-four engine. The XJ550H Maxim was designed to meet the needs of the cruiser buyer while the XJ550RH Seca was for the sport bike fan.

The Maxim used the pullback bars, an exaggerated teardrop tank and two-level saddle to fulfill its mission. The Seca used more traditional fittings. The Seca included a small sport fairing that wrapped around the headlight and turn signals and was finished in white with red stripes. Cast wheels were used on both, but the Maxim's were more of a spiral pattern while the Seca's featured a more angular design. The XJ550 engine was only a half-inch wider than the XS400 twin, the most compact design available.

Two versions of a slightly larger Maxim were found in the XJ650H and XJ650LH. The LH was finished in the black and gold theme of the Midnight Special, and joined the ranks of that hand-made faction.

A larger iteration of the Seca was the XJ750RH. It more than made up for the loss in technology and electronics. The inline-four engine measured only

New for 1981 was the XJ-550 Seca, bringing new life to the middleweight sport bike arena. Barbara Pugh

337

YAMAHA

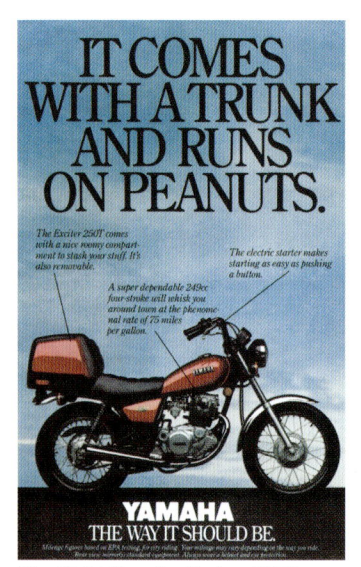

The 1981 Yamaha Exciter 250T was highlighted in this comparison with elephants. Yamahas don't spray water—but they can take you through puddles!

18 inches across, rivaling some two-and three-cylinder entries. The 750 Seca was also driven by a shaft but this feature only added convenience, taking nothing away in the power department. The styling of the 750 was a bit more "standard," but still fairly rakish.

The instrument array included a liquid crystal display. In addition to the usual RPM and speed, the lights and gauges monitored the position of the side stand, fuel and battery levels as well as brake fluid. When compared to other offerings of the day, the Seca 750 ranked near the top in almost every sector, and bested them all in fuel mileage. At $3,199, it was the priciest as well, but only by a few hundred dollars. The level of technology and shaft drive more than compensated for that.

Another new 750 was the Virago. Instead of the Seca inline-four, the Virago featured a V-twin mill with cylinders at a 75-degree spread. By offsetting the rear cylinder's location, better cooling was achieved. Using the engine as a stressed member eliminated the need for a lower frame tube and provided a seat height of only 29.5 inches. At the rear of the Virago, a shaft drive, and the industry's first mono-shock suspension, were found. A drum brake on the rear wheel was augmented by a disc on the front wheel. The spokes on the front wheel were held in a spiral pattern.

The standard issue models of the XS850 and XS1100 were gone, leaving only the Special and Midnight Specials in the catalog. New versions of the touring machines were the Venturers. Full fairings, complete with lowers, were bolted to the frames of the big XS models and chrome case guards were thrown in to protect the fragile bits in the event of tip over. Heavier suspension in the rear helped to support the hard-sided saddlebags when fully loaded. A chrome luggage rack was capable of holding added gear and diamond stitched saddles were unique to the Venturers. Keeping a Venturer out of the hands of thieves was achieved by using the wheel locking chain as part of the standard equipment list. The XS1100 Venturer also had a larger 6.3-gallon fuel tank, extending the cycle's range on the open road.

1981 YAMAHA

Model	Engine	Displacement	Transmission
DT100H	Single cylinder	98cc	Five-Speed
DT125H	Single cylinder	125cc	Four-Speed
DT175H	Single cylinder	175cc	Five-Speed
DT250H	Single cylinder	250cc	Five-Speed
SR250H Exciter	Single cylinder	249cc	Five-Speed
SR250TH Exciter	Single cylinder	249cc	Five-Speed
XS400H Special II	Two-cylinder	358cc	Five-Speed
XS400SH	Two-cylinder	358cc	Five-Speed
SR500H	Single cylinder	499cc	Five-Speed
XJ550H Maxim (New for 1981)	Four-cylinder	528cc	Six-Speed
XJ550RH Seca (New for 1981)	Four-cylinder	528cc	Six-Speed
XT500H	Two-cylinder	499cc	Five-Speed
XJ650H Maxim	Four-cylinder	653cc	Five-Speed
XJ650LH Maxim Midnight Special	Four-cylinder	653cc	Five-Speed
XS650H	Two-cylinder	653cc	Five-Speed
XS750RH Seca (New for 1981)	Four-cylinder	748cc	Five-Speed
XV750 Virago (New for 1981)	Two-cylinder	750cc	Five-Speed
XS850H Venturer (New for 1981)	Three-cylinder	826cc	Five-Speed
XS850LH	Three-cylinder	826cc	Five-Speed
XS850SH	Three-cylinder	826cc	Five-Speed
XS1100H Venturer (New for 1981)	Four-cylinder	1101cc	Five-Speed
XS1100LH Midnight Special	Four-cylinder	1101cc	Five-Speed
XS1100SH	Four-cylinder	1101cc	Five-Speed

YAMAHA 1982

The 400cc Seca was new for 1982 and appealed to experienced and beginning riders with its broad power band and low seat height.

Yamaha Motors

The 1982 model year would see the dismissal of several of Yamaha's smaller mounts and a bevy of fresh blood was transfused into the operation. First of the latest arrivals was the XJ400R Seca. Unlike the 550 and 750 variants, the 400 was powered by a parallel twin engine that displaced 399cc. Styled much like the Maxim models, it featured sleek bodywork on the tank and side panels. The 400 had a low seat height of only 30.7 inches. The cycle had a sub 400-lb. weight when it was half-filled with fuel. The light weight and low saddle made it a perfect entry level machine but its features enticed more experienced riders. The 55-inch wheelbase and steep rake delivered precise handling but lacked any form at the front fork adjustment. A single shock was found at the rear, keeping the design clean and uncluttered. It only took $1,999 to bring one home.

The XZ550R Vision was another new entry on the 1982 logbooks and featured a 70-degree V-twin engine and final shaft drive. A drum brake on the single shock rear swing arm was teamed with a solitary disc up front. No fork adjustments were available. The Vision was hefty, weighing 462 lbs. when filled with a half tank of fuel. Of the 550cc machines sold for 1982, the Vision was the most expensive at $2,849, eclipsing its own brethren the 550 Seca at $2,659.

Yamaha rolled out a puffer bike, the XJ650L Seca Turbo. By adding a turbocharger to the 653cc, inline-four, big things happened when the throttle was twisted.

In place of the rush of whacking the twist grip

YAMAHA

In between the returning 550 and new 1100 models was the 750 Maxim.

Owner/Photo: Chris Bednas

of a race bike, the turbo gained power, delivering a rush of power. Once the 6000 RPM range was reached, it was time to hold on tightly as the boost reached maximum velocity, rocketing the turbo model forward. They cloaked the Turbo in space age trim and sharply creased panels.

A full fairing was part of the plan and added to the style and 567 lbs. of weight. The engine and the entire exhaust were cloaked in black, adding to the beast's sinister nature. By adding a turbo to the 653cc engine, Yamaha achieved output usually reserved for much bigger machines. Sadly, no sooner had the appearance of turbocharged machines shown up than higher than usual insurance premiums were applied. The Seca Turbo disappeared after 1983. A larger 750 Maxim joined the fray for 1982 as well and appealed to riders who sought a bigger machine with plenty of style.

Model year 1982 also saw the time-tested XS850 and 1100 pulled from the production lines. Both machines enjoyed a full life, but it was time to debut some fresh faces.

The Virago clan was enhanced by a larger 920cc version. Using more traditional styling for the bigger Virago, Yamaha hoped to capture more of the sport touring audience. The staggered-cylinder, V-twin engine remained an integral part of the chassis and rode beneath a sloping fuel tank that led directly to the two-tier saddle. Cast wheels with spiral spokes held the rubber in position. Taking the Maxim formula to the highest degree, an 1100 version was introduced for 1982. Style of the big Maxim was similar to the smaller units with an elongated teardrop tank, deeply contoured saddle and short sissy bar at the rear of the seat. The inline-four engine fed the power through a shaft drive and used a four-into-two chrome exhaust. A round headlight was seen and mild pullback bars made the reach for grips an easier.

1982 YAMAHA

Model	Engine	Displacement	Transmission
SR185 Exciter	Single cylinder	185cc	Five-Speed
SR250 Exciter	Single cylinder	249cc	Five-Speed
XS400R Seca	Two-cylinder	399cc	Six-Speed
XS400S Special	Two-cylinder	358cc	Five-Speed
SR500H	Single cylinder	499cc	Five-Speed
XT500H	Two-cylinder	499cc	Five-Speed
XJ550 Maxim	Four-cylinder	528cc	Six-Speed
XT550R Vision (New for 1982)	Two-cylinder	550cc	Six-Speed
XJ650 Maxim	Four-cylinder	653cc	Five-Speed
XJ650L Seca Turbo (New for 1982)	Four-cylinder	653cc	Five-Speed
XS650R Seca	Four-cylinder	653cc	Five-Speed
XS650S	Two-cylinder	653cc	Five-Speed
XV750 Maxim (New for 1982)	Four-cylinder	748cc	Five-Speed
XJ750R Seca	Four-cylinder	748cc	Five-Speed
XS750 Virago	Two-cylinder	750cc	Five-Speed
XV920 Virago (New for 1982)	Two-cylinder	902cc	Five-Speed
XJ1100 Maxim (New for 1982)	Four-cylinder	1100cc	Five-Speed

YAMAHA 1983

The 550 Vision returned in an all-new configuration for 1983 with more power and a great frame-mounted fairing that provided style and function.

Owner/Photo: Chris Bednas

Neither the 185 nor 250 version of the Exciter found too much enthusiasm from buyers and both were pulled from the floor for 1983. At the other end of the rainbow, the big 1100 Maxim was also a goner after only a single year of sales. The insurance industry had driven the final nail into the XJ650 Seca Turbo's life as well, and after 1983 it would slip into oblivion.

Not all news for 1983 was of departing machines as several entries made their debut in the same year.

A 500cc version of the Virago was the smallest of the new iron, and although displacing fewer ccs, and having less size than the others, it remained a stylish cruiser. A saddle height of only 29.5 inches for the rider and a weight when filled halfway with fuel at just over 400 lbs., the XV500 was a great way to get your riding experience started. A single disc up front and a drum brake out back allowed stopping with ease. Some 2.9 gallons of fossil fuel could be stored in the tank when full which allowed for a bit over 120 miles before switching to reserve. The $2,299 price tag added to the value of the baby Virago.

The 750 and 920cc Viragos were still found and were also sold in the ominous black and gold Midnight livery. The rest of this Yamaha was the same but the glistening black paint was accented by bits of gold, including the cast wheels.

Almost every variant in the 1983 Yamaha cruiser family had their electronic gauge clusters replaced with traditional instruments, saving cost and confusion.

The middleweight XZ550R Vision was back, but featured more power and a slew of new hardware, making it a far better motorcycle than its debut version only a year before. Changes to the airbox, engine specs and carburetors all resulted in far more power being gleaned from the 552cc V-twin. The 34mm carbs were replaced with 36mm units allowing the Vision to breathe easier. The

YAMAHA

New for 1983 was the 900 Seca. It joined the smaller variants and offered the rider sport-bike power.

Matt Jonas

larger airbox also aided the Vision in this department, and brought a lot more fun to the table. The sleek fairing was both functional and stylish with vents that could duct heat towards the rider when the mercury fell low in the thermometer. All of this glitz and glitter came at a price though, and the 1983 Vision also carried a price tag of $3,299 that was $500 to $600 more than the competition. While it was pricier, the Yamaha Vision did bring an enhanced package to the game.

For the Seca buyer who wanted more than the others could provide, a 900 version was enrolled in the '83 class for Yamaha. Actually displacing 853cc, the new Seca featured a raft of go-fast bits and claimed a dry weight of only 483 lbs. These numbers gave the big Seca a terrific power-to-weight ratio that was immediately appreciated by the rider.

Heavily contoured bodywork included a quarter fairing mounted to the bars and a spacious, well-padded saddle. The inline-four engine was mostly black with polished fins and case covers. A chrome four-into-two exhaust handled the spent fumes with style.

Having witnessed the success of the Honda Gold Wing from afar, 1983 would see Yamaha toss its hat into the upper echelon touring ring with their Venture and Venture Royale. Both fully-equipped touring machines were pushed along by a V-four engine that displaced 1198cc and sent the power to the rear wheel via shaft drive.

The big lump was mounted to the frame with rubber bushings reducing vibration to nearly nothing. A hydraulic clutch, downdraft carburetors and electronically controlled ignition advance made the Venture a smooth operator. Rear suspension was provided by a single shock that was air-assisted and adjustable.

Air-adjusted front forks were also fitted with anti-dive technology, allowing the rider to bring the colossus to a halt with minimum fuss.

A full array of electronics and comfort features adorned the Venture with even more on the Royale edition. The full fairing, saddlebags and rear travel box were all included in the Venture's domain and were unique to the 1200cc touring machine.

1983 YAMAHA

Model	Engine	Displacement	Transmission
XS400 Maxim	Two-cylinder	358cc	Five-Speed
XS400R Seca	Two-cylinder	399cc	Six-Speed
XS500 Virago (New for 1983)	Two-cylinder	500cc	Five-Speed
XJ550 Maxim	Four-cylinder	528cc	Six-Speed
XJ550R Seca	Four-cylinder	528cc	Six-Speed
XZ550R Vision	Two-cylinder	550cc	Five-Speed
XJ650 Maxim	Four-cylinder	653cc	Five-Speed
XJ650L Seca Turbo (Final Year)	Four-cylinder	653cc	Five-Speed
XJ650R Seca	Four-cylinder	653cc	Five-Speed
XS650S	Two-cylinder	653cc	Five-Speed
XJ750 Maxim	Four-cylinder	748cc	Five-Speed
XJ750R Seca	Four-cylinder	748cc	Five-Speed
XV750 Virago	Two-cylinder	750cc	Five-Speed
XV750M Midnight Virago (New for 1983)	Two-cylinder	750cc	Five-Speed
XJ900 Seca (New for 1983)	Four-cylinder	853cc	Five-Speed
XV920 Virago	Two-cylinder	920cc	Five-Speed
XV920M Midnight Virago (New for 1983)	Two-cylinder	920cc	Five-Speed
XVZ1200T Venture (New for 1983)	Four-cylinder	1198cc	Five Speed
XVZ1200TD Venture Royale (New for 1983)	Four-cylinder	1198 cc	Five-Speed

YAMAHA
1984

After a robust year of new model introductions, 1984 would see a greatly reduced catalog but did offer some brand new machinery. Seventeen models that were seen in 1983 were now gone including every version of the Maxim, Seca and Vision. The returning Viragos were both fitted with different motors, so in theory even the Viragos of 1983 were gone.

Making a comeback for 1984 was a two-stroke machine, the RZ350. Yamaha had spent countless hours in the R&D lab to overcome the restrictions applied to the two-stroke engine's use, and delivered a great new sport bike in the process. The liquid-cooled engine was quieter and ran without killing mosquitoes as the previous version did, allowing its sale in the USA. It had been sold in Europe before reaching our shores, although the crowd across the pond didn't get the yellow and black Kenny Roberts paint.

A trio of disc brakes slowed the 330-lb. craft and a single shock at the rear wheel provided the suspension. Yamaha's Power Valve technology helped boost power while keeping things clean and $2,399 was all it took to ride one home. In addition to the Kenny Roberts livery, there was a version that was white with red stripes, much like the 1979 edition sold here.

Now lacking the Seca sport machines, Yamaha rolled out their new FJ600 for 1984. Learning from all of their past experience with sport machines and borrowing a few bits of hardware, the true sport bike FJ600 was created.

Hoping to placate the buyers who missed their powerful two-stroke street machines, Yamaha released the RZ350 for 1984 and used a cleaner, quieter engine.

The inline-four engine breathed through valves that were sized for bigger machines, thus delivering potent breathing. The 32mm carburetors fed the fuel and air mixture smoothly and departing gases traveled through a four-into-two exhaust. Six cogs were on hand, sending the power to the rear wheel via a drive chain. Three slotted brake discs were on duty to slow the 415-lb. FJ600 and De Carbon suspension at the rear provided race ready stability. The frame-mounted half-fairing was augmented by a separate chin spoiler and added to the sporting nature of the small FJ.

For the sport bike rider who wanted to take to the highway from time to time, the larger FJ1100 could easily succeed when it wasn't strafing corners around town. Created in the same pattern as the FJ600 the bigger version, it displaced 1097cc and shifted through a five-speed box. Its 16-inch wheels under both fenders helped to give the 501-lb. machine some quick moves when it was at speed. Adjustable suspension at both ends allowed a tailored ride whether alone on the bike or with a passenger. Similar bodywork on the FJ1100 included a frame mounted fairing and chin spoiler. Selling for a dollar under $5,000, the new FJ was a great bargain with plenty of power and style.

Two versions of the Virago were found on the 1984 order sheet, but both were nothing like the two editions they replaced. Sold as a 700 or 1000, the new versions were redesigned for cleaner operation and rode with revised sheet metal. The XV1000 used a stylish peanut fuel tank but also had a second fuel storage housing that sat beneath the seat, adding to the capacity without taking away any points for style. The XV700 was built to stay within the boundaries of the latest tariff on motorcycles over 700cc that were imposed by the government. The XV700 was also completely restyled for 1984 with revisions at every corner.

Introduced for 1983 and instantly winning the hearts of the media and buyers alike, the Venture was back in two levels of trim for 1984. The Venture—and its more lavish brother the Venture Royale—were grafted with a wide range of small improvements but the primary composition remained as before. Taller windscreens, enhanced electronics and adjustable suspension kept the Venture at the top of the hill in the ultra touring division.

Making its debut for 1984 was the tiny RX50. The 49cc, two-stroke engine propelled the 165-lb. cruiser along smartly. Done in a cruiser format, the RX50 featured tall bars and a two-level seat. A solo disc on the front and drum on the rear wheel slowed the $649 model with confidence.

1984 YAMAHA

Model	Engine	Displacement	Transmission
RX50 (New for 1984)	Single cylinder	49cc	Five-Speed
RZ350L (New for 1984)	Two-cylinder	347cc	Six-Speed
FJ600 (New for 1984)	Four-cylinder	598cc	Six-Speed
XV700 Virago Tariff Beater	Two-cylinder	699cc	Five-Speed
XV1000 Virago (New for 1984)	Two-cylinder	981cc	Five-Speed
XVZ1200T Venture	Four-cylinder	1198cc	Five-Speed
XVZ1200TD Venture Royale	Four-cylinder	1198 cc	Five-Speed

STANDARD CATALOG OF ® JAPANESE MOTORCYCLES   YAMAHA

1985

Several additions were seen for the 1985 model year and there were a few subtractions. Gone were the RX50 and the standard Venture.

The Maxim name returned to the fold and was seen in two versions of 700cc cruisers. The Maxim 700 carried an air-cooled four cylinder in the frame while the Maxim 700X utilized the more potent liquid-cooled mill from the FZ750, but was resized at 697cc. The 20-valve head was carried over from the FZ as well, upping the performance of the laid-back cruiser. Both Maxims used the same chassis and styling, making the motor and cost of entry the only difference. The Maxim X sold for $3,499, a $500 premium over the air-cooled version. Both machines came in under the tariff triggering 700cc limit, saving the buyer some green.

The power for the FZ750, Yamaha's newest sport bike, came from a 20-valve, four- cylinder engine that displaced 749cc. The mill was tilted at an extreme angle of 45 degrees, placing much of its weight on the front wheel. This radical arrangement produced fewer wheelies and enhanced the handling of the chassis. A lean angle of 51 degrees was listed in period ads, making it as close to a race bike as we've seen. A 16-inch hoop up front was teamed with an 18-inch on the rear and a six-speed gearbox was included. At least 5.3 gallons of fuel could be stored in the tank

All new for 1985 was the FZ-750. The sport bike was powered by a four-cylinder, 20-valve engine that was canted at a radical 45 degrees for better weight distribution.

Yamaha Motors

The Maxim name returned, but was attached to two different motorcycles for 1985. The standard Maxim was more traditional with its air-cooled engine.

Yamaha Motors

345

Crashing onto the scene in 1985 was the amazing V-Max. Powered by a V-4 engine from the Venture Royale, the V-Max was listed at 135 hp.

Matt Kallas

and the FZ750 came stock with a frame-mounted half-fairing and blacked-out engine and exhaust.

An entirely new class of motorcycles was created with the debut of the V-Max. Slung into a muscle bike frame was the same 1198cc V-four engine as in the Venture Royale. A pair of non-functioning air intakes was affixed to each side of the faux fuel tank, making a bold statement about the V-Max's intentions.

The super-wide 150 series tire shoved under the rear fender furthered this aggression, and with a claimed horsepower of 135, very few could argue the point. The engine may have begun its life as the one used in the touring model, but extensive revisions within boosted the power to unseen figures. When accelerating about 6000 RPM, the V-Boost system was activated, allowing the cylinders to draw an increased volume of air and fuel. A five-speed gearbox was linked to a final shaft drive, and the actual fuel storage was held beneath the low 30.1-inch saddle. Four gallons could be held at once, but high-speed runs could quickly devour that quantity. Oddly enough, no one seemed to care. The price of $5,299 was required before riding the new V-Max home, but it became a legend overnight and would enjoy a long life.

With the standard issue Venture gone, the remaining Venture Royale received an even bigger bag of electronic trickery. The cruise control was now electronic as was the AM/FM/Cassette/CD system. Air leveling was also the job of the on-board computer and better anti-dive brakes were a part of the 1985 model's DNA. At $8,299 it was higher priced than the Gold Wing Aspencade and Interstate, but less expensive than the limited edition anniversary model.

1985 YAMAHA

Model	Engine	Displacement	Transmission
RZ350	Two-cylinder	347cc	Six-Speed
FJ600	Four-cylinder	598cc	Six-Speed
XJ700 Maxim (New for 1985)	Four-cylinder	697cc	Five-Speed
XJ700 Maxim X (New for 1985)	Four-cylinder	697cc	Five-Speed
XV700 Virago	Two-cylinder	699cc	Five-Speed
FZ750R (New for 1985)	Four-cylinder	749cc	Six-Speed
XV1000 Virago	Two-cylinder	981cc	Five-Speed
FJ1100	Four-cylinder	1097cc	Five-Speed
V-Max (New for 1985)	Four-cylinder	1198cc	Five-Speed
XVZ1200TD Venture Royale	Four-cylinder	1198 cc	Five-Speed

YAMAHA 1986

The Yamaha Radian was new for 1986 and featured a racy engine with standard styling that suited many levels of riders.
Yamaha Motors

Model year 1986 was full of changes for the Yamaha team with new models, dropped motorcycles and revised examples of returning units.

The FJ600 was pulled from the shelf to make room for the sportier FZ600. The new model was ridden in the shadows of its big brother the FZ750, which returned for 1986. Taking a cue from the FZ400, a Yamaha that was not sold in the USA, the same square-section tube frame was applied to the FZ600 equation. The FZ600 was virtually the same machine as the smaller FZ400, only with a bigger and more powerful engine hidden beneath the race ready fairing and bodywork. Four Mikuni BS30 carburetors fed the 598cc mill and sent the power to the six-speed box. As expected from a sport bike, final drive was by chain.

New in the 600cc division were several very different offerings. The SRX600 had a single-cylinder 595cc mill hung from a tubular steel frame and was fairly conventional in its design and layout. The SOHC engine was attached to a five-speed gearbox and the whole thing was started by kicking the pedal. Triple disc brakes hauled the SRX600 down in a hurry and part of that was due to its low 329-lb. dry weight.

Next in the new 600cc machine parade was the Radian. Using the styling of a standard model and the power of a 598cc inline-four engine, the Radian satisfied both ends of the spectrum. A dry weight of 408 lbs., a six-speed box and chain drive were part of the vitals of this bike. The brakes were two discs on the front

Also new for 1986 was the one-lunged SRX 600. It provided a simple platform with plenty of power. Yamaha Motors

YAMAHA

The big Virago was back, but now was powered by an 1100cc engine where a 1000cc version had rested in 1985.

Yamaha Motors

wheel and a drum in the rear. A black engine was highlighted with gold colored cylinder heads and a chrome exhaust. Apple Red or Bluish Black were the listed hues for 1986.

Moving to the 700cc class, there was a new version of the Virago offered alongside the returning 1985 model and both flavors of the Maxim. The Virago 700C held the tires in place using cast rims while the 700S sported wire wheels in their stead. The C was offered in two shades, Deep Violet or Miyabi Maroon while the C was only sold in New Black Blue. The Virago 1000 grew in displacement to reach 1100 for 1986 and was the only liter-sized cruiser in the Yamaha family for this year. Marshall Gold and Apple Red were the choices in the paint department.

Back to the sportier side of the coin, the FJ1100 had grown into the FJ1200 for the latest year. A sleeker fairing and a clock in the instrument array were also new for 1986 with Silky White being listed as the paint with red accents and a blacked-out exhaust.

The touring crowd would find fixed saddlebags on their Venture Royale with removable liners that added space to the previous examples. Improved electronics made life simpler and more precise, and the Venture Royale continued to steal the thunder of the Honda Gold Wing.

1986 YAMAHA

Model	Engine	Displacement	Transmission
RZ350	Two-cylinder	347cc	Six-Speed
FZ600 (New for 1986)	Four-cylinder	598cc	Six-Speed
XY 600 Radian (New for 1986)	Four-cylinder	598cc	Six-Speed
SRX600 (New for 1986)	Single cylinder	595cc	Five-Speed
XJ700 Maxim	Four-cylinder	697cc	Five-Speed
XJ700X Maxim X	Four-cylinder	697cc	Five-Speed
FZX700 Fazer (New for 1986)	Four-cylinder	697cc	Six-Speed
XV700 Virago C (Cast wheels)	Two-cylinder	699cc	Five-Speed
XV700 Virago B (Wire wheels)	Two-cylinder	699cc	Five-Speed
XV1100 Virago (New for 1986)	Two-cylinder	1063cc	Five-Speed
FJ1200 (More displacement)	Four-cylinder	1188cc	Five-Speed
V-Max	Four-cylinder	1198cc	Five-Speed
XVZ1200TD Venture Royale	Four-cylinder	1198cc	Five-Speed

YAMAHA 1987

A variety of changes greeted buyers at Yamaha dealerships for 1987 with some fresh entries, a few losses and, as nearly always, some returning models.

Having been introduced for 1985, the V-Max was missing from the catalog for 1987. Eager buyers would not be denied for long as the muscle bike returned for 1988. The RZ350 was also pulled, but would not return to the playing field. The wire wheel version of the Virago 700 was another no-show for 1987 as people seemed to prefer the cast wheel version.

Making a return for 1987 was the base model of the Venture. Still opulently equipped, it was missing a few of the accoutrements of the Royale and saved the buyer a few sheckles in the process.

Turning our attentions to the new models we find the SRX250 stepping in where the RZ350 had been. The SRX250 was a four-stroke, single-cylinder engine in lieu of the RZ's two-stroke, so EPA restrictions were not an issue. Electric start and a set of six cogs made the SRX appealing from the mechanical standpoint and the frame-mounted fairing brought a look of sport bike to the equation. A red frame and wheels set off the Silky White and Red bodywork nicely and the entire thing only weighed 271 lbs. The SRX600 was no longer sold.

The FZ-700 was new for 1987 and its 697cc engine fell within the guidelines of the government's tariffs on larger cycles.

Yamaha Motors

Moving in for 1987 was the 535 Virago, offering the cruiser buyer a fully-equipped bike at a lower cost and weight than some other machines being sold.

Yamaha Motors

YAMAHA

Boasting an impressive 989cc engine and an even more dramatic weight of only 450 lbs., the FZR-1000 was a fearsome sport bike.

Yamaha Motors

The Venture was again seen in two flavors for 1987, the base model seen here and the more lavishly equipped Royale.

Yamaha Motors

In the sport bike class, an FZ700 made its appearance. The tariff-beating 697cc engine was installed in a racing-inspired frame and wrapped in equally sporty bodywork. Three disc brakes slowed the FZ700 and six-speeds pushed it forward. When devoid of fuel, the FZ700 clocked in at 452 lbs., a few more than its even more aggressive FZR750R sibling. The FZR750R weighed 448 lbs. dry and was joined by an even bigger variant for 1987.

New for 1987 was the FZR1000. With an inline four that displaced 989cc, and a dry weight of only 450 lbs., the math was easy. The FZR1000 only carried five gears in its box but the bigger motor offered enough power at almost any RPM to satisfy riders of all stripes. Yamaha's five-valve technology was present on the liter-sized FZR as had become customary in their sport machines.

The Fazer, Radian and FJ1200 all returned with cosmetic changes.

The cruiser division may have lost the wire wheeled XV700 Virago but gained the Virago 535 in the process. The smaller Virago rode with all the style of the bigger versions but weighed nearly 100 lbs. less than the 700cc model. A single disc on the front wheel and a drum on the rear slowed the 386-lb. (dry weight) 535 smoothly and the five-speed gearbox provided ample selections. Deep Scarlet or Greenish Black were listed as the 1987 hues.

Only the cast wheel version of the XV700 Virago was seen and the XV1100 Virago was also a repeat for 1987.

1987 YAMAHA

Model	Engine	Displacement	Transmission
SRX250 (New for 1987)	Single cylinder	249cc	Six-Speed
XV535 Virago (New for 1987)	Two-cylinder	535cc	Five-Speed
FZ600	Four-cylinder	598cc	Six-Speed
XY600 Radian	Four-cylinder	598cc	Six-Speed
FZX700 Fazer	Four-cylinder	697cc	Six-Speed
XV700 Virago	Two-cylinder	699cc	Five-Speed
FZ700 (New for 1987)	Four-cylinder	697cc	Six-Speed
FZR750R	Four-cylinder	749cc	Six-Speed
FZR1000 (New for 1987)	Four-cylinder	989cc	Five-Speed
XV1100 Virago	Two-cylinder	1063cc	Five-Speed
FJ1200	Four-cylinder	1188cc	Five-Speed
XVZ1200T Venture (Returned for 1987)	Four-cylinder	1198cc	Five-Speed
XVZ1200TD Venture Royale	Four-cylinder	1198 cc	Five-Speed

YAMAHA
1988

With the over 700cc tariff lifted, the FZ-750 was no longer a crime to ride and delivered the enhanced power the extra 50cc brought.

Yamaha Motors

With the tariff on motorcycles over 700cc lifted, Yamaha returned to normalcy and brought back some 750cc machines. Gone were the under 700cc offerings that were trimmed to meet guidelines as they were no longer required.

New for 1988 was the Route 66 cruiser. With a 249cc V-twin motor, and all the classic styling cues, the Route 66 was a great entry-level machine. A dry weight of 302 lbs. and super low saddle height of only 27 inches made it an easy choice for beginning or vertically challenged riders. Despite its smaller dimensions, the Route 66 didn't miss a trick when it came to design. Pullback bars, a stepped saddle and teardrop tank were all present. Staggered shotgun exhaust pipes played their part and a five-cog box was on hand. A single disc brake up front and drum brake at the rear brought the 66 to safe stops. Splendid Beige or Melting Black were your options in the paint department.

The previously trimmed Virago 700 was now back as a full-fledged 750, and was seated along-

Looking every inch the big-boy cruiser, the Route 66 was actually quite compact and made a great entry-level buy. Yamaha Motors

351

YAMAHA

After a year long hiatus, the mighty V-Max returned wearing new paint for 1988.

Yamaha Motors

side the 535 and 1100 variants. Both versions of the luxo-barge Venture were available as well, keeping the pressure on the Gold Wing.

After a year-long sabbatical, the V-Max returned for 1988. Besides the new Apple Red hue, no alterations were seen on the V-four muscle bike.

The FZ700 was one of the machines no longer required to meet with regulations and was replaced by the FZ750. While basically the same machine as the 700, the 750 carried 749cc and shifted through a six-speed gearbox. The FZR750R and FZR1000 were repeats for 1988 with only new graphics to show for their efforts.

The Fazer was another model yanked out of the catalog after a brief production run.

Gaining no weight for the 1988 model year, the FZR-1000 was still a force to be reckoned with and sported new graphics.

Yamaha Motors

1988 YAMAHA

Model	Engine	Displacement	Transmission
Route 66 (New for 1988)	Two-cylinder	249cc	Five-Speed
SRX250	Single cylinder	249cc	Six-Speed
FZR400 (New for 1988)	Four-cylinder	399cc	Six-Speed
XV535 Virago	Two-cylinder	535cc	Five-Speed
FZ600	Four-cylinder	598cc	Six-Speed
XY600 Radian	Four-cylinder	598cc	Six-Speed
XV750 Virago	Two-cylinder	748cc	Five-Speed
FZ750	Four-cylinder	749cc	Six-Speed
FZR750R	Four-cylinder	749cc	Six-Speed
FZR1000	Four-cylinder	989cc	Five-Speed
XV1100 Virago	Two-cylinder	1063cc	Five-Speed
FJ1200	Four-cylinder	1188cc	Five-Speed
V-Max (Returning Model)	Four-cylinder	1198cc	Five-Speed
XVZ1200T Venture	Four-cylinder	1198cc	Five Speed
XVZ1200TD Venture Royale	Four-cylinder	1198 cc	Five-Speed

YAMAHA
1989

With the loss of some other standards, the Radian was left behind to carry on the naked bike tradition.

Yamaha Motors

Yamaha did some serious culling of the herd for 1989 and nearly every division was affected by the cuts. The only segment not feeling the pinch was the cruisers with every 1988 model coming back for another turn. The 535 Virago was the 1988 model with no actual 1989 units sold.

The Venture Royale was again the only version offered and remained an opulent choice for the long-distance rider who demanded every creature comfort. Dull Blue Cocktail and Graceful Maroon were the latest shades offered.

Having taken a year off for 1987, the V-Max was back for 1989 but bore no alterations including color for 1989.

The Route 66 was another repeat with Melting Black and Luminous Red the only changes listed for 1989. All three sizes of the Virago were seen with "Previous year model available" being shown for the 535 on the 1989 brochure.

Sport bike riders found the SRX250 gone as were every version of the 750 machines. The FZ600 of 1988 was back as a FZR600 for 1989 as performance was enhanced. Silky White or New Yamaha Black were the colors for 1989. The FZR400 and FZR1000 both had Silky White shown as the only hue offered but both featured the diagonal red slashes as part of their

Yamaha went back and forth with their entries in the luxury category and the 1989 version found only the Venture Royale being listed. Yamaha Motors

YAMAHA

Three variations of the Virago remained with the 1100 sitting at the top of the heap.

Yamaha Motors

The FZR-400 was a potent choice for the sport-bike buyer who wanted something a bit smaller than the 600cc or higher models from Yamaha.

Yamaha Motors

graphics. The sport touring FJ1200 now wore a choice of Silky White with Silver trim or Shiny Black with Blue accents.

The naked Radian continued to be seen in your choice of New Yamaha Black or Dark Purplish Blue Cocktail.

1989 YAMAHA

Model	Engine	Displacement	Transmission
Route 66	Two-cylinder	249cc	Five-Speed
FZR400	Four-cylinder	399cc	Six-Speed
XV535 Virago (1988 Model)	Two-cylinder	535cc	Five-Speed
FZR600	Four-cylinder	598cc	Six-Speed
XY600 Radian	Four-cylinder	598cc	Six-Speed
XV750 Virago	Two-cylinder	748cc	Five-Speed
FZR1000	Four-cylinder	989cc	Five-Speed
XV1100 Virago	Two-cylinder	1063cc	Five-Speed
FJ1200	Four-cylinder	1188cc	Five-Speed
V-Max	Four-cylinder	1198cc	Five-Speed
XVZ1200TD Venture Royale	Four-cylinder	1198cc	Five-Speed

YAMAHA
1990

The 1990 model year would appear as a duplicate of 1989 with only prices and a few minor features were the alterations. No changes in the model listing were seen after a serious trimming of the model selection was applied the year before.

The 535 Virago for 1989 was actually the 1988 version, so for 1990 we got a slightly better copy that utilized some fresh features. The 1988 edition held only 2.2 gallons of fuel, and was somewhat limiting when it came time for rides of any length. The 1990 version had the usual tank joined by a second cell that held an extra 1.2 gallons in check, thus boosting the distance between stops. New emission regulations were met with the installation of Yamaha's air-induction system. Seating was also revised for both rider and passenger.

The Virago 750 saw only an increase in price of $200 and the 1100 gained $300 along with Metallic Black paint. Ivory was added to the roster for the Route 66, as was another $300 to the MSRP.

Without a single dime added to its price, the V-Max was back in Black and as mean as ever. The more mannerly FJ1200 would set its buyer back an extra $300 but again carried no changes from the previous year.

The upper class touring mount, the Venture Royale, saw a boost of $500, bringing the new total to $10,299 for 1990. For the trouble, a digitally controlled ignition was available and so were new color choices.

Sport bike fans were forced to ante up more money and the FZR600 increased by $500, the FZR1000 by $350 and the FZR400 cost $300 more to gain entry. Even the naked Radian would see an increase of $200, making its cost $3,699 without options.

1990 YAMAHA

Model	Engine	Displacement	Transmission
Route 66	Two-cylinder	249cc	Five-Speed
FZR400	Four-cylinder	399cc	Six-Speed
XV535 Virago	Two-cylinder	535cc	Five-Speed
FZR600	Four-cylinder	598cc	Six-Speed
XY600 Radian	Four-cylinder	598cc	Six-Speed
XV750 Virago	Two-cylinder	748cc	Five-Speed
FZR1000	Four-cylinder	989cc	Five-Speed
XV1100 Virago	Two-cylinder	1063cc	Five-Speed
FJ1200	Four-cylinder	1188cc	Five-Speed
V-Max	Four-cylinder	1198cc	Five-Speed
XVZ1200TD Venture Royale	Four-cylinder	1198 cc	Five-Speed

YAMAHA

1991

The 1991 model year for Yamaha would be a lean one with respect to the models that remained in the catalog. Every street machine under 600cc was now gone, and several within that displacement range were also pulled.

A unique feature on every street-legal 1991 Yamaha was the insurance that was included. All that was required to get the insurance was a driver's license and payment or financing for the bike. For a period of one year, Yamaha covered the insurance fee, eliminating one of the obstacles to buying a motorcycle. Maybe it was the limited scale of the 1991 catalog that made this feasible, but it was a different approach regardless of the reasoning.

Missing from the 1991 lineup were the Route 66, FZR400 and Virago 535. The Radian was also a no-show, leaving only seven models from the previous offering. About the only true change was the boost in displacement for the Venture Royale. It grew from 1198 to 1294cc but was still of the V-four configuration.

The FZR1000 remained a darling to the sport bike crowd as it continued to rack up victories on race tracks across the USA, and was just as potent when ridden on the streets.

1991 YAMAHA

Model	Engine	Displacement	Transmission
FZR600	Four-cylinder	598cc	Six-Speed
XV750 Virago	Two-cylinder	748cc	Five-Speed
FZR1000	Four-cylinder	989cc	Five-Speed
XV1100 Virago	Two-cylinder	1063cc	Five-Speed
FJ1200	Four-cylinder	1188cc	Five-Speed
V-Max	Four-cylinder	1198cc	Five-Speed
XVZ1300D Venture Royale (1300cc)	Four-cylinder	1294cc	Five-Speed

1992

The Yamaha camp had some new players for 1992, along with an option of ABS brakes on the FJ1200.

Making the scene for 1992 was the Seca II. By combining features from the previous Seca models and adding some modern tricks, the II was born. A 599cc inline-four engine was canted forward, placing more of the weight on the front wheel for enhancing handling. Fitted with Yamaha's own direct intake and downdraft carburetors, the Seca II drew breath more easily than other middleweight machines. A six-cog box provided ample ratios to keep the II in the sweet spot. Staunch 38mm front fork legs also helped keep the Seca II tracking true with compliant suspension to smooth out the bumps in the road. Slippery bodywork included a frame mounted, half-fairing that included a deflection flap on the windscreen to effectively steer the wind around and over the rider. A spacious and well-padded pillion provided plenty of room for the rider to move around a bit or to easily carry a passenger in style. Weighing 401 lbs. when it was dry, the fuel tank held 4.49 gallons of fuel. Your choice of Vivid Red Cocktail or Black was on the menu with dark silver alloy wheels on both.

Taking a cue from Europe, the TDM850 was introduced to handle all forms of sport riding, even that with no paved road. Powered by an 849cc parallel-twin engine, the TDM was liquid cooled and featured the Genesis 5-valve design. Torque at the bottom and middle of the scale was enormous, playing right into the hands of those who might take the TDM off road.

Three disc brakes were on hand to provide as much stopping power as was needed regardless of the riding conditions. A pair of round headlights peered out from the half-fairing that was bolted to the frame, and any color you wished was available, as long as it was Vivid Red Cocktail. At 439 lbs. when dry, the TDM850 also included 6.3 inches of ground clearance to take on the uneven terrain found off road.

For the first time ever, the FJ1200 was sold in two varieties, one of which included anti-lock brakes, also known as ABS. This system kept the wheels from locking under extreme braking, helping to control the big FJ's weight and size. The ABS system brought a new dimension of safety to riding and added 15 lbs. to the weight of the FJ. Sold in Marble Silver with blue and black accents the 1992 FJ1200 continued to be a favorite of the sport touring crowd. For the true touring fans, the Venture Royale was back and still offered an expansive array of comfort and convenience features.

The Virago could be had in your choice of 750cc or 1100cc, the former in Graceful Maroon, the latter in Blue. The V-Max was sold in a dark red but bore no other changes from the previous year.

The sporty FZR family kept both of its members who measured 600cc and 1000cc in size.

The Seca II was a brand-new model for 1992 and embodied what we loved about the first Secas, along with some modern technology.

Yamaha Motors

1992 YAMAHA

Model	Engine	Displacement	Transmission
FZR600R	Four-cylinder	599cc	Six-Speed
XJ600 Seca II (New for 1992)	Four-cylinder	599cc	Six-Speed
XV750 Virago	Two-cylinder	748cc	Five-Speed
TDM850	Two-cylinder	748cc	Five-Speed
FZR1000	Four-cylinder	989cc	Five-Speed
XV1100 Virago	Two-cylinder	1063cc	Five-Speed
FJ1200	Four-cylinder	1188cc	Five-Speed
FJ1200 ABS	Four-cylinder	1188cc	Five-Speed
V-Max	Four-cylinder	1198cc	Five-Speed
XVZ1300D Venture Royale (1300cc)	Four-cylinder	1294cc	Five-Speed

YAMAHA
1993

About the only news for the 1993 line was the introduction of the amazing and radical GTS1000R. With the sport touring market as their target, Yamaha created a machine like nothing the world had seen before. Of course it had two wheels and an engine, but replacing the front fork was a unique and unusual arrangement. Taking over where the fork tubes would normally be, a single leading arm held the front wheel in place and handled both suspension and steering duties. This futuristic approach also dealt with personal riding style by being fully adjustable for preload, compression and rebound. A large diameter, 330mm disc brake was bolted to the front rim and grabbed by a six-piston caliper. A second disc of 282mm was found on the rear wheel and was squeezed by a two-piston caliper. Both brakes were linked with ABS to maintain control under severe braking.

Powering the GTS1000R was an engine that began life as a 1000cc unit from the race proven FZR1000. Adding fuel injection and a catalytic converter in the exhaust made for quick starts and seamless power. The engine was cradled in an Omega shaped frame that gave the GTS a lower center of gravity and provided ample stability for the do-it-all front end. A full coverage fairing and hard saddlebags made the GTS comfortable at any speed and provided storage space for weekend getaways.

The entire package of style and technology weighed in at 553 lbs. dry and could hold 5.28 gallons of fuel in the tank. Yamaha left the remaining model line unchanged for 1993, save for altered hues and graphics. While some of the smaller variations would eventually be removed from the catalog, the RD350 would grow into bigger models that were transformed into race bikes with headlights by eager riders all around the world.

1993 YAMAHA

Model	Engine	Displacement	Transmission
FZR600R	Four-cylinder	599cc	Six-Speed
XJ600 Seca II	Four-cylinder	599cc	Six-Speed
XV750 Virago	Two-cylinder	748cc	Five-Speed
TDM850	Two-cylinder	748cc	Five-Speed
FZR1000	Four-cylinder	989cc	Five-Speed
GTS1000R (New for 1993)	Four-cylinder	1003cc	Five-Speed
XV1100 Virago	Two-cylinder	1063cc	Five-Speed
FJ1200	Four-cylinder	1188cc	Five-Speed
FJ1200 ABS (ABS Brakes)	Four-cylinder	1188cc	Five-Speed
V-Max	Four-cylinder	1198cc	Five-Speed
XVZ1300D Venture Royale	Four-cylinder	1294cc	Five-Speed

YAMAHA
1994

Taking their sport-bike game to the next threshold, Yamaha released the YZF-750R for 1994, unleashing their most powerful sport machine ever.

Yamaha Motors

After a quiet year in 1993, the 1994 Yamaha plan showed us some excitement beyond the GTS1000R.

In the sport bike division, an entirely new YZF750R made its presence known. Using their legendary Genesis five-valve design as a basis, the new engine was fed by a set of four 38mm Mikuni carbs that were helped by an electronic fuel pump. Held in a position that was almost vertical, the fuel and air mix had a straight shot into the waiting cylinders. The 11.5:1 compression was achieved by using racing slugs in the engine further aiding the creation of power. Keeping the whole blend cool was a large capacity radiator with two electronically activated fans that maintained a constant temperature regardless of the pace of the ride. Six cogs were installed in the gearbox completing the race ready package.

Rear suspension was in the form of a single shock, with a monocross design that suspended the swing arm with precision. A 17-inch tire and wheel had a 245mm drilled disc brake and two-puck caliper. Front forks were aluminum sliders and inverted.

Fully adjustable, they held another 17-inch wheel in check and with a pair of 320mm drilled rotors, halted by a six-piston caliper. Before

YAMAHA

adding the five gallons of fuel and fluids, the YZF750R tipped the scales at a paltry 428 lbs. Yellow wheels were offset by bodywork that was covered in a graphic display of blue, purple, white and yellow.

Yamaha didn't spend all of their attention on the YZF750R and spruced up the FZR1000 with a few tricks. A revised front fairing now held the same "cat eye" headlights used on the YZF for a more aggressive look. Further attention was focused on the front forks that were 41mm and inverted. More powerful front brakes were fitted with six-piston calipers and the engine was modified for better shifting and improved clutch function. Keeping all of this new technology out of a crook's hands was accomplished by incorporating a theft prevention system that used only an authorized key for operation.

The Seca II was still drawing rave reviews and the 1994 edition had an improved front fairing and a larger windscreen. Reddish Yellow Cocktail or Faraway Blue were the new colors. The V-Max was also delivered in an eye-popping Reddish Yellow Cocktail hue, drawing even more attention to the tire shredding power it possessed.

The Virago clan listed four variations for 1994 with two of those being versions of the 535. The 535 Special wore more chrome than the entry level 535 and sported a saddle that was tufted with deeply recessed buttons. A wide range of official Yamaha options could be bolted on to the Virago to make it more of a personal statement.

The GTS1000R broke enough rules when it made its debut and was left unchanged for 1994. Both versions of the FJ1200 and the Venture Royale were missing.

1994 YAMAHA

Model	Engine	Displacement	Transmission
XV535 Virago	Two-cylinder	535cc	Five-Speed
XV535 Virago SP (Low Cost Virago 535)	Two-cylinder	535cc	Five-Speed
FZR600R	Four-cylinder	599cc	Six-Speed
XJ600 Seca II	Four-cylinder	599cc	Six-Speed
XV750 Virago	Two-cylinder	748cc	Five-Speed
YZF750R (New for 1994)	Four-cylinder	749cc	Six-Speed
FZR1000	Four-cylinder	989cc	Five-Speed
GTS1000R	Four-cylinder	1003cc	Five-Speed
XV1100 Virago	Two-cylinder	1063cc	Five-Speed
V-Max	Four-cylinder	1198cc	Five-Speed

STANDARD CATALOG OF® JAPANESE MOTORCYCLES

YAMAHA
1995

The FZR-1000 was another 1995 Yamaha that was the same as the year before but wore new paint and graphics.
Yamaha Motors

Although a picture of the 1994 YZF750R was seen in the '95 catalog, it would not be offered for sale that model year. If a dealer had one lying around it could still be purchased but no upgraded version was seen.

Instead of the YZF750R, there was a brand new 1995 YZF600R in the lineup. It took Yamaha engineers 20 months to create a 599cc engine that out powered the rest of the field, then wrapped it in sleek race-inspired bodywork. A six-speed was included for greater flexibility and a 41mm Kayaba fork kept it on the straight and narrow, no matter how twisty the road got. On the MSRP was $6,999, making it $800 more than its sibling the FZR600R. The FZR600R returned but was only given new paint for 1995. Except for revised graphics and colors, the FZR1000 was also unchanged from its last version.

After being fitted with a sleeker fairing and taller windscreen for 1994, the Seca II would only get new graphics and paint for 1995. The all around motorcycle continued to garner positive feedback from the media despite the fact it had been little changed in four years.

YAMAHA

Offered as one of the two machines in Yamaha's 600cc class, the FZR-600 was a returning model with only new paint as a differentiator from the previous versions.

Yamaha Motors

Proving its worth by continuing to return with no changes, the V-Max rolled into the showrooms wearing Fire Red paint for 1995. The unique styling and forkless front end GTS1000R was no longer available. Its quirkiness failed to draw enough buyers.

After a four-year vacation, the VX250 Virago was back. The low saddle height of 27 inches, combined with a curb weight of only 301 lbs. made the Lilliputian Virago a great starter bike. The 249cc V-twin continued to impress and sold for only $3,699, a bargain considering the features and style it delivered at that price.

The dual listing for the 535 Virago was seen and both versions were stopped by using a revised front-disc brake that was squeezed by a twin-piston caliper. The big 1100 Virago had its foot pegs moved forward and set low with no other changes shown. The 750 variant was the same as before except for the new hues.

1995 YAMAHA

Model	Engine	Displacement	Transmission
XV250 Virago (New for 1995)	Two-cylinder	250cc	Five-Speed
XV535 Virago	Two-cylinder	535cc	Five-Speed
XV535 Virago SP (Low Cost Virago 535)	Two-cylinder	535cc	Five-Speed
FZR600R	Four-cylinder	599cc	Six-Speed
YZF600R (New for 1995)	Four-cylinder	599cc	Six-Speed
XJ600 Seca II	Four-cylinder	599cc	Six-Speed
XV750 Virago	Two-cylinder	748cc	Five-Speed
YZF750R (1994 model)	Four-cylinder	749cc	Six-Speed
FZR1000	Four-cylinder	989cc	Five-Speed
XV1100 Virago	Two-cylinder	1063cc	Five-Speed
V-Max	Four-cylinder	1198cc	Five-Speed

YAMAHA
1996

Almost every inch of the 1996 catalog was filled with returning models, as Yamaha felt comfortable with their blend of sport and cruiser models. Bolstering the cruiser segment was a new machine that was sold in two versions for the latest model year.

Both the Royal Star and Tour Classic edition carried 1294cc, V-4 engines in the frames. Fed by a bank of four, 28mm carburetors, the power was sent to five-speed gearboxes complete with overdrive. Final shaft drive kept things neat and quiet. With 82.5 lbs.-ft. of torque at 3500RPM, the pull of the new power train was undeniable. All of this power was dressed in two levels of cool.

With a powerful 79 cubic inch V-4 engine hung in the frame, the new Royal Star was dressed to fit the classic cruiser design.
Yamaha Motors

By adding the retro-style saddlebags, windshield and revised saddle to the Royal Star, Yamaha produced the Tour Classic. Yamaha Motors

At 408 lbs. dry, the YZF-600R proved to be a potent performer in the 600cc division and was capable of being ridden all day. Yamaha Motors

YAMAHA

The low saddle height and classic cruiser style of the Virago 250 made the model appealing to a wide variety of riders. Yamaha Motors

The Virago 750 still delivered on the promise of power and attitude and was complete with two-tone hues and cast wheels. Yamaha Motors

The base Royal Star featured heavily contoured fenders, cast wheels and three selections of paint to accent the heavily chromed theme. A comfortable saddle with individual passenger pillion provided hours of pain-free riding for one or two adults. A low saddle height of 28.5 inches put boots flat on the pavement and gave the Royal Star an easy to maneuver stance.

The Tour Classic took that same formula and blended in a pair of saddlebags, large windshield and a backrest for the passenger. A pair of two-tone color choices was on tap along with extra bits of chrome. The Tour Classic tipped the scales at 725 lbs. while the Royal Star was 673 lbs.

The sporty YZF750R was treated to a long list of minor refinements, all of which sharpened the focus of the already cutting edge performer.

Returning to the field was the race-proven YZR-750R. It was still worthy of the praise heaped upon it by both the motorcycle media and loyal riders.

Yamaha Motors

1996 YAMAHA

Model	Engine	Displacement	Transmission
XV250 Virago	Two-cylinder	250cc	Five-Speed
XV535 Virago	Two-cylinder	535cc	Five-Speed
XV535 Virago SP	Two-cylinder	535cc	Five-Speed
FZR600R	Four-cylinder	599cc	Six-Speed
YZF600R	Four-cylinder	599cc	Six-Speed
XJ600 Seca II	Four-cylinder	599cc	Six-Speed
XV750 Virago	Two-cylinder	748cc	Five-Speed
YZF750R	Four-cylinder	749cc	Six-Speed
FZR1000	Four-cylinder	989cc	Five-Speed
XV1100 Virago	Two-cylinder	1063cc	Five-Speed
V-Max	Four-cylinder	1198cc	Five-Speed
Royal Star (New for 1996)	Four-cylinder	1294cc	Five-Speed
Royal Star Tour Classic (New for 1996)	Four cylinder	1294cc	Five-Speed

YAMAHA
1997

One of the many versions of the Yamaha Royal Star used these Western-style saddlebags to create an entirely new feeling for the massive cruiser.

The 1997 team for Yamaha was again mostly a repeat of 1996, but saw changes throughout with a few new members seated on the bench. Both versions of the 535 Virago claimed new paint with all black on the standard and a two-tone black and silver on the SP. The larger 1100 was also seen in two editions with the SP being the new version. The 1100 SP had black paint accented by a chrome headlight eyebrow, three-dimensional tank badges and chrome covers over the rear shocks.

After a quick sellout in 1996, the 1997 version of the V-Max was released early. Except for the altered release date and two-tone black and silver paint the '97 was a copy of the '96.

The sport bike class found an improved YZF1000R filling the seat left vacant by the departed FZR1000. The latest liter capacity Yamaha lost none of the usefulness of the previous version while providing higher levels of sport bike tact and handling.

A more responsive engine held forged slugs and a lighter crank along with 38mm Mikuni carbs, feeding the energy through a five-cog gearbox. Weighing in at 437 lbs. dry, the new YZF1000R delivered potent power and was finished in choices of red with white or black and silver. This Yamaha was priced at $9,799.

YAMAHA

STANDARD CATALOG OF ® JAPANESE Motorcycles

ONE RIDE AND YOU'LL DISCOVER
ITS DISTINCT CRUISING SPIRIT.

Yamaha offered potential buyers a demonstration ride in this magazine ad.

Yamaha Motors

Having been refined for the previous model year the YZF750R was unchanged for 1997 and sold for $1,000 less than the 1000. The YZF600R and FZR600 were also duplicates of their former selves with only new colors and graphics being added.

After their triumphant debut for 1996, the Royal Star line was untouched, but did find self-canceling turn-signals being added to their long list of standard features.

1997 YAMAHA

Model	Engine	Displacement	Transmission
XV250 Virago	Two-cylinder	250cc	Five-Speed
XV535 Virago	Two-cylinder	535cc	Five-Speed
XV535 Virago SP	Two-cylinder	535cc	Five-Speed
FZR600	Four-cylinder	599cc	Six-Speed
YZF600R	Four-cylinder	599cc	Six-Speed
XJ600 Seca II	Four-cylinder	599cc	Six-Speed
XV750 Virago	Two-cylinder	748cc	Five-Speed
YZF750R	Four-cylinder	749cc	Six-Speed
YZF1000R (New for 1997)	Four-cylinder	989cc	Five-Speed
XV1100 Virago	Two-cylinder	1063cc	Five-Speed
XV1100 SP Virago (New for 1997)	Two-cylinder	1063cc	Five-Speed
V-Max	Four-cylinder	1198cc	Five-Speed
Royal Star	Four-cylinder	1294cc	Five-Speed
Royal Star Tour Classic	Four-cylinder	1294cc	Five-Speed

YAMAHA
1998

> ONE RIDE AND YOU'LL DISCOVER ITS DISTINCT CRUISING SPIRIT.

1-888-Demo-Ride
TOLL FREE

Every Royal Star features a 5-Year Unlimited Mileage Warranty and a 5-year Road Star™ Service Membership

YAMAHA

Two new entries in the captain's log for 1998 grabbed all the headlines as the rest of the Yamaha crew stayed on board.

The Royal Star models had made an immediate impression on the cruiser market and on those who bought and rode them. As impressive as the Royal Star was, there were some who were put off by its shear size, heft and cost. To meet with the demands of those who wanted it all for less, the V-Star was created.

By installing a V-twin engine of only 649cc into the frame of the V-Star, all of the issues of the bigger Royal Star were addressed. While it powered by a much smaller engine, the V-Star lacked nothing in its appearance. At more than 60 inches in length, the V-Star was not a mini-bike by any means.

Aiding in its appearance was the 35-degree rake of the front forks, and rear suspension that

The beautiful Royal Star by Yamaha was ready and waiting for riders according to this 1998 ad.
Yamaha Motors

The rakish profile of the 1998 Yamaha YZF-R1 was evident in this magazine ad. Yamaha Motors

367

YAMAHA

STANDARD CATALOG OF JAPANESE Motorcycles

The Yamaha Royal Star was available in the Boulevard edition during the 1998 model year.
Yamaha Motors

The elegant lines of the Yamaha V-Star Custom were displayed in 1998.
Yamaha Motors

was hidden from view. Sculpted fenders, both front and rear, added a degree of couture to the downsized cruiser. A five-speed box and shaft drive made things convenient and quiet. A set of chrome plated, staggered exhaust mufflers added to the low slung look of the V-Star and kept the noise within limits. By using the engine from the 535 Virago as their platform, the cost of developing the V-Star was kept low and the savings were passed along to the buyer.

Upping the ante in the sport bike arena, Yamaha replaced their already amazing YZF1000R with the all-new YZF R1. Buy putting 998cc of power into a motorcycle that was only a shade larger than their 600cc entries, the R1 was an impressive package. A dry weight of only 390 lbs. was another factor that played into the handling and speed of this new class-leading model. A six-speed box was included to ensure the proper gear ratio was always on call, no matter what your riding style demanded.

1998 YAMAHA

Model	Engine	Displacement	Transmission
XV250 Virago	Two-cylinder	250cc	Five-Speed
XV535 Virago	Two-cylinder	535cc	Five-Speed
XV535 Virago SP	Two-cylinder	535cc	Five-Speed
FZR600	Four-cylinder	599cc	Six-Speed
YZF600R	Four-cylinder	599cc	Six-Speed
XJ600 Seca II	Four-cylinder	599cc	Six-Speed
V-Star (New for 1998)	Two-cylinder	649cc	Five-Speed
XV750 Virago	Two-cylinder	748cc	Five-Speed
YZF750R	Four-cylinder	749cc	Six-Speed
YZF1000R1 (New for 1998)	Four-cylinder	989cc	Six-Speed
XV1100 Virago	Two-cylinder	1063cc	Five-Speed
XV1100 SP Virago	Two-cylinder	1063cc	Five-Speed
V-Max	Four-cylinder	1198cc	Five-Speed
Royal Star	Four-cylinder	1294cc	Five-Speed
Royal Star Tour Classic	Four-cylinder	1294cc	Five-Speed

YAMAHA
1999

For 1999, Yamaha brought back the Venture name and applied it to their flagship touring machine, complete with V-4 power and plenty of class.

Yamaha Motors

The quiet years that preceded 1999 were over, and Yamaha unleashed a bevy of new hardware in the cruiser and sport bike categories. Gone for 1999 were the SP versions of the Virago 535 and 1100 Viragos. The same trio of options in the standard issue range remained, and other models joined the expanding Yamaha cruiser listing.

A new version of the 1998 V-Star was the V-Star Custom. Using the same 649cc engine as the now named V-Star Classic, the Custom wore a trimmer fender over a taller front wheel and a duck tail unit over the rear donut. The 25.6-inch saddle height was listed as the lowest in its class, and made the V-Star Custom feel lighter than it was.

Taking the Star listing to the next step was the all-new V-Star 1100. Designing a brand new, 1063cc V-twin for use in the bigger V-Star was the first step. Bolting it into a tubular frame and hanging shapely fuel tank and fenders completed the picture. A five-speed box sent the selected gear to the rear wheel via shaft drive. This Yamaha edition had a low saddle height of only 27.5 inches off the tarmac.

Royal Star listings grew to three with the addition of the Boulevard and Tour Deluxe models. The Boulevard wore a small windscreen along with the full coverage fenders and cast wheels. The same V-4 engine throbbed in the frame as the year before.

The Royal Star Tour Deluxe was fully equipped with hard-sided saddlebags that matched the bike's primary hue, a backrest for the passenger and a large clear windshield to block the rider from the elements. Whitewall tires and a four-into-two exhaust, finished in chrome topped off the unique features to the new Tour Deluxe.

The Venture name was pulled off the shelf and

A 79-cid V-4 engine was surrounded by all the stylish sheet metal one could handle. There was plenty of touring gear on the Royal Star Tour Deluxe model.

Yamaha Motors

YAMAHA

Finished in Forest Green and Titanium Gray, the Silverado was a tasteful and powerful way to enter the cruising scene.

Yamaha Motors

dusted off for 1999 and applied to a completely different machine than it had last been used on. The new Venture was powered by a 1294cc V-4 engine that was mounted in a class leading 67.1-inch wheelbase. Rider and passenger had floor boards for their boots and the rider was shielded from the wind by a handlebar mounted fairing that extended across the front of the forks.

Hard-sided saddlebags were joined by a rear mounted travel trunk, boosting storage capacity to almost 130 liters. The audio system sent the sound through a set of four speakers mounted in the front and back to satisfy rider and passenger alike.

The final new entries in the '99 cruiser range were the Road Star and Road Star Silverado. In this writer's opinion, the Road Star was as close to mimicking Harley's Fat-Boy as Yamaha could get. A big 1602cc V-twin engine, complete with exposed pushrod tubes, pounded away in the frame, and sleek fenders adorned both tires.

Although the Road Star lacked the solid aluminum wheels of its Milwaukee counterpart, the design theme was clearly an attempt to make one of their own. A pair of shotgun exhaust mufflers took the departing fumes away and a two-level saddle made a comfortable perch for rider and passenger. Wire wheels and whitewall tires completed the package. The Silverado trim included studded seats and matching saddlebags, a backrest for the passenger and a large windscreen mounted to the bars.

The sport bike regime lost its favorite Seca II but gained a reduced sized version of their 1998 released R1 in the YZF-R6. By melding 120 hp and a 370-lb. dry weight into a compact layout, Yamaha produced the all-new R6. The 599cc engine was fed by four 37mm carbs and exhaled through a four-into-one exhaust.

Ram-Air induction and a 15,500 rpm redline made the R6 a real screamer on the track, or around town when the gendarmes weren't looking. All of this mechanical fun was wrapped in wind cheating bodywork that looked a lot like that used on the R1, making them hard to distinguish from one another.

1999 YAMAHA

Model	Engine	Displacement	Transmission
XV250 Virago	Two-cylinder	250cc	Five-Speed
XV535 Virago	Two-cylinder	535cc	Five-Speed
XV535 Virago SP	Two-cylinder	535cc	Five-Speed
FZR600	Four-cylinder	599cc	Six-Speed
YZF600R	Four-cylinder	599cc	Six-Speed
Y2F-R6 (New for 1999)	Four-cylinder	599cc	Six-Speed
V-Star Classic	Two-cylinder	649cc	Five-Speed
V-Star Custom (New for 1999)	Two-cylinder	649cc	Five-Speed
XV750 Virago	Two-cylinder	748cc	Five-Speed
YZF1000R1	Four-cylinder	989cc	Six-Speed
XJ1100 Virago	Two-cylinder	1063cc	Five-Speed
V-Star 1100 (New for 1999)	Two-cylinder	1063cc	Five-Speed
V-Max	Four-cylinder	1198cc	Five-Speed
Royal Star Boulevard (New for 1999)	Four-cylinder	1294cc	Five-Speed
Royal Star Tour Classic	Four-cylinder	1294cc	Five-Speed
Royal Star Tour Deluxe (New for 1999)	Four-cylinder	1294cc	Five-Speed
Venture	Four-cylinder	1294cc	Five-Speed
Road Star	Two-cylinder	1602cc	Five-Speed
Road Star Silverado	Two-cylinder	1602cc	Five-Speed

STANDARD CATALOG OF ® JAPANESE MOTORCYCLES

YAMAHA
2000

After a blockbuster year of new models in 1999, 2000 would see mostly reductions in the catalog, along with two special Millennium Edition cruisers that were sold for 2000 only.

The long lives of the Virago 750 and 1100 came to an end as the new Yamaha Star models took control. Last year's V-Star 1100 was back in two forms for 2000. A Classic and Custom were seen, both wearing different duds but powered by the same 1063cc V-twin engine. As expected, the Custom sported trimmer fenders at both ends, along with a taller front wheel, while the Classic bore full coverage tin on the wheels and wider tires at each axle.

Commemorating the new millennium, Yamaha presented several of their Star motorcycles in a limited-edition color and equipment package. Yamaha Motors

The Yamaha V-Star 1100 Classic and V-Star Classic were together in this 2000 ad. Yamaha Motors

371

YAMAHA

STANDARD CATALOG OF JAPANESE MOTORCYCLES

By throwing in whitewall tires, a studded seat, saddlebags and a clear windscreen, the Road Star Silverado was born.

Yamaha Motors

The middle-of-the-road Royal Star was the Tour Classic that was equipped with saddlebags, an enhanced pillion and a protective windscreen.

Yamaha Motors

Several Royal Star models were also sold in 2000 with the Boulevard being the starting point of the progression.

Yamaha Motors

For the rider who wanted something a little less costly than the bigger Road Star and Royal Star, the V-Star 1100 was sold in two trim levels.

Yamaha Motors

The Millennium Edition of the Venture was mechanically the same as the standard issue version but was finished in Radiant Pearl and White paint with handsome tan trim on the saddle, backrest and tank strap. Further separating the Millennium edition from the rest were the "MM Limited" badges found on the saddlebag hinges and brass serial number badges on the trunk and ignition key.

A similar treatment was seen on the Road Star MM Limited edition, including the unique paint, badging and studded seat.

Only three bikes were left in the Yamaha sport bike corral in the YZF600R, YZF-R6 and the potent YZF-R1. After only two years, the R1 was highly modified to improve its already amazing performance. More than 150 components were upgraded, and the changes affected the engine, suspension, brakes and gearbox along with the bodywork, lighting and saddle. It seemed like the R1 was already a leading machine in its class, but to stay at the top of the game, constant changes were required.

2000 YAMAHA

Model	Engine	Displacement	Transmission
XV250 Virago	Two-cylinder	250cc	Five-Speed
XV535 Virago	Two-cylinder	535cc	Five-Speed
YZF600R	Four-cylinder	599cc	Six-Speed
Y2F-R6	Four-cylinder	599cc	Six-Speed
V-Star Classic	Two-cylinder	649cc	Five-Speed
V-Star Custom	Two-cylinder	649cc	Five-Speed
YZF-R1	Four-cylinder	989cc	Six-Speed
V-Star 1100 Classic	Two-cylinder	1063cc	Five-Speed
V-Star 1100 Custom	Two-cylinder	1063cc	Five-Speed
V-Max	Four-cylinder	1198cc	Five-Speed
Royal Star Boulevard	Four-cylinder	1294cc	Five-Speed
Royal Star Tour Classic	Four-cylinder	1294cc	Five-Speed
Royal Star Tour Deluxe	Four-cylinder	1294cc	Five-Speed
Venture	Four-cylinder	1294cc	Five-Speed
Venture MM Limited Millennium Edition	Four-cylinder	1294cc	Five-Speed
Road Star	Two-cylinder	1602cc	Five-Speed
Road Star MM Limited Millennium Edition	Two-cylinder	1602cc	Five-Speed
Road Star Silverado	Two-cylinder	1602cc	Five-Speed

YAMAHA
2001

The Yamaha V-Star motorcycles were on display in this 2001 magazine ad.

Yamaha Motors

Radical changes in the 2001 lineup were few and far between with most of the same machines returning for a fresh year.

Joining the three carry-over sport bikes was the new semi-naked FZ1. The FZ1 ran with a slightly detuned R1 engine in its frame and featured a far more comfortable seating posture. Still a sport bike at heart, the FZ1 included adjustable suspension at both ends and a racy little handlebar-mounted fairing. A heavier, less exotic frame than on the R1 boosted the weight of the FZ1 to 455 lbs. or 70 lbs. more than the razor's edge R1. The FZ1 delivered on its promise to offer comfort and terrific performance to the rider who wanted both in his street machine.

The Midnight Star edition of the Road Star

The 2001 Road Star series offered a classic look combined with 21st century technology.

Yamaha Motors

featured a blacked-out engine with highlights on the cooling fins, a bright front fork and exhaust and black paint throughout. At first glance, whatever wasn't black was chrome, and that's just how the cruiser market liked it.

An all new saddle and backrest adorned the big Venture, adding more comfort to an already well-padded perch. Your choice of two-tone paint was also seen for 2001: Cherry and Bordeaux Red or Stardust Silver with Forest Green. Changes to the rest of the legion were in the offered colors, leaving the nuts and bolts as they were.

2001 YAMAHA

Model	Engine	Displacement	Transmission
XV250 Virago	Two-cylinder	250cc	Five-Speed
XV535 Virago	Two-cylinder	535cc	Five-Speed
YZF600R	Four-cylinder	599cc	Six-Speed
Y2F-R6	Four-cylinder	599cc	Six-Speed
V-Star Classic	Two-cylinder	649cc	Five-Speed
V-Star Custom	Two-cylinder	649cc	Five-Speed
FZ1 (New for 2001)	Four-cylinder	998cc	Six-Speed
YZF-R1	Four-cylinder	989cc	Six-Speed
V-Star 1100 Classic	Two-cylinder	1063cc	Five-Speed
V-Star 1100 Custom	Two-cylinder	1063cc	Five-Speed
V-Max	Four-cylinder	1198cc	Five-Speed
Royal Star Boulevard	Four-cylinder	1294cc	Five-Speed
Royal Star Tour Classic	Four-cylinder	1294cc	Five-Speed
Royal Star Tour Deluxe	Four-cylinder	1294cc	Five-Speed
Venture	Four-cylinder	1294cc	Five-Speed
Road Star	Two-cylinder	1602cc	Five-Speed
Road Star Midnight Star (New for 2001)	Two-cylinder	1602cc	Five-Speed
Road Star Silverado	Two-cylinder	1602cc	Five-Speed

YAMAHA

STANDARD CATALOG OF JAPANESE MOTORCYCLES

Power to burn.

THE ALL-NEW ROAD STAR WARRIOR.

Hungry for power? Good, 'cause we've got just the thing to hit the spot. Start with the world's biggest production pushrod air-cooled V Twin ever - 102 cubic inches of pure, unadulterated muscle. Add one aluminum frame with YZF-R1-derived suspension. Wrap it in incomparably stunning Star fit and finish. Throw in an all-new electronic fuel injection with 40mm twin cross-bore throttle bodies and ultra-light pistons. Rev briskly and serve. The all-new Road Star Warrior.

Special thanks to Mike Alderson, Tom Brashier, Roger Cicconi, Brian Coughlin, Gary Engles, Jay Melton, Kurt Switters, Dale Tait and all the Yamaha owners and STAR members who helped in the making of this ad. Shot on location at Star Days 2001, Bowling Green, Kentucky.

Dress properly for your ride with a helmet, eye protection, long-sleeved shirt, long pants, gloves and boots. Yamaha and the Motorcycle Safety Foundation encourage you to ride safely and respect the environment. For more information regarding the MSF rider course, call 1-800-446-9227. Do not drink and ride. It is illegal and dangerous. © 2002 Yamaha Motor Corporation, U.S.A. Cypress, CA 90630. Professional rider depicted on a closed course. Do not attempt. • For the Yamaha dealer nearest you call: 1-800-88-YAMAHA. • yamaha-motor.com

YAMAHA

The 2002 Yamaha Road Star Warrior exuded power. And it was real—not just an advertising image.

YAMAHA 2002

Model year 2002 would prove to be another quiet year for Yamaha shoppers, but changes to the R1 and a few new models in the cruiser clan would add some spice to an otherwise timid period. The 535 Virago was no longer sold, nor were the Royal Star models. Considering the popularity of the V-Star 1100, the Royal Stars were just a bit too close to being redundant and thus were removed. Even with nearly 150 changes applied to the 2001 R1, it was not enough to keep the machine on the cutting edge, so for 2002, additional tweaks were made to the chassis, steering and fuel injection system. Revised panels on the fairing and altered gauges were also found on the latest edition of the race ready R1. Pricing on the 2002 version was seen as $10,299.

Both the 650 and 1100 versions of the V-Star found another sibling in their crib for 2002. The Silverado package had been an oft-selected choice in the Road Star division, so the same cosmetic treatment was applied to the smaller V-Star machines.

The addition of the adjustable windscreen, leather saddlebags and passenger backrest made the V-Stars even more appealing for those seeking a lower cost entry into the cruiser world. The V-Star Silverado carried a tag of $6,899 and the larger 1100 was set at $9,299.

With the exception of a single year's hiatus, the V-Max had been in the Yamaha yearbook since 1985. Its position as a muscle bike was always a solo spot, but that was to change as the Road Star Warrior was sent into battle.

By joining forces of the brute power of the 1670cc V-twin and chassis bits from the R1, a new class of bike was born. The Warrior not only sounded aggressive, its style and hunkered down stance told the world of its intentions at a single glance.

Beefy inverted forks and a trio of drilled disc brakes were not commonly seen on an cruiser, but the Warrior had them all and more. Each cylinder had its own chrome exhaust tube that then merged into a single pipe, finished off with a massive canister at the end. The entire system snaked upwards, increasing ground clearance during hard cornering, another facet not usually addressed in a cruiser. At $11,999 it wasn't the cheapest model in the case, but by no means the most expensive.

2002 YAMAHA

Model	Engine	Displacement	Transmission
XV250 Virago	Two-cylinder	250cc	Five-Speed
YZF600R	Four-cylinder	599cc	Six-Speed
YZF-R6	Four-cylinder	599cc	Six-Speed
V-Star Classic	Two-cylinder	649cc	Five-Speed
V-Star Custom	Two-cylinder	649cc	Five-Speed
V-Star Silverado (New for 2002)	Two-cylinder	649cc	Five-Speed
FZ1	Four-cylinder	998cc	Six-Speed
YZF-R1 (Revised for 2002)	Four-cylinder	989cc	Six-Speed
V-Star 1100 Classic	Two-cylinder	1063cc	Five-Speed
V-Star 1100 Custom	Two-cylinder	1063cc	Five-Speed
V-Star 1100 Silverado (New for 2002)	Two-cylinder	1063cc	Five-Speed
V-Max	Four-cylinder	1198cc	Five-Speed
Venture	Four-cylinder	1294cc	Five-Speed
Road Star	Two-cylinder	1602cc	Five-Speed
Road Star Midnight Star	Two-cylinder	1602cc	Five-Speed
Road Star Silverado	Two-cylinder	1602cc	Five-Speed
Road Star Warrior (New for 2002)	Two-cylinder	1670cc	Five-Speed

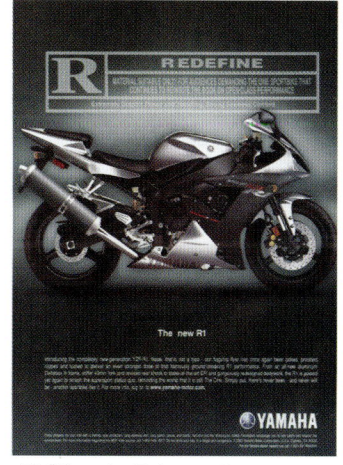

The Yamaha R-1 was all new and very modern looking as it was presented to prospective buyers in 2002.

YAMAHA
2003

Only a single new entry was seen for 2003, while another version of the jam-packed Venture also joined the fray for Yamaha.

The sport touring rider had been denied access to anything from Yamaha since the death of the FJ1200. It had proven itself to be a worthy machine on both long and short jaunts, regardless of the speed demanded. Stepping in try to fill its shoes was the new FJR1300 for 2003. A 1298cc, inline-four engine was hung in the frame and fed the horsepower to the rear wheel via shaft drive. The FJR1300 was released early for 2003 due to the excitement generated by the word of its coming. Ensconced in slippery, yet angular bodywork, no one would mistake the FJR for the FJ it replaced. At 571 lbs. dry and an MSRP of $11,499, the FJR1300 made a terrific buy for a rider and his passenger to eat up huge miles at speed and in total comfort.

The other mount in Yamaha's barn that was capable of devouring pavement in great gobs was the Venture. It was one of the most comfortable full-sized bikes on the market and was mechanically unaltered for 2003. For the long distance rider with a darker side, the Midnight Venture was right up his darkened alley. Finished in large expanses of black, and trimmed with a studded saddle and backrest, only a smattering of chrome was used. The Midnight Venture also carried a tag that was $500 higher than the base Venture, but for those who desired a more sinister touring bike, it was alone in its class.

The Warrior had made its debut for 2002 and was back for another set in 2003. As an option, you could spend an extra $100 and get your evil Warrior finished in black with a factory flame job of blue. Nothing says "hot rod" like flames, and the Warrior stayed on as one of Yamaha's two hot rod bikes.

The V-Star 1100 Classic was still one of three variations in that range, and cast wheels could supplant the factory wires for an added $400 in 2003. The Silverado and Custom were the other options for the 1100, and the 650 was also sold in all three flavors.

2003 YAMAHA

Model	Engine	Displacement	Transmission
XV250 Virago	Two-cylinder	250cc	Five-Speed
YZF600R	Four-cylinder	599cc	Six-Speed
Y2F-R6	Four-cylinder	599cc	Six-Speed
V-Star Classic	Two-cylinder	649cc	Five-Speed
V-Star Custom	Two-cylinder	649cc	Five-Speed
V-Star Silverado	Two-cylinder	649cc	Five-Speed
FZ1	Four-cylinder	998cc	Six-Speed
YZF-R1	Four-cylinder	989cc	Six-Speed
V-Star 1100 Classic	Two-cylinder	1063cc	Five-Speed
V-Star 1100 Custom	Two-cylinder	1063cc	Five-Speed
V-Star 1100 Silverado	Two-cylinder	1063cc	Five-Speed
V-Max	Four-cylinder	1198cc	Five-Speed
Venture	Four-cylinder	1294cc	Five-Speed
Midnight Venture (New for 2003)	Four-cylinder	1294cc	Five-Speed
FJR1300 (New for 2003)	Four-cylinder	1298cc	Five-Speed
Road Star	Two-cylinder	1602cc	Five-Speed
Road Star Silverado	Two-cylinder	1602cc	Five-Speed
Road Star Warrior	Two-cylinder	1670cc	Five-Speed

YAMAHA 2004

Midnight madness had gripped Yamaha, and for 2004 there was a Road Star Silverado Midnight in the offing. By joining the black and chrome motif with the Silverado's long list of accoutrements, the resulting machine was both dark and accommodating.

The Warrior was offered in solid Indigo or Cerulean Silver with flames. A revised saddle provided more comfort and the foot peg location and handlebars were altered for a more ergonomic posture for the rider.

The Road Star gang all received the bigger 1670cc engine that the Warrior used along with numerous improvements to the valve train for enhanced power and durability. The saddle now carried more width and interior padding and the floorboards floated in their mounts for an added measure of comfort for your feet and derriere.

Weight was reduced by installing new nine-spoke cast wheels and a drive pulley that matched. An LED taillight was brighter and more modern and the face of the speedometer was designed to be more retro than the one it replaced.

Major revisions had been made to the R1 in both years leading up to 2004, but for 2004 it was all new again. The new motor still displaced 998cc, but produced more horsepower, making the R1 the king of the power-to-weight ratio wars.

Weight was lowered by adding an under seat

Turning their attention to the sport bike crowd, the YZF-R1 was a cutting-edge machine that showed its dominant side both on and off the track.

Yamaha Motors

YAMAHA

Still considered the flagship of the fleet, the Royal Star Venture was an opulent touring mount that also carried a high level of panache for its riders.

Yamaha Motors

exhaust that was crafted of titanium. The proven Delta box chassis was also retooled for added stiffness with fewer ounces. Even the five-spoke wheels were revised to drop some weight, bringing the new total to a staggering 379 lbs. when dry.

The FZ1 had been an immediate hit with buyers, but some still dreamed of a smaller naked sport bike. Responding to their demands, the FZ6 made its debut for 2004. Like the FZ1 design that used a detuned motor from the R1, the FZ6 took its power from an R6 mill. The revised engine was suspended from an alloy cradle and was put to use as a stressed member of the rigid platform. The under seat exhaust design was borrowed from the R1 adding some extra "sport" to the equation. At 423 lbs. dry, the FZ6 delivered a nimble, yet powerful motorcycle to the middleweight class and received a stylish bar-mounted fairing to boot.

Yamaha did its best to appeal to every faction of the riding community and the Virago 250 was a great fit for the beginning rider or one who liked smaller cycles.

Yamaha Motors

2004 YAMAHA

Model	Engine	Displacement	Transmission
XV250 Virago	Two-cylinder	250cc	Five-Speed
YZF600R	Four-cylinder	599cc	Six-Speed
Y2F-R6	Four-cylinder	599cc	Six-Speed
FZ6 (New for 2004)	Four-cylinder	600cc	Six-Speed
V-Star Classic	Two-cylinder	649cc	Five-Speed
V-Star Custom	Two-cylinder	649cc	Five-Speed
V-Star Silverado	Two-cylinder	649cc	Five-Speed
FZ1	Four-cylinder	998cc	Six-Speed
YZF-R1	Four-cylinder	989cc	Six-Speed
V-Star 1100 Classic	Two-cylinder	1063cc	Five-Speed
V-Star 1100 Custom	Two-cylinder	1063cc	Five-Speed
V-Star 1100 Silverado	Two-cylinder	1063cc	Five-Speed
V-Max	Four-cylinder	1198cc	Five-Speed
Venture	Four-cylinder	1294cc	Five-Speed
Midnight Venture	Four-cylinder	1294cc	Five-Speed
FJR1300	Four-cylinder	1298cc	Five-Speed
Road Star	Two-cylinder	1602cc	Five-Speed
Road Star Midnight	Two-cylinder	1602cc	Five-Speed
Road Star Silverado	Two-cylinder	1602cc	Five-Speed
Road Star Midnight Silverado (New for 2004)	Two-cylinder	1602cc	Five-Speed
Road Star Warrior	Two-cylinder	1670cc	Five-Speed

STANDARD CATALOG OF ® JAPANESE Motorcycles

YAMAHA

2005

Feel free to dress it, or undress it, as you see fit.
The all-new Royal Star Tour Deluxe.

The Star series from Yamaha offered the type of motorcycles that brought out the dreamer in many owners.
Yamaha Motors

The R1 was lavished with new bits and praise in the last three years of production while the equally sporty R6 was left untouched. This fact would change for 2005 as the middleweight was revamped to be better than before. Beefier 43mm inverted forks led the way, as did thinner brake rotors that shaved ounces off the new curb weight. The chassis on the 2005 R6 has also been enhanced to provide more stiffness without any weight gain.

Alterations to the power plant resulted in three additional ponies being forced into the corral, putting the total at 108 at the rear wheel. Considering the Honda CBX of 1979 delivered 105 at the crank from a 1079cc six cylinder engine, you can see how far we've come in the world of sport bike design.

Cosmetics for the latest R6 include the optional all-black paint scheme that features red pinstripes on the equally black wheels to break up the monochrome theme.

The balance of the Yamaha lineup was mostly unchanged with a few subtle upgrades being found throughout the line.

The R6 offered a new generation of Yamaha motorcycle that was offered to the public for the first time during the 2005 model year.

2005 YAMAHA

Model	Engine	Displacement	Transmission
XV250 Virago	Two-cylinder	250cc	Five-Speed
YZF600R	Four-cylinder	599cc	Six-Speed
Y2F-R6	Four-cylinder	599cc	Six-Speed
FZ6	Four-cylinder	600cc	Six-Speed
V-Star Classic	Two-cylinder	649cc	Five-Speed
V-Star Custom	Two cylinder	649cc	Five-Speed
V-Star Silverado	Two-cylinder	649cc	Five-Speed
FZ1	Four-cylinder	998cc	Six-Speed
YZF-R1	Four-cylinder	989cc	Six-Speed
V-Star 1100 Classic	Two-cylinder	1063cc	Five-Speed
V-Star 1100 Custom	Two-cylinder	1063cc	Five-Speed
V-Star 1100 Silverado	Two-cylinder	1063cc	Five-Speed
V-Max	Four-cylinder	1198cc	Five-Speed
Venture	Four-cylinder	1294cc	Five-Speed
Midnight Venture	Four-cylinder	1294cc	Five-Speed
FJR1300	Four-cylinder	1298cc	Five-Speed
Road Star	Two-cylinder	1602cc	Five-Speed
Road Star Midnight	Two-cylinder	1602cc	Five-Speed
Road Star Silverado	Two-cylinder	1602cc	Five-Speed
Road Star Midnight Silverado	Two-cylinder	1602cc	Five-Speed
Road Star Warrior	Two-cylinder	1670cc	Five-Speed

STANDARD CATALOG OF *JAPANESE* MOTORCYCLES   YAMAHA

2006

The 2006 model year would be far more exciting, as far as new Yamaha's showing up would go, and new versions of some returning faces added some extra spice to the punch.

Taking their cruiser formula to the extreme, Yamaha introduced two machines powered by 1854cc V-twin engines and heaped with fresh style and features.

The Roadliner was offered in three trim packages: Roadliner, Roadliner S and Midnight Roadliner. All three were built around the same stump-pulling 1854cc, fuel injected V-twin engine but wore a different wardrobe. The Roadliner S added gobs of chrome and polished wheels while the Midnight edition sported Raven paint to offset the shiny parts. A five-speed tranny sent power to the rear wheel via belt drive and the frame and swing arm were created in aluminum to save weight. Despite these efforts to shave ounces, the Roadliner still rolled in at 705 lbs. before adding fuel and fluids.

The Stratoliner took the running gear and style of the Roadliner and added some necessary touring gear for long days on the road. An easy to detach windshield gave the rider respite from the weather when needed.

The big bruiser V-Max rolled on for another year but in 2006 it featured pinstriped wheels and a more sinister, blacked-out appearance.

Yamaha Motors

Taking their cruiser family to the next level, Yamaha introduced the Road Liner group. It offered a high degree of style with awesome performance.

Yamaha Motors

383

Almost a member of the naked-bike category, the FZ-1 was powered by a detuned R1 engine and provided the rider with a more comfortable posture for street riding.

Yamaha Motors

A pair of removable saddlebags were available to carry the rider's swag. A passenger backrest was also easy to install or remove, depending on your needs. The S also added more chrome and polished rims while the Midnight was finished in black as the name suggests. The Stratoliner was the second costliest cruiser in the Yamaha field for 2005 carrying an MSRP of $15,180. The only one more expensive was the tour de force Venture with a tag of $16,799.

Taking over where the legendary FJ-1200 left off, the FJR-1300 was a much sportier way to tour the country or simply blast around town. Yamaha Motors

Not everything new and shiny was for the cruiser fan as the YZF-R6S made its debut. Still bristling with sporting attitude, it lacked the cutting edge performance and riding posture of its sibling the R6. Less costly at $8,199, the R6S weighed a tad more and didn't carry quite the punch of the R6 but was still a highly capable 600cc machine complete with six-speed gearbox and wind-cheating fairing.

The R1 was sold in a Limited Edition livery that was destined for track use right out of the box. It still carried all required lighting for street legal use, but the suspension and wheels were revised for optimum performance. Ohlins front forks were designed in conjunction with the company engineers to provide sure-footed handling regardless of the road conditions.

Ultra light Marchesini wheels also played a role in the handling as they shaved weight off of the running gear. Special badges and additional gold colored components throughout contrasted nicely with the black and yellow 50th anniversary paint of the LE. The standard issue R1 was also given some added attention for 2006, resulting in a heart stopping 180 hp figure and under seat exhaust.

Wrapping up the new model listing for 2006 is the FJR1300RE. Not only does the RE use the same linked braking as on the R, but features an electric shifter that eliminates the need for a traditional clutch, by flipping a switch on the handlebar telling the FJR to take over. The standard issue FJR sold for $13,499 while the RE required $15,299 to be ridden home.

2006 YAMAHA

Model	Engine	Displacement	Transmission
XV250 Virago	Two-cylinder	250cc	Five-Speed
YZF600R	Four-cylinder	599cc	Six-Speed
Y2F-R6	Four-cylinder	599cc	Six-Speed
YZF-R6S (New for 2006)	Four-cylinder	600cc	Six-Speed
FZ6	Four-cylinder	600cc	Six-Speed
V-Star Classic	Two-cylinder	649cc	Five-Speed
V-Star Custom	Two-cylinder	649cc	Five-Speed
V-Star Silverado	Two-cylinder	649cc	Five-Speed
FZ1	Four-cylinder	998cc	Six-Speed
YZF-R1	Four-cylinder	989cc	Six-Speed
V-Star 1100 Classic	Two-cylinder	1063cc	Five-Speed
V-Star 1100 Custom	Two-cylinder	1063cc	Five-Speed
V-Star 1100 Silverado	Two-cylinder	1063cc	Five-Speed
V-Max	Four-cylinder	1198cc	Five-Speed
Royal Star Tour Deluxe	Four-cylinder	1294cc	Five-Speed
Venture	Four-cylinder	1294cc	Five-Speed
FJR1300R	Four-cylinder	1298cc	Five-Speed
FJR1300RE (New Electric Shift)	Four-cylinder	1298cc	Five-Speed
Road Star	Two-cylinder	1602cc	Five-Speed
Road Star Silverado	Two-cylinder	1602cc	Five-Speed
Road Star Warrior	Two-cylinder	1602cc	Five-Speed
Star Roadliner (New for 2006)	Two-cylinder	1854cc	Five-Speed
Star Roadliner Midnight (New for 2006)	Two-cylinder	1854cc	Five-Speed
Star Stratoliner (New for 2006)	Two-cylinder	1854cc	Five-Speed
Star Stratoliner S (New for 2006)	Two-cylinder	1854cc	Five-Speed
Star Stratoliner Midnight (New for 2006)	Two-cylinder	1854cc	Five-Speed

YAMAHA
2007

STANDARD CATALOG OF® JAPANESE Motorcycles

Images: Yamaha Motors

The classic look of the Yamaha V-Star 1300 Tourer on the street was offered as a stimulus to potential owners in 2007 company literature.

The 2007 Yamaha V-Star Silverado showed its color choices—Galaxy Blue (top) and Raven (bottom).

The 2007 FZ1 by Yamaha was a striking-looking vehicle on the road, as shown in this image.

Things didn't get much better than a cruise on a Yamaha Road Star Silverado motorcycle in 2007.

The 2007 RF1 by Yamaha was a sleek motorcycle that was ready for street or racing action.

Japanese Motorcycle Values

How to Use This Price Guide

The prices listed here are a sampling of the motorcycles with the top values today from the Krause Publications database and our publication *Vintage Motorcycles*. Please refer to *Vintage Motorcycles* for a complete list of motorcycle values.

Motorcycle Condition Scale

1 Excellent: Restored to current maximum professional standards of quality in every area or perfect original with components operating and appearing as new. A 95-plus point motorcycle that is not ridden. In national show judging, motorcycle in number one condition is likely to win top honors in its class.

2 Fine: Well-restored or a combination of superior restoration and excellent original parts. An extremely well-maintained original showing minimal wear. It may be ridden limited miles each year.

3 Very Good: Completely operable original or older restoration. A good amateur restoration, or a combination of well-done restoration and good operable components or partially restored motorcycle with parts necessary to complete and/or valuable NOS parts. Generally, most motorcycles on display at shows are in number three condition.

4 Good: A rideable vehicle needing no work or only minor work to be functional. A deteriorated restoration or poor amateur restoration. All components may need restoration to be "excellent" but the motorcycle is usable "as is." It does need some help. A "rider" that may be in the process of restoration.

5 Restorable: Needs complete restoration. May or may not be running. Isn't weathered or stripped to the point of being useful only for parts. May have some original parts in boxes. It is essentially all there with little or no surface rust.

6 Parts Bike: May or may not be running but is weathered, wrecked and/or stripped to the point of being useful primarily for parts. This is a deteriorated, perhaps rusty vehicle. It usually comes in the form of a frame and parts.

PRICE GUIDE

HONDA

1959	6	5	4	3	2	1
CB92 Benly Super Sport 125 (124cc twin)	2,400	3,600	5,400	7,200	9,600	12,000
CA71 Dream Touring 250 (247cc twin)	1,300	1,950	2,930	3,900	5,200	6,500
CE71 Dream Sport 250 (247cc twin)	2,400	3,600	5,400	7,200	9,600	12,000
C76 Dream Touring 300 (305cc twin)	1,300	1,950	2,930	3,900	5,200	6,500
CA76 Dream Touring 300 (305cc twin)	1,280	1,920	2,880	3,840	5,120	6,400

1960	6	5	4	3	2	1
CB92 Benly Super Sport 125 (124cc twin)	2,400	3,600	5,400	7,200	9,600	12,000
CA71 Dream Touring 250 (247cc twin)	1,300	1,950	2,930	3,900	5,200	6,500
CE71 Dream Sport 250 (247cc twin)	2,200	3,300	4,950	6,600	8,800	11,000
C76 Dream Touring 300 (305cc twin)	1,300	1,950	2,930	3,900	5,200	6,500
CS76 Dream Sport 300 (305cc twin)	2,200	3,300	4,950	6,600	8,800	11,000
CSA76 Dream Sport 300 (305cc twin)	1,800	2,700	4,050	5,400	7,200	9,000

1961	6	5	4	3	2	1
CB92R Benly SS Racer 125 (124cc twin)	4,400	6,600	9,900	13,200	17,600	22,000
C72 Dream Touring 250 (247cc twin)	1,180	1,770	2,660	3,540	4,720	5,900
CA72 Dream Touring 250 "Early" (247cc twin)	940	1,410	2,120	2,820	3,760	4,700
CB72 Hawk 250 (247cc twin)	960	1,440	2,160	2,880	3,840	4,800
CSA77 Dream Sport 305 (305cc twin)	1,000	1,500	2,250	3,000	4,000	5,000

1962	6	5	4	3	2	1
CB92R Benly SS Racer 125 (124cc twin)	4,400	6,600	9,900	13,200	17,600	22,000
CA72 Dream Touring 250 "Early" (247cc twin)	940	1,410	2,120	2,820	3,760	4,700
CB72 Hawk 250 (247cc twin)	1,000	1,500	2,250	3,000	4,000	5,000
CB77 Super Hawk 305 (305cc twin)	900	1,350	2,030	2,700	3,600	4,500
CSA77 Dream Sport 305 (305cc twin)	1,000	1,500	2,250	3,000	4,000	5,000

1963	6	5	4	3	2	1
CA72 Dream Touring 250 "Early" (247cc twin)	940	1,410	2,120	2,820	3,760	4,700
CA72 Dream Touring 250 "Late" (247cc twin)	940	1,410	2,120	2,820	3,760	4,700
CA77 Dream Touring 305 "Early" (305cc twin)	850	1,280	1,910	2,550	3,400	4,250
CA77 Dream Touring 305 "Late" (305cc twin)	850	1,280	1,910	2,550	3,400	4,250
CSA77 Dream Sport 305 (305cc twin)	1,000	1,500	2,250	3,000	4,000	5,000

1964	6	5	4	3	2	1
CA72 Dream Touring 250 "Late" (247cc twin)	940	1,410	2,120	2,820	3,760	4,700
CB72 Hawk 250 (247cc twin)	800	1,200	1,800	2,400	3,200	4,000
CL72 Scrambler 250 (247cc twin)	700	1,050	1,580	2,100	2,800	3,500
C77 Dream Touring 305 (305cc twin)	820	1,230	1,850	2,460	3,280	4,100
CA77 Dream Touring 305 "Late" (305cc twin)	820	1,230	1,850	2,460	3,280	4,100

1965	6	5	4	3	2	1
CA72 Dream Touring 250 "Late" (247cc twin)	900	1,350	2,030	2,700	3,600	4,500
CB72 Hawk 250 (247cc twin)	800	1,200	1,800	2,400	3,200	4,000
CL72 Scrambler 250 (247cc twin)	700	1,050	1,580	2,100	2,800	3,500
CA77 Dream Touring 305 "Late" (305cc twin)	820	1,230	1,850	2,460	3,280	4,100
CL77 Scrambler 305 (305cc twin)	700	1,050	1,580	2,100	2,800	3,500
CB450 Super Sport 450 (444cc twin)	800	1,200	1,800	2,400	3,200	4,000

1966	6	5	4	3	2	1
CA72 Dream Touring 250 "Late" (247cc twin)	800	1,200	1,800	2,400	3,200	4,000
CB72 Hawk 250 (247cc twin)	800	1,200	1,800	2,400	3,200	4,000
CA77 Dream Touring 305 "Late" (305cc twin)	820	1,230	1,850	2,460	3,280	4,100
CL77 Scrambler 305 (305cc twin)	800	1,200	1,800	2,400	3,200	4,000
CB450 Super Sport 450 (444cc twin)	840	1,260	1,890	2,520	3,360	4,200

PRICE GUIDE

HONDA

1967	6	5	4	3	2	1
CA77 Dream Touring 305 "Late" (305cc twin)	820	1,230	1,850	2,460	3,280	4,100
CB77 Super Hawk 305 (305cc twin)	800	1,200	1,800	2,400	3,200	4,000
CL77 Scrambler 305 (305cc twin)	800	1,200	1,800	2,400	3,200	4,000
CB450 Super Sport 450 (444cc twin)	900	1,350	2,030	2,700	3,600	4,500
CB450D Super Sport 450D (444cc twin)	800	1,200	1,800	2,400	3,200	4,000
CL450 Scrambler 450 (444cc twin)	820	1,230	1,850	2,460	3,280	4,100

1968	6	5	4	3	2	1
CA77 Dream Touring 305 "Late" (305cc twin)	800	1,200	1,800	2,400	3,200	4,000
CB77 Super Hawk 305 (305cc twin)	900	1,350	2,030	2,700	3,600	4,500
CL77 Scrambler 305 (305cc twin)	800	1,200	1,800	2,400	3,200	4,000
CB450 Super Sport 450 (444cc twin)	820	1,230	1,850	2,460	3,280	4,100
CB450K1 Super Sport 450 (444cc twin)	840	1,260	1,890	2,520	3,360	4,200
CL450K1 Scrambler 450 (444cc twin)	840	1,260	1,890	2,520	3,360	4,200

1969	6	5	4	3	2	1
CB450K1 Super Sport 450 (444cc twin)	900	1,350	2,030	2,700	3,600	4,500
CL450K1 Scrambler 450 (444cc twin)	800	1,200	1,800	2,400	3,200	4,000
CL450K2 Scrambler 450 (444cc twin)	800	1,200	1,800	2,400	3,200	4,000
CB750 Four "Sandcast" (736cc four)	3,900	5,850	8,780	11,700	15,600	19,500
CB750 Four "Diecast" (736cc four)	1,600	2,400	3,600	4,800	6,400	8,000

1970	6	5	4	3	2	1
CB350K2 Super Sport 350 (325cc twin)	580	870	1,310	1,740	2,320	2,900
CL350K2 Scrambler 350 (325cc twin)	580	870	1,310	1,740	2,320	2,900
CB450K3 Super Sport 450 (444cc twin)	640	960	1,440	1,920	2,560	3,200
CL450K3 Scrambler 450 (444cc twin)	650	980	1,460	1,950	2,600	3,250
CB750 750 Four "Diecast" (736cc four)	1,600	2,400	3,600	4,800	6,400	8,000
CB750K1 750 Four (736cc four)	1,600	2,400	3,600	4,800	6,400	8,000

1971	6	5	4	3	2	1
CB350K3 Super Sport 350 (325cc twin)	540	810	1,220	1,620	2,160	2,700
CL350K3 Scrambler 350 (325cc twin)	550	830	1,240	1,650	2,200	2,750
CB450K4 Super Sport 450 (444cc twin)	640	960	1,440	1,920	2,560	3,200
CL450K2 Scrambler 450 (444cc twin)	640	960	1,440	1,920	2,560	3,200
CB500 500 Four (498cc four)	700	1,050	1,580	2,100	2,800	3,500
CB750K1 750 Four (736cc four)	1,600	2,400	3,600	4,800	6,400	8,000

1972	6	5	4	3	2	1
XL250 Motosport 250 (248cc single)	450	680	1,010	1,350	1,800	2,250
CB350F (347cc four)	480	720	1,080	1,440	1,920	2,400
CB450K5 Super Sport 450 (444cc twin)	400	600	900	1,200	1,600	2,000
CL450K5 Scrambler 450 (444cc twin)	400	600	900	1,200	1,600	2,000
CB500K1 500 Four (498cc four)	640	960	1,440	1,920	2,560	3,200
CB750K2 750 Four (736cc four)	1,600	2,400	3,600	4,800	6,400	8,000

1973	6	5	4	3	2	1
SL350K2 Motosport 350 (325cc twin)	390	590	880	1,170	1,560	1,950
CB350F (347cc four)	440	660	990	1,320	1,760	2,200
CL450K5 Scrambler 450 (444cc twin)	440	660	990	1,320	1,760	2,200
CB500K2 500 Four (498cc four)	600	900	1,350	1,800	2,400	3,000
CB750K3 750 Four (736cc four)	1,400	2,100	3,150	4,200	5,600	7,000

1974	6	5	4	3	2	1
CB350F1 (347cc four)	380	570	860	1,140	1,520	1,900
CB450K7 Super Sport 450 (444cc twin)	380	570	860	1,140	1,520	1,900
CL450K6 Scrambler 450 (444cc twin)	380	570	860	1,140	1,520	1,900
CB550 550 Four (544cc four)	400	600	900	1,200	1,600	2,000
CB750K4 750 Four (736cc four)	1,400	2,100	3,150	4,200	5,600	7,000

PRICE GUIDE

HONDA

1975	6	5	4	3	2	1
TL250 Trails 250 (248cc single)	400	600	900	1,200	1,600	2,000
CB400F Super Sport 400 Four (408cc four)	400	600	900	1,200	1,600	2,000
CB550F Super Sport 550 Four (544cc four)	400	600	900	1,200	1,600	2,000
CB550K1 550 Four (544cc four)	400	600	900	1,200	1,600	2,000
CB750F 750 Super Sport (736cc four)	900	1,350	2,030	2,700	3,600	4,500
CB750K5 750 Four (736cc four)	600	900	1,350	1,800	2,400	3,000
GL1000 Gold Wing (999cc four)	1,000	1,500	2,250	3,000	4,000	5,000

1976	6	5	4	3	2	1
CB750A 750 Hondamatic (736cc four)	600	900	1,350	1,800	2,400	3,000
CB750F 750 Super Sport (736cc four)	600	900	1,350	1,800	2,400	3,000
CB750K 750 Four K (736cc four)	600	900	1,350	1,800	2,400	3,000
GL1000 Gold Wing (999cc four)	660	990	1,490	1,980	2,640	3,300
GL1000LTD Gold Wing Limited Edition (999cc four)	760	1,140	1,710	2,280	3,040	3,800

1977	6	5	4	3	2	1
CB400F Super Sport 400 Four (408cc four)	400	600	900	1,200	1,600	2,000
CB550F Super Sport 550 Four (544cc four)	400	600	900	1,200	1,600	2,000
CB550K 550 Four K (554cc four)	400	600	900	1,200	1,600	2,000
CB750A 750 Hondamatic (736cc four)	600	900	1,350	1,800	2,400	3,000
CB750F 750 Super Sport (736cc four)	600	900	1,350	1,800	2,400	3,000
CB750K 750 Four K (736cc four)	600	900	1,350	1,800	2,400	3,000
GL1000 Gold Wing (999cc four)	660	990	1,490	1,980	2,640	3,300

1978	6	5	4	3	2	1
CR250R Elsinore (247cc single)	400	600	900	1,200	1,600	2,000
CB400A Hawk Hondamatic (395cc twin)	400	600	900	1,200	1,600	2,000
CB750A 750 Hondamatic (736cc four)	550	830	1,240	1,650	2,200	2,750
CB750F 750 Super Sport (736cc four)	550	830	1,240	1,650	2,200	2,750
CB750K 750 Four K (736cc four)	550	830	1,240	1,650	2,200	2,750
GL1000 Gold Wing (999cc four)	640	960	1,440	1,920	2,560	3,200

1979	6	5	4	3	2	1
CB750F 750 Super Sport (749cc four)	640	960	1,440	1,920	2,560	3,200
CB750K 750 Four K (749cc four)	540	810	1,220	1,620	2,160	2,700
CB750K Limited Edition (749cc four)	600	900	1,350	1,800	2,400	3,000
GL1000 Gold Wing (999cc four)	640	960	1,440	1,920	2,560	3,200
CBX Super Sport (1,047cc six)	1,800	2,700	4,050	5,400	7,200	9,000

1980	6	5	4	3	2	1
CB750C 750 Custom (749cc four)	500	750	1,130	1,500	2,000	2,500
CB750F 750 Super Sport (749cc four)	640	960	1,440	1,920	2,560	3,200
CB750K 750 Four K (749cc four)	500	750	1,130	1,500	2,000	2,500
CB900C 900 Custom (902cc four)	500	750	1,130	1,500	2,000	2,500
CBX Super Sport (1,047cc six)	1,800	2,700	4,050	5,400	7,200	9,000
GL1100 Gold Wing (1,085cc four)	700	1,050	1,580	2,100	2,800	3,500
GL1100I Gold Wing Interstate (1,085cc four)	840	1,260	1,890	2,520	3,360	4,200

1981	6	5	4	3	2	1
GL500 Silver Wing (496cc V-twin)	600	900	1,350	1,800	2,400	3,000
GL500I Silver Wing Interstate (496cc V-twin)	600	900	1,350	1,800	2,400	3,000
CB900F 900 Super Sport (902cc four)	600	900	1,350	1,800	2,400	3,000
CBX Super Sport (1,047cc six)	1,800	2,700	4,050	5,400	7,200	9,000
GL1100 Gold Wing (1,085cc four)	700	1,050	1,580	2,100	2,800	3,500
GL1100I Gold Wing Interstate (1,085cc four)	840	1,260	1,890	2,520	3,360	4,200

PRICE GUIDE
HONDA

1982	6	5	4	3	2	1
CX500TC 500 Turbo (497cc turbo V-twin)	1,200	1,800	2,700	3,600	4,800	6,000
FT500 Ascot (498cc single)	900	1,350	2,030	2,700	3,600	4,500
CB750SC Nighthawk 750 (749cc four)	1,000	1,500	2,250	3,000	4,000	5,000
CBX Super Sport (1,047cc six)	1,800	2,700	4,050	5,400	7,200	9,000
GL1100A Gold Wing Aspencade (1,085cc four)	920	1,380	2,070	2,760	3,680	4,600

1983	6	5	4	3	2	1
CX650T 650 Turbo (674cc turbo V-twin)	1,100	1,650	2,480	3,300	4,400	5,500
VF750F V45 Interceptor (748cc V-four)	940	1,410	2,120	2,820	3,760	4,700
CB750SC Nighthawk 750 (749cc four)	960	1,440	2,160	2,880	3,840	4,800
CB1100F Super Sport (1,067cc four)	940	1,410	2,120	2,820	3,760	4,700
GL1100A Gold Wing Aspencade (1,085cc four)	920	1,380	2,070	2,760	3,680	4,600
GL1100I Gold Wing Interstate (1,085cc four)	940	1,410	2,120	2,820	3,760	4,700

1984	6	5	4	3	2	1
VT500FT Ascot (491cc V-twin)	900	1,350	2,030	2,700	3,600	4,500
VF750F V45 Interceptor (748cc V-four)	880	1,320	1,980	2,640	3,520	4,400
VF1000F 1000 Interceptor (998cc V-four)	1,000	1,500	2,250	3,000	4,000	5,000
GL1200A Gold Wing Aspencade (1,182cc four)	940	1,410	2,120	2,820	3,760	4,700
GL1200I Gold Wing Interstate (1,182cc four)	840	1,260	1,890	2,520	3,360	4,200

1985	6	5	4	3	2	1
VF1000R (998cc V-four)	1,000	1,500	2,250	3,000	4,000	5,000
VT1100C Shadow 1100 (1,099cc V-twin)	840	1,260	1,890	2,520	3,360	4,200
GL1200A Gold Wing Aspencade (1,182cc four)	960	1,440	2,160	2,880	3,840	4,800
GL1200I Gold Wing Interstate (1,182cc four)	840	1,260	1,890	2,520	3,360	4,200
GL1200L Gold Wing Limited Edition (1,182cc four)	920	1,380	2,070	2,760	3,680	4,600

1986	6	5	4	3	2	1
VFR750F 750 Interceptor (748cc V-four)	800	1,200	1,800	2,400	3,200	4,000
VF1000R (998cc V-four)	1,000	1,500	2,250	3,000	4,000	5,000
VT1100C Shadow 1100 (1,099cc V-twin)	820	1,230	1,850	2,460	3,280	4,100
GL1200A Gold Wing Aspencade (1,182cc four)	920	1,380	2,070	2,760	3,680	4,600
GL1200I Gold Wing Interstate (1,182cc four)	800	1,200	1,800	2,400	3,200	4,000
GL1200SE-i Gold Wing Aspencade SE-i (1,182cc four)	980	1,470	2,210	2,940	3,920	4,900

1987	6	5	4	3	2	1
VFR700F2 Interceptor (698cc V-four)	740	1,110	1,670	2,220	2,960	3,700
CBR1000F 1000 Hurricane (998cc four)	800	1,200	1,800	2,400	3,200	4,000
VT1100C Shadow 1100 (1,099cc V-twin)	800	1,200	1,800	2,400	3,200	4,000
GL1200A Gold Wing Aspencade (1,182cc four)	920	1,380	2,070	2,760	3,680	4,600
GL1200I Gold Wing Interstate (1,182cc four)	800	1,200	1,800	2,400	3,200	4,000

1988	6	5	4	3	2	1
VT600C Shadow VLX (583cc V-twin)	700	1,050	1,580	2,100	2,800	3,500
VT800C Shadow 800 (800cc V-twin)	1,000	1,500	2,250	3,000	4,000	5,000
CBR1000F 1000 Hurricane (998cc four)	820	1,230	1,850	2,460	3,280	4,100
VT1100C Shadow 1100 (1,099cc V-twin)	800	1,200	1,800	2,400	3,200	4,000
GL1500 Gold Wing (1,520cc six)	1,200	1,800	2,700	3,600	4,800	6,000

1989	6	5	4	3	2	1
GB500 Tourist Trophy (499cc single)	1,300	1,950	2,930	3,900	5,200	6,500
XL600V TransAlp (583cc V-twin)	1,000	1,500	2,250	3,000	4,000	5,000
PC800 Pacific Coast (800cc V-twin)	800	1,200	1,800	2,400	3,200	4,000
VT1100C Shadow 1100 (1,099cc V-twin)	800	1,200	1,800	2,400	3,200	4,000
GL1500 Gold Wing (1,520cc six)	1,200	1,800	2,700	3,600	4,800	6,000

PRICE GUIDE

HONDA

1990	6	5	4	3	2	1
GB500 Tourist Trophy (499cc single)	1,300	1,950	2,930	3,900	5,200	6,500
XL600V TransAlp (583cc V-twin)	1,000	1,500	2,250	3,000	4,000	5,000
*VFR750R RC30 (748cc V-four)	1,700	2,550	3,830	5,100	6,800	8,500
GL1500 Gold Wing (1,520cc six)	1,200	1,800	2,700	3,600	4,800	6,000
GL1500SE Gold Wing SE (1,520cc six)	1,300	1,950	2,930	3,900	5,200	6,500

KAWASAKI

1963	6	5	4	3	2	1
B8/B8T (125cc single)	700	1,050	1,580	2,100	2,800	3,500

1964	6	5	4	3	2	1
B8/B8T (125cc single)	640	960	1,440	1,920	2,560	3,200
SG (250cc single)	740	1,110	1,670	2,220	2,960	3,700

1965	6	5	4	3	2	1
J1 (85cc single)	400	600	900	1,200	1,600	2,000
J1T (85cc single)	400	600	900	1,200	1,600	2,000
B8/B8T (125cc single)	600	900	1,350	1,800	2,400	3,000
B8S (150cc single)	620	930	1,400	1,860	2,480	3,100
SG (250cc single)	740	1,110	1,670	2,220	2,960	3,700

1966	6	5	4	3	2	1
B8S (150cc single)	480	720	1,080	1,440	1,920	2,400
F1TR (175cc single)	450	680	1,010	1,350	1,800	2,250
F2 (175cc single)	460	690	1,040	1,380	1,840	2,300
SG (250cc single)	600	900	1,350	1,800	2,400	3,000
W1 (624cc twin)	1,400	2,100	3,150	4,200	5,600	7,000

1967	6	5	4	3	2	1
A1 Samurai (247cc twin)	600	900	1,350	1,800	2,400	3,000
A1R (247cc twin)	2,000	3,000	4,500	6,000	8,000	10,000
A1SS Samurai (247cc twin)	600	900	1,350	1,800	2,400	3,000
SG (250cc single)	600	900	1,350	1,800	2,400	3,000
A7 Avenger (338cc twin)	700	1,050	1,580	2,100	2,800	3,500
A7SS Avenger (338cc twin)	700	1,050	1,580	2,100	2,800	3,500
W1 (624cc twin)	1,400	2,100	3,150	4,200	5,600	7,000

1968	6	5	4	3	2	1
A1R (247cc twin)	2,000	3,000	4,500	6,000	8,000	10,000
F21M (250cc single)	700	1,050	1,580	2,100	2,800	3,500
A7 Avenger (338cc twin)	700	1,050	1,580	2,100	2,800	3,500
A7SS Avenger (338cc twin)	700	1,050	1,580	2,100	2,800	3,500
W1 (624cc twin)	1,100	1,650	2,480	3,300	4,400	5,500
W1SS (624cc twin)	1,160	1,740	2,610	3,480	4,640	5,800
W2SS Commander (624cc twin)	1,400	2,100	3,150	4,200	5,600	7,000

1969	6	5	4	3	2	1
H1 Mach III (498cc triple)	1,400	2,100	3,150	4,200	5,600	7,000
H1R Roadracer (498cc triple)	5,200	7,800	11,700	15,600	20,800	26,000
W1SS (624cc twin)	1,100	1,650	2,480	3,300	4,400	5,500
W2SS Commander (624cc twin)	1,160	1,740	2,610	3,480	4,640	5,800
W2TT Commander (624cc twin)	1,320	1,980	2,970	3,960	5,280	6,600

1970	6	5	4	3	2	1
A7A Avenger (247cc twin)	700	1,050	1,580	2,100	2,800	3,500
F21M (250cc single)	700	1,050	1,580	2,100	2,800	3,500
H1 Mach III (498cc triple)	1,400	2,100	3,150	4,200	5,600	7,000
H1R Roadracer (498cc triple)	5,200	7,800	11,700	15,600	20,800	26,000
W1SS (624cc twin)	1,080	1,620	2,430	3,240	4,320	5,400
W2SS Commander (624cc twin)	1,160	1,740	2,610	3,480	4,640	5,800

PRICE GUIDE

KAWASAKI

1971	6	5	4	3	2	1
A1B Samurai (247cc twin)	520	780	1,170	1,560	2,080	2,600
A1SSB Samurai (247cc twin)	520	780	1,170	1,560	2,080	2,600
H1 Mach III (498cc triple)	1,300	1,950	2,930	3,900	5,200	6,500
H1R Roadracer (498cc triple)	5,200	7,800	11,700	15,600	20,800	26,000
W1SS (624cc twin)	1,080	1,620	2,430	3,240	4,320	5,400

1972	6	5	4	3	2	1
S1 Mach I (249cc triple)	360	540	810	1,080	1,440	1,800
F8A Bison (250cc single)	400	600	900	1,200	1,600	2,000
F11 (250cc single)	360	540	810	1,080	1,440	1,800
S2 Mach II (350cc triple)	400	600	900	1,200	1,600	2,000
H1B Mach III (498cc triple)	600	900	1,350	1,800	2,400	3,000
H2 Mach IV (750cc triple)	1,100	1,650	2,480	3,300	4,400	5,500

1973	6	5	4	3	2	1
F9A Big Horn (350cc single)	400	600	900	1,200	1,600	2,000
S2A Mach II (350cc triple)	360	540	810	1,080	1,440	1,800
H1D Mach III (498cc triple)	600	900	1,350	1,800	2,400	3,000
H2A Mach IV (750cc triple)	980	1,470	2,210	2,940	3,920	4,900
Z1 (900cc four)	3,000	4,500	6,750	9,000	12,000	15,000

1974	6	5	4	3	2	1
KX250 (250cc single)	400	600	900	1,200	1,600	2,000
F9B Big Horn (350cc single)	400	600	900	1,200	1,600	2,000
S3 (400cc triple)	400	600	900	1,200	1,600	2,000
KX450 (450cc single)	420	630	950	1,260	1,680	2,100
H1E Mach III (498cc triple)	700	1,050	1,580	2,100	2,800	3,500
H2B Mach IV (750cc triple)	1,000	1,500	2,250	3,000	4,000	5,000
Z1A (900cc four)	2,600	3,900	5,850	7,800	10,400	13,000

1975	6	5	4	3	2	1
KH250-B1 Mach I (249cc triple)	400	600	900	1,200	1,600	2,000
KH400-A3 (400cc triple)	560	840	1,260	1,680	2,240	2,800
KX400 (400cc single)	340	510	770	1,020	1,360	1,700
KH500-A8 Mach III (498cc triple)	600	900	1,350	1,800	2,400	3,000
Z1-B (900cc four)	2,600	3,900	5,850	7,800	10,400	13,000

1976	6	5	4	3	2	1
KH250-A5 (249cc triple)	380	570	860	1,140	1,520	1,900
KH500-A8 (498cc triple)	400	600	900	1,200	1,600	2,000
KZ750-B1 (750cc twin)	400	600	900	1,200	1,600	2,000
KZ900-A4 (903cc four)	1,200	1,800	2,700	3,600	4,800	6,000
KZ900-B1 LTD (903cc four)	1,000	1,500	2,250	3,000	4,000	5,000

1977	6	5	4	3	2	1
KH400-A4 (398cc triple)	400	600	900	1,200	1,600	2,000
KZ650 (652cc four)	400	600	900	1,200	1,600	2,000
KZ650-B1 (652cc four)	420	630	950	1,260	1,680	2,100
KZ900-A5 (903cc four)	660	990	1,490	1,980	2,640	3,300
KZ1000-A1 (1,015cc four)	640	960	1,440	1,920	2,560	3,200
KZ1000-B1 LTD (1,015cc four)	550	830	1,240	1,650	2,200	2,750

1978	6	5	4	3	2	1
KZ650-C2 (652cc four)	420	630	950	1,260	1,680	2,100
KZ650-D1 SR (652cc four)	480	720	1,080	1,440	1,920	2,400
KZ1000-A2 (1,015cc four)	550	830	1,240	1,650	2,200	2,750
KZ1000-D1 (1,015cc four)	700	1,050	1,580	2,100	2,800	3,500
KZ1 RTC Turbo (1,015cc four)	1,600	2,400	3,600	4,800	6,400	8,000

PRICE GUIDE

KAWASAKI

1979	6	5	4	3	2	1
KZ650-D2 (652cc four)	480	720	1,080	1,440	1,920	2,400
KZ1000-A3 (1,015cc four)	540	810	1,220	1,620	2,160	2,700
KZ1000-B3 LTD (1,015cc four)	660	990	1,490	1,980	2,640	3,300
KZ1000-E1 (1,015cc four)	620	930	1,400	1,860	2,480	3,100
KZ1300-A1 (1,286cc six)	680	1,020	1,530	2,040	2,720	3,400

1980	6	5	4	3	2	1
KZ1000-E2 Shaft (1,015cc four)	620	930	1,400	1,860	2,480	3,100
KZ1 RTC Turbo (1,015cc four)	1,600	2,400	3,600	4,800	6,400	8,000
KZ1300-A2 (1,286cc six)	680	1,020	1,530	2,040	2,720	3,400
KZ1300-B2 (1,286cc six)	680	1,020	1,530	2,040	2,720	3,400
SFC 750 racer (750cc twin)	2,000	3,000	4,500	6,000	8,000	10,000

SUZUKI

1963	6	5	4	3	2	1
RM63 (50cc single)	11,000	16,500	24,750	33,000	44,000	55,000
RT63 (124cc twin)	10,000	15,000	22,500	30,000	40,000	50,000
S31 (124cc twin)	220	330	500	660	880	1,100
S250 Colleda (248cc twin)	300	450	680	900	1,200	1,500
TC250 El Camino (248cc twin)	300	450	680	900	1,200	1,500

1964	6	5	4	3	2	1
M12 Sports 50 (50cc single)	220	330	500	660	880	1,100
K11 Sports 80 (79cc single)	220	330	500	660	880	1,100
T10 (246cc twin)	300	450	680	900	1,200	1,500

1965	6	5	4	3	2	1
K11 Sports 80 (79cc single)	180	270	410	540	720	900
B100 (118cc single)	180	270	410	540	720	900
S10 (124cc twin)	220	330	500	660	880	1,100
S32 (149cc twin)	240	360	540	720	960	1,200
T20 (247cc twin)	300	450	680	900	1,200	1,500
X-6 Super Six (247cc twin)	320	480	720	960	1,280	1,600

1966	6	5	4	3	2	1
M15 (49cc single)	180	270	410	540	720	900
K11 P Challenger (79cc single)	180	270	410	540	720	900
A100 (98cc single)	180	270	410	540	720	900
B120 (118cc single)	240	360	540	720	960	1,200
S32 II (149cc twin)	240	360	540	720	960	1,200
T20 (247cc twin)	300	450	680	900	1,200	1,500

1967	6	5	4	3	2	1
RK67 Racer (50cc twin)	9,000	13,500	20,250	27,000	36,000	45,000
B105 P Bearcat (118cc single)	280	420	630	840	1,120	1,400
T20 Super Six (247cc twin)	300	450	680	900	1,200	1,500
T21 Super (247cc twin)	300	450	680	900	1,200	1,500
TC250 Hustler (247cc twin)	700	1,050	1,580	2,100	2,800	3,500

1968	6	5	4	3	2	1
TC250 (247cc twin)	300	450	680	900	1,200	1,500
TM250 (249cc single)	440	660	990	1,320	1,760	2,200
T305 (305cc twin)	500	750	1,130	1,500	2,000	2,500
TC305 (305cc twin)	500	750	1,130	1,500	2,000	2,500
T500 Cobra (492cc twin)	600	900	1,350	1,800	2,400	3,000

PRICE GUIDE

SUZUKI

1969	6	5	4	3	2	1
T250 Hustler (247cc twin)	440	660	990	1,320	1,760	2,200
T305 Raider (305cc twin)	480	720	1,080	1,440	1,920	2,400
T350 Rebel (315cc twin)	520	780	1,170	1,560	2,080	2,600
T500 II Titan (492cc twin)	600	900	1,350	1,800	2,400	3,000
TR500 (500cc twin)	600	900	1,350	1,800	2,400	3,000

1970	6	5	4	3	2	1
T125II Stinger (124cc twin)	340	510	770	1,020	1,360	1,700
TS250II Savage (246cc single)	400	600	900	1,200	1,600	2,000
T250II Hustler (247cc twin)	440	660	990	1,320	1,760	2,200
T350II Rebel (315cc twin)	520	780	1,170	1,560	2,080	2,600
T500III Titan (492cc twin)	600	900	1,350	1,800	2,400	3,000

1971	6	5	4	3	2	1
T125II Stinger (124cc twin)	340	510	770	1,020	1,360	1,700
TS250II Savage (246cc single)	400	600	900	1,200	1,600	2,000
T250II Hustler (247cc twin)	440	660	990	1,320	1,760	2,200
T350II Rebel (315cc twin)	520	780	1,170	1,560	2,080	2,600
T500III Titan (492cc twin)	600	900	1,350	1,800	2,400	3,000

1972	6	5	4	3	2	1
T250J Hustler (247cc twin)	420	630	950	1,260	1,680	2,100
GT380J Sebring (371cc triple)	400	600	900	1,200	1,600	2,000
TS400J (396cc twin)	420	630	950	1,260	1,680	2,100
T500J Titan (492cc twin)	520	780	1,170	1,560	2,080	2,600
GT550J Indy (543cc triple)	440	660	990	1,320	1,760	2,200
GT750J Le Mans (739cc triple)	1,000	1,500	2,250	3,000	4,000	5,000

1973	6	5	4	3	2	1
T250K Hustler (247cc twin)	440	660	990	1,320	1,760	2,200
GT380K Sebring (371cc triple)	420	630	950	1,260	1,680	2,100
TS400K Apache (396cc single)	420	630	950	1,260	1,680	2,100
T500K Titan (492cc twin)	480	720	1,080	1,440	1,920	2,400
GT750K Le Mans (739cc triple)	940	1,410	2,120	2,820	3,760	4,700

1974	6	5	4	3	2	1
T250L Hustler (247cc twin)	440	660	990	1,320	1,760	2,200
GT380L Sebring (371cc triple)	420	630	950	1,260	1,680	2,100
TS400L Apache (396cc single)	420	630	950	1,260	1,680	2,100
T500L Titan (492cc twin)	480	720	1,080	1,440	1,920	2,400
GT750L Le Mans (739cc triple)	920	1,380	2,070	2,760	3,680	4,600

1975	6	5	4	3	2	1
TS185M Sierra (183cc single)	420	630	950	1,260	1,680	2,100
T250M Hustler (247cc twin)	440	660	990	1,320	1,760	2,200
TS400M Apache (396cc single)	420	630	950	1,260	1,680	2,100
T500M Titan (492cc twin)	480	720	1,080	1,440	1,920	2,400
RE5M (497cc single, Wankel)	1,140	1,710	2,570	3,420	4,560	5,700
GT750M Le Mans (739cc triple)	880	1,320	1,980	2,640	3,520	4,400

1976	6	5	4	3	2	1
T250A Hustler (247cc twin)	440	660	990	1,320	1,760	2,200
TS400A Apache (396cc single)	420	630	950	1,260	1,680	2,100
T500A Titan (492cc twin)	480	720	1,080	1,440	1,920	2,400
RE5A (497cc single, Wankel)	1,100	1,650	2,480	3,300	4,400	5,500
GT750A Le Mans (739cc triple)	880	1,320	1,980	2,640	3,520	4,400

PRICE GUIDE

SUZUKI

1977	6	5	4	3	2	1
T250B Hustler (247cc twin)	440	660	990	1,320	1,760	2,200
GT380B Sebring (371cc triple)	400	600	900	1,200	1,600	2,000
TS400B Apache (396cc single)	400	600	900	1,200	1,600	2,000
T500B Titan (492cc twin)	420	630	950	1,260	1,680	2,100
GT750B Le Mans (739cc triple)	400	600	900	1,200	1,600	2,000
GS750B (748cc four)	880	1,320	1,980	2,640	3,520	4,400

1978	6	5	4	3	2	1
GS550C (549cc four)	440	660	990	1,320	1,760	2,200
GS550EC (549cc four)	440	660	990	1,320	1,760	2,200
GS750C (748cc four)	580	870	1,310	1,740	2,320	2,900
GS750EC (748cc four)	580	870	1,310	1,740	2,320	2,900
GS1000C (997cc four)	600	900	1,350	1,800	2,400	3,000

1979	6	5	4	3	2	1
GS850GN (843cc four)	460	690	1,040	1,380	1,840	2,300
GS1000EN (997cc four)	600	900	1,350	1,800	2,400	3,000
GS1000LN (997cc four)	600	900	1,350	1,800	2,400	3,000
GS1000N (997cc four)	600	900	1,350	1,800	2,400	3,000
GS1000SN (997cc four)	700	1,050	1,580	2,100	2,800	3,500

1979	6	5	4	3	2	1
GS1000ET (997cc four)	600	900	1,350	1,800	2,400	3,000
GS1000GLT (997cc four)	600	900	1,350	1,800	2,400	3,000
GS1000GT (997cc four)	600	900	1,350	1,800	2,400	3,000
GS1000ST (997cc four)	680	1,020	1,530	2,040	2,720	3,400
GS1100ET (1,074cc four)	660	990	1,490	1,980	2,640	3,300
GS1100LT (1,074cc four)	660	990	1,490	1,980	2,640	3,300

YAMAHA

1961	6	5	4	3	2	1
MF1 (50cc single)	500	750	1,130	1,500	2,000	2,500
MF2 (50cc single)	500	750	1,130	1,500	2,000	2,500
YA2 (125cc single)	500	750	1,130	1,500	2,000	2,500
YA3 (125cc single)	500	750	1,130	1,500	2,000	2,500
YC1 (175cc single)	540	810	1,220	1,620	2,160	2,700
YD2 (250cc twin)	900	1,350	2,030	2,700	3,600	4,500
YDS1 (250cc twin)	900	1,350	2,030	2,700	3,600	4,500

1962	6	5	4	3	2	1
MJ2 (55cc single)	420	630	950	1,260	1,680	2,100
YA5 (125cc single)	520	780	1,170	1,560	2,080	2,600
YD3 (250cc twin)	920	1,380	2,070	2,760	3,680	4,600
YDS2 (250cc twin)	920	1,380	2,070	2,760	3,680	4,600

1963	6	5	4	3	2	1
YG1 (73cc single)	520	780	1,170	1,560	2,080	2,600
YG1T (73cc single)	520	780	1,170	1,560	2,080	2,600
YDT1 (250cc twin)	920	1,380	2,070	2,760	3,680	4,600

1964	6	5	4	3	2	1
MG1T (73cc single)	520	780	1,170	1,560	2,080	2,600
YA5 (125cc single)	520	780	1,170	1,560	2,080	2,600
YA6 (125cc single)	520	780	1,170	1,560	2,080	2,600
YD3 (250cc twin)	920	1,380	2,070	2,760	3,680	4,600
YDS2 (250cc twin)	1,200	1,800	2,700	3,600	4,800	6,000
TDS3 (250cc twin)	1,400	2,100	3,150	4,200	5,600	7,000
YDT1 (250cc twin)	1,000	1,500	2,250	3,000	4,000	5,000

PRICE GUIDE

YAMAHA

1965	6	5	4	3	2	1
TD1B (250cc twin)	2,600	3,900	5,850	7,800	10,400	13,000
TD1C (250cc twin)	2,600	3,900	5,850	7,800	10,400	13,000
YD3C Big Bear Scrambler (250cc twin)	1,140	1,710	2,570	3,420	4,560	5,700
YDS3 (250cc twin)	1,400	2,100	3,150	4,200	5,600	7,000
YM1 (305cc twin)	800	1,200	1,800	2,400	3,200	4,000

1966	6	5	4	3	2	1
MJ1T Omaha Trail (80cc single)	500	750	1,130	1,500	2,000	2,500
YL1 (98cc twin)	500	750	1,130	1,500	2,000	2,500
TD1 Daytona Road Racer (247cc twin)	2,600	3,900	5,850	7,800	10,400	13,000
YDS3C Big Bear (250cc twin)	1,000	1,500	2,250	3,000	4,000	5,000
YDSM Ascot Scrambler (250cc twin)	1,000	1,500	2,250	3,000	4,000	5,000
YM1 Big Bear Scrambler (305cc twin)	800	1,200	1,800	2,400	3,200	4,000

1967	6	5	4	3	2	1
YL2C (90cc single)	500	750	1,100	1,500	2,000	2,500
YA6 Santa Barbara (125cc single)	500	750	1,130	1,500	2,000	2,500
TD1 Daytona (247cc twin)	2,600	3,900	5,850	7,800	10,400	13,000
YM1 Cross Country (305cc twin)	540	810	1,220	1,620	2,160	2,700
YM2C (305cc twin)	500	750	1,130	1,500	2,000	2,500
YR1 Grand Prix (350cc twin)	600	900	1,350	1,800	2,400	3,000

1968	6	5	4	3	2	1
TD1 Daytona (247cc twin)	2,600	3,900	5,850	7,800	10,400	13,000
DT1 Enduro (250cc single)	900	1,350	2,030	2,700	3,600	4,500
YM1 Cross Country (305cc twin)	540	810	1,220	1,620	2,160	2,700
YR2 Grand Prix (350cc twin)	600	900	1,350	1,800	2,400	3,000
YR2C Street Scrambler (350cc twin)	540	810	1,220	1,620	2,160	2,700

1969	6	5	4	3	2	1
YAS1-C Street Scrambler (125cc twin)	510	770	1,150	1,530	2,040	2,550
CT1 Trail (175cc single)	500	750	1,130	1,500	2,000	2,500
YDS6C Street Scrambler (250cc twin)	540	810	1,220	1,620	2,160	2,700
YM1 (305cc twin)	600	900	1,350	1,800	2,400	3,000
R3 (347cc twin)	600	900	1,350	1,800	2,400	3,000
YR2-C Street Scrambler (350cc twin)	540	810	1,220	1,620	2,160	2,700

1970	6	5	4	3	2	1
AS2C (125cc twin)	500	750	1,130	1,500	2,000	2,500
AT1B Enduro (125cc single)	500	750	1,130	1,500	2,000	2,500
AT1BMX (125cc single)	500	750	1,130	1,500	2,000	2,500
CT1B Enduro (175cc single)	500	750	1,130	1,500	2,000	2,500
TD2 (247cc twin)	2,700	4,050	6,080	8,100	10,800	13,500
RT1 Enduro (250cc single)	620	930	1,400	1,860	2,480	3,100
R5 (347cc twin)	520	780	1,170	1,560	2,080	2,600
XS1 (654cc twin)	1,000	1,500	2,250	3,000	4,000	5,000

1971	6	5	4	3	2	1
TD2B (247cc twin)	2,700	4,050	6,080	8,100	10,800	13,500
R5B (347cc twin)	540	810	1,220	1,620	2,160	2,700
RT1B Enduro (360cc single)	540	810	1,220	1,620	2,160	2,700
XS1B (654cc twin)	1,000	1,500	2,250	3,000	4,000	5,000

1972	6	5	4	3	2	1
CS5 (198cc twin)	510	770	1,150	1,530	2,040	2,550
TD3 (247cc twin)	2,700	4,050	6,080	8,100	10,800	13,500
R5C (347cc twin)	540	810	1,220	1,620	2,160	2,700
RT2 Enduro (360cc single)	540	810	1,220	1,620	2,160	2,700
XS2 (654cc twin)	1,000	1,500	2,250	3,000	4,000	5,000

PRICE GUIDE

YAMAHA

1973	6	5	4	3	2	1
TA250 (247cc twin)	2,100	3,150	4,730	6,300	8,400	10,500
TZ350 (347cc twin)	2,600	3,900	5,850	7,800	10,400	13,000
RT3 (360cc single)	700	1,050	1,580	2,100	2,800	3,500
TX650 (654cc twin)	1,000	1,500	2,250	3,000	4,000	5,000
TX750 (743cc twin)	800	1,200	1,800	2,400	3,200	4,000

1974	6	5	4	3	2	1
TA125A (125cc twin)	1,700	2,550	3,830	5,100	6,800	8,500
TZ250A (247cc twin)	2,400	3,600	5,400	7,200	9,600	12,000
TZ350A (347cc twin)	2,600	3,900	5,850	7,800	10,400	13,000
TX650A (654cc twin)	1,000	1,500	2,250	3,000	4,000	5,000
TZ700A (698cc four)	4,000	6,000	9,000	12,000	16,000	20,000

1975	6	5	4	3	2	1
TA1 (125cc twin)	1,800	2,700	4,050	5,400	7,200	9,000
TZ250B (247cc twin)	2,400	3,600	5,400	7,200	9,600	12,000
TZ350B (347cc twin)	2,600	3,900	5,850	7,800	10,400	13,000
XS650B (654cc twin)	800	1,200	1,800	2,400	3,200	4,000
TZ750B (750cc four)	3,800	5,700	8,550	11,400	15,200	19,000

1976	6	5	4	3	2	1
TZ250C (247cc twin)	2,400	3,600	5,400	7,200	9,600	12,000
RD400C (399cc twin)	550	830	1,240	1,650	2,200	2,750
XT500C (499cc single)	600	900	1,350	1,800	2,400	3,000
XS650C (654cc twin)	800	1,200	1,800	2,400	3,200	4,000
TZ750C (750cc four)	3,800	5,700	8,550	11,400	15,200	19,000

1977	6	5	4	3	2	1
TZ250D (247cc twin)	2,200	3,300	4,950	6,600	8,800	11,000
YZ400D (399cc single)	2,400	3,600	5,400	7,200	9,600	12,000
XS650D (654cc twin)	800	1,200	1,800	2,400	3,200	4,000
XS750D (747cc triple)	700	1,050	1,580	2,100	2,800	3,500
TZ750D (750cc four)	3,400	5,100	7,650	10,200	13,600	17,000

1982	6	5	4	3	2	1
TZ250E (247cc twin)	2,400	3,600	5,400	7,200	9,600	12,000
XS650E (654cc twin)	800	1,200	1,800	2,400	3,200	4,000
XS650SE (654cc twin)	800	1,200	1,800	2,400	3,200	4,000
TZ750E (750cc four)	3,400	5,100	7,650	10,200	13,600	17,000
XS1100E (1,101cc four)	1,000	1,500	2,250	3,000	4,000	5,000

1979	6	5	4	3	2	1
RD400F Daytona Special (399cc twin)	660	990	1,490	1,980	2,640	3,300
XT500F (499cc twin)	800	1,200	1,800	2,400	3,200	4,000
XS650-2F (654cc twin)	800	1,200	1,800	2,400	3,200	4,000
XS1100F (1,101cc four)	1,000	1,500	2,250	3,000	4,000	5,000
XS1100SF (1,101cc four)	1,000	1,500	2,250	3,000	4,000	5,000

1980	6	5	4	3	2	1
XT500G (499cc single)	480	720	1,080	1,440	1,920	2,400
XS650G (654cc twin)	800	1,200	1,800	2,400	3,200	4,000
XS650SG (654cc twin)	800	1,200	1,800	2,400	3,200	4,000
XS850G (826cc triple)	800	1,200	1,800	2,400	3,200	4,000
XS1100G (1,101cc four)	800	1,200	1,800	2,400	3,200	4,000
XS1100SG (1,101cc four)	800	1,200	1,800	2,400	3,200	4,000

Expand Your Two-Wheel Knowledge

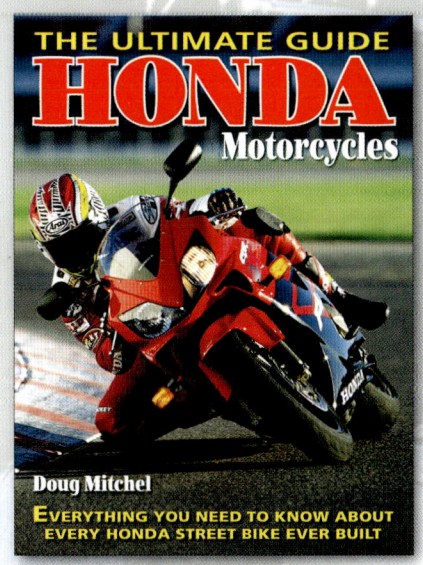

Honda Motorcycles
Everything You Need to Know About Every Honda Motorcycle Ever Built
by Doug Mitchel
Get the full story of Soichiro Honda's innovative approach to motorcycle design, performance data and options for every model from the collectible 750-Four and Super Hawks to today's CBX models, as well as up-to-date collector values.
Softcover • 8 1/4 x 10 7/8 • 224 pages • 250 color photos
Item# HDAM • $24.99

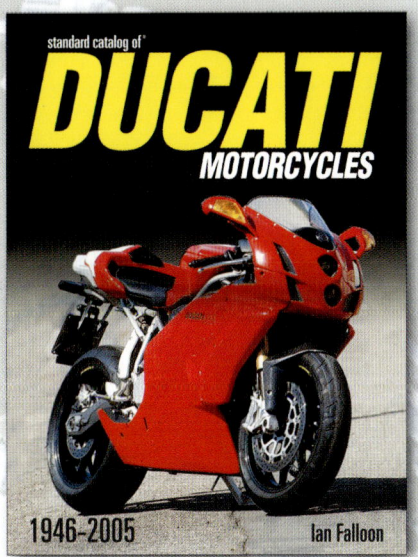

Standard Catalog of® Ducati Motorcycles 1947-2005
by Ian Falloon
Provides a detailed look at each model of Ducati from the Cucciolo to today's 999, with weights, specifications, displacements and performance and production data, and spectacular photographs.
Softcover • 8 1/4 x 10 7/8 • 224 pages • 250 color photos
Item# DUCM1 • $24.99

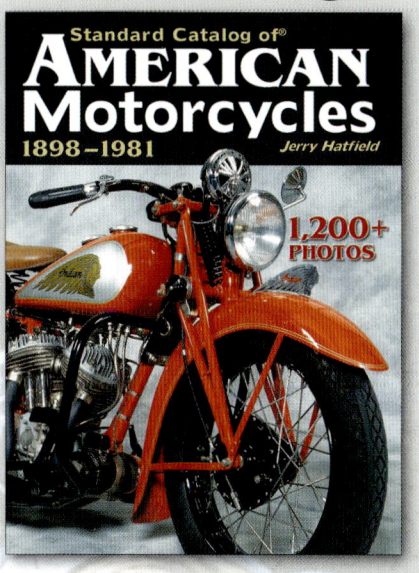

Standard Catalog of® American Motorcycles 1898-1981
The Only Book to Fully Chronicle Every Bike Ever Built
by Jerry H. Hatfield
Rediscover the reasons you love your favorite model of motorcycle with the help of 1,200 photos, and historical details featured in this comprehensive guide to American-made motorcycles.
Softcover • 8 1/2 x 11 • 448 pages • 1,200 b&w photos
Item# ACYL • $29.99

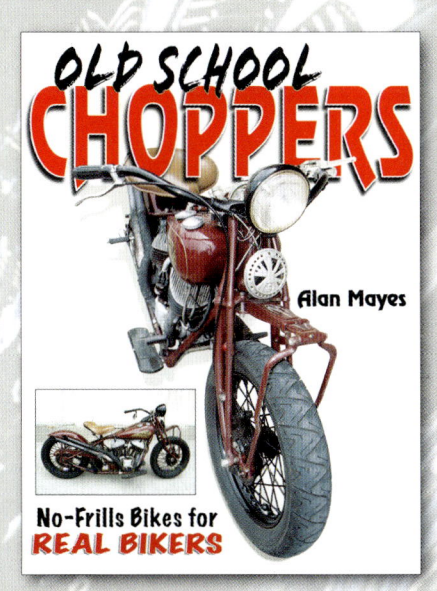

Old School Choppers
No-Frills Bikes for Real Bikers
by Alan Mayes
Features 30+ bobbers and old school choppers built with the techniques and attitude of early chopper building; showcased in 400 brilliant color photos.
Softcover • 8 1/4 x 10 7/8 • 176 pages • 600 color photos
Item# OHCH • $24.99

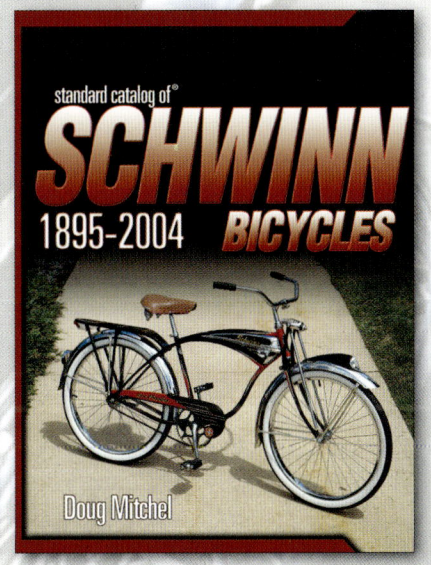

Standard Catalog of® Schwinn Bicycles 1895-2004
by Doug Mitchel
More than 350 stunning full-color photos document Schwinn bikes from the best vintage models, to today's latest releases, including the new chopper-style Sting Ray. The narrative discusses color, frame sizes, and other options available.
Softcover • 8 1/4 x 10 7/8 • 224 pages • 350+ color photos
Item# SWNB • $24.99

Order directly from the publisher by calling
800-258-0929
M-F 8 am – 5 pm

Online at
www.krausebooks.com
or from booksellers and auto parts shops nationwide

Please reference offer
AUB7
with all direct-to-publisher orders.

kp krause publications
An imprint of F+W Publications, Inc.
P.O. Box 5009, Iola, WI 54945-5009
www.krausebooks.com

Subscribe to Old Cars WEEKLY NEWS & MARKETPLACE Today!

ONLY 81¢ PER ISSUE

Old Cars Weekly covers the entire field of collectible automobiles—from the classic touring cars and roadsters of the early 1900s, to the popular muscle cars of the 1960s and '70s!

Inside each info-packed issue, you'll get:

- Technical tips and expert restoration advice
- A classified marketplace for cars, parts, and accessories
- Hot news on car shows, swap meets, and auctions
- Personal collectible stories and old car photos
- And much, much more!

Subscribe and save 73% off the cover price!

Act now—subscribe today and get 1 YEAR (52 BIG issues) for just $41.98!

To order online, visit **www.oldcarsweekly.com**

To order by phone, call 877-300-0243— offer J7AHAD
(Outside the U.S. and Canada call 386-246-3431)

To order by mail, P.O. Box 420235, Palm Coast, FL 32142

In Canada: add $67 (includes GST/HST). Outside the U.S. and Canada: add $92 and remit payment in U.S. funds with order. Please allow 4-6 weeks for first-issue delivery. Annual newsstand rate $155.48